Lecture Notes
in Business Information Processing   **432**

More information about this series at http://www.springer.com/series/7911

Estefanía Serral · Janis Stirna · Jolita Ralyté ·
Jānis Grabis (Eds.)

The Practice of Enterprise Modeling

14th IFIP WG 8.1 Working Conference, PoEM 2021
Riga, Latvia, November 24–26, 2021
Proceedings

Editors
Estefanía Serral (iD)
KU Leuven, LIRIS
Leuven, Belgium

Jolita Ralyté (iD)
University of Geneva
Carouge, Switzerland

Janis Stirna (iD)
Stockholm University
Kista, Sweden

Jānis Grabis (iD)
Riga Technical University
Riga, Latvia

ISSN 1865-1348   ISSN 1865-1356 (electronic)
Lecture Notes in Business Information Processing
ISBN 978-3-030-91278-9   ISBN 978-3-030-91279-6 (eBook)
https://doi.org/10.1007/978-3-030-91279-6

This Springer imprint is published by the registered company Springer Nature Switzerland AG
The registered company address is: Gewerbestrasse 11, 6330 Cham, Switzerland

Preface

The 14th IFIP WG 8.1 Working Conference on the Practice of Enterprise Modeling (PoEM 2021) was aimed at improving the understanding of the practice of enterprise modeling and architecture. PoEM offers a forum for sharing experiences and knowledge between the academic community and practitioners from industry and the public sector.

This year, the theme of the conference was the use of enterprise modeling and enterprise architecture towards ensuring sustainability and resilience of enterprises and societies. The theme is aligned to the increasing demand for businesses, services, and products to be more environmentally friendly and efficient, as well as to last longer and be more robust to unexpected changes. The field of enterprise modeling should seek to support these challenges by providing methods and tools, as well as investigating and reporting on the current state of the art in practice.

PoEM 2021 took place during November 24–26, 2021. It was organized by the Riga Technical University (RTU), Latvia, as a hybrid conference - partially at the newly enhanced Ķīpsala campus of RTU and partially online.

Following its tradition, PoEM 2021 was open for submissions in three categories that also form part of this proceedings: 1) research papers describing original research contributions in enterprise modeling; 2) practitioner/experience papers presenting problems, challenges, or experience related to any aspect of enterprise modeling encountered in practice; and 3) short papers presenting work in progress and emerging enterprise modeling challenges.

In total, we received 47 submissions for the main conference, including research papers, experience papers, and short papers. Based on three reviews by members of the Program Committee, we selected 14 full papers (a 30% acceptance rate) and six short papers (a 43% acceptance rate for full and short papers combined). Accepted papers are grouped by the following topics: enterprise modeling and enterprise architecture; methods and method engineering; business process modeling and management; requirements for privacy, security and governance; and case studies and experiences.

In addition to the main conference, PoEM 2021 featured three workshops: The 2nd Workshop on Blockchain and Enterprise Systems (BES 2021) organized by Andrea Morichetta and Petra Maria Asprion; The 1st Workshop on AI Native Enterprises organized by Vinay Kulkarni, Henderik Proper, Tony Clark, and Sreedhar Reddy; and The 1st Workshop on Enterprise Modeling for the Digital Transformation (EM4DT) organized by Samedi Heng and Saïd Assar. Also, a tutorial on "Hands-on Artefact-Centric Business Process Modelling with MERODE" was given by Monique Snoeck, and a PoEM Forum was organized by Balbir Bern and Kurt Sandkuhl.

PoEM 2021 also featured two keynotes, namely, "Software Sustainability: the Challenges and Opportunities for Enterprises and their Researchers" by Patricia Lago and "Design Science for Constructive Enterprise Modelling" by Paul Johannesson and Erik Perjons.

We thank the speakers for the keynotes and tutorial, as well as all the authors who submitted their work, and the Program Committee members who ensured a high-quality selection of papers while providing insightful advice for improving the contributions. Moreover, we thank the organizers of workshops and the Forum for making PoEM 2021 such a diverse and active event. We also thank IFIP WG 8.1 for allowing this conference series to evolve under its auspices.

Last but not least, we would like to thank the organization team at RTU led by Zane Solovjakova, Krišjānis Pinka, Kristaps P. Rubulis, and Evita Roponena for their hard work in ensuring the success of this event.

October 2021   Estefanía Serral
                                                                      Janis Stirna
                                                                      Jolita Ralyté
                                                                      Jānis Grabis

Organization

General Chairs

Jolita Ralyté   University of Geneva, Switzerland
Jānis Grabis   Riga Technical University, Latvia

Program Committee Chairs

Estefanía Serral   KU Leuven, Belgium
Janis Stirna   Stockholm University, Sweden

Forum Chairs

Balbir Barn   Middlesex University, UK
Kurt Sandkuhl   University of Rostock, Germany

Workshop Chairs

Beatriz Marín   Universidad Politécnica de Valencia, Spain
Yves Wautelet   KU Leuven, Belgium

Steering Committee

Anne Persson   University of Skövde, Sweden
Kurt Sandkuhl   University of Rostock, Germany
Janis Stirna   Stockholm University, Sweden

Program Committee

Raian Ali   Hamad Bin Khalifa University, Qatar
Joao Paulo Almeida   Federal University of Espirito Santom, Brazil
Steven Alter   University of San Francisco, USA
Dominik Bork   TU Wien, Austria
Rimantas Butleris   Kaunas University of Technology, Lithuania
Sybren De Kinderen   University of Luxembourg, Luxembourg
Paul Drews   Leuphana University of Lüneburg, Germany
Michael Fellmann   University of Rostock, Germany
Hans-Georg Fill   University of Fribourg, Switzerland
Ana-Maria Ghiran   Babes-Bolyai University of Cluj-Napoca, Romania

Additional Reviewers

Isaac da Silva-Torres
Anne Gutschmidt
Simon Hacks
Nafe Moradkhani
Jack Daniel Rittelmeyer
Emre Süren
Rafika Thabet
Johannes Wagner

Abstracts of Invited Keynote Talks

Software Sustainability: The Challenges and Opportunities for Enterprises and their Researchers

Patricia Lago

Department of Computer Science, Vrije Universiteit Amsterdam, The Netherlands
p.lago@vu.nl

Abstract. The need for sustainability is crucial for all aspects of society, as framed by the Sustainable Development Goals (SDGs) of the United Nations and increasingly prioritized by Governments and Global Organizations. Thanks to digital transformation, most enterprises in all sectors are facing incredible challenges to embrace sustainability as related to their software portfolios. Similarly, they struggle in identifying the opportunities that software sustainability can bring. This talk introduces the role of software for sustainability and related research. It also discusses some challenges and opportunities for modern enterprises in both research and practice, among which how to make sure the enterprise understands the necessity for sustainability. Examples from collaboration with various industries and sectors are used to illustrate the main takeaways.

Keywords: Sustainable development · Software sustainability · Enterprise sustainability

Design Science for Constructive Enterprise Modelling

Paul Johannesson and Erik Perjons

Department of Computer and Systems Sciences, Stockholm University, Sweden
{pajo, perjons}@dsv.su.se

Abstract. Within design science, models are considered one of the most important kinds of contributions, if not the most important one. We will compare the notion of a model in design science with the view of models as it has emerged in the enterprise modelling practice. One issue is whether models in design science and enterprise modelling solely have a prescriptive function or whether they also can have descriptive and explanatory functions. This issue raises the question of the relationship between models in design and science. Another issue is how enterprise models today take a constructive role instead of a purely representative one, as reality is not only described but also constructed through models in digital systems. We will discuss how these issues can be addressed by distinguishing between real and imagined systems, models, model types, and model descriptions.

Keywords: Design Science · Enterprise modeling · Research methods

Contents

Enterprise Modeling and Enterprise Architecture

Enterprise Coherence with GEA – *A*
15 year Co-evolution of Practice and Theory

Henderik A. Proper[1,2]([⊠]), Roel Wagter[3], and Joost Bekel[4]

[1] Luxembourg Institute of Science and Technology, Luxembourg, Luxembourg
e.proper@acm.org
[2] University of Luxembourg, Luxembourg, Luxembourg
[3] Solventa B.V., Nieuwegein, The Netherlands
roel.wagter@solventa.nl
[4] Radboud University, Nijmegen, The Netherlands
joost.bekel@ru.nl

Abstract. GEA (General Enterprise Architecting) is an enterprise architecture method which has been developed and matured over the past 15 years. The GEA method has emerged out of needs from practice, and differs from other enterprise architecture approaches in that it has a strong focus on enterprise coherence and the explicit governance thereof. This focus followed from the observed need to move beyond the Business-IT alignment and 'Business-to-IT' stack thinking that is embodied in most of the existing enterprise architecture approaches.

In this paper, we reflect on the development of the GEA method (so-far), which involved a co-evolution between theory and practice. We then present the core elements of (the current version of) GEA, and illustrate these in terms of a real-world (social housing) case. Finally, we also discuss some of the lessons learned in applying GEA across different organizations.

1 Introduction

The environment in which modern day enterprises (including commercial companies, government agencies, etc.) need to operate, changes constantly. As a result, enterprises transform almost continuously to keep up with these changes. One could even go as far as to say that enterprises need to stay 'in motion' [19]. The involved transformations may range from changes in value propositions and business processes, via changes to the information systems used to support the business processes, to changes of the underlying IT infrastructures. Furthermore, the transformations may be the result of a 'premeditated' (strategy driven) desire to change, but they can also be the outcome of numerous 'spontaneous' changes as a result of locally needed/induced changes. Enterprise transformations are also likely to touch upon a rich mix of aspects of the enterprise, such as human resourcing, finance, organizational structures, reporting structures, etc.; i.e. not just 'Business' and 'IT'. As a consequence, enterprise transformations typically

E. Serral et al. (Eds.): PoEM 2021, LNBIP 432, pp. 3–18, 2021.
https://doi.org/10.1007/978-3-030-91279-6_1

involve many stakeholders [35] with differing stakes and interests, who (should) influence the direction and/or speed of the transformation.

To make (premeditated) enterprise transformations feasible and manageable, they are typically managed as a portfolio of transformation programs, where these programs are split further into projects. Such a portfolio of programs and projects, together with the 'spontaneous' (bottom-up) changes, all need to be mutually *coordinated* while, at the same time, also maintaining alignment to the enterprise's strategy. A lack of such a coordination will likely lead to 'local optimizations' favoring short term and/or local interests over the overall interests of the enterprise. The latter ultimately leads to a degradation of the enterprise's *coherence* [12,13,20,23], which GEA defines as *the extent to which all relevant aspects of an enterprise are interconnected, such that these connections facilitate an enterprise in achieving its management's desired results* [20,23].

Traditionally, project management and program management are put forward as being responsible for such coordination tasks. However, these approaches focus primarily on the management of typical project parameters such as budgets, resource use, deadlines, etc.; i.e. "on time and within budget". When being too focused on such project parameters, one runs the risk of conducting only local and or partial improvements at the level of specific projects [20]. For example, when making design decisions that have an impact which transcends a specific project, projects are likely to aim for solutions that provide the best cost/benefits trade-off within the scope of that specific project, while not looking at the overall picture [18,20]. Regretfully, however, in practice such local optimizations do not just remain a potential risk. More often than not, this risk materializes, and consequently results in reduced structural coherence of important aspects of the enterprise (such as human resources, services, customers, processes, marketing, finance, physical infrastructures, IT, etc.). As a result, enterprises often fail to actually realize the *desired* transformation; even when the involved projects may have finished on time and within budget.

As an answer to this, enterprise architecture has been positioned as a *means* to enable such coordination and associated governance of enterprise coherence [6,18,20,26]. At the same time, however, one has to observe how most existing enterprise architecture approaches, such as Zachman [22], DYA [28], TOGAF [24], IAF [45], and ArchiMate [8,11], follow a rather 'engineering oriented' style towards enterprise transformation [14,27,35,42]. This engineering oriented style is typically embodied in an underlying architecture/design framework (typically involving of several columns and/or rows) in terms of which one is expected to architect/design the enterprise. This is also where we find the traditional Business-IT alignment and the Business-to-IT-stack thinking. These engineering-style approaches correspond to what De Caluwé [5] refers to as the Blue-print style of thinking regarding change.

To coordinate change, and ultimately ensure enterprise coherence [12,13], stakeholder interests, formal and informal power structures within enterprises and its context, as well as the associated processes of creating win-win situations and forming coalitions, should be taken as a starting point [14,27,35,42]; i.e. not just as an afterthought in terms of stakeholder specific 'viewpoints'. In terms of De Caluwé [5], a more Yellow-print style of thinking about change needs to be embraced (while also involving the other 'colors'). Where the more traditional engineering-style approaches involve a set of pre-determined aspects of an enterprise that should be aligned, the notion of *enterprise coherence* aims to go beyond this by focusing on "the extent to which all relevant aspects of an enterprise are interconnected" [20,23], where the set of *relevant aspects* is highly organisation specific.

In 2006, these insights triggered the Dutch consultancy firm Ordina to initiate a multi-client research program to develop an enterprise architecture method that would indeed focus on *enterprise coherence* and the need to more explicitly govern this coherence during enterprise transformations. By 2007 this resulted in the formal establishment of a multi-party[1] research and development program[2]. This program has resulted in the development (and ongoing evolution) of the GEA method [23,26,30]. Even though the group (See footnote 1) of (Netherlands based) organizations participating in the development of the GEA includes e.g. banks, pension funds, and logistic companies, there is a strong presence of governmental agencies. This may be a natural consequence of three factors. Firstly, the specific branch of Ordina that initiated the development of GEA was Ordina Public, which specifically targets clients in the public sector. Secondly, enterprise/digital transformation in the (e)governmental/public context typically involve multiple stakeholder across different organizational entities. Thirdly, government-related organizations generally (certainly within the Netherlands) are open to collaborative improvement and maturation of enterprise/digital transformation.

The goal of this paper is to (1) reflect on the development of GEA as a co-evolution between theory and practice, while also (2) presenting the core of (the current version of) GEA and illustrating this in terms of a real-world (social housing) case, as well as (3) discuss several lessons learned in applying GEA across different organizations. In line with this, the remainder of this paper is structured as follows. We start, in Sect. 2, with a discussion of the core elements of the (current version of) the GEA method, where we will use the real-world case of a Social Housing Foundation (De Key[3]) to illustrate these elements. We then continue in Sect. 3 with a brief report on the development of the GEA method as a co-evolution of practice and theory, and some of the lessons learned related to this. In doing so, we will also clarify why we prefer to speak about co-evolution, and why we put practice before theory. In Sect. 4, we then reflect on the use of GEA across multiple (large) cases. Finally, in concluding, we will also discusses some further directions in which we plan/expect GEA to (co)evolve further.

---

[1] During different stages of the GEA research program, the following client organizations participated: ABN-AMRO Bank; ANWB; Achmea; Belastingdienst – Centrum voor ICT; ICTU; ING; Kappa Holding; Ministerie van Binnenlandse Zaken en Koninkrijksrelaties; Ministerie van Defensie; Ministerie van Justitie – Dienst Justitiële Inrichtingen; Ministerie van Landbouw, Natuur en Voedselkwaliteit – Dienst Regelingen; Nederlandse Spoorwegen; PGGM; Politie Nederland; Prorail; Provincie Flevoland; Rabobank; Rijkswaterstaat; UWV; Wehkamp.

[2] https://www.groeiplatformgea.nl.

[3] https://www.dekey.nl.

2   Main Elements of GEA

In this Section, we present the main elements of the GEA method [23], covering the notion of *enterprise issue*, the overall perspectives of the enterprise's *level of purpose* and *level of design*, and the *integral solution contour*. In doing so, we will also illustrate these elements in terms of a recent case in which GEA was applied, involving a social housing foundation *De Key* (See footnote 3). This case also features as an illustrative case in [23].

Enterprise Issue – The main driver for enterprises to apply GEA is to deal with an *enterprise issue*, since such issues either trigger enterprise transformations, or *emerge* during an ongoing transformation. In general, an *enterprise issue* is a problem, bottleneck, challenge, or alleged solution, which is considered and controlled from the context of different perspectives within an enterprise. An enterprise issue can be a 'positive' issue, such as the desire to innovate, move towards new markets, apply new technologies to become more efficient, etc. It can also be a 'negative' issue, such as a need become more efficient, reduce costs, manage/avoid a loss of market share, become GDPR compliant, etc.

Enterprise issues can have both external and internal 'causes'. Examples of external causes include the need to respond to changes in the *environment*, such as legislation, technological developments, demographic trends or changing competitive relationships. Examples of internal causes include a need to increase efficiency, cost control, and compliance with (legal) norms and standards.

─────────────────────── De Key: The enterprise issue ───────────────────────

De Key is a large social housing corporation in Amsterdam with two offices. It had an issue that, in short, could be best described as "a required strengthening of the financial function". The underlying causes of this issue concerned changes in Dutch financial legislation, which imposed new requirements with respect to financial accountability for enterprises, as well as from the perspective of the supervisory bodies that controlled these aspects that required De Key to produce more detailed financial reports.

De Key's responsible financial director immediately realized that this issue could not be solved within the financial discipline only, but that a strong dependency existed with other disciplines within De Key and that solving these 'financial' issues would require the active cooperation of all managers of the involved disciplines.

──

In solving enterprise issues, the GEA method suggests the roadmap as shown in Fig. 1. This suggested roadmap may, of course, need situational adjustments to a specific enterprise context. In the case of De Key, for now, only the first four steps of the roadmap have been performed (the dark gray elements in Fig. 1). It should be noted that this roadmap is part of a broader framework [27], provided by GEA, for the governance of enterprise coherence. For instance, the (organisation specific) GEA framework, as will be illustrated below in terms of Fig. 4, can also be used to monitor the coherence of an enterprise while it is 'in motion' (due to bottom-up and/or top-down changes).

The roadmap as shown in Fig. 1 largely speaks for itself, so due to space limitations, we take the liberty of not discussing it in detail and only highlight some key considerations. A first aspect to note is (in step 1) the role of the

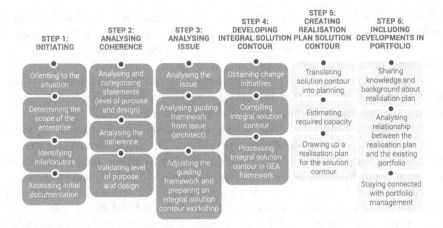

Fig. 1. Generic GEA roadmap [23]; In dark gray the steps performed at De Key so-far

interlocutors, who represent (with mandate) the different stakes, interests, and concerns, that need to be taken into consideration. As mentioned before, the key difference between GEA and existing enterprise approaches lies in GEA's focus on enterprise coherence. Therefore, step 2 involves an analysis of the existing enterprise coherence. It does so, both at the *level of purpose* and the *level of design*, which we will discuss below. This analysis is then used in the further steps to direct/guide the further analysis of the enterprise issue at hand (step 3), and then gradually develop and implement a 'solution' (steps 4 to 6).

Fig. 2. The elements of coherence at level of purpose [23]

Level of Purpose – The level of purpose is the consideration level where GEA considers the meaning and purpose of an enterprise. At this level, GEA essentially adopts the "Strategic Development Process Model" as proposed by Kaplan & Norton [10], the "Strategy Formulation" approach by Thenmozhi [25] and the notion of endless pursuit of a company's mission from "Building Your Company's Vision" by Collins & Porras [4]. Based on these theories we distinguish five key concepts: *mission, vision, core values, goals* and *strategy*, see Fig. 2.

The *mission* involves a brief, typically one sentence, statement that defines the fundamental purpose of the organization [10] that is "enduringly pursued but never fulfilled" [4]. It should include what the organization provides to its clients and inform executives and employees about the overall goal they have come together to pursue [10]. The "enduringly pursued but never fulfilled" qualification refers to the fact that the act of *achieving* a mission is never finished; realising the fundamental purpose is an ongoing effort.

The *vision* is a concise statement that operationalizes the mission in terms of the mid to long-term goals of the organization. The vision should be external and market oriented and should express – preferably in aspirational terms – how the organization wants to be perceived by the world [10]. *Core value statements* prescribe a desired behaviors, character and culture [10] and are required for an enterprise to be, or become, successful within its formulated vision. *Goal statements* involve a formulation of a desired stage of development for an enterprise working towards achieving the enterprise's vision [10]. The *strategy* involves a comprehensive master plan in which it is stated how an enterprise will achieve its goals. It should also maximize the competitive advantages and minimize competitive disadvantages [25].

Vision statements	Mission elements					
	De Key	Dynamics of the city	Ring A10	People	First steps	Housing market
We are in line with current developments and remain true to values that have traditionally determined De Key's identity.	x	x				
Spatial the urbanisation has consequences: for example, to build homes, more high-rise buildings are needed.		x	x			x
Our contribution to the dynamism in Amsterdam is to create and manage affordable forms of housing that are attractive to people who want to take their first steps in the housing market.	x	x		x	x	x
We continue to build current home ownership with active portfolio management, innovative housing concepts and by supporting initiatives.		x			x	x

Fig. 3. Excerpt of De Key's Mission-Vision matrix [23]

———————————— De Key: Level of purpose ————————————

The mission of De Key is[4] (translated from Dutch): "De Key contributes to the dynamics of the city of Amsterdam by enabling people to take their first steps on the housing market, inside, or just outside the A10 ring." (The A10 is a highway around the core of the city.) In capturing the level of purpose, in terms of Fig. 2, all elements were captured, and confronted to each other using matrices 'flowing' down the triangle. In other words, core elements from the mission were confronted to the statements of the vision, these were then confronted with statements capturing the core values, etc.

At De Key, this involved: 1 mission statement, 14 vision statements, 4 core values, 8 goal statements, and 15 strategy statements. Fig. 3 provides an excerpt of the matrix linking vision statements to key elements in the mission.

---

[4] https://www.dekey.nl/Media/9b0b72d9c89e08f9232917106b273dc0/original/ ruimte_voor_beweging.pdf/

Level of Design – The level of design, is concerned with a (high level perspective) on the design of the enterprise, by which the level of purpose is instantiated. This level concerns *perspectives, core concepts, guiding statements, core models,* and *relevant relationships.*

Perspectives concern the angles from which one wishes to contemplate and to govern the enterprise. The set of perspectives used in a specific enterprise depend very much on its formal and informal power structures. Both internally, and externally. Typical examples are culture, customer, products/services, business processes, information provision, finance, value chain, corporate governance, etc. *Core concepts* concern the core concepts in terms of which one wishes to contemplate and to govern a perspective. *Guiding statements* are internally agreed and published statements which give direction to desirable behavior. They may involve overall policy statements, more specific objectives, as well as principles. *Core models* are models of one or more perspectives, based on and in line with the guiding statements of the corresponding perspective(s). *Relevant relationships* are descriptions of the connections between guiding statements from different perspectives.

Combined, this leads to the structure as exemplified in Fig. 4. The perspectives as shown there are just illustrative. The actual set of relevant perspectives in a specific situation is organization specific.

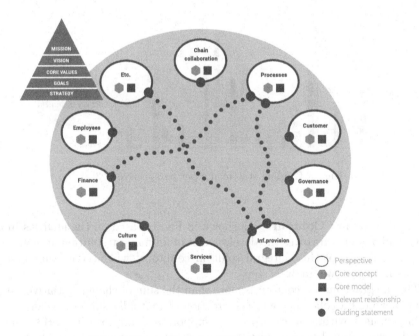

Fig. 4. Elements of the GEA framework, [23]

——————————————— De Key: Level of design ———————————————

At De Key, ten perspectives were identified: *Finance, Customer, Real estate, Services, Suppliers, Governance, Employees, Stakeholders, Processes,* and *Information provision.* As an illustration, Fig. 5 shows for each of the identified perspectives the number, and kinds of, guiding statements that were formulated.

What was interesting is that for the *Real estate* and *Stakeholders* perspectives no principles were formulated, while for the *Suppliers* perspective no objectives were formulated. These observations raised concerns for the respective perspective owners. For instance, for a social housing foundation it is rather 'odd' to manage real estate without clear (business) principles. Similarly, one would expect that for the management of suppliers there to be clear objectives.

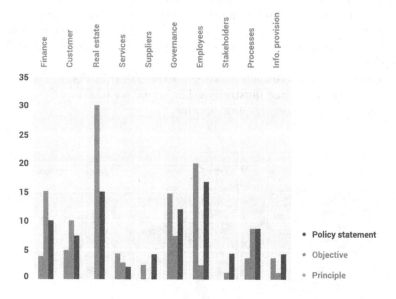

Fig. 5. Guiding statements per perspective, [23]

Integral Solution Contour – As shown in Fig. 1, based on the analysis from step 2 and 3, step 4 involves the development of an integral solution at 'contour' level. The design of this 'integral solution countour' will need to answer the insights from the two analysis steps.

The integral solution contour is more than the sum of change initiatives, it is about meaningful coherence and the creation of mutually supportive and reinforcing changes within an enterprise to support and improve its performance. Initially, there may be contradictions with other change initiatives, there may be overlap, and change initiatives may clash with guiding statements from other perspectives. All change initiatives, starting with the initiatives with the highest priority must be examined for these problems. Any disagreements must be brought to the attention of the relevant perspective owners who must decide how these matters will be resolved. Once the disagreements have been solved, an integral solution contour can be described and submitted to the board of the enterprise for decision making.

―――――――――― De Key: Developing the integral solution contour ――――――――――

A one-day workshop was organized, which included the perspective owners from De Key, issue owners, some De Key board members and two GEA supervisors.

Once the GEA supervisors had explained the workshop and making the aforementioned items available, the issue owners explained the results of the issue analysis (Fig. 1, step 3) in depth using their (earlier) prepared presentation.

Once all the issues of the participants had been addressed, the workshop moved to a level where it became clear that all the participants really understood the issue, and its degree of importance and urgency. Subsequently, the integral solution contour for the relevant issue as described above was co-created.

3   The Development of GEA

In this Section, we discuss the experiences in the development of GEA. We start with short discussion of the general background, and then structure the remainder of this Section around some of the key lessons learned.

As discussed in the introduction, the initiative to develop the GEA method was taken by the Dutch consultancy firm Ordina in 2006. As a prelude to the actual start of the development, a survey was conducted among the participating organizations to identify the requirements on the desired outcomes. It also validated the need to more explicitly govern *enterprise coherence*, beyond mere Business-IT Alignment. More recent publications [12,13] provide further (a posteri) support for this motivation.

Organize the Need – From the start out, the ambition of the GEA research program was to follow a science-driven approach. From a research methodological perspective [43], the development of GEA involved a design science [7] effort, with an important role for cases studies [46] as a way to drive the iterations. It was, therefore, also important to have a good understanding of the needs for/requirements on GEA in practice, and it was necessary to have access to real-world cases. Therefore, the next step was the creation of the multi-client (See footnote 1) research program (See footnote 2) involving clients (i.e. future 'users' of the method) that saw a real need for the method.

Validation of Need by Financial Commitment – In the initial stages (i.e. the first five years) of the research program, the participating members were also required to provide a financial contribution to the program. This financial contribution was not only meant to cover (some) of the costs of the program. Requiring a substantial financial contribution also implied a (1) validation of the shared understanding of the need to develop GEA, and (2) commitment to the development of GEA (e.g. by way of real-world cases).

Value for Practice Before Rigor for Science – Next to the industrial partners, the research program also involved an advisory board involved five senior researchers from different Universities, covering management sciences, organizational sciences, and business informatics. This is also where a first interaction between practice and theory took place. The need for the development of GEA was clearly born in practice. However, already at the start, the senior researchers in the advisory board were then able to already provide input regarding relevant existing theories/methods that could be integrated into the design of the GEA method. This resulted in a series of white papers [30,31,33] (in Dutch) documenting the need for GEA, its initial design, as well as positioning in relation to existing related instruments (such as the balanced score card [9], and McKinsey's 7s model [3]). Next to the advisory board with senior researchers, there was also a clear intention (and commitment from Ordina) to sponsor a part-time PhD candidate [27].

Nevertheless, soon it became clear that for the GEA program to succeed from the perspective of the industrial partners, and thus for the *continuity* of the program, it was necessary to first focus on *establishing value for practice*. This also meant that, e.g. towards the research needed for the part-time PhD project, the primary focus had to be on doing real-world cases (in real-world circumstances) with the project partners, and then at a later stage leverage these towards scientific reflection and publications. This also resulted in additional white papers (e.g. [29,32]) documenting the cases (which were also beneficial in attracting additional project partners). At a later stage, once the program was well on its way, and the first version of GEA had been documented in terms of a book [26], there was room for more scientific reflection and rigor [34–44]. This also resulted in the finalization of the PhD project [27] sponsored by the GEA program.

Loosely Coupled Co-evolution of Practice and Theory – Next to the previous lesson learned on *value for practice before rigor for science*, the ongoing work in the GEA program also resulted in a series of parallel research activities. These research activities were formally separate from the GEA program, but partly inspired by the findings within the GEA program, while some of the findings of these parallel research activities flowed back to the GEA program.

For instance, an important concept in GEA is the notion of *guiding statement*, which involves of *policy statements*, *objectives*, and *principles*. The need for a better understanding of these concepts also triggered more explicit work on the concept of *architecture principles*, which a.o. resulted in [6]. The latter then, in its turn, also enabled the GEA program to further mature these concepts within the GEA context.

The need for more coordination in enterprise transformation to ensure enterprise coherence, was also one of the triggers for the *Architectural Coordination of Enterprise Transformation* project [20]. PhD candidates involved in the latter project also interacted with the project members of the GEA program, to obtain case material for their work. Conversely, different results reported in [20] provide(d) more theoretical underpinning(s) of the GEA method.

The need to involve multiple stakeholders in a collaborative setting, also inspired work towards an approach to use collaboration engineering concepts to structure such interactions [16,17]. These results are expected to be integrated into future versions of GEA, in particular when developing more explicit tool support for the method (see the discussion on future research in Sect. 5).

Finally, now that the GEA method is well established (and also internationally available [23]) there is a growing need (and ambition) to be able to more explicitly *quantify* enterprise coherence and its impact on the performance of enterprises. First steps in this direction have already been published [1,2].

In each of these examples, the needs from GEA-related *practices* inspired the development of new concepts and theories, while some of the latter then flow(ed) back towards the further development of GEA. As such, we also prefer to speak about co-evolution from practice and theory, consciously putting practice first (rather than the often used order of theory and practice), while using the word 'co-evolution' rather than the often used "from practice to theory and back".

Controlled Initiation; Independent Growth – As mentioned the GEA program was initiated by the consultancy firm Ordina. Having one organization in clear control of the development proved valuable in order to organize the need, financial commitments towards the joint development, etc.

However, after the establishment of a first stable version, and making this widely accessible [26] (to a professional audience), enterprise architects working at other consultancy firms also became interested in co-developing the GEA method. This then triggered the transfer of the GEA method to an independent foundation. This foundation[5] now manages the further development of GEA from a more neutral position.

4   Lessons Learned from Applying GEA in Practice

Over the past 10 to 15 years, GEA has been applied to several cases. This includes several smaller cases, but also a number of larger cases. Table 1 shows (partially anonimized) some of the key figures of the larger cases. Case 5 to 7, were conducted at the early stages of the development of GEA. For those stages, no detailed breakdown of the number of guiding statements is available.

On average these cases involved 2.5 person-month involvement of two external consultants, and on average 0.25 person-month per perspective owners. Combined, this is an average of $2.5 \times 2 + 0.25 \times 10 = 7.5$ person-months in total, per case.

Applying GEA in each of the (larger and smaller) cases has resulted in several lessons learned. In the remainder of this Section, we discuss some of these lessons.

Good Inputs for Level of Purpose – The presence of a good documented enterprise mission, vision, core values, goals and strategy are preconditions to be able to determine the content of the cohesive elements on the design level of the organization and they are the essential resources for this determination.

---

[5] https://www.groeiplatformgea.nl/groeiplatform-gea/stichting/.

Table 1. Overall indicators per project

Case	Perspectives	Guiding statements #				Guiding statements %			
		Policy statements	Objectives	Case Principle	Total	Policy statements	Objectives	Principle	Total
1 [38,40]	12	111	51	73	235	47	22	31	100
2	10	75	64	152	291	26	22	52	100
3	9	347	93	20	460	75	20	5	100
4 [23]	10	108	95	66	269	40	35	25	100
5 [44]	10								
6	11								
7	10								

Benchmark in Numbers – Based on the experience across the different cases the following average numbers seem to be relevant benchmarks for larger (1000+ employees) enterprises:

1. The number of perspectives will be between 9 and 11.
2. The average number of key concepts will be 4 to 8 per perspective.
3. The number of guiding statements for a large enterprise will be between 200 and 400.
4. The distribution of the guiding statements will be approximately 10 to 25% principles, 30 to 45% policy statements and 30 to 45% objectives.

Without assuming these numbers to represent an absolute truth, they provide important indicators of when a strong deviation from the patterns is visible in an enterprise. When strong deviations do occurs, it is important to discuss these deviations with those responsible, such as the perspective owners, and to see whether it is necessary to change, to remove or to add elements at the level of design. In the case of De Key, we already saw (in Sect. 2) that there were less than expected principles for the *real estate* perspective, while there were no objectives formulated for the *suppliers* perspective. In another case, a GEA survey found that there to be 198 policy statements, 1 principle statement and 1 objective statement. This is a striking example of a not very result-oriented enterprise, which is stuck in policy-making processes.

Of course, an interesting question is what the *added value* is of using GEA in practice. Given the size, the complexity, and situatedness, of enterprise transformations in general, a comparative study between transformations that applied GEA and transformations that did not, is difficult. However, across the projects in which GEA was applied, several 'feats of arms' can be identified, such as:

- With the help of GEA, the EU-accreditation of a large agency, which had gotten completely out of control, was safeguarded within one year.
- At a Dutch ministry, the unnecessary start up of a large (and costly) project, initially triggered by a change of a law, was prevented.
- In the context of a large digitization program at a ministry, GEA was used to break (within two months) a stalemate in a decision-making process that had been stuck for a year.

– With the help of GEA, the financial function of a large housing corporation was brought up to the level required by regulators within 3 months.

5   Conclusion and Further Research

In this paper, we reported on the GEA method for enterprise architecture, and its development as a co-evolution (so-far) between practice and theory, as well as associated lessons learned. We presented the core elements of (the current version of) GEA, and illustrate these in terms of a real-world (social housing) case. Finally, we also discussed some of the lessons learned in applying GEA across different organizations.

Towards the future, we see several challenges for further co-evolution between practice and theory. Firstly, there is a need to better quantify the notion of enterprise coherence. Initial work in this direction has already been reported in [1,2], but much more work remains. Once the notion of enterprise coherence has been quantified more explicitly, it also becomes possible to find causal relations between (the level of) enterprise coherence and the concept of EBIT(D)A; i.e. an enterprise's economical performance in terms of *earnings before interest, taxes, (depreciation), and amortization.*

A second challenge involves the growing desire to develop more tool support for GEA. Doing so, however, requires a more explicit meta-model. As one of the next steps, we also foresee the development of more explicit meta-models.

A third challenge involves the integration with existing enterprise architecture approaches. The fact that GEA differs from other enterprise architecture approaches by its strong orientation towards the governance of enterprise coherence, does not mean that existing enterprise modeling/architecting/engineering approaches cannot be combined. Even more, we see potential benefit in doing so in terms of e.g. the core models used at the *level of design*, as well as the elaboration of such models towards actual solutions. These models may, for instance, provide some (organization specific) standardization of the modeling constructs used to express core models.

Finally, we also see opportunities to more explicitly support collaborative processes involved in gathering guiding statements across the different perspectives (and stakeholders), and the development of the integral solution contour. There we plan to investigate the integration of existing work regarding collaborative approaches to enterprise architecture (e.g. CAEDA [17]) and support by collaborative tools for policy formulation [15].

References

1. Bekel, J., Wagter, R.: Measurement of enterprise coherence by means of the gea C-index-a first investigation. In: 22nd IEEE Conference on Business Informatics, CBI 2020, Antwerp, Belgium, June 22–24, 2020, vol. 2, pp. 57–64. IEEE (2020)

2. Bekel, J., Wagter, R.: Enterprise coherence metrics in enterprise decision making. In: Aveiro, D., Guizzardi, G., Pergl, R., Proper, H.A. (eds.) EEWC 2020. LNBIP, vol. 411, pp. 213–227. Springer, Cham (2021). https://doi.org/10.1007/978-3-030-74196-9_12
3. Channon, D.F., Caldart, A.A.: McKinsey 7S model. Strateg. Manage. J. **12** (2015)
4. Collins, J., Porras, J.: Building Your Company's Vision. Harvard Business Review (1996)
5. De Caluwé, L., Vermaak, H.: Learning to Change: A Guide for Organization Change Agents. Sage Publications, London (2003)
6. Greefhorst, D., Proper, H.A.: Architecture Principles - The Cornerstones of Enterprise Architecture. Springer (2011). https://doi.org/10.1007/978-3-642-20279-7
7. Hevner, A.R.: A three cycle view of design science research. Scand. J. Inf. Syst. **19**(2), 87–92 (2007)
8. Iacob, M.E., Jonkers, H., Lankhorst, M.M., Proper, H.A.: ArchiMate 1.0 Specification. The Open Group (2009)
9. Kaplan, R.S., Norton, D.P.: The balanced scorecard - measures that drive performance. Harvard Bus. Rev. **70**, 71–79 (1992)
10. Kaplan, R.S., Norton, D.P., Barrows, E.A.: Developing the Strategy: Vision, Value Gaps, and Analysis. Balanced Scorecard Review, January-February 2008
11. Lankhorst, M.: Enterprise Architecture at Work. TEES, Springer, Heidelberg (2013). https://doi.org/10.1007/978-3-642-29651-2
12. Leinwand, P., Mainardi, C.: The Coherence Premium. Harvard Business Review (2010)
13. Leinwand, P., Mainardi, C.R.: The Essential Advantage: How to Win with a Capabilities-Driven Strategy. Harvard Business Review Press (2010)
14. Magalhães, R., Proper, H.A.: Model-enabled Design and Engineering of Organisations. Organisational Design and Enterprise Engineeering **1**(1), 1–12 (2017)
15. Nabukenya, J., Bommel, P.v., Proper, H.A.: A theory-driven design approach to collaborative policy making processes. In: 42st Hawaii International International Conference on Systems Science (HICSS-42 2009), pp. 1–10. IEEE Computer Society, California (2009)
16. Nakakawa, A., Bommel, P.v., Proper, H.A.: Definition and validation of requirements for collaborative decision-making in enterprise architecture creation. Int. J. Coop. Inf. Syst. **20**(1), 83–136 (2011)
17. Nakakawa, A., van Bommel, P., Proper, H.A., Mulder, J.B.F.: A situational method for creating shared understanding on requirements for an enterprise architecture. Int. J. Coop. Inf. Syst. **27**(4), 1850010 (2018)
18. Op 't Land, M., Proper, H.A., Waage, M., Cloo, J., Steghuis, C.: Enterprise Architecture - Creating Value by Informed Governance. Springer (2008). https://doi.org/10.1007/978-3-540-85232-2
19. Proper, H.A.: Enterprise architecture: informed steering of enterprises in motion. In: Hammoudi, S., Cordeiro, J., Maciaszek, L.A., Filipe, J. (eds.) ICEIS 2013. LNBIP, vol. 190, pp. 16–34. Springer, Cham (2014). https://doi.org/10.1007/978-3-319-09492-2_2
20. Proper, H.A., Winter, R., Aier, S., Kinderen, S.d. (eds.): Architectural Coordination of Enterprise Transformation. Springer (2018). https://doi.org/10.1007/978-3-319-69584-6
21. Rinderle-Ma, S., Sanz, J.L., Bai, X.Y. (eds.): 14th IEEE International Conference on Commerce and Enterprise Computing, CEC 2012, Hangzhou, China, 9–11 September 2012. IEEE Computer Society Press, California, September 2012

22. Sowa, J., Zachman, J.A.: Extending and formalizing the framework for information systems architecture. IBM Syst. J. **31**(3), 590–616 (1992)
23. Stovers, R., Ruijter, J.d., Wagter, R.: GEA Enterprise Architecture in Practice - Better Performance by Managing Coherence. Dialoog, Zaltbommel, the Netherlands (2021)
24. The Open Group: TOGAF Version 9. Van Haren Publishing, Zaltbommel, the Netherlands (2009)
25. Thenmozhi, M.: Module 9 - Strategic Management. Lecture Notes, Department of Management Studies, Indian Institute of Technology, Madras, India (2009)
26. Wagter, R.: Sturen op samenhang op basis van GEA - Permanent en event driven. Van Haren Publishing, Zaltbommel, the Netherlands (2009).in Dutch
27. Wagter, R.: Enterprise Coherence Governance. Ph.D. thesis, Radboud University, Nijmegen, the Netherlands (2013)
28. Wagter, R., van den Berg, M., Luijpers, J., van Steenbergen, M.E.: Dynamic Enterprise Architecture. How to make it work. Wiley, New York (2005)
29. Wagter, R., Nijkamp, G., Proper, H.A.: Applying GEA to a business issue. White Paper GEA-5, Ordina, the Netherlands (2007). in Dutch
30. Wagter, R., Nijkamp, G., Proper, H.A.: Overview 1th Phase - General Enterprise Architecturing. White Paper GEA-1, Ordina, the Netherlands (2007). in Dutch
31. Wagter, R., Nijkamp, G., Proper, H.A.: The Elements of the "GEA-Structure". White Paper GEA-2, Ordina, the Netherlands (2007). in Dutch
32. Wagter, R., Nijkamp, G., Stovers, R., Proper, H.A.: E-Government using GEA and NORA. White Paper GEA-4, Ordina, the Netherlands (2007). in Dutch
33. Wagter, R., Nijkamp, G., Witte, D., Proper, H.A.: GEA in relation to other steering instruments. White Paper GEA-8, Ordina, the Netherlands (2008). in Dutch
34. Wagter, R., Proper, H.A.: Coherence management dashboard for ACET. In: Proper et al. [20], chap. 18, pp. 183–191
35. Wagter, R., Proper, H.A.: Involving the right stakeholders - enterprise coherence governance. In: Proper et al. [20], chap. 10, pp. 99–110
36. Wagter, R., Proper, H.A.E., Witte, D.: Enterprise coherence assessment version. In: Harmsen, F., Grahlmann, K., Proper, E. (eds.) PRET 2011. LNBIP, vol. 89, pp. 28–52. Springer, Heidelberg (2011). https://doi.org/10.1007/978-3-642-23388-3_2
37. Wagter, R., Proper, H.A., Witte, D.: Enterprise architecture: a strategic specialism. In: Rinderle-Ma et al. [21], pp. 1–8
38. Wagter, R., Proper, H.A.E., Witte, D.: Enterprise coherence in the dutch ministry of social affairs and employment. In: Bajec, M., Eder, J. (eds.) CAiSE 2012. LNBIP, vol. 112, pp. 600–607. Springer, Heidelberg (2012). https://doi.org/10.1007/978-3-642-31069-0_50
39. Wagter, R., Proper, H.A., Witte, D.: The extended enterprise coherence-governance assessment. In: Aier, S., Ekstedt, M., Matthes, F., Proper, E., Sanz, J.L. (eds.) PRET/TEAR -2012. LNBIP, vol. 131, pp. 218–235. Springer, Heidelberg (2012). https://doi.org/10.1007/978-3-642-34163-2_13
40. Wagter, R., Proper, H.A., Witte, D.: On the use of GEA at the dutch ministry of social affairs and employment. In: Rinderle-Ma et al. [21], pp. 115–119
41. Wagter, R., Proper, H.A.E., Witte, D.: A practice-based framework for enterprise coherence. In: Proper, E., Gaaloul, K., Harmsen, F., Wrycza, S. (eds.) PRET 2012. LNBIP, vol. 120, pp. 77–95. Springer, Heidelberg (2012). https://doi.org/10.1007/978-3-642-31134-5_4

42. Wagter, R., Proper, H.A., Witte, D.: A Theory for Enterprise Coherence Governance. In: Saha, P. (ed.) A Systematic Perspective to Managing Complexity with EA. IGI Publishing, Hershey, Pennsylvania (2013)

43. Wagter, R., Proper, H.A., Witte, D.: Developing the GEA method – design science and case-study research in action. In: Franch, X., Soffer, P. (eds.) CAiSE 2013. LNBIP, vol. 148, pp. 43–57. Springer, Heidelberg (2013). https://doi.org/10.1007/978-3-642-38490-5_4

44. Wagter, R., Proper, H.A., Witte, D.: Enterprise coherence governance in the public sector – custodial institutions agency of the dutch ministry of security and justice. In: IEEE 15th Conference on Business Informatics, CBI 2013, Vienna, Austria, 15–18 July, 2013, pp. 117–124. IEEE Computer Society Press, California (2013)

45. Wout, J.v., Waage, M., Hartman, H., Stahlecker, M., Hofman, A.: The Integrated Architecture Framework Explained. Springer, Heidelberg (2010). https://doi.org/10.1007/978-3-642-11518-9

46. Yin, R.K.: Case Study Research: Design and Methods (Applied Social Research Methods). Sage Publications, London (2013)

Machine Learning-Based Enterprise Modeling Assistance: Approach and Potentials

Nikolay Shilov[1]([✉]) [iD], Walaa Othman[2] [iD], Michael Fellmann[3] [iD],
and Kurt Sandkuhl[3] [iD]

[1] SPC RAS, St. Petersburg, Russia
nick@iias.spb.su
[2] ITMO University, St. Petersburg, Russia
walaa_othman@itmo.ru
[3] University of Rostock, Rostock, Germany
{michael.fellmann,kurt.sandkuhl}@uni-rostock.de

Abstract. Today, enterprise modeling is still a highly manual task that requires substantial human effort. Human modelers are not only assigned the creative component of the process, but they also need to perform routine work related to comparing the being developed model with the existing ones. Although the huge amount of information available today (big data) makes it possible to analyze more best practices, it also introduces difficulties since a person is often not able to analyze all of it. In this work, we analyze the potential of using machine learning methods for assistance during enterprise modeling. An illustrative case study proves the feasibility and potentials of the proposed approach, which can potentially significantly affect the modern modeling methods, and also has long-term prospects for the creation of new technologies, products, and services.

Keywords: Enterprise modeling · Assisted modeling · Machine learning · Graph neural networks · Decision support

1 Introduction

Today, the high speed of scientific and technological progress as well as globalization have led to the need to often develop and modify enterprise models (e.g., [1]), which are usually described using graph-based structures. At the same time, even though the human engineer is usually assigned the creative component of the process, he/she still needs to perform routine work related to comparing the being developed model with the existing ones (best practice). Although the huge amount of information available today (big data) makes it possible to analyze more existing models, it also introduces difficulties since a person is often not able to analyze all of it.

Usage of modeling patterns is currently one of the trends [2, 3]. However, patterns sometimes can be an inefficient solution due to their diversity, specialization for specific conditions, and the same need to analyze the available patterns "manually".

© IFIP International Federation for Information Processing 2021
Published by Springer Nature Switzerland AG 2021
E. Serral et al. (Eds.): PoEM 2021, LNBIP 432, pp. 19–33, 2021.
https://doi.org/10.1007/978-3-030-91279-6_2

Efficient use of big data is a global challenge today, which is emphasized by the popularity of research in this area. In the view of significant development of information technologies, machine learning methods using, for example, deep neural networks, have made a significant qualitative leap in the past few years.

As mentioned in [4] "...a human actor will more easily adapt decision making to context specific factors, while an automated service will only address context if this was explicitly included in its design". The capability of such machine learning models as deep neural networks to take into account and generalize the whole available information (e.g., the entire enterprise model) might help to overcome this limitation. As a result, the application of such machine learning techniques to support design decisions might enable modelers to take into account the context and various aspects of the being built model when comparing it with numerous (hundreds, thousands, or even millions) available models (best practices). So, slightly rephrasing the question from [4], the research question considered is "Can graph-based machine learning discover tacit enterprise model patterns from existing solutions to support enterprise modelers?".

The goal of the presented work is to analyze the potential of using machine learning methods for assistance during enterprise modeling. This approach can potentially significantly affect the modern modeling methods, and also has long-term prospects for the creation of new technologies, products, and services.

The paper is structured as follows. The next section introduces the state of the art in the areas of decision support and assistance for enterprise modeling and similar domains, as well as machine learning techniques capable of dealing with graph-based structures. It is followed by the approach description. Section 4 presents the experimental evaluation of the developed approach. The research results are discussed in sec. 5 followed by conclusions.

2 State of the Art Review

2.1 Recommender System Techniques in Conceptual Modelling

Today, assistance for configuration and modeling processes is in great demand, since in addition to the creative component, such processes include tasks related to the analysis of existing solutions for possible reuse, which is a very laborious process. Existing research efforts intending to aid the modeler when designing an enterprise model are works in the intersection of Recommender Systems (RS) and conceptual modeling. In the most general sense, RS "generate meaningful recommendations to a collection of users" [15]. While RS are quite well-known in domains such as e-commerce, not much research is available so far in the domain of enterprise modeling. Modeling is still a highly manual task that requires substantial human effort e.g. in order to decide which label is appropriate for a model element, to determine where to start and stop modeling (scope of the model), and to model on a consistent abstraction level since guidance is lacking in current tools [16].

Hence some initial techniques and prototypes have been developed that are capable of generating suggestions on how to complete a model currently being edited. These approaches mainly have been developed in the context of business process modeling. They are geared towards different assistance features such as to *ease the completion of a partially constructed model* e.g. by presenting relevant fragments of already existing models [17], using pattern-based knowledge for completion [18], or other auto-completion mechanisms [19], by adding required information for model execution [20] or assist in applying the modeling syntax [21].

Another form of recommendation-based support is *suggestions for concrete modeling actions* also denoted as auto-suggest features [22]. Regarding the latter, an initial evaluation of a knowledge-based paradigm for suggestion generation led to promising results [23]. Finally, some approaches also intend to *improve the model quality* [24] or *provide domain-specific knowledge-support* in the case of modeling for software engineering where constraints have to be satisfied [25] or where support regarding model changes is sought e.g. to inform the user about untypical model changes that potentially lead to errors based on a large data set about model evolutions [26]. In general, the cited works develop task-specific recommendation approaches that often differ from classical recommender system implementations and paradigms. Recently, also the incorporation of machine learning e.g. to learn parameters for the recommendation approach is discussed as future work [25].

All the above approaches are mainly based on utilizing predefined patterns, what on the one hand makes the modeling process more reliable and predictable, but on the other hand less flexible and creative. This limitation is addressed by the proposed use of machine learning.

2.2 Machine Learning in Modeling

Application of machine learning (which is basically about finding tacit modeling patterns) to support configuration tasks resulted from usage of pattern libraries built manually or semi-automatically. For example, in paper [5], the ability to use patterns is considered an essential functionality of enterprise modeling tools in the modern era of digitalization. The authors of [3] propose a complex system for organizing patterns with an evaluation of their consistency, and the authors of [6] – a system of recommendations for specific patterns or known models. The efficiency and promising outlook of using patterns in enterprise modeling is also emphasized in work [2].

The patterns are also used in other modeling domains, for example, when configuring complex products [7]. In work [8], co-authored by one of the authors of this work, a method was proposed for configuring complex systems (namely, a network of information and computing resources to solve a specific problem) based on an analysis of the functionality of resources and existing constraints. However, since a significant part of the resources remained unchanged from task to task, and the tasks belonged to one problem area, the use of machine learning models could potentially speed up the configuration process, but this opportunity was not considered. A recommender system proposed in [9] is focused on supporting the configuration process (configuring production for the release of a software product) and uses collaborative filtering techniques to select similar resources for the release of similar software products. Quite interesting is the work [10], the authors of which represent robotic industrial systems in the form of graphs and use the analysis of embeddings to select the most suitable components. This approach is the closest to the idea proposed in this paper, however, it uses algorithmic optimization and not machine learning methods.

A review of methodologies for creating ontologies (which are semantic models of a problem area described as graph-like structures) in an industrial context [11] showed that only one of the considered methodologies used today in the field of enterprise modeling considers methods of reusing ontologies, and only on the level of standards and fixed fragments. The authors of [12] provide an overview of various existing systems for supporting business process modeling, but machine learning methods are not mentioned among them. The same is also true for the survey of research in enterprise modeling [13].

The necessity of balancing between pattern flexibility/diversity and the number of patterns to be analyzed manually is emphasized in paper [14], the authors of which proposed to expand the patterns to the concept of "bag of fragments" (a set of fragments), which are compared with the current configuration. It can be said that this work serves as a kind of link between the use of patterns and machine learning methods. Machine learning methods that allow both to identify such patterns by analyzing and summarizing the available big data, and to select and offer them to the user, depending on the situation, can be useful for solving this problem.

Today there already exist machine learning models, including those based on deep neural networks, which are focused on working with network-like structures and with graphs as particular. Paper [27] proposes a method for representing a graph in a form suitable for use in machine learning models and supporting parallelization of the learning process for efficient use of GPUs in order to increase the speed and performance of the learning process. In [28], the authors use the random forest machine learning paradigm to analyze the main flows within a transport network, representing the latter in the form of a graph. Such models are often successfully used today in chemistry. In [29], the authors use a graph to represent chemical compounds to use machine learning methods to generalize and predict their properties. A similar problem is solved in [30], with the use of machine learning methods. The authors of [31] apply machine learning to assist modeling particle processes.

Graph Neural Networks (GNN). Analyzing graphs using machine learning has received a lot of attention due to the great expressive power of the graphs. Graph neural networks can be defined as deep learning-based methods that operate on graphs. According to [32], GNN can be categorized into four groups: convolutional graph neural networks, recurrent graph neural networks, graph autoencoders, and spatial-temporal graph neural networks. The main tasks for graph learning are:

1. Node level: includes node classification, regression, and clustering tasks. While the first task aims to classify the nodes into several classes, the regression task predicts a continuous value of the node. The clustering task splits nodes into disjoint groups.
2. Edge-level: the main tasks are to predict whether there is an edge between two nodes (edge prediction or link prediction) and to classify edges.
3. Graph-level: includes graph matching, graph classification, and graph regression.

To solve the *edge prediction* task for knowledge graph, there have been developed several models with the main focus on transforming the graph into low dimensional space while preserving the semantic information or graph embedding based models. These models can be categorized into three groups [33]:

1. Translational-distance-based models inspired by word2vec [34] based on representing each word by a vector of length n that represents the coordinates of this word in the n-dimensional space (like TransE [35], TransH [36], TransM [37], and TransR [38]), however, these models are reported to have a low capability of capturing the semantic information.
2. Semantic-matching-based models (like DistMult [39] and Complex [40]) embed both the relations and the entities into a unified vector space and define a scoring function to measure the validity. Although these models capture more semantic information, they still have some drawbacks which make them inefficient when deep semantic information is needed.
3. Neural-network-based models (like ConvE [41], HypER [42], CNN-BiLSTM [43]).

The neural-network-based models take into consideration the node type and the path information, and use convolution layers and attention mechanisms for enhancing the embeddings. ConvE was the first model to use a convolutional neural network for graph completion. It uses 2D convolution for the entity and relation embedding after reshaping and concatenating them. HypER introduces "hypernetworks" based on ConvE to generate convolutional filter weights for each relation. HypER uses 1D filters for entity embeddings to simplify the interaction between entities and relational embeddings. CompGCN [44] is a novel GCN that performs a composition operator over each edge in the neighborhood of the central node. The composed embeddings are convolved using two filters representing the inverse and the original relations. The aggregated messages of the neighbors represent the updated embedding of the central node. CNN-BiLSTM combines bidirectional long short-term memory (BiLSTM) and convolutional neural network (CNN) modules with an attention mechanism. The CNN followed by BILSTM modules are used to embed relations into a low space dimension. The attention layer is used to capture the semantic correlation between the candidate relation and each path between the two entities, and extracts reasoning evidence from the representation of the paths to predict whether two nodes should be connected by the candidate relation or not.

While multiple models aimed at operating on graphs exist, there is still a lack of those aimed at work with enterprise models. With this research, we would like to bridge the gap between the models themselves and the application area of EM, and in this paper we are checking the fundamental possibility of this.

3 Proposed Approach

3.1 Machine Learning-Based Assistance of EM

In this section, we suggest main potential assistance scenarios during EM that can be supported by machine learning technologies based on the application of GNN.

Generally, GNNs are aimed at solving the following four tasks taking the entire available graph as the input:

1. Edge prediction: the model calculates the probability of the given edge.
2. Edge class prediction: the model classifies the given edge.
3. Node class prediction: the model classifies the given node.
4. Graph classification: the model classifies the entire graph.

Based on these tasks, the following EM tasks that can be potentially assisted with machine learning have been identified (Table 1):

Table 1. Association between tasks solved by GNN and EM processes

Task solved by GNN	Associated EM assistance suggestions
Edge prediction	1. Suggestion of edges 2. Identification of likely wrong edges
Edge class prediction	3. Suggestion of edge class 4. Identification of edges of likely wrong types or with wrong labels
Node class prediction	5. Suggestion of node class 6. Identification of nodes of likely wrong types or with wrong labels 7. Suggestion of nodes
Graph classification	8. Model verification 9. Model validation

1. Suggestion of possibly existing connections: given a partially defined EM, a number of connections can be randomly generated (or all possible connections can be generated) and those with high probability can be suggested to the modeler.
2. Identification of likely wrong edges: the probability of a newly added by the modeler edge can be evaluated and if it is low enough, the corresponding warning can be presented to the modeler.
3. Suggestion of the edge class: the model can suggest the class of the newly added edge (edge type, label, etc.).

At this point, it is worth mentioning that the "class" from the machine learning point of view is not necessarily only the class (or type) of an item in the modeling domain. This term can equally apply to various other characteristics of the item such as functions it performs, requirements it meets, or associated text labels. Besides, an item can be related to several classes simultaneously.

1. Identification of edges of likely wrong types or with wrong labels: the probability of the type or text label of a newly added by the modeler edge can be evaluated and if it is low enough, the corresponding warning can be presented to the modeler together with a suggestion of better fitting type or label.
2. Suggestion of the node class: the model can suggest the class of the newly added node (node type, label, etc.).

3. Identification of nodes of likely wrong types or with wrong labels: the probability of the type or text label of a newly added by the modeler node can be evaluated and if it is low enough, the corresponding warning can be presented to the modeler together with a suggestion of better fitting type or label.
4. Suggestion of nodes: in this scenario, a node needs to be generated first (for example, connected to a newly added by the modeler node), then classified, and then the probability of its edge(s) is evaluated; if the probability is high enough, the appropriate suggestion is shown to the modeler.
5. Model verification (checking for consistency, correctness, and meeting given standards): classification of the model to consistent/inconsistent, correct/incorrect, meeting the given standards or not.
6. Model validation (checking that the model fulfills the requirements and achieves the goal): classification of the model against the requirements.

While the first seven scenarios are clear and potentially possible given the sufficient training data (that does not seem to be impossible), the last two scenarios are subject of more remote future, since they require trusted training data in rather narrow domains, and the question "what data sources can be credibly used in this process" raised in [4] becomes important.

Summarizing the above scenarios, Fig. 1 illustrates the approach as a whole. The numbers in parenthesis correspond to the scenarios described above. The text labeling of edges and nodes can additionally be extended with using Natural Language Processing (NLP) machine learning models for text analysis, matching, and suggesting better naming during the modeling (cf. [45]), however, this issue is currently out of the scope of the current research.

3.2 GNN Models for Approach Feasibility Evaluation

In order to evaluate the validity of the above-described approach, two models have been built: the node classification model and the edge prediction model.

Node Classification Model. The node classification model is used to determine the node class (e.g., concept, resource, rule, etc.). The input of the model is the enterprise model graph represented by the node names and the edges connecting them. The output is the node class.

Before feeding the graph into the network, the label encoding has to be used to encode both the node name and the node's class name.

The model consists of two sage convolution layers [46] followed by three fully connected layers. The rectified linear unit (relu) function is used as the activation function for all the layers except the last layer where the sigmoid function is used. The sage convolution layers (SAGEConv) get the information from the neighbors and aggregate them using the mean function. The architecture used is shown in Fig. 2.

Edge Prediction Model. The edge prediction model is aimed at the prediction of missing edges in the enterprise model. The input of the model is a graph, where the nodes of the graph represent the main entities of the enterprise model (like concepts, organizational units, resources, rules, etc.) and the edges represent the connections between these entities. For each node, there are two attributes that describe the node (the class name, and the node description).

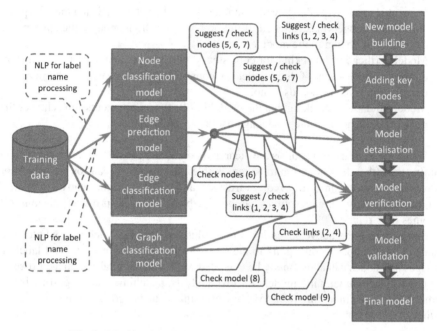

Fig. 1. Machine learning-based support of different EM stages.

Fig. 2. The architecture of the neural network used for node classification.

Before feeding the graph into the model, first, all its nodes have to be embedded. In the current version of the model, all nodes' names and the nodes' attributes in the graph are embedded using word2vec technique with Skip-gram architecture [47] using the word window of size 2.

For node description, the text is preprocessed by dropping all the stop words and mapping different forms of the word to the source using Snowball's stemming algorithm. Although this embedding is simple, which is essential for the proof of concept, it has a number of drawbacks for use in production. The main one is the need to recompute the embedding, every time a new node is added to the graph.

To keep things simple, in our approach, for now, we drop the description information and only use the node name alongside with the node class. The label encoding method is used to encode both the node class and the node name.

The edge prediction model consists of three graph convolutional layers (GCNConv) with rectified linear unit (relu) activation function. The similarity between the nodes is calculated using the cosine measure (Fig. 3).

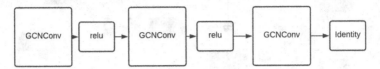

Fig. 3. The architecture of the neural network used for edge prediction task.

4 Experimental Evaluation

The overall experiment scheme is shown in Fig. 4.

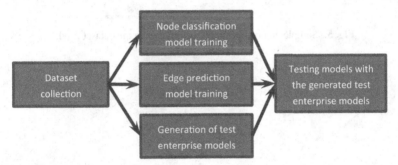

Fig. 4. The scheme of experimentation for testing the feasibility of the approach.

The dataset based on models built during the EM university course consists of 55 enterprise models with 1728 edges and 35 node classes. Figure 5 shows a sample model from the dataset. This set is not sufficient for productive use but can be still enough for the proof of the concept. Based on this test, two models have been trained: the node classification model and the edge prediction model.

The node classification model was trained for 200 epochs with the loss function negative log likelihood loss, Adam optimizer, and learning rate 0.005. Figure 6 shows the loss/accuracy graph during the training of node classification model.

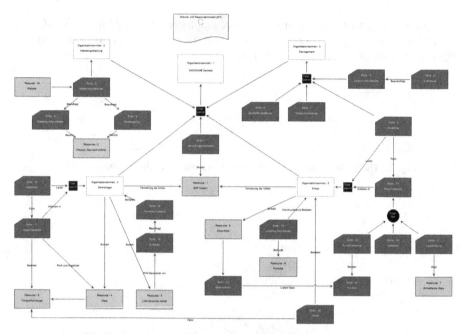

Fig. 5. Sample enterprise model example from the dataset used.

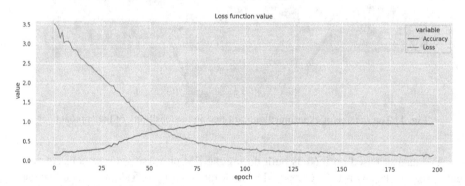

Fig. 6. The accuracy/loss graph during node classification model training.

The edge prediction model was trained for 1000 epochs with the loss function Binary Cross Entropy, Adam optimizer, and learning rate 0.01. Figure 7 shows the loss/accuracy graph during the edge prediction model training.

At this point, no hyperparameters tuning has been done. In future work, such hyperparameters as the learning rate, the number of epochs, and the batch size ca be adjusted.

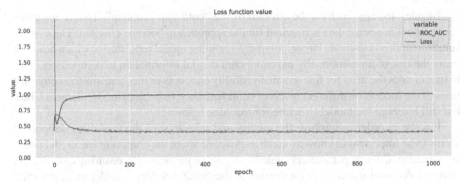

Fig. 7. The accuracy/loss graph during edge prediction model training.

For testing purposes, several enterprise models were built with definitely correct and wrong elements. Out of 1000 tested elements, the models correctly classified 962 elements resulting in an accuracy of 96.2%, precision of 0.9354, and the F1 score of 0.956.

5 Discussion

In our work, we presented a machine learning-based enterprise modeling support approach and analyzed its potentials. Our approach consists in application of machine learning models (GNN in particular) to support the modeler during the enterprise modelling process. We have also outlined the potential assistance scenarios and carried out proof of concept experiment.

All in all, we have demonstrated the feasibility and potentials of leveraging machine learning for enterprise modeling. On the positive side, such an approach would be capable of analyzing large amounts of available models up to a volume that could be considered as "Big Data" (i.e. thousands of models). This could be used to extract common patterns or to extract best practices, if any indication of the model's quality or other performance attribute is available. It would also prevent the modeler from untypical or rare solutions that might be prone to errors or simply superseded by improved solutions that the modeler is not aware of.

On the negative side however, such features always bear the risk of "nudging" the modeler towards mainstream solutions. This could lead to novel, original and innovative solutions being unnoticed or, even worse, considered as inferior or non-efficient. Hence additional research is required how to improve this situation.

The model can also suffer from the problem of data imbalance. By that we mean, that some enterprise models can have elements that occur only once like some resources and processes, and others that appear much often like some organizational units. This can lead to poor performance on the low frequent elements. To overcome this problem, as a start, we included data from several enterprises' models, so each training model consists of several similar models. Also in some models, we duplicated these elements. In that case, we increased the number of the low-frequent elements. In future work, more experiments will be conducted to overcome this problem.

Besides, the approach can be affected by the "cold start problem". That is, a significant amount of source data is required for the approach to become efficient. The evident solution for this is to create larger, company-spanning model repositories which however bears the risk of unintentionally exposing confidential information to competitors. This in turn creates the need for fine-grained visibility concepts or mechanisms to anonymize parts of the models on different levels of confidentiality, (e.g. blind model element labels but still leverage the model structure for machine learning).

Finally, in order to improve the quality and relevance of the modelling support, it seems to be important to know as much as possible about the context of the model under construction. Context parameters could be its *goal* or *purpose* (e.g. ensuring compliance, strategic decision making), *requirements* to the being developed model (e.g., ensuring model's flexibility), *subject matter* (e.g. procurement, production, marketing, finance, HR), enterprise-specific *enforced modeling conventions and constraints* (e.g. preferred terms, styles of expression, colors, formatting) or *intended addressees* (e.g. business experts, developers, lawyers, customers). Even though such context can potentially be identified based on already existing model elements, the problem is still critical when the modeler begins to model and the model contains only a few elements. In this situation, it is next to impossible to provide adequate modelling support without knowing this context parameters. Having the context as one of the input parameters for machine learning models is possible, however, this makes the problem of cold start more critical and requires additional research.

6 Conclusions and Future Work

The paper proposes application of machine learning (graph neural networks in particular) to assist a modeler during the enterprise modelling process and analyses its potentials. The main assistance scenarios associated with tasks solved by GNN have been identified. Some of them have been implemented to evaluate the feasibility of the approach.

It has been found that modelling support using machine learning techniques is feasible and has a significant potential. However, it still suffers the problems of suggesting mainstream solutions and identification of novel or unusual ones as incorrect. Besides, there is a problem of finding enough credible training data that is essential for building reliable and efficient models.

Planned future work is aimed at two main directions. First, deeper text analysis techniques can be used for dealing with labels and descriptions of enterprise model elements. This can be addressed with application of natural language processing techniques. The other direction is developing a prototype and collecting feedback from modelers to evaluate the effectiveness of the approach.

Acknowledgements. The paper is due to State Research no. 0073–2019-0005.

References

1. Riss, U.V., Maus, H., Javaid, S., Jilek, C.: Digital twins of an organization for enterprise modeling. In: PoEM 2020: The Practice of Enterprise Modeling. Lecture Notes in Business Information Processing. Springer, pp. 25–40 (2020)

2. Fayoumi, A.: Toward an Adaptive Enterprise Modelling Platform. In: Buchmann, R.A., Kara-giannis, D., Kirikova, M. (eds.) PoEM 2018. LNBIP, vol. 335, pp. 362–371. Springer, Cham (2018). https://doi.org/10.1007/978-3-030-02302-7_23
3. Awadid, A., Bork, D., Karagiannis, D., Nurcan, S.: Toward generic consistency patterns in multi-view enterprise modelling. In: ECIS 2018 Proceedings. AIS eLibrary, p. 146 (2018)
4. Snoeck, M., Stirna, J., Weigand, H., Proper, H.A.: Panel discussion: artificial intelligence meets enterprise modelling. In: The 12th IFIP Working Conference on The Practice of Enterprise Modeling, PoEM 2019. CEUR (2019)
5. van Gils, B., Proper, H.A.: Enterprise Modelling in the Age of Digital Transformation. In: Buchmann, R.A., Karagiannis, D., Kirikova, M. (eds.) PoEM 2018. LNBIP, vol. 335, pp. 257–273. Springer, Cham (2018). https://doi.org/10.1007/978-3-030-02302-7_16
6. Khider, H., Hammoudi, S., Meziane, A.: Business process model recommendation as a transformation process in MDE: conceptualization and first experiments. In: Proceedings of the 8th International Conference on Model-Driven Engineering and Software Development. SciTePress, pp. 65–75 (2020)
7. Rasmussen, J.B., Hvam, L., Kristjansdottir, K., Mortensen, N.H.: Guidelines for structuring object-oriented product configuration models in standard configuration software. J. Univ. Comput. Sci. **26**, 374–401 (2020)
8. Smirnov, A., Shchekotov, M., Shilov, N., Ponomarev, A.: Decision support service based on dynamic resource network configuration in human-computer cloud. In: 2018 23rd Conference of Open Innovations Association (FRUCT). IEEE, pp. 362–368 (2018)
9. Pereira, J.A., Schulze, S., Krieter, S., et al.: A context-aware recommender system for extended software product line configurations. In: Proceedings of the 12th International Workshop on Variability Modelling of Software-Intensive Systems. ACM, New York, NY, USA, pp. 97–104 (2018)
10. Hildebrandt, M., Sunder, S.S., Mogoreanu, S., Thon, I., Tresp, V., Runkler, T.: Configuration of industrial automation solutions using multi-relational recommender systems. In: Brefeld, U., et al. (eds.) ECML PKDD 2018. LNCS (LNAI), vol. 11053, pp. 271–287. Springer, Cham (2019). https://doi.org/10.1007/978-3-030-10997-4_17
11. Tarasov, V., Seigerroth, U., Sandkuhl, K.: Ontology development strategies in industrial contexts. In: Abramowicz, W., Paschke, A. (eds.) BIS 2018. LNBIP, vol. 339, pp. 156–167. Springer, Cham (2019). https://doi.org/10.1007/978-3-030-04849-5_14
12. Elkindy, A.I.A.: Survey of Business Process Modeling Recommender Systems. University of Koblenz - Landau (2019)
13. Vernadat, F.: Enterprise modelling: research review and outlook. Comput. Ind. **122**, 103265 (2020). https://doi.org/10.1016/j.compind.2020.103265
14. Wang, J., Gui, S., Cao, B.: A process recommendation method using bag-of-fragments. Int. J. Intell. Internet Things Comput. **1**, 32 (2019). https://doi.org/10.1504/IJIITC.2019.104734
15. Melville, P., Sindhwani, V.: Recommender systems. In: Sammut, C., Webb, G.I. (eds) Encyclopedia of Machine Learning. Springer US, Boston, MA, pp. 829–838 (2011)https://doi.org/10.1007/978-1-4471-5604-8_4
16. Fellmann, M., Metzger, D., Jannaber, S., et al.: Process modeling recommender systems - a generic data model and its application to a smart glasses-based modeling environment. Bus. Inf. Syst. Eng. **60**, 21–38 (2018)
17. Koschmider, A., Hornung, T., Oberweis, A.: Recommendation-based editor for business process modeling. Data Knowl. Eng. **70**, 483–503 (2011). https://doi.org/10.1016/j.datak.2011.02.002
18. Kuschke, T., Mäder, P.: Pattern-based auto-completion of UML modeling activities. In: Proceedings of the 29th ACM/IEEE International Conference on Automated Software Engineering. ACM, New York, NY, USA, pp. 551–556 (2014)

19. Wieloch, K., Filipowska, A., Kaczmarek, M.: Autocompletion for business process modelling. In: Abramowicz, W., Maciaszek, L., Węcel, K. (eds.) BIS 2011. LNBIP, vol. 97, pp. 30–40. Springer, Heidelberg (2011). https://doi.org/10.1007/978-3-642-25370-6_4

20. Born, M., Brelage, C., Markovic, I., Pfeiffer, D., Weber, I.: Auto-completion for executable business process models. In: Ardagna, D., Mecella, M., Yang, J. (eds.) BPM 2008. LNBIP, vol. 17, pp. 510–515. Springer, Heidelberg (2009). https://doi.org/10.1007/978-3-642-00328-8_51

21. Mazanek, S., Minas, M.: Business process models as a showcase for syntax-based assistance in diagram editors. In: Schürr, A., Selic, B. (eds.) MODELS 2009. LNCS, vol. 5795, pp. 322–336. Springer, Heidelberg (2009). https://doi.org/10.1007/978-3-642-04425-0_24

22. Clever, N., Holler, J., Shitkova, M., Becker, J.: Towards auto-suggested process modeling – prototypical development of an auto-suggest component for process modeling tools. In: Enterprise Modelling and Information Systems Architectures (EMISA 2013). Gesellschaft für Informatik e.V., pp. 133–145 (2013)

23. Fellmann, M., Zarvić, N., Thomas, O.: Business processes modelling assistance by recommender functionalities: a first evaluation from potential users. In: Johansson, B., Møller, C., Chaudhuri, A., Sudzina, F. (eds.) BIR 2017. LNBIP, vol. 295, pp. 79–92. Springer, Cham (2017). https://doi.org/10.1007/978-3-319-64930-6_6

24. Li, Y., Cao, B., Xu, L., et al.: An efficient recommendation method for improving business process modeling. IEEE Trans. Industr. Inf. **10**, 502–513 (2014). https://doi.org/10.1109/TII.2013.2258677

25. Nair, A., Ning, X., Hill, J.H.: Using recommender systems to improve proactive modeling. Softw. Syst. Model. **20**(4), 1159–1181 (2021). https://doi.org/10.1007/s10270-020-00841-2

26. Kögel, S.: Recommender system for model driven software development. In: Proceedings of the 2017 11th Joint Meeting on Foundations of Software Engineering. ACM, New York, NY, USA, pp. 1026–1029 (2017)

27. Jangda, A., Polisetty, S., Guha, A., Serafini, M.: Accelerating graph sampling for graph machine learning using GPUs. In: Proceedings of the Sixteenth European Conference on Computer Systems. ACM, New York, NY, USA, pp. 311–326 (2021)

28. Valera, M., et al.: Machine learning for graph-based representations of three-dimensional discrete fracture networks. Comput. Geosci. **22**(3), 695–710 (2018). https://doi.org/10.1007/s10596-018-9720-1

29. Chen, C., Ye, W., Zuo, Y., et al.: Graph networks as a universal machine learning framework for molecules and crystals. Chem. Mater. **31**, 3564–3572 (2019). https://doi.org/10.1021/acs.chemmater.9b01294

30. Na, G.S., Chang, H., Kim, H.W.: Machine-guided representation for accurate graph-based molecular machine learning. Phys. Chem. Chem. Phys. **22**, 18526–18535 (2020). https://doi.org/10.1039/D0CP02709J

31. Nielsen, R.F., Nazemzadeh, N., Sillesen, L.W., et al.: Hybrid machine learning assisted modelling framework for particle processes. Comput. Chem. Eng. **140**, 106916 (2020). https://doi.org/10.1016/j.compchemeng.2020.106916

32. Wu, Z., Pan, S., Chen, F., et al.: A comprehensive survey on graph neural networks. IEEE Trans. Neural Netw. Learn. Syst. **32**, 4–24 (2021). https://doi.org/10.1109/TNNLS.2020.2978386

33. Wang, M., Qiu, L., Wang, X.: A survey on knowledge graph embeddings for link prediction. Symmetry **13**, 485 (2021). https://doi.org/10.3390/sym13030485

34. Mikolov, T., Sutskever, I., Chen, K., et al.: Distributed Representations of Words and Phrases and their Compositionality (2013)

35. Bordes, A., Usunier, N., Garcia-Duran, A., et al.: Translating embeddings for modeling multi-relational dat. Adv. Neural Inf. Process. Syst. (NIPS 2013) 26 (2013)

36. Wang, Z., Zhang, J., Feng, J., Chen, Z.: Knowledge graph embedding by translating on hyperplanes. In: AAAI 2014: Proceedings of the Twenty-Eighth AAAI Conference on Artificial Intelligence, pp. 1112–1119 (2014)
37. Fan, M., Zhou, Q., Chang, E., Zheng, T.F.: Transition-based knowledge graph embedding with relational mapping properties. In: Proceedings of the 28th Pacific Asia Conference on Language, Information and Computing. Department of Linguistics, Chulalongkorn University, pp. 328–337 (2014)
38. Lin, Y., Liu1, Z., Sun, M., et al.: Learning entity and relation embeddings for knowledge graph completion. In: Proceedings of the Twenty-Ninth AAAI Conference on Artificial Intelligence, pp. 2181–2187 (2015)
39. Yang, B., Yih, W., He, X., et al.: Embedding Entities and Relations for Learning and Inference in Knowledge Bases (2014)
40. Trouillon, T., Welbl, J., Riedel, S., et al.: Complex Embeddings for Simple Link Prediction (2016)
41. Dettmers, T., Minervini, P., Stenetorp, P., Riedel, S.: Convolutional 2D Knowledge Graph Embeddings (2017)
42. Balažević, I., Allen, C., Hospedales, T.M.: Hypernetwork knowledge graph embeddings. In: Tetko, I.V., Kůrková, V., Karpov, P., Theis, F. (eds.) ICANN 2019. LNCS, vol. 11731, pp. 553–565. Springer, Cham (2019). https://doi.org/10.1007/978-3-030-30493-5_52
43. Jagvaral, B., Lee, W.-K., Roh, J.-S., et al.: Path-based reasoning approach for knowledge graph completion using CNN-BiLSTM with attention mechanism. Expert Syst. Appl. **142**, 112960 (2020). https://doi.org/10.1016/j.eswa.2019.112960
44. Vashishth, S., Sanyal, S., Nitin, V., Talukdar, P.: Composition-based Multi-Relational Graph Convolutional Networks (2019)
45. Sonntag, A., Hake, P., Fettke, P., Loos, P.: An approach for semantic business process model matching using supervised machine learning. In: European Conference on Information Systems (ECIS) (2016)
46. Hamilton, W.L., Ying, R., Leskovec, J.: Inductive Representation Learning on Large Graphs (2017)
47. Mikolov, T., Chen, K., Corrado, G., Dean, J.: Efficient estimation of word representations in vector space. In: Proceedings of the International Conference on Learning Representations (ICLR 2013) (2013)

The Models for Knowledge Acquisition in PMI Specific Requirements Engineering

Ksenija Lace[(⊠)] and Marite Kirikova[(⊠)]

Riga Technical University, Riga, Latvia
ksenija.lace@edu.rtu.lv, marite.kirikova@rtu.lv

Abstract. Knowledge acquisition is an important part of any requirements engineering activity, as it builds the foundation for all decisions and actions performed. In PMI activities knowledge acquisition is equally important and more complicated as in requirements engineering in general. This leads us to the conclusion that PMI initiative should have an additional focus on the knowledge acquisition. This paper explores requirements elicitation for PMI as a knowledge acquisition process and proposes models for its accomplishment. It covers the following research steps - required characteristics of an effective PMI requirements elicitation are identified, corresponding existing research is analyzed, possible adjustments to the previously presented requirements elicitation model are identified, enhanced knowledge acquisition model is proposed, and the proposed model is illustrated with a real application example. As a result of this research the adjusted and detailed PMI specific knowledge acquisition model for PMI specific requirements engineering has been created that consists of two parts – the knowledge acquisition process model and the knowledge acquisition data model.

Keywords: Mergers & acquisitions · Knowledge management · Requirements Engineering · Elicitation

1 Introduction

Nowadays one of the main approaches for business growth is merge of several companies to create one bigger and stronger company, with more resources and higher potential. Merge initiative is a complex and long process with the extensive planning phase. Planning includes merge goal definition, search for potential merge partners, discussions, and agreements. But once planning is finished and the deal is signed, a merge should be executed. Practical execution of a merge initiative is called post-merger integration (PMI) and during this process companies are combined to form one union [24]. PMI covers all different aspects of the organizational architecture, including technical perspective, social perspective, and cyber perspective. This makes PMI a process for integration of several socio-cyber -physical systems (SCPSs) [25].

Knowledge acquisition is an important part of any requirements engineering (RE) activity, as it builds the foundation for all decisions and actions performed. If some knowledge is missing, under-evaluated or misinterpreted, there is a high risk that requirements

© IFIP International Federation for Information Processing 2021
Published by Springer Nature Switzerland AG 2021
E. Serral et al. (Eds.): PoEM 2021, LNBIP 432, pp. 34–47, 2021.
https://doi.org/10.1007/978-3-030-91279-6_3

will not represent the real need [4]. This becomes even more important in the scope of PMI activity, as it has additional difficulties to the knowledge acquisition, such as cultural barriers, strict time limitations, high complexity, and limited ability to learn from previous projects [5]. In the recent research [23], the authors of this paper, by studying existing RE models from the perspective of their applicability for the requirements identification of PMI initiatives, detected required improvements, and proposed a generic RE Model for PMI contexts [23]. The proposed model was verified through its application for the PMI initiative example. This model covers both static and dynamic perspectives of the PMI RE and includes three stages of PMI project, namely, Initial Assessment, Decisions and Plan, and Plan Execution. In the model, the initial assessment phase of PMI corresponds to the RE elicitation phase. The model was feasible in general, but further improvements were required including more detailed description of each RE activities. In this paper, the Initial Assessment phase of PMI Specific RE Model, i.e., RE elicitation phase is explored in detail from the point of view of knowledge acquisition.

Thus, the goal of this paper is defining a detailed knowledge acquisition process and main concepts relevant in requirements elicitation in PMI context. To achieve this goal, the following research method was used: PMI requirements elicitation related literature was reviewed regarding PMI specific requirement elicitation quality criteria, PMI elicitation related quality criteria, and exiting approaches how these criteria are achieved; after that the most promising approaches were selected and adopted into the previously proposed PMI specific RE model [23]; then, the adjusted model was applied to the PMI project example to verify its applicability and identify possible improvements.

The rest of the paper is structured as follows: Sect. 2 is focused on the definition of a quality criteria for PMI specific requirement elicitation and review of most suitable existing requirements elicitation approaches; Sect. 3 proposes PMI RE elicitation specific model; Sect. 4 presents the demonstration of the proposed model applicability; brief summary is provided in Sect. 5.

2   PMI Requirements Elicitation Quality Criteria and Literature Review

In this section the most suitable requirements elicitation approaches are reviewed from the perspective of an applicability for PMI RE.

From the elicitation process organizational perspective, PMI Specific RE Model includes the following high-level requirement elicitation activities [23]:

- Identify related information resources
- Gather knowledge on goals
- Gather knowledge on the context
- Gather knowledge on architectures

Existing requirements engineering approaches covering one or several of the elicitation activities were reviewed in [23]. Additionally, SCPS specific and PMI specific elicitation approaches were investigated.

From elicitation process related risks and issues perspective, if we look on the PMI as the SCPS initiative with a major part being social elements, there are the following open questions that need to be addressed in the scope of PMI specific requirement elicitation [6, 21]:

- How to elicit both tacit and explicit knowledge
- How to elicit SCPS specific requirements
- How to elicit merge & acquisition specific requirements

In total 53 research papers were reviewed for the publication period from 2000 or later. The following research libraries were used – Science Direct, Springer, IEEE Xplore. The following key words were searched – elicitation & SCPS, elicitation & mergers and acquisitions, knowledge & mergers and acquisitions, tacit knowledge & mergers and acquisitions. Research did not follow any specific methodology. First, all papers were explored to filter out papers discussing M&A knowledge related challenges. Selected papers were investigated in more details to define main issues that need to be solved for the effective M&A knowledge elicitation. To get more deep understanding, authors additionally explored research papers identified as a research foundation for papers focusing on knowledge elicitation issues. After that, additional search was executed to find papers focusing on the solutions for more efficient knowledge elicitation in general, as well as on the solutions for previously identified M&A knowledge elicitation issues. All found papers were evaluated from the point of solution applicability to M&A context. Below are summarized the findings from the existing research, which is related to required requirements elicitation adjustments for SCPS and PMI specifics, by focusing on the above-mentioned questions. Additionally, research works exploring other risks and issues for PMI related requirements elicitation were reviewed.

Goal information elicitation is one of the first steps in RE. In [16] the goal, question, and answer approach is proposed. This approach focuses on the acquiring detailed information about goals, as well as creating tree-like goals decomposition structure. The approach uses required and anticipated functions perspective to define and formulate project goals. In PMI it is important to state clear and detailed goals, as this defines overall PMI initiative direction. In [9] authors describe the method how to organize goal related knowledge acquisition using the perspectives challenge – goal- function. This helps to focus on real problems and not create non required goals. In [14], overconfidence of involved leaders is stated as one of the reasons for PMI failure, meaning that often PMI related risks are underestimated. Research describes the way how PMI related risks can be identified early in a project, and corresponding action plan created. It is advised to start risk identification as soon as goals are defined.

After goals are defined, next step is to identify corresponding information sources. As finding tacit knowledge is one of the biggest challenges for requirements elicitation, stakeholders should be identified very carefully, as well as each of them should be assessed from the perspective how tacit knowledge can be gathered. In [18] the approach for stakeholder identification is described. In addition to common practices, the research points out the necessity to gather additional information about stakeholders, as well as to use information about relationships between stakeholders to find out additional stakeholders for the PMI initiative.

After all information sources are defined, it is time to plan for the elicitation. In [8] the importance of the assessment of data availability and quality prior any elicitation activities are highlighted, so that required adjustments in the elicitation can be planned. In [2] authors propose the approach for identification of unknown by using adjusted elicitation techniques. Challenges for tacit knowledge identification, as well as appropriate elicitation techniques are described in [19]. In PMI it is important to define all known knowns and known unknowns prior the elicitation, as well as elaborate on the list after each elicitation activity to find new known unknowns and plan the elicitation for them. Knowing goals, risks, related information sources and issues with data accessibility and quality helps to find the most effective elicitation techniques. Possible elicitation techniques are described also in [17]. But [13] gives the method how to apply efficiency criteria for elicitation technique selection procedures. As PMI initiatives usually have time and resource availability constraints, it is important to choose the most effective techniques to acquire the knowledge with minimum required effort.

In [1] authors discuss the importance of predefined standardized questionaries during elicitation activities, as well as the process of lessons learned. As software integration plays important role in the overall PMI success, in [12] specific questions for software related knowledge identification are defined. As for tacit knowledge acquisition, as well as for respecting cultural aspect, it is required to identify stakeholders' perspectives on the elicited knowledge. This topic is elaborated in [10] by incorporating opinions and rationales as part of acquired knowledge on the previously identified information. As for cultural perspective importance, [7] stresses out the value of cultural aspects in scope of PMI, as well es defines the approach how to identify cultural aspects which can become blockers for PMI success. Crucial element during the elicitation is also constant evaluation of gathered information quality and planning adjustments in the elicitation. Method for the elicitation results evaluation is explored in [15].

Elicited information should be structured so that it can be analyzed in the next requirement engineering phases. Structuring approaches are defined in the following articles:

- [11] – incorporation domain ontology
- [3] – statement of all three perspectives: economic, social and technical
- [20] – depiction of embedded systems specifics
- [22] – representation of enterprise architecture

None of the above reviewed research works covers all elicitation activities and takes into account all PMI and SCPS specifics. However, each of them can contribute to the PMI specific RE knowledge acquisition models for requirements elicitation.

3   PMI Specific Knowledge Acquisition Model

This section describes how previously defined PMI specific high abstractions level elicitation [23] can be detailed and enhanced, based on the findings in the existing research.

As stated before, there is no one holistic approach for PMI requirements elicitation, however, generic knowledge acquisition process can be enhanced by incorporating activities focused on solving the identified PMI issues and risks (as illustrated in Fig. 1):

- During PMI goal identification – create more detailed goal-trees [9, 16], as well as identify all known knowns and known unknowns [2]
- During identification of related information sources – focus more on the identification of stakeholders and related information [18]
- During planning elicitation – incorporate data accessibility and quality evaluation [8], state elicitation challenges and come up with corresponding elicitation techniques [13, 17, 19]
- During conducting elicitation – use standardized elicitation questionaries [1, 12], pay attention to stakeholder perspectives and rationales [10]
- During analysis of elicitation results – structure knowledge per economic, technical, social, and cultural perspectives [7, 10], use gathered knowledge to identify new known unknowns [2], evaluate gathered data quality and plan additional elicitation if necessary [15], as well as define goals related risks [14]

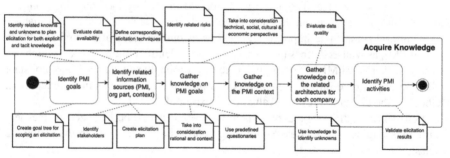

Fig. 1. Possible enhancements in the knowledge acquisition process (6 steps, UML activity diagram)

Based on the defined possible enhancements, Initial 6-step knowledge acquisition process model was reworked and transformed into 5-step model (as illustrated in Fig. 2) where:

- Initially, goals tree for PMI initiative should be created
- For each goal, related information sources (stakeholders, documents, and systems in operations) are defined
- For each information source the elicitation is planned – known knowns and known unknowns are defined, elicitation techniques are selected, potential elicitation challenges are defined, and corresponding solutions selected. All previously mentioned issues are summarized in an elicitation plan
- For each planned elicitation activity elicitation is conducted – additional information about known knowns and known unknowns is gathered, stakeholders' perspectives

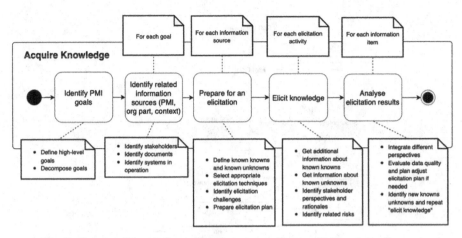

Fig. 2. Enhanced knowledge acquisition process (5 steps, UML activity diagram)

together with their rationales are identified, respecting related risks, which can block goal achievements

- For each acquired information item – gathered information is structured into economic, technical, social and cultural perspectives. Information quality is evaluated and required action items are planned. Finally, new known unknowns are defined, and additional elicitation activities are planned

Together with process changes, adjustments in initial class (sub) model of PMI RE model [23] also were required (see Fig. 3).

The initial model contained the information and knowledge artefacts related to PMI initiative, current organizational structure perspectives, context perspectives, as well as future merge decisions and related changes. PMI goal and PMI initiative are the only elements reused from the previous model. The following additional elements were added:

- To cover elicitation information source elements - Stakeholder, Document and System in operation elements were added, as well as related Known known and Known unknown elements
- To include elicitation planning - Elicitation technique, Elicitation challenge, Elicitation challenge solution and Elicitation plan elements were added
- To keep data about knowledge evaluation - Quality evaluation and Elicitation challenge solution elements were added
- To accumulate knowledge gathered during the elicitation - Information item element was added
- To structure gathered knowledge - Economic perspective, Technical perspective, Social perspective, and Cultural perspective elements were added
- To highlight identified risks for goal achievement - Risk element was added

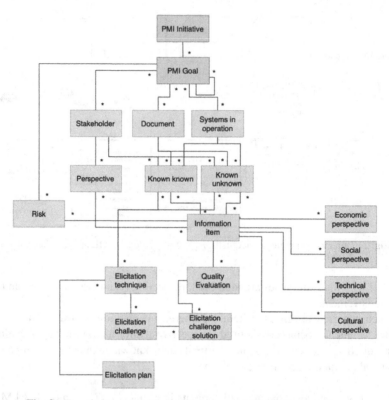

Fig. 3. Knowledge acquisition related class model (UML class diagram)

4   Demonstration of the Applicability of the Proposed Model

In this section the proposed model was used for the real-life example to verify model's applicability, as well as find possible model improvements. The process of model application, as well as the resulting artefacts in a form of object models are described below.

During "Identify PMI goals" step, initial goal "Align practices and optimize resources" was initially divided into two separate goals "Use same common processes" and "Optimize resources". After that "Optimize resources" was parted into two sides of optimization "Merge resources" and "Improve resources efficiency". Then "Merge resources" was decomposed into more tangible goals "Merge human resources", "Merge IS resources" and "Merge other resources". The results are illustrated in Fig. 4.

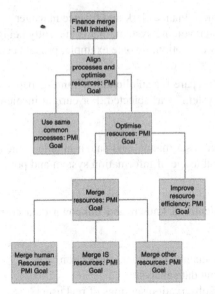

Fig. 4. Goal identification artefacts - goal tree (UML object diagram)

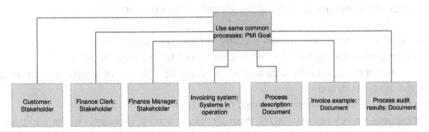

Fig. 5. Information sources artefacts – stakeholder, document, and systems in operation (UML object diagram)

For the next step - "Identify information sources", goal "Use same common processes" was selected for illustrative purpose in scope of this article. For the simplicity, this paper covers elicitation in scope of one company only – acquiring company. But in real life the same activities should be performed also for the acquired company. For this goal the following information sources were identified (illustrated in Fig. 5):

- Stakeholders – customer, finance clerk and finance manager
- Systems in operation – invoicing system, that is currently being used
- Documents - process description, invoice example, process audit results

For the next step - "Prepare for an elicitation", in this paper, one specific information source "Invoicing system" was selected. For current invoicing system known and unknown data is identified:

- Known known – system user manual and data available in the information system
- Known unknown – real usage of information system and possible improvements for this system

Then for each of identified known and unknown data corresponding elicitation technique was selected:

- System user manual – manual document inspection
- Data in the IS – existing data analysis
- Real usage of the IS – observation sessions of real users
- Possible improvements for IS – survey and interviews of stakeholders

For each elicitation technique, respecting also information that should be elicited, challenges and solutions for solving these challenges were identified:

- Outdated version of user manual – verify version relevance
- Non structured data in the IS – create data model to structure IS data
- Too many approaches how data is entered in the IS – prioritize approaches to focus on the most important
- No trust from user to share real usage of IS – build trust relationships
- Ambiguous survey results – walk through results with respondents to get additional comments
- Too many and too different opinions about IS improvements – analyze and prioritize stakeholders to prioritize their input
- Conflicting opinions about IS improvements – apply conflict resolution techniques to find agreement

All artefacts are illustrated in Fig. 6.

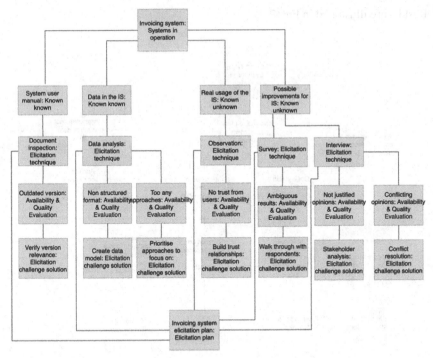

Fig. 6. Preparation for elicitation artefacts - known knowns, known unknowns, related elicitation techniques, information evaluation and elicitation challenge solutions, as well as overall elicitation plan (UML object diagram)

One specific known unknown "Real usage of the IS" was selected for the next step "Elicit knowledge" illustration. After selected elicitation techniques were executed, the following information items were created – "Observation video" and "Observation protocols".

Each of this information items were analyzed in order to identify risks related to the ability to achieve stated goal "Use same common processes". The following risks were identified:

- System requires comprehensive learning for new users
- System contains only part of required data
- Additional licenses are required to use the system for both companies
- For each information item stakeholder perspectives were additionally elicited:
- Finance clerk - comments from user perspective about the observation video
- Finance manager – additional comments from user perspective about the observation video and the opinion on required IS changes for observation protocol
- Customer – opinion on observation protocol about IS issues from a customer perspective

Results are illustrated in Fig. 7.

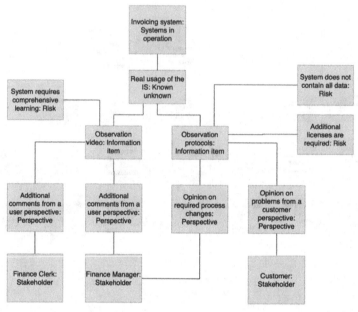

Fig. 7. Knowledge acquisition artefacts - information items, related risks and stakeholder perspectives (UML object diagram)

"Observation protocols" information item was selected for the illustration of the next step "Analyze elicitation results". Firstly, information item data was divided into different perspectives:

- Economic perspective - cost of required system changes and financial loses due to system issues
- Technical perspective – system functionality
- Social perspective – user characteristics
- Cultural perspective – attitudes towards the system usage

Information item data quality was evaluated and "No statistical data" represented in the protocols issue was identified. To solve this issue, solution "Observe mode users" was selected. This solution requires additional elicitation sessions to be executed using the process described previously.

Additionally, related new known unknowns were identified – "Priority of found issues" and "User competence level". For each of them elicitation activity should be planned and executed as it was described earlier.

The results are illustrated in Fig. 8.

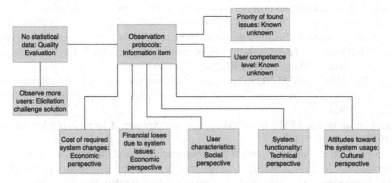

Fig. 8. Elicitation results analysis artefacts - information item evaluation and elicitation challenge solutions, as well as economic, technical, social, and cultural perspectives (UML object diagram)

5 Summary

This article explores the elicitation part of PMI specific requirements engineering model. Authors defined the required elicitation quality criteria, reviewed existing research works and identified possible solutions for the adjustments and elaborations of the previously defined high-level PMI specific elicitation process.

PMI specific elicitation requires enhanced goal analysis, proper planning with potential issue resolution plan. All these aspects are included in the proposed PMI RE elicitation model with a dedicated goal model, and elicitation plan model as crucial elements of PMI RE. Additionally, PMI RE as SCPS RE requires structured information covering all economic, technical, social, and cultural perspectives. All SCPS perspectives are incorporated into proposed model. With a high risk to miss PMI related tacit knowledge, which simultaneously is one of core components for PMI success, model's cultural perspective, includes also eliciting stakeholder opinions on the gathered information. The proposed models also support iterative elicitation approach, through uncovering new known unknowns during the elicitation process and repeating elicitation activities for them.

For the future research the following improvements and additions to the model could be made:

- Describe in more details process of information sources identification and sources related information structure
- Detailed description of elicitation technique selection (including technique selection criteria)
- List of standardized elicitation questions
- Checklist for possible PMI goals related risks
- Templates for artefacts contents
- Incorporate into data model relationships to enterprise architecture and context

References

1. Butler, S.: The standardisation of due diligence questionnaires: practical ambition or dream?. Pensions: Int. J. **11**(2), 120–129 (2006). https://doi.org/10.1057/palgrave.pm.5940013
2. Sutcliffe, A., Sawyer, P.: Requirements elicitation: towards the unknown unknowns. In: 2013 21st IEEE International Requirements Engineering Conference, RE 2013 - Proceedings, 92–104 (2013). https://doi.org/10.1109/RE.2013.6636709
3. Dey, S., Lee, S.W.: REASSURE: requirements elicitation for adaptive socio-technical systems using repertory grid. Inf. Softw. Technol. **87**, 160–179 (2017). https://doi.org/10.1016/j.infsof.2017.03.004
4. Nääs, I., et al. (eds.): APMS 2016. IAICT, vol. 488. Springer, Cham (2016). https://doi.org/10.1007/978-3-319-51133-7
5. Knauss, A.: On the usage of context for requirements elicitation: end-user involvement in IT ecosystems. In: 2012 20th IEEE International Requirements Engineering Conference, RE 2012 - Proceedings, 345–348 (2012). https://doi.org/10.1109/RE.2012.6345835
6. Raza, S.A.: Managing ethical requirements elicitation of complex socio-technical systems with critical systems thinking: a case of course-timetabling project. Technol. Soc. **66**(June), 101626 (2021). https://doi.org/10.1016/j.techsoc.2021.101626
7. Burke, D., Kovela, S.: ITMA - IT integration in mergers and acquisitions. Int. J. Bus. Manage. **12**(11), 16 (2017). https://doi.org/10.5539/ijbm.v12n11p16
8. Capgemini.: IT in M&A: The way we see it (2015)
9. Kancherla, A.K., Kummamuru, S.: Framework for post merger integration using systems principles. In: Proceedings - 2011 Annual IEEE India Conference: Engineering Sustainable Solutions, INDICON-2011 (2011). https://doi.org/10.1109/INDCON.2011.6139602
10. Al-Alshaikh, H.A., Mirza, A.A., Alsalamah, H.A.: Extended rationale-based model for tacit knowledge elicitation in requirements elicitation context. IEEE Access **8**, 60801–60810 (2020). https://doi.org/10.1109/ACCESS.2020.2982837
11. Lee, Y., Zhao, W.: Domain requirements elicitation and analysis - an ontology-based approach. In: Alexandrov, V.N., van Albada, G.D., Sloot, P.M.A., Dongarra, J. (eds.) ICCS 2006. LNCS, vol. 3994, pp. 805–813. Springer, Heidelberg (2006). https://doi.org/10.1007/11758549_108
12. Schenkhuizen, J., van Langerak, R., Jansen, S., Popp, K.M.: Defining the process of acquiring product software firms. In: Lassenius, C., Smolander, K. (eds.) ICSOB 2014. LNBIP, vol. 182, pp. 100–114. Springer, Cham (2014). https://doi.org/10.1007/978-3-319-08738-2_8
13. Van Der Merwe, A., Kotzé, P.: Criteria used in selecting effective requirements elicitation procedures. ACM Int. Conf. Proc. Ser. **226**, 162–171 (2007). https://doi.org/10.1145/1292491.1292510
14. Asaoka, D.: Behavioral analysis of mergers and acquisitions decisions. Corp. Board Role Duties Compos. **15**(3), 8–16 (2019). https://doi.org/10.22495/cbv15i3art1
15. Tsao, C.T.: Applying a fuzzy multiple criteria decision-making approach to the M&A due diligence. Expert Syst. Appl. **36**(2 PART 1), 1559–1568 (2009). https://doi.org/10.1016/j.eswa.2007.11.041
16. Zhi, Q., Zhou, Z., Morisaki, S., Yamamoto, S.: An approach for requirements elicitation using goal, question, and answer. In: Proceedings - 2019 8th International Congress on Advanced Applied Informatics, IIAI-AAI 2019, pp. 847–852 (2019). https://doi.org/10.1109/IIAI-AAI.2019.00172
17. Dar, H., Lali, M.I., Ashraf, H., Ramzan, M., Amjad, T., Shahzad, B.: A systematic study on software requirements elicitation techniques and its challenges in mobile application development. IEEE Access **6**, 63859–63867 (2018). https://doi.org/10.1109/ACCESS.2018.2874981

18. Pacheco, C., Garcia, I.: A systematic literature review of stakeholder identification methods in requirements elicitation. J. Syst. Softw. **85**(9), 2171–2181 (2012). https://doi.org/10.1016/j.jss.2012.04.075
19. Sandhu, R.K., Weistroffer, H.R.: A review of fundamental tasks in requirements elicitation. In: Wrycza, S., Maślankowski, J. (eds.) SIGSAND/PLAIS 2018. LNBIP, vol. 333, pp. 31–44. Springer, Cham (2018). https://doi.org/10.1007/978-3-030-00060-8_3
20. Pereira, T., Sousa, A., Oliveira, R., Albuquerque, D., Alencar, F., Castro, J.: A metamodel to guide a requirements elicitation process for embedded systems. In: Proceedings - 2018 International Conference on the Quality of Information and Communications Technology, QUATIC 2018, 101–109 (2018). https://doi.org/10.1109/QUATIC.2018.00023
21. Kumari, s.N., Pillai, A.S.: A study on the software requirements elicitation issues - Its causes and effects. In: 2013 3rd World Congress on Information and Communication Technologies, WICT 2013, pp. 245–252 (2014). https://doi.org/10.1109/WICT.2013.7113143
22. Escalona, M.J., Aragón, G., Linger, H., Lang, M., Barry, C., Schneider, C. (eds.): Information system development. Springer, Cham (2014). https://doi.org/10.1007/978-3-319-07215-9
23. Buchmann, R.A., Polini, A., Johansson, B., Karagiannis, D. (eds.): BIR 2021. LNBIP, vol. 430. Springer, Cham (2021). https://doi.org/10.1007/978-3-030-87205-2
24. Riedel, L., Asghari, R.: Mergers and acquisitions as enabler of digital business transformation: introducing an integrated process. In: Sangwan, K.S., Herrmann, C. (eds.) Enhancing Future Skills and Entrepreneurship. SPLCEM, pp. 271–279. Springer, Cham (2020). https://doi.org/10.1007/978-3-030-44248-4_27
25. Motta, M., Peitz, M.: Big tech mergers. Inf. Econ. Policy **54**, 100868 (2021). https://doi.org/10.1016/j.infoecopol.2020.100868

Using Knowledge Graphs to Detect Enterprise Architecture Smells

Muhamed Smajevic[1], Simon Hacks[2,3], and Dominik Bork[1(✉)]

[1] TU Wien, Business Informatics Group, Vienna, Austria
e11742556@student.tuwien.ac.at, dominik.bork@tuwien.ac.at
[2] Division of Network and Systems Engineering, KTH Royal Institute of Technology, Stockholm, Sweden
shacks@kth.se
[3] The Maersk Mc-Kinney Moller Institute, University of Southern Denmark, Odense, Denmark
shacks@mmmi.sdu.dk

Abstract. Hitherto, the concept of Enterprise Architecture (EA) Smells has been proposed to assess quality flaws in EAs and their models. Together with this new concept, a catalog of different EA Smells has been published and a first prototype was developed. However, this prototype is limited to ArchiMate and is not able to assess models adhering to other EA modeling languages. Moreover, the prototype is not integrateable with other EA tools. Therefore, we propose to enhance the extensible Graph-based Enterprise Architecture Analysis (eGEAA) platform that relies on Knowledge Graphs with EA Smell detection capabilities. To align these two approaches, we show in this paper, how ArchiMate models can be transformed into Knowledge Graphs and provide a set of queries on the Knowledge Graph representation that are able to detect EA Smells. This enables enterprise architects to assess EA Smells on all types of EA models as long as there is a Knowledge Graph representation of the model. Finally, we evaluate the Knowledge Graph based EA Smell detection by analyzing a set of 347 EA models.

Keywords: Enterprise architecture · Model transformation · ArchiMate · Knowledge graph · Analysis

1 Introduction

With the increasing complexity of today's enterprises and enterprise ecosystems, creating, using, and maintaining a model representation thereof becomes increasingly challenging. Enterprise Architecture Management (EAM) with the de-facto industry standard modeling language ArchiMate [28] provides a high-level view of different enterprise domains (e.g., business, application, and technology) as well as their interrelationships. However, ArchiMate has also limitations, especially with respect to its semantic specificity [30] and the capabilities it offers to process the modeled information [7].

© IFIP International Federation for Information Processing 2021
Published by Springer Nature Switzerland AG 2021
E. Serral et al. (Eds.): PoEM 2021, LNBIP 432, pp. 48–63, 2021.
https://doi.org/10.1007/978-3-030-91279-6_4

Naturally, with the increasing complexity of the modeled system under study, also the complexity of the model itself increases. Although Enterprise Architecture (EA) modeling is widely adopted in industry and much research is conducted in the field, the analysis of EA models is surprisingly underrepresented [2, 19]. Generally, two analysis approaches can be distinguished: manual and automated. Given the discussed complexity of EA models, manual analysis *"can be complicated and omissions or miscalculations are very likely."* [10] Automated model analysis can mitigate this problem by scaling well and by providing interactive analysis means that extend static ones [22]. Aside from first attempts to equip EA modeling by advanced visualization and analysis techniques [5, 12, 17, 21, 31, 40], automated analysis of EA models is still underdeveloped.

The value of EA models is of course threatened by the shortcomings stressed at the outset. To mitigate parts of these problems, in the paper at hand, we concentrate on the use and maintenance of EA models. In particular, we want to automatically and efficiently analyze even large EA models with the aim to detect *EA Smells*. EA Smells have been recently proposed as a novel and promising research direction [33]. EA Smells are inspired by Code Smells, which are a common means to indicate possible Technical Debts [8]. Generally, a smell describes a qualitative issue that effects future efforts (e.g., maintenance) and not the functionality. While Code Smells analyze source code, EA Smells analyze an organization from a more holistic point of view and go beyond a technical scope. Hitherto, first EA Smells and tool prototypes have been proposed aiming to detect possible flaws in EA models [24, 33, 41].

To also allow the analysis of other EA models than ArchiMate and to realize a scalable approach, we generalize the EA model to a Knowledge Graph (KG) [9] and provide queries representing respective EA Smells. Hence, the detection of EA Smells can be applied to all EA models, which can be represented as a KG – which is not uncommon in EA research [2]. We propose a *generic* and *extensible* platform that facilitates the transformation of EAs into KG representations. The platform can be easily extended to support further modeling languages. Once a transformation is realized, the existing EA Smells queries can be efficiently executed even on very large models and model corpora.

Combining the discussed challenges with the sketched solution characteristics mentioned at the outset, the research presented in the remainder of this paper aims to contribute to the following research objectives:

i) Transforming Enterprise Architecture models into Knowledge Graphs
ii) Using Knowledge Graphs to automatically detect EA Smells

The rest of the paper is organized as follows. Background information on graph-based analysis of EA models and EA Smells is presented in Sect. 2. The transformation of EA models into KGs is then discussed in Sect. 3. Section 4 reports on how the KG can facilitate the automated detection of EA Smells. A comprehensive evaluation of our approach is presented in Sect. 5 where we report on the transformation and analysis of a huge corpora of openly available ArchiMate models. We conclude this paper in Sect. 6 with a discussion and some directions for future research.

2   Background

In this section, we will first introduce the foundations and related works on graph-based analysis of enterprise architecture models (Sect. 2.1) before introducing the backgrounds of EA Smells (Sect. 2.2).

2.1   Graph-Based Analysis of EA Models

Recently, the concept of Knowledge Graphs (KG) was proposed [9], which is continuously gaining more attention – also driven by the prominent use by Google in presenting the search results to its users. KGs realize an integrated representation on heterogeneous data that is ready for automated and efficient reasoning starting from (complex) graph queries toward the application of machine learning algorithms (e.g., Graph Neural Networks). At the core, a Knowledge Graph is a labelled graph that connects nodes by edges. More generally, a Knowledge Graph is *"a large network of entities, and instances for those entities, describing real world objects and their interrelations, with specific reference to a domain or to an organization"* [4, p. 27].

Interpreting EA models as graphs is a common approach in EA research [2]. For example, Garg et al. [13] propose a 3-tier architecture that allows defining EAs and their transformation into a graph structure to enable stakeholders with different visual analysis capabilities. Aier [1] propose the *EA Builder* tool that supports the identification of clusters in graphs which can then be considered as candidates for services in a service-oriented architecture. Similarly, Iacob et al. [19] quantitatively analyze layered, service-oriented EA models.

Santana et al. [36] propose to combine manual inspection by enterprise architects with automated analysis of graphs. Johnson et al. [20] interpret modeling of EAs as a probabilistic state estimation problem. They propose to facilitate Dynamic Bayesian Networks and to observe a computer network in order to predict the likeliest representation of the EA's technology layer. This was later implemented and refined in [3]. Similarly, Hacks and Lichter [16] use the graph representation to plan for future evolutions of the EA by considering different scenarios with underlying probabilities to become reality.

Taking a step further, several efforts have been taken to use graphs for maintaining and optimizing EAs. Giakoumakis et al. [14] replace existing services with new services while aiming not to disrupt the organization. Therefore, they formalize the EA as a graph and solve the resulting problem by means of multi-objective optimization. Similarly, Franke et al. [11] use a binary integer-programming model to optimize the relation between IT systems and processes based on needed functionalities. In contrast, MacCormack et al. [26] use Design Structure Matrices to analyze the coupling between the EA components. Moreover, they consider future states of the EA and generate measures that can be used to predict performance.

Further, there are also works using graph structures in the background without naming it explicitly. Österlind et al. [29] extend selected ArchiMate concepts with variables that are computed for structural analysis of the EA. Alike, Singh et al. [38] develop seven metrics to measure criticality and impact of any element in an EA model. Holschke et al. [18] perform failure impact analysis with Bayesian Belief Networks and Buschle et al. [7] adapt ArchiMate by fault trees to analyze the availability of EA components.

2.2   EA Smells

Previously, Hacks et al. [15] proposed to combine the concept of Technical Debt [8] with the concept of EA to so called *EA Debts*. EA Debts do not solely cover technical aspects but provide a more holistic view on the entire organization including for example flaws related to organizational structures. However, their proposal lacks an effective means to measure EA Debts. Therefore, Salentin and Hacks [33] facilitated the concept of Code Smells, which is popular to measure Technical Debt, and adapted it to EA models. They started with 56 Code Smells and ended up with a catalogue of 45 EA Smells [34]. This catalog was further extended by Lehmann et al. [24] and Tieu and Hacks [41], who took inspiration from process anti-patterns and software architecture smells, respectively.

In the aforementioned catalog [34], each EA Smell is documented in the same manner [33]: First, each EA Smell has an associated *name*, possible *synonyms*, and a *description*. The *context* provides further information such as the underlying concept from other domain smells (e.g., Code Smells). An *example* is provided to ease the understanding of the EA Smell. Second, the *cause* describes the reasons for an EA Smell, while the *consequences* illustrate the negative influence on the organization. Additionally, a short description is provided how the EA Smell could be *detected*. Third, a *possible solution* is proposed to solve the EA Smell. Finally, for each EA Smell *meta-information* is provided, which eases the searching for certain EA Smells, e.g., by filtering for EA layers.

An example for an EA Smell is *Weakened Modularity* [33]. It is adapted from the Code Smell with the same name that desires each module for high cohesion and low coupling. To detect this EA Smell, for each element and all successive sub-elements the modularity ratio is calculated by dividing the number of internal references (cohesion) by the number of external references (coupling).

Figure 1 illustrates three examples of EA Smells in an EA model. Firstly, a *Cyclic dependency* in which three services build on each other. Secondly, a *Dead Component*, which has no relations to the rest of the model. Lastly, a *Strict Layers Violation* where elements of the business layer are directly linked to an element of the technology layer. Figure 1 contains even more flaws such as other EA Smells, underlying issues behind the smells themselves (i.e., EA Debts [15] causing EA Smells to arise), or issues with ArchiMate. However, as the focus of this work is to automate the identification of EA Smells using Knowledge Graphs, we do not elaborate further on these aspects.

To achieve an automated detection of EA Smells, Salentin and Hacks [33] developed a prototype [32] that is capable to detect 14 EA Smells listed in the catalog. Therefore, it takes an ArchiMate Exchange File as input and prints the found EA Smells. Accordingly, the prototype can only analyze ArchiMate

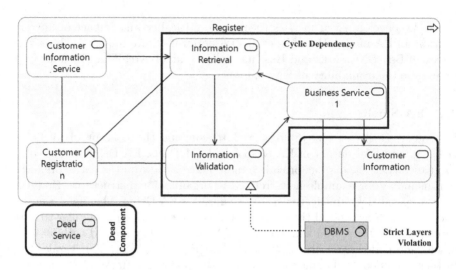

Fig. 1. Three examples for EA Smells [33]

models and integration with other tools is not possible. Moreover, the detection of EA Smells is implemented in Java and, thus, the tool needs to be compiled every time an EA Smell is added or removed and the scalability of the detection mechanism for large EA graphs is limited.

In this paper, we therefore aim to develop a *generic, extensible,* and *scalable* approach that supports *i*) the transformation of EA models into KGs and *ii*) the automated detection of EA Smells by means of KG queries. In the following, we will first elaborate on the transformation in Sect. 3. Section 4 will then report on the realization of EA Smells detection by means of KG queries. Eventually, applicability and scalability of our approach will be evaluated in Sect. 5.

3   Transforming EA Models into Knowledge Graphs

In order to analyze the EA in a graph-based manner, we propose an enhancement of the *extensible Graph-based Enterprise Architecture Analysis (eGEAA)* platform (see Fig. 2). The core platform, initially proposed by Smajevic and Bork [6,40], allows the transformation of ArchiMate models into graph structures. In this paper, we enhance this platform with the capability to transform EA models conforming to the Open Group Exchange format to a KG. In contrast to the initial proposal, which only comprised basic graph analysis metrics like *Centrality* and *Betweenness*, we furthermore enhance eGEAA by means of semantic queries to automatically detect EA Smells (detailed in Sect. 4).

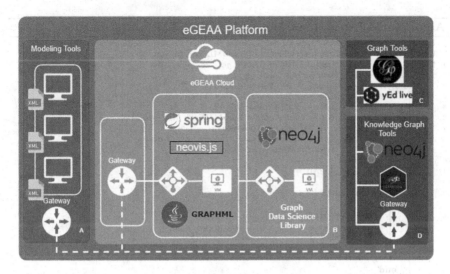

Fig. 2. eGEAA platform architecture – adapted from [40].

Compared to the related works (see Sect. 2), the eGEAA platform is generic and extensible in two ways: First, it builds upon the conceptual models produced by state-of-the-art metamodeling platforms like Ecore and ADOxx instead of being realized on – and being thus constrained to – one modeling language or tool. This enables the transformation of any conceptual model created with these platforms into a KG. Second, we transform the conceptual model into GraphML, a standardized graph representation format [27] that enables interchangeability with many graph analysis (e.g., Gephi, yEd) and KG tools (e.g., neo4j, Star-dog). Consequently, eGEAA builds a bridge between powerful modeling (and metamodeling platforms) and graph analysis and reasoning tools.

Listing 1 presents the pseudo-code for the transformation of EA models into KGs. The transformation combines two parts, the generic part responsible for transforming any conceptual model derived from the Ecore metamodel into a graph structure, and the second part, that takes care of the specifics of the Archi-Mate modeling language and the specific implementation of the Ecore metamodel in Archi.

The first rule transforms a *Grouping*, *Folder*, or *View* element into a nested *Graph* thereby overriding the generic transformation that would have resulted in a Node. All contents connected with that grouping through a *nested element* relation in the ArchiMate (ArchiMate) model will be added as *Node*s in the nested graph. Secondly, since Archi stores the ArchiMate relationships as entities (i.e., *IArchimateRelationshipEntity*s), the generic transformation rule needs to be overridden to transform an IArchimateRelationshipEntity into an *Edge* with an additional edge data to store the relationship endpoints.

Algorithm 1: Archi ArchiMate model to GraphML transformation.

Input: Archi-based ArchiMate model instance in Open Group Exchange xml format.
Output: Knowledge Graph serialized in GraphML xml format.

```
 1  for EObject package : input.eAllContents().getPackages() do
 2  │   Graph g ← transformPackage(package)
 3  │   for EObject eo : package.eAllContents() do
 4  │   │   if eo instanceof Grouping, Folder, View then
 5  │   │   │   Graph subg ← createSubgraph(eo)
 6  │   │   │   for EObject eo : subg.getEAllNestedElements() do
 7  │   │   │   │   Node n ← transformNode(eo)
 8  │   │   │   │   for EAttribute a : eo.getEAllAttributes() do
 9  │   │   │   │   │   n.addAttribute(transformAttribute(a))
10  │   │   │   │   end
11  │   │   │   │   subg.add(n)
12  │   │   │   end
13  │   │   │   g.add(subg)
14  │   │   else
15  │   │   │   Node n ← transformNode(eo)
16  │   │   │   for EAttribute a : eo.getEAllAttributes() do
17  │   │   │   │   n.addAttribute(transformAttribute(a))
18  │   │   │   end
19  │   │   │   g.add(n)
20  │   │   end
21  │   end
22  │   for EObject eo : package.eAllContents() do
23  │   │   if eo instanceof IArchimateRelationshipEntity then
24  │   │   │   Edge edge ← transformEdge(eo)
25  │   │   else
26  │   │   │   for EReference ref : eo.getEAllReferences() do
27  │   │   │   │   Edge edge ← transformEdge(ref)
28  │   │   │   end
29  │   │   end
30  │   │   edge.source ← findNode(eo)
31  │   │   edge.target ← findNode(eo.get(ref))
32  │   │   for EAttribute a : ed.getEAllAttributes() do
33  │   │   │   edge.addAttribute(transformAttribute(a))
34  │   │   end
35  │   │   g.add(edge)
36  │   end
37  │   output.add(g)
38  end
39  return output
```

Figure 3 visualizes the conceptual view on the model transformation approach. It shows that the transformation itself is specified on the metamodel-level, i.e., using elements of the Archi metamodel and elements of the GraphML metamodel when specifying the transformation rules. This enables the execution of the transformation on any source Archi-based EA model which will transform the conceptual model into a KG representation. From a technical point of view, the source and target model are stored as xml documents – the former in the Open Group Exchange format, the latter in the GraphML format.

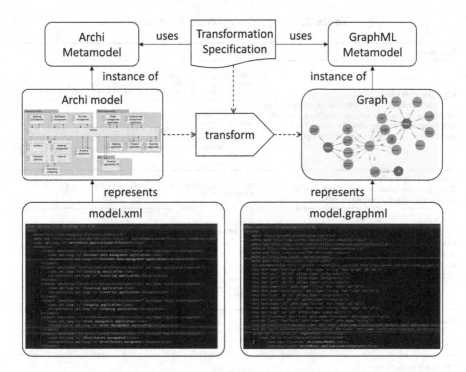

Fig. 3. Archi to Knowledge Graph transformation example.

4   Knowledge Graph Based EA Smells Detection

Once the transformation of ArchiMate models into GraphML is achieved, enterprise architects can visually explore the graph structure or apply basic graph analysis techniques as e.g., reported in [40]. More advanced analysis by means of reasoning is required for larger models and where the interests go beyond basic structural questions. This latter case is followed upon in the remainder of this paper, where we use KG queries to automatically detect EA Smells.

Table 1 lists already in Java implemented EA Smells [32, 33] and maps them to KG queries that are capable to automatically detect them. The presented smells hereafter emphasize structural characteristics such as circular dependencies while semantic aspects like the relation of data elements to service elements are also considered. Of course, future extensions of the catalogue will most likely be dominated by even more complex semantic smells (cf. [35]).

Table 1. KG queries resolving EA Smells

EA Smell [34]	KG Query
Chatty Service A high number of operations is required to complete one abstraction. Such operations are typically rather simple tasks that needlessly slow down an entire process.	```MATCH (a)-[r]-(b)
WHERE a.ClassName contains 'Service'
and b.ClassName contains 'Service'
and not r.Label contains 'Composition
'
with a,count(r) as cnt
where cnt>4
MATCH (a)-[r1]-(b1)
WHERE a.ClassName contains 'Service' and b1
.ClassName contains 'Service'
return a,b1, cnt```
Cyclic Dependency Two or more abstractions directly or indirectly depend on each other.	```MATCH (a)-[r1]->(b)-[r2]->(c)-[]->(a)
return a,b,c```
Data Service A service that exclusively performs information retrieval and typically provides only simple read operations.	```MATCH (a)-[r1]-(b1)
WHERE a.ClassName contains 'Service'
and (b1.ClassName = 'BusinessObject'
or b1.ClassName = 'DataObject'
or b1.ClassName = 'SystemSoftware
')
with a,r1,b1
match (a)
where not (a)--(:BusinessService)
return a```
Dead Component A component is no longer used or used to support potential future behavior.	```MATCH (n)
WHERE not (n)--()
return n```
Dense Structure An EA repository has dense dependencies without any particular structure.	```MATCH (p)
RETURN CASE WHEN avg(apoc.node.degree(p))
>1.75 THEN 1 ELSE 0 END AS result;```
Documentation A lengthy documentation often points to unnecessary complex structures.	```MATCH (n)
where size(n.documentation)>256
RETURN n```
Duplication Two or more abstractions with highly similar functionality exist.	```MATCH (a),(b)
where a<>b and a.ClassName = b.ClassName
and apoc.text.jaroWinklerDistance(a.
Label, b.Label)>0.8
RETURN a,b,apoc.text.jaroWinklerDistance(a.
Label, b.Label) as similarNameScore```
Hub-like Modularization This smell arises when an abstraction has dependencies (both incoming and outgoing) with a large number of other abstractions, being a single point of failure.	```match (a)-[r]-(b)
where (r.Label contains 'Aggregation' or r.
Label contains 'Realization' or r.Label
contains "Composition" or r.Label
contains "Assignment")
and a.ArchimateLayer = b.ArchimateLayer
with a, collect(r) as rels, a+collect(b) as
cluster
match (m)-[r1]-(n)
where not (r1.Label contains 'Aggregation'
or r1.Label contains 'Realization' or
r1.Label contains "Composition" or r1.
Label contains "Assignment") and
(m in cluster and not n in cluster)
with a, cluster, collect(r1) as fanout
match (m)-[r2]-(n)
where not (r2.Label contains 'Aggregation'
or r2.Label contains 'Realization' or
r2.Label contains "Composition" or r2.
Label contains "Assignment") and
(not m in cluster and n in cluster)
with a, cluster, fanout, collect(r2) as
fanin
where size(fanout) > 7 and size(fanin)>7
return a, cluster, size(fanout), size(fanin)```

(*continued*)

Table 1. (*continued*)

Lazy Component
A component that is not doing enough to pay for itself should be eliminated. Those components often only pass messages on to another.

```
MATCH (n)
where n.Label contains 'controller' or n.
     Label contains 'manager'
RETURN n
```

Message Chain
A number of services that rely on each other, while providing similar functionality.

```
MATCH (a)-[r1]->(b)-[r2]->(c)-[]->(d)-[]->(e
     )
where a.ClassName contains 'Service'
     and b.ClassName contains 'Service'
     and c.ClassName contains 'Service'
     and d.ClassName contains 'Service'
     and e.ClassName contains 'Service'
return a,b,c,d,e
```

Shared Persistency
Different services access the same database. In the worst case, different services access the same entities of the same schema.

```
MATCH (a)-[r]-(b)
WHERE a.ClassName='SystemSoftware' and (r.
     Label='AssociationRelationship' or r.
     Label='RealizationRelationship' or r.
     Label='AssignmentRelationship')
with a,count(r) as cnt
MATCH (a)-[r1]-(b1)
where cnt>1 and (r1.Label='
     AssociationRelationship' or r1.Label='
     RealizationRelationship' or r1.Label='
     AssignmentRelationship')
return a,b1
```

Strict Layers Violation
An element skips the EA layer directly beneath and accesses a layer further below instead.

```
MATCH (a)-[r]-(b)
where a.ArchimateLayer contains 'Business'
     and b.ArchimateLayer contains '
     Technology' //example
return a,b,r
```

Weakened Modularity
Each module must strive for high cohesion and low coupling. This smell arises when a module exhibits high coupling and low cohesion.

```
match (a)-[r]-(b)
where (r.Label contains 'Aggregation' or r.
     Label contains 'Realization' or r.Label
     contains "Composition" or r.Label
     contains "Assignment")
     and a.ArchimateLayer = b.ArchimateLayer
with a, collect(r) as rels, a+collect(b) as
     cluster
match (m)-[r1]-(n)
where m in cluster and n in cluster
with a, cluster, collect(r1) as internal
match (m)-[r2]-(n)
where not (r2.Label contains 'Aggregation'
     or r2.Label contains 'Realization' or
     r2.Label contains "Composition" or r2.
     Label contains "Assignment") and
(not m in cluster and n in cluster) or (m
     in cluster and not n in cluster)
with a, cluster, internal, collect(r2) as
     external
where size(internal) < size(external) and
     size(internal)>3
return a, cluster, size(internal), size(
     external)
```

5 Evaluation

For evaluating our approach, we refer to the openly available model corpora of the MAR search engine [25]. In summary, we found 369 ArchiMate models which were created with the Archi modeling tool. In average, a model in the corpus comprised 51.41 ± 97.04 Nodes and 47.14 ± 70.23 Edges. We transformed these models using the eGEAA platform and executed the EA Smells queries defined in Table 1. The evaluation aimed to respond to the following research questions:

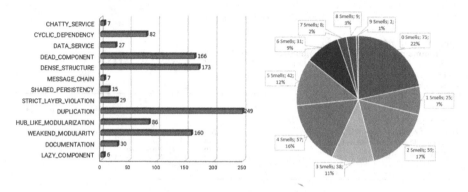

Fig. 4. Detected EA Smells.

RQ.1 – Feasibility Is our approach feasible to automatically detect EA Smells in ArchiMate models? If yes, how often do specific smells (co-) occur?

RQ.2 – Performance How efficient is our Knowledge Graph based approach in detecting EA Smells?

RQ.1 – Feasibility. For evaluating the feasibility, we collected a set of openly available ArchiMate models [25] and transformed them initially into the Open Group Exchange format using Archi. From the resulting set of 369 models, the eGEAA platform was able to automatically transform 347 of them (94%) into a KG stored in GraphML. The few models that were not transformed had some encoding issues or the source model was corrupt. As can be derived from Fig. 4 (left), we found all implemented EA Smells in the data set. In future research, we plan to extend the data set and to also involve real models form practitioners. In an action design research setting, we could then investigate, how practitioners value our EA Smell detection approach.

The results of applying the EA Smells queries of Table 1 are summarized in Fig. 4. The detailed analysis showed that 78.38% of the EA models had at least one smell. Figure 4 (right) shows, how many EA Smells have been found in how many of the analyzed EA models. It can be derived, that 45.82% of the models had at most two smells, whereas the majority of the EA models had three or more smells. Noteworthy, this is only an indicator of the smell's existence in a model, not the number of incarnations of the smell in a model.

We then were also interested to see, which smells occur most often and which smells co-occur most often. The data showed, that DUPLICATION (249 hits), DENSE_STRUCTURE (173 hits), DEAD_COMPONENT (166 hits), and WEAKEND_MODULARITY (160 hits) together make up for almost 75% of all detected EA Smells. When analyzing the relationships between the detected EA Smells, the following three co-occurrences were most frequent in the data set: 162 co-occurrences (46.68%) of DENSE_STRUCTURE and DUPLICATION, 155 co-occurrences (44.66%) of DUPLICATION and WEAKEND_MODULARITY, and 153 co-occurrences (44.09%) of DEAD_COMPONENT and DUPLICATION.

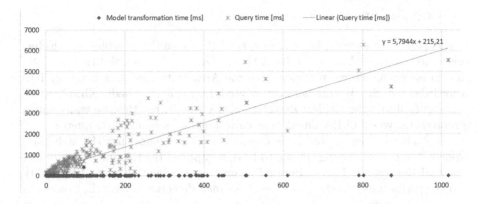

Fig. 5. Performance of the EA Smells detection. (Color figure online)

RQ.2 – Performance. Past research has indicated that Knowledge Graph queries can be executed highly efficiently also on huge graphs with many thousands or even millions of nodes [4]. With our experiments, we can confirm this observation also for our Knowledge Graph based EA Smell detection. Figure 5 plots the relationship between the size of the Knowledge Graph (x-axis) and the model transformation time (blue) and the KG query time (orange) on the y-axis, both measured in milliseconds.

It can be derived, that the performance is stable even when analyzing KGs with more than 1000 elements (nodes and edges). In reality, it is unlikely to see larger EA models (cf. [23,37]), we can therefore conclude, that the performance of our solution is promising to tackle the complexity of the task at hand. While the model transformation time remains stable even for large KGs with an average time of 7.46 ms ± 23.85 ms, the query execution time naturally increases with the size of the KG with an average of 786.31 ms ± 1044.09 ms.

To show also the relative performance of our solution compared to the prototype presented in [32], we used the same set of experimental models and compared the query execution times. These early investigations yielded interesting insights and confirmed, that our approach is stable with respect to time in executing smell detection while it is a bit slower in detecting EA Smells than the previous solution. However, the results vary depending on the smell (i.e., the complexity of the query itself). Moreover, these first results may not tell the true story since the tracked time in our experiments involved setting up a connection to a database and transporting from and to a database server instead of the pure query execution time as for the previous solution. In our future research we will, amongst others, therefore conduct further experiments to investigate the performance of our approach more rigorously and comparatively.

6 Conclusion

In this paper, we showed, how we enhanced the extensible Graph-based Enterprise Architecture Analysis (eGEAA) platform to automatically transform Enterprise Architectures modeled with the ArchiMate modeling language into Knowledge Graphs. We furthermore showed, how this Knowledge Graph structure can facilitate the efficient detection of EA Smells. For this, we transformed a representative set of EA Smells into corresponding semantic KG queries.

For evaluating our approach, we created a data set comprising 347 ArchiMate models. After transforming them into KGs, we applied the EA Smell queries and analyzed the results. This elaborated quantitative evaluation proved feasibility and the performance of the KG based EA Smell detection approach. Compared to existing solutions, our proposal is *generic*, i.e., it can be easily adopted for different EA modeling languages and tools [39], and *extensible*, i.e., further EA Smells or different EA analysis techniques can be easily realized by means of KG queries. However, a qualitative assessment of the smell identification is missing and needs to be addressed to ensure that it is complete and correct. Such an evaluation would require a curated set of EA models which still needs to be developed.

In our future work, we aim to further extend the catalog of EA Smells. Furthermore, we plan to conduct empirical experiments with enterprise architects. We expect that through such experiments, we can not only evaluate the ease of use and usability of the platform, but also the intention to use EA Smells in practice. Eventually, we perceive this work as a foundation for an entire stream of research that concerns adding knowledge to the Knowledge Graph (e.g., KG embeddings) and applying advanced reasoning (e.g., Graph Neural Networks).

The presented platform is available open source [6], enabling the enterprise modeling and enterprise architecture communities to use the platform for realizing their specific EA analysis purpose and to provide valuable feedback. We are also currently working on a plug-in that enables the execution of our KG based EA Smell detection directly within the Archi modeling tool.

References

1. Aier, S.: How clustering enterprise architectures helps to design service oriented architectures. In: 2006 IEEE International Conference on Services Computing (SCC 2006), pp. 269–272. IEEE (2006)
2. Barbosa, A., Santana, A., Hacks, S., Stein, N.V.: A taxonomy for enterprise architecture analysis research. In: 21st International Conference on Enterprise Information Systems, vol. 2, pp. 493–504. SciTePress (2019)
3. Bebensee, B., Hacks, S.: Applying dynamic bayesian networks for automated modeling in archimate: a realization study. In: 23rd IEEE International Enterprise Distributed Object Computing Workshop, EDOC Workshops 2019, Paris, France, 28–31 October 2019, pp. 17–24. IEEE (2019)
4. Bellomarini, L., Fakhoury, D., Gottlob, G., Sallinger, E.: Knowledge graphs and enterprise ai: the promise of an enabling technology. In: 2019 IEEE 35th International Conference on Data Engineering (ICDE), pp. 26–37. IEEE (2019)

5. Bork, D., et al.: Requirements engineering for model-based enterprise architecture management with ArchiMate. In: Pergl, R., Babkin, E., Lock, R., Malyzhenkov, P., Merunka, V. (eds.) EOMAS 2018. LNBIP, vol. 332, pp. 16–30. Springer, Cham (2018). https://doi.org/10.1007/978-3-030-00787-4_2

6. Bork, D., Smajevic, M.: Source code repository of the eGEAA platform (2021). https://github.com/borkdominik/eGEAA

7. Buschle, M., Johnson, P., Shahzad, K.: The enterprise architecture analysis tool - support for the predictive, probabilistic architecture modeling framework, pp. 3350–3364 (2013)

8. Cunningham, W.: The wycash portfolio management system. SIGPLAN OOPS Mess. 4(2), 29–30 (1992)

9. Fensel, D., et al.: Knowledge Graphs - Methodology, Tools and Selected Use Cases. Springer, Germany (2020). https://doi.org/10.1007/978-3-030-37439-6

10. Florez, H., Sánchez, M., Villalobos, J.: A catalog of automated analysis methods for enterprise models. SpringerPlus 5(1), 1–24 (2016)

11. Franke, U., Holschke, O., Buschle, M., Narman, P., Rake-Revelant, J.: It consolidation: an optimization approach. In: 2010 14th IEEE International Enterprise Distributed Object Computing Conference Workshops, pp. 21–26 (2010)

12. Gampfer, F., Jürgens, A., Müller, M., Buchkremer, R.: Past, current and future trends in enterprise architecture-a view beyond the horizon. Comput. Ind. **100**, 70–84 (2018)

13. Garg, A., Kazman, R., Chen, H.M.: Interface descriptions for enterprise architecture. Sci. Comput. Program. **61**(1), 4–15 (2006)

14. Giakoumakis, V., Krob, D., Liberti, L., Roda, F.: Technological architecture evolutions of information systems: trade-off and optimization. Concurr. Eng. **20**(2), 127–147 (2012). https://doi.org/10.1177/1063293X12447715

15. Hacks, S., Hofert, H., Salentin, J., Yeong, Y.C., Lichter, H.: Towards the definition of enterprise architecture debts. In: IEEE 23rd International Enterprise Distributed Object Computing Workshop (EDOCW), pp. 9–16. IEEE (2019). https://doi.org/10.1109/EDOCW.2019.00016

16. Hacks, S., Lichter, H.: A probabilistic enterprise architecture model evolution. In: 22nd IEEE International Enterprise Distributed Object Computing Conference, EDOC 2018, Stockholm, Sweden, 16–19 October 2018, pp. 51–57. IEEE Computer Society (2018)

17. Hinkelmann, K., Gerber, A., Karagiannis, D., Thoenssen, B., Van der Merwe, A., Woitsch, R.: A new paradigm for the continuous alignment of business and it: Combining enterprise architecture modelling and enterprise ontology. Comput. Ind. **79**, 77–86 (2016)

18. Holschke, O., Närman, P., Flores, W.R., Eriksson, E., Schönherr, M.: Using enterprise architecture models and bayesian belief networks for failure impact analysis. In: Feuerlicht, G., Lamersdorf, W. (eds.) ICSOC 2008. LNCS, vol. 5472, pp. 339–350. Springer, Heidelberg (2009). https://doi.org/10.1007/978-3-642-01247-1_35

19. Iacob, M.E., Jonkers, H.: Quantitative analysis of enterprise architectures. In: Konstantas, D., Bourrieres, J.P., Leonard, M., Boudjlida, N. (eds.) Interoperability of Enterprise Software and Applications, pp. 239–252. Springer, Heidelberg (2006). https://doi.org/10.1007/1-84628-152-0_22

20. Johnson, P., Ekstedt, M., Lagerström, R.: Automatic probabilistic enterprise IT architecture modeling: a dynamic bayesian networks approach. In: Franke, U., Lapalme, J., Johnson, P. (eds.) 20th International Enterprise Distributed Object Computing Workshop (EDOCW), pp. 123–129 (2016)

21. Jugel, D.: An integrative method for decision-making in EA management. In: Zimmermann, A., Schmidt, R., Jain, L.C. (eds.) Architecting the Digital Transformation. ISRL, vol. 188, pp. 289–307. Springer, Cham (2021). https://doi.org/10.1007/978-3-030-49640-1_15

22. Jugel, D., Kehrer, S., Schweda, C.M., Zimmermann, A.: Providing EA decision support for stakeholders by automated analyses. In: Digital Enterprise Computing 2015, pp. 151–162. GI (2015)

23. Lagerström, R., Baldwin, C., MacCormack, A., Dreyfus, D.: Visualizing and measuring enterprise architecture: an exploratory BioPharma case. In: Grabis, J., Kirikova, M., Zdravkovic, J., Stirna, J. (eds.) PoEM 2013. LNBIP, vol. 165, pp. 9–23. Springer, Heidelberg (2013). https://doi.org/10.1007/978-3-642-41641-5_2

24. Lehmann, B.D., Alexander, P., Lichter, H., Hacks, S.: Towards the identification of process anti-patterns in enterprise architecture models. In: 8th International Workshop on Quantitative Approaches to Software Quality in conjunction with the 27th Asia-Pacific Software Engineering Conference (APSEC 2020), vol. 2767, pp. 47–54. CEUR-WS (2020)

25. López, J.A.H., Cuadrado, J.S.: MAR: a structure-based search engine for models. In: Syriani, E., Sahraoui, H.A., de Lara, J., Abrahão, S. (eds.) MoDELS '20: ACM/IEEE 23rd International Conference on Model Driven Engineering Languages and Systems, Virtual Event, Canada, 2020, pp. 57–67. ACM (2020)

26. Maccormack, A.D., Lagerstrom, R., Baldwin, C.Y.: A methodology for operationalizing enterprise architecture and evaluating enterprise it flexibility. Harvard Business School working paper series# 15–060 (2015)

27. Messina, A.: Overview of standard graph file formats. Technical Report, RT-ICAR-PA-2018-06 (2018). http://dx.doi.org/10.13140/RG.2.2.11144.88324

28. OMG: ArchiMate® 3.1 Specification. The Open Group (2019). http://pubs.opengroup.org/architecture/archimate3-doc/

29. Österlind, M., Lagerström, R., Rosell, P.: Assessing modifiability in application services using enterprise architecture models – a case study. In: Aier, S., Ekstedt, M., Matthes, F., Proper, E., Sanz, J.L. (eds.) PRET/TEAR -2012. LNBIP, vol. 131, pp. 162–181. Springer, Heidelberg (2012). https://doi.org/10.1007/978-3-642-34163-2_10

30. Pittl, B., Bork, D.: Modeling digital enterprise ecosystems with ArchiMate: a mobility provision case study. In: ICServ 2017. LNCS, vol. 10371, pp. 178–189. Springer, Cham (2017). https://doi.org/10.1007/978-3-319-61240-9_17

31. Roelens, B., Steenacker, W., Poels, G.: Realizing strategic fit within the business architecture: the design of a process-goal alignment modeling and analysis technique. Softw. Syst. Model. 18(1), 631–662 (2019)

32. Salentin, J., Hacks, S.: Enterprise architecture smells prototype (2020). https://git.rwth-aachen.de/ba-ea-smells/program

33. Salentin, J., Hacks, S.: Towards a catalog of enterprise architecture smells. In: Gronau, N., Heine, M., Krasnova, H., Poustcchi, K. (eds.) Entwicklungen, Chancen und Herausforderungen der Digitalisierung: Proceedings der 15. Internationalen Tagung Wirtschaftsinformatik, WI 2020, Potsdam, Germany, 9–11 March 2020, Community Tracks, pp. 276–290. GITO Verlag (2020)

34. Salentin, J., Lehmann, B., Hacks, S., Alexander, P.: Enterprise architecture smells catalog (2021). https://swc-public.pages.rwth-aachen.de/smells/ea-smells/

35. Sales, T.P., Guizzardi, G.: Ontological anti-patterns: empirically uncovered error-prone structures in ontology-driven conceptual models. Data Knowl. Eng. 99, 72–104 (2015)

36. Santana, A., Fischbach, K., Moura, H.: Enterprise architecture analysis and network thinking: A literature review. In: 2016 49th Hawaii International Conference on System Sciences (HICSS), pp. 4566–4575. IEEE (2016)
37. Schoonjans, A.: Social network analysis techniques in enterprise architecture management. Ph.D. thesis, PhD thesis, Ghent University, Ghent (2016)
38. Singh, P.M., van Sinderen, M.J.: Lightweight metrics for enterprise architecture analysis. In: Abramowicz, W. (ed.) BIS 2015. LNBIP, vol. 228, pp. 113–125. Springer, Cham (2015). https://doi.org/10.1007/978-3-319-26762-3_11
39. Smajevic, M., Bork, D.: From conceptual models to knowledge graphs: a generic model transformation platform. In: MoDELS'21: ACM/IEEE 24th International Conference on Model Driven Engineering Languages and Systems (MODELS) - Tools & Demonstrations. ACM/IEEE (2021). (in press)
40. Smajevic, M., Bork, D.: Towards graph-based analysis of enterprise architecture models. In: Proceedings of the 40th International Conference on Conceptual Modeling (2021). (in Press)
41. Tieu, B., Hacks, S.: Determining enterprise architecture smells from software architecture smells. In: 23rd IEEE International Conference on Business Informatics Workshops (to be published). IEEE (2021)

Mind the Gap!: Learning Missing Constraints from Annotated Conceptual Model Simulations

Mattia Fumagalli[1(✉)], Tiago Prince Sales[1], and Giancarlo Guizzardi[1,2]

[1] Conceptual and Cognitive Modeling Research Group (CORE),
Free University of Bozen-Bolzano, Bolzano, Italy
{mattia.fumagalli,tiago.princesales,giancarlo.guizzardi}@unibz.it
[2] Services and Cybersecurity, University of Twente, Enschede, The Netherlands

Abstract. Conceptual modeling plays a fundamental role to capture information about complex business domains (e.g., finance, healthcare) and enables semantic interoperability. To fulfill their role, conceptual models must contain the exact set of constraints that represent the worldview of the relevant domain stakeholders. However, as empirical results show, modelers are subject to cognitive limitations and biases and, hence, in practice, they produce models that fall short in that respect. Moreover, the process of formally designing conceptual models is notoriously hard and requires expertise that modelers do not always have. This paper falls in the general area concerned with the development of artificial intelligence techniques for the enterprise. In particular, we propose an approach that leverages *model finding* and *inductive logic programming (ILP)* techniques. We aim to move towards supporting modelers in identifying domain constraints that are missing from their models, and thus improving their precision w.r.t. their intended worldviews. Firstly, we describe how to use the results produced by the application of model finding as input to an inductive learning process. Secondly, we test the approach with the goal of demonstrating its feasibility and illustrating some key design issues to be considered while using these techniques.

Keywords: Conceptual modeling · Model validation · Inductive learning · Model simulation

1 Introduction

Conceptual modeling plays a fundamental role in information systems engineering. In complex and sensitive scenarios (e.g., finance, healthcare), domain models are paramount in supporting critical semantic interoperability tasks. To fulfill this role, modelers must be able to systematically produce models that precisely articulate the worldview of the relevant domain stakeholders [16].

Technically speaking, domain models should only admit *instantiations* (e.g., *model interpretations, instance populations*) that correspond to state-of-affairs

© IFIP International Federation for Information Processing 2021
Published by Springer Nature Switzerland AG 2021
E. Serral et al. (Eds.): PoEM 2021, LNBIP 432, pp. 64–79, 2021.
https://doi.org/10.1007/978-3-030-91279-6_5

that are admissible according to the conceptualizations these models are supposed to represent. However, as empirical results show, modelers are subject to cognitive limitations and biases, and, in practice, they are often unable to create domain models endowed with this property, also due to a lack of expertise [16,18,19,24,31]. In particular, these results show that such models are often *underconstrained*, thus admitting interpretations their designers did not intend.

The issue of repairing underconstrained models has been investigated in the past [6,9,12], however, none has been able to automatically learn complex domain constraints yet. Some of us have developed a validation technique that combines model finding with visual simulation to automatically generate admissible model instances, which one could analyze to manually derive missing constraints [1]. In this paper, we combine this technique with a machine learning algorithm from *inductive logic programming* (ILP) to automate this process.

With our validation technique, one naturally generates a dataset of *allowed (positive) and forbidden (negative) examples* from admissible model interpretations. By combining this dataset with the constraints already embedded in the model and feeding them to an ILP learner [2], we can automatically uncover missing constraints. The main advantage of this approach is that it does not require modelers to formulate the constraints themselves. Instead, they simply need to judge whether model interpretations should be allowed or forbidden.

The remainder of this paper is organized as follows. In Sect. 2, by introducing a running example, we explain how visual model simulation allows us to determine whether a model is *underconstrained*. In Sect. 3, we describe our approach, and, in Sect. 4, we evaluate its capacity to learn complex constraints that would be needed in practice. In Sect. 5, we discuss related work. Finally, in Sect. 6, we make some final considerations, including implications to practice.

2 Model Validation

Conceptual modeling is an error-prone activity [31]. Modelers often dedicate a significant amount of time to testing and debugging their models in order to increase their reliability [7]. To cope with that, research efforts have been devoted to devising engineering tools for model validation, which consists of assessing if a model is: (i) *overconstrained*, namely, if it excludes interpretations intended by the modeler; or (ii) *underconstrained*, namely, if it admits interpretations that are not intended by the modeler.

Checking if a domain model is overconstrained can be easily represented as a classical *model checking* problem, namely, as the activity of *verifying* whether a given state of affairs *holds* in a given model [4]. Take, for instance, the OntoUML[1] model depicted in Fig. 1 (a fragment of a model about vehicles and their parts, which could be used to devise a *vehicle dealer* knowledge base). Model-checking allows one to detect whether a given state of affairs like *"x is both a wheel and an engine"* violates the *logical rules* encoded by the model. In this example, it is

---

[1] OntoUML is a version of UML designed in accordance with the UFO foundational ontology principles and axiomatization [15,17].

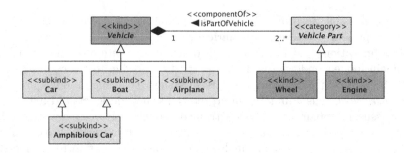

Fig. 1. An OntoUML model on (a subset of) the vehicle dealership domain.

trivial to see that such a state-of-affairs is not allowed[2], but that is not always the case. Nonetheless, if this state-of-affairs was intended by the author of this model, and yet not allowed by it, the model would be considered *overconstrained*. To adjust it, one would need to "relax" it by removing or "weakening" some of its constraints [33].

Checking whether a conceptual model is *underconstrained* is another model validation task, but one that cannot be handled via model checking. It can be informally expressed as follows: *"check if the model only allows instantiations representing the state of affairs intended by the modeler"*. Let us come back to the example in Fig. 1. Suppose we have a state of affairs like *"x is both a car and a boat, but it is not an amphibious car"*. While running model checking, this statement does not violate the model, but still, the modeler may consider it a violation of her domain conceptualization.

From now on we use the terms "admitted state of affair", "configuration", and "simulation run" interchangeably, where a simulation run is the result of *an interpretation function satisfying the conceptual model*. In other words: if we take the (Onto)UML diagram of Fig. 1 as a M1-model (in OMG's MDA sense), a configuration is a M0-model that could instantiate that M1-model; if we take the UML diagram as a logical specification, then a configuration is a logical model of that specification. Finding these valid configurations given a specification is the classical task performed by a *model finder*.

While the two aforementioned tasks are both important when validating conceptual models, there are important differences between them. On the one hand, the task of checking whether a given state of affairs holds in a given model can be algorithmically addressed by *satisfiability solvers* [20]. On the other hand, as anticipated in [11], the task of identifying *what* in a conceptual model allows for an unintended state of affairs, implies that the intended model, which is assumed to be implicit in the mind of the modeler, is involved in the validation phase. This enables an empirical process where humans cannot be left outside the loop. The latter challenge is what we focus on in this paper.

---

[2] In OntoUML, all *kinds* are mutually disjoint [15].

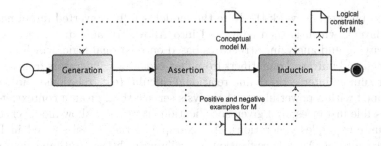

Fig. 2. Approach overview.

3 From Model Finding to Inductive Learning

An overview of the proposed approach is summarized in Fig. 2 below. Besides the domain model M, the ILP process takes as input a list of negative (neg) and positive (pos) examples, which are elicited by applying model finding. The final output is a set of logical constraints that can be used by the modeler to complete the input domain model.

The core steps involved in the approach we envision are like from the pseudocode represented in Listing 1. These steps can be grouped into three main phases, namely the *generation*, the *assertion* and the *induction* phase.

Listing 1. Model Finding and ILP combination process.

```
    Result: Set of logical constraints L^M
 1  get input conceptual model M;
 2  for conceptual model M do
        /* (1) Generation */
 3      convert conceptual model into model finder specifications M^F;
 4      execute model finding;
 5      store simulations files into S^M;
 6      for unintended and intended simulations S^M admitted by M^F do
            /* (2) Assertion */
 7          combine S^M with M^F;
 8          elicit positive and negative examples E^{-/+};
            /* (3) Induction */
 9          run ILP with E^{-/+} and M as inputs;
10          store ILP outputs into set L^M;
11      end
12  end
```

(1) Generation. The first task here is to take a domain model [15] as input and convert it into a format (see step 3 in Listing 1) so that it can be validated through model finding. We achieved this by using a *compiler* that runs a transformation on the input (OntoUML) model, and relies on the mappings

proposed by previous work [1]. Here the model is fully converted into a neutral logical layer[3], which is then converted into Alloy [21], an expressive language for specifying and analyzing structures based on relational logic, which includes existential and universal quantifiers from first-order logic, operators from set theory (e.g., union, intersection), and relational calculus (e.g., relational join). Alloy is equipped with a powerful model analysis service that, given a context, generates possible instances for a given specification (it can also allow model checking and counterexamples generation). An example of the model showed in Fig. 1 converted into an Alloy specification is available in https://github.com/unibz-core/Mind-the-Gap/blob/main/CarDL.als. After converting the input conceptual model, the Alloy Analyzer APIs are applied to validate the model (step 4 in Listing 1). The analysis is performed to simulate arbitrary instances that conform to the model constraints. This step requires a definition of the *scope* of the analyzer, which consists of the *type* of concepts to be analyzed and the *number* of instances to be produced.

Once a set of configurations is produced (S^M in Listing 1), the modeler can classify them into *intended* or *unintended*. For the validation of the model configurations, we followed the strategy in [31]. If some unintended configurations are found the process continues, otherwise it terminates (meaning by this that the input conceptual model is correct according to the modeler scope).

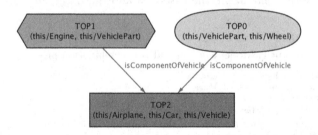

Fig. 3. Example of vehicle parts model simulation.

Figure 3 presents an example of configuration generated out of the model represented in Fig. 1, with three instances. The colors of the boxes represent the different kinds of objects involved in the simulation. Notice that "this/..." refers to a class, and the values "*TOPx*" refer to its generated instances. So if TOP2 is marked with this/Car and this/Airplane then this individual is both a 'Car' and a 'Airplane' at the same time. This simulation could be, for instance, annotated as unintended, since we may do not want to allow for a "Car (TOP2) to be also an Airplane". Notice that all the output configurations collected in S^M are saved in a file collecting all the information generated through the Alloy analyzer visualization tool.

---

[3] Currently, the logical layer can be encoded by First Order Logic FOL syntax or by Description Logic (DL) syntax, covering ALC, SHOIQ, and SROIQ expressivity.

(2) Assertion. Once the set of intended and unintended configurations is generated, we apply another conversion step. Here we use the trace of the original domain model as input and all the files of the annotated simulations to create a new output. The file generated out of this step is the domain model and all the instances coming from the intended and unintended simulations. This is what can be used by the modeler to elicit negative and positive examples. Each imported configuration, indeed, involves a mix of allowed and proscribed relations (i.e., particular individuals that instantiate a class in the model). For example, in Fig. 3, the instance 'TOP2' may be proscribed, while 'TOP1' may be allowed. The assertion step allows the modelers to mark which instances in the unintended simulations represent negative (proscribed) or positive (allowed) examples. Notice that the plan is to use an *ad hoc* editor to support the annotation process together with the example set generated in the assertion step. In particular, we will employ the capabilities embedded in the OntoUML editor [10] with some additional features, such as i) exploration of Alloy simulations; ii) simulations annotation; iii) neg/pos example set generation.

(3) Induction. In this phase, the elicited negative and positive examples, along with the structure of the original conceptual model, are given as input to a learning system. Considering the scope of this paper, the learning process we set up must accounts for the ability of *identifying missing formal constraints* in a way that is easily accessible to the modeler, which should be able, then, to process the suggested output and repair the input source model. For this particular goal, we adopted the CELOE algorithm, an extended version of the OCEL [25] algorithm. This is considered one of the best available state-of-the-art *Inductive Logic Programming* (ILP)[28] options for *Class Expression Learning*, and has been applied to a large number of cases [2]. Notice that, multiple ILP algorithms are available. Accurate analysis and benchmark of the existing options for our task is out of the scope of this paper, and is part of immediate future work.

An illustrative case of a populated model transformation for this particular task can be represented as follows (this case reuses the car simulation output of Fig. 3, along with elicited neg/pos examples):

* $E^+ = \{Engine(TOP1),\ Wheel(TOP0),\ VehiclePart(TOP1),\ VehiclePart(TOP0)\}$
* $E^- = \{Car(TOP2),\ Airplane(TOP2),\ Vehicle(TOP2)\}$
* $PCM = \{E^+, E^-, \forall x.(Airplane(x) \rightarrow Vehicle(x)), \forall x.(Car(x) \rightarrow Vehicle(x)),$ $\forall x.(Engine(x) \rightarrow VehiclePart(x)), \forall x.(Wheel(x) \rightarrow VehiclePart(x)), \forall x.(VehiclePart(x) \rightarrow \exists y.(Vehicle(y) \wedge isComponentOfVehicle(x,y)))\}$

where E^+ represents the set of positive examples, namely the examples that are admitted by the intended models as well as (e.g., in this case) allowed fragments in unintended models; where E^- represents the set of negative examples, namely those instances that are proscribed in unintended models; and where *PCM* (Populated Conceptual Model) represents the model file, with the model axioms and all its instances along with negative and positive examples. By using the model, the positive examples and the negative examples, the algorithm is able to highlight the rule(s) describing the non-admitted instance(s):

* *Structural error* $= \exists x.(Car(x) \wedge Airplane(x))$
* *Suggested constraint* $= \forall x.(Car(x) \rightarrow \neg Airplane(x))$

The axiom identified by the algorithm uncovers that the problem is due to an overlap between the class 'Car' and the class 'Airplane'. Once possible underconstraing problems are uncovered, in order to forbid the unintended instance(s), the axioms are then simply negated.

4   Evaluation

We evaluate the proposed approach by addressing the two following research questions: (1) *To which extent the proposed combination between model finding and ILP is able to discover constraints that can be used to avoid unintended configurations in practice?* (2) *To which extent the process we propose is able to produce constraints that are expected?*

The first question aims at assessing the feasibility of the approach, namely if the two technologies together can be used to find useful constraints. The second question aims at assessing performance issues from a qualitative perspective, namely if the design choices we adopted in the presented process allow us to identify the constraints that are expected.

4.1   Setup

Method. To address both questions we ran an experiment involving a simple example model.[4] We take here the general methodological practice employed in natural sciences of starting with simple models to explore a fuller extent of the ideas at hand [3]. In this particular case, irrespective of its size, the conceptual model used in this experiment allows for the investigation of relevant constraints, which are likely to be needed in practice. For this goal, we used, as a preliminary "litmus test"[5] recurrent modeling issues that appear in models of

---

[4] All data used for the case study described in this section are available for research purposes at https://github.com/unibz-core/Mind-the-Gap.

[5] A litmus test is "a critical indicator of future success or failure". A is a litmus test for B if A can be effectively used to measure some property of B [5].

all sizes, namely: i) a possible occurrence of *completeness error*, usually caused by the difficulty of balancing the *flexibility* and *consistency* of the model [24, 26]; ii) a possible occurrence of *"or" operator misuse*, usually caused by the *overlap between the linguistic and logical usage of "and" and "or"* [30] ; iii) a possible occurrence of *imprecise association*, usually caused by the fact that the range of an association is too broad, thus allowing to miss some domain-specific constraints [31]. The evaluation is performed in a controlled environment, in which we know in advance the constraints to be learned. The configurations to be assessed are generated randomly through Alloy, and, to force the analyzer in creating the unintended configurations, the target constraints were negated.

To answer question (1) we checked whether the approach can learn constraints able to avoid occurrences of issues like *i)*, *ii)* and *iii)*. To answer the research question (2) we analyzed the process we followed to derive the expected constraint with 100% *accuracy*, as the sum of all the *true* elicited positive examples and all the *true* elicited negative examples divided by all the examples.

Data. The model we used in the experiment is the one depicted in Fig. 1. We firstly highlighted three kinds of error (e) that can be hosted by the input model and. Secondly, we identified possible target constraints (c). Selected errors and constraints were paired as follows:

(1.e) *"some vehicles are neither cars, boats nor airplanes"*
(2.e) *"some vehicles are both cars and boats, but not amphibious cars"*
(3.e) *"some vehicles have no engines"*
(1.c) *"all vehicles are either cars, boats or airplanes"*
(2.c) *"all vehicles which are both cars and boats are amphibious cars"*
(3.c) *"all vehicles have at least one engine"*

(1.e) is generated by the fact that the specialization of the class "Vehicle" is not complete. (2.e) occurs because the class "AmphibiousCars" is taken as a sub-class of "Car" *"or"* "Boat" instead of being equivalent to the intersection between "Car" *"and"* "Boat". (3.e) is generated by the fact that the "componentOf" relation is used at a very abstract level, namely between "Vehicle" and "VehiclePart", thus missing the specific constraint between "Vehicle" and "Engine". To check whether we are able to learn constraints for avoiding errors (1.e-2.e-3.e), we ran *15 simulations* and collected a total of *17 examples*. For each error, we then created a populated model by selecting the negative examples highlighting each error and the related positive example. This was in order to test if we are able to learn the constraints (1.c-2.c-3.c).

4.2   Results

Question 1. We firstly highlighted the error (1) by selecting instances of the concept 'Vehicle' that are neither cars, nor boats, and nor airplanes. The output constraint was the following:

$$\forall x.(Vehicle(x) \rightarrow (Airplane(x) \vee Boat(x) \vee Car(x)))\qquad(1)$$

The rule was straightforwardly derived with 100% of *accuracy*.[6] Secondly, we selected negative examples highlighting error (2) where the elicited negative examples were both 'Cars' and 'Boats', but not 'Amphibious Cars'. The derived rule was the following:

$$\forall x.((Boat(x) \wedge Car(x)) \rightarrow AmphibiousCar(x))\qquad(2)$$

The output constraint was straightforwardly derived with 100% of *accuracy*. Finally, we learned a constraint for defining a target class through a target relation. Here we highlighted vehicles without an engine as negative examples. The final output axiom was the following:

$$\forall x.(Vehicle(x) \rightarrow \exists y.(Engine(y) \wedge isComponentOfVehicle(y,x)))\qquad(3)$$

Again, the output constraint was derived with 100% of *accuracy*. The selection of the target classes for the above trials worked as a scope restriction to focus on the part of the model we wanted to analyze and repair.

Question 2. The amount of data we generated to identify the target constraints was relatively small. As anticipated before, we just needed to generate 15 simulations and 17 example instances. The amount of time used to run the transformation steps and the induction of the constraints was trifling, in the order of few milliseconds. However, in order to avoid not useful, i.e., noisy, simulations (e.g., simulations with concepts, such as 'Wheel', which are not related to the errors), during the model finding step, we had to manage the scope of the analyzer. Moreover, before learning the expected constraints with 100% accuracy we had to go through each input populated model and identify possibly conflicting negative/positive examples. For instance, in order to learn rule (1), we had to exclude negative examples highlighting other possible errors. By running the first trial we got indeed 66% for the target constraint rule. This was because we firstly selected a total of 6 examples, which, with the provided annotation, returned 4 true positive examples, two false-positive examples, and, accordingly, 2 false-negative examples and 4 true negative examples. The two 'outliers' (annotated as negative examples) in this case, were selected to avoid overlapping issues (e.g., a 'Vehicle' which is both an 'Airplane' and a 'Boat', thus allowing for a negative and a positive example for both 'Airplane' and a 'Boat'), which were not directly connected to error 1.e.

---

[6] Notice that the output provided by the applied algorithm can be taken as a *rule* composed by axioms encoded in Description Logic (DL) or *manchester owl syntax* (www.w3.org/owl2-manchester-syntax/), and in order to map the output into FOL language, a further mapping must be applied. For instance, the output resulting from the conjunction of the first three axioms provided as solution by the algorithm applied for the rule (1) above was: $(Vehicle \sqsubseteq ((Airplane) \sqcup (Boat) \sqcup (Car)))$.

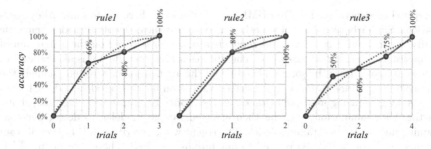

Fig. 4. Number of trials and accuracy trends.

Figure 4 shows the trials we run, for each rule, to get 100% accuracy. The chart shows how the deletion of the given outliers improves the accuracy of the learning task (for sake of clarity we showed the improvement by deleting an example per trial). The conclusion we can draw from this experience is that, in order to get the best from the learning task and allowing the modeler to decrease the effort of trial-and-error activities, a set of formal guidelines for the annotation and the ILP set-up must be provided (for instance, processing sub-fragments of the model, focusing on associations and generalization relations separately, deleting irrelevant instances, minimizing the set of examples). The definition of these guidelines will be part of the immediate future work.

4.3 Threats to Validity

As for any experimental evaluation, some threats can affect the validity of our findings. These threats are mainly concerned with the generalization of the observed results to a real-case scenario.

Firstly, we did not account for random annotation. In this experiment, indeed, the errors we found in the configurations were generated by knowing in advance the rules to be learned. The main focus here is on assessing whether the given approach is valid in learning the selected repairing solutions. In order to check the types of rules that can be learned when the modeler does not know in advance the required output, an experiment considering a larger population of modelers and, possibly, a larger set of conceptual models should be conducted. Moreover, to make the approach usable by teams of engineers that may vary in size and complexity, the proposal must be evaluated across a breadth of annotation data sets, both varying in size and complexity, to also provide a precise assessment of the limits of the new technique. Secondly, in the experiment we did not compare the observed results with what could be obtained by using alternative ILP algorithms. We recognize that the approach could potentially benefit from assessing different algorithms in terms of what types of rules can be learned (or not) and *how* efficiently they can be learned. We intend to do this as future work after gathering more data from concrete models in different domains.

5   Related Work

Model Validation. Our work builds primarily upon the large amount of work done in the recent years on *conceptual model validation*. [1] proposed a solution to assess conceptual models defined in OntoUML by transforming these models into Alloy specifications. Similarly, [32] devised a methodology to test the conceptual models semantic quality, in terms of *correctness* and *completeness*, which is based on the generation of *automated conceptual test cases* [23]. The approach presented in [13] is also related to what we propose. Here the solution is based on the application of a system, namely the USE system, that allows for a model-driven validation of UML models and OCL constraints, by generating multiple instances of the model, or snapshots. These snapshots, like the Alloy simulations, can be then assessed by the modeler to detect overconstraining and underconstraining issues. The recent work described in [14], even if from a higher-level perspective, is related to our proposal as well. There, the main goal is to formalize the process by which modelers analyze and modify the model as a sort of "dialogue", which must be iterated in order to better identify and capture the final intended worldview.

Compared to these key works, the main difference in our approach is the exploitation and the integration of model finding and statistical relational learning techniques, like ILP, in order to identify refactoring solutions.

Constraint Learning. Our work can be also placed in the general research area of *constraint learning for conceptual models*. In this respect, of direct relevance to our effort on using the validation process to then infer model constraints, is also the work in [29]. This approach aims at identifying and solving possible (UML) model design flaws, by exploiting model finding and adopting *constraint logic* [22]. Similarly, the work in [9] proposes a genetic algorithm [27] in order to generate Object Constraint Language (OCL) invariants from examples. Moreover, the work in [6] propose an approach to infer OCL invariants from valid/invalid snapshot by checking the relevance of the generated outputs. Another work that is close in spirit to ours is discussed in [18,31], where the main goal is to efficiently identify recurrent error-prone structures across conceptual models and then manually uncover possible missing constraints. Compared to these pivotal works, the main difference in our approach are the following: i) we employ ILP (as opposed to CSP as, e.g., in [6]) to address the constraint learning problem. As discussed in [8], there might be some relevant advantages in addressing CSP problems from an ILP perspective; ii) we support multiple representational languages for the input conceptual model to be assessed and repaired, namely, OWL, UML and OntoUML (approaches like the ones present in [6,27], for instance account for UML models only). In fact, our aim is to build an infrastructure for learning: a) *ontological constraints* such as the ones expressible in OntoUML [15]; b) anti-patterns for that language [31]; iii) we provide a set-up of the model finding facility that can be used to curate a database of positive and negative examples for conceptual models, covering different application domains. In fact, our approach seamlessly leverages and extends on the existing methodological and computational support for model validation via visual simulation (visual model finding) provided by the OntoUML toolset [1,10]. In that sense, it requires less intrusive manual interventions for eliciting and curating examples and counterexamples than, for example, [6].

6   Discussion

In the sequel, we discuss the implications of this novel approach. Moreover, by identifying the limitations of our current setting, we also discuss opportunities for future work.

Implications. A first central implication is that the proposed approach can support the modelers in better exploiting the analysis they run with the model finding model simulator. Indeed, by collecting and annotating the simulations generated through the application of the model finder, a large data set of intended/unintended simulations can be generated, and then (re-)used to derive possible repair options. This can be taken as a backup facility that allows storing and keeping track of information that may be lost during the run-time analysis.

Secondly, another key point is that, by enabling modelers to generate populated models with a related set of elicited negative/positive examples, the proposed framework paves the way to a large number of case studies, especially on the application of different learning approaches, to identify constraints, or to address other tasks that can support the conceptual modeling activities (like for instance the identification of unintended instances across models, exploiting the annotation of previous activities). In the current setting, we adopted one single algorithm, but the same algorithm can be tuned in multiple ways and can produce different kinds of outputs. A benchmark of the available technologies and the possible configurations is out of the scope of this paper, but it is still a pivotal research issue, especially to check *what* kind of constraints can be learned and *how* easily they can be understood and reused to repair the model.

Thirdly, by adopting ILP the constraint learning task can leverage on a very small amount of data. Similarly, relying on ILP allows inducing human-understandable logical rules. Still, this does not prevent us to exploit a much larger amount of data. Even just by applying the CELOE algorithm, we selected, indeed, we can measure the *accuracy* of each derived rule, thus leveraging the feedback provided by multiple annotations and/or users.

Fourthly, the application of the automated steps of the framework, see for instance the conversion of the conceptual model into Alloy specifications, or the automatic identification of possible erroneous axioms, along with the suggestion of possible repair solutions, return to be useful allies in the conceptual modeling process. While they cannot be seen as alternatives to most of the modelers' activities, still they can be seen as useful means for improving the efficiency of some key steps. For instance, the modeler does not need to know how to encode its model into Alloy specifications, or she can start from a set of multiple repair suggestions, before deciding how to change the source model, this being particularly helpful in a scenario with very complex models, or involving non-expert (i.e., novice) modelers.

Limitations. Applying the presented framework over OntoUML configurations, and then learning more complex constraints is our long-term objective and it triggers the agenda for the immediate future work. In order to achieve this goal, with the current set-up, there is still a gap that needs to be bridged.

The model in Fig. 5 provides an example of one of the problems that we may want to address in the future, but that cannot be solved without human intervention with our current approach. In this model, while 'Purchase' defines a certain *kind* of relationship (i.e., "Relator", according to the OntoUML terminology), 'Buyer' and 'Seller' represents two *roles* that can be played by instances of the *kind* 'Person'. Supposing that we run a simulation by reducing the scope to 'Purchase', 'Buyer', 'Seller' and 'Purchasable Item', it is possible to have an instance that is involved as both a 'Buyer' and 'Seller' in the same 'Purchase' relationship. An example of an unintended simulation that can be generated would be then when an instance of 'Purchase' (suppose this/TOP0) is the source of both 'involvesSeller' and 'InvolvesBuyer', and these relations have the same instance (suppose `this/TOP1`) as the target. The constraints to be learned to avoid this problem can be then represented by the formula (4) below.

$$\forall x.y.z((Purchase(x) \wedge involvesBuyer(x,y) \wedge involvesSeller(x,z)) \rightarrow y \neq z) \quad (4)$$

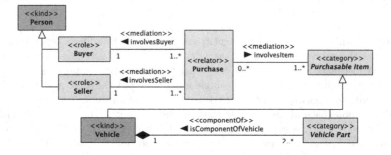

Fig. 5. An extension of the OntoUML model represented in Fig. 1.

Currently, we are not able to learn the exact constraints for this type of error. This is primarily due to the fact that the algorithm we selected is limited to DL expressivity. CELOE, indeed, is an efficient solution if the goal is to support modelers in constructing models and resources, used to devise, for instance, reasoning systems, or *Semantic Web* applications. Moreover, it is widely applied in a lot of ontology engineering case studies and it is also implemented as part of the DL-learner framework [2]. Still, learning complex rules, such as (4), is out of the scope of this algorithm and, hence, will require the investigation of complementary ILP approaches. Moreover, this kind of more complex problems brings challenges for the annotation step. We may have cases, indeed, where to highlight a possible problematic structure we may need to annotate as negative multiple instances involved in multiple relations, thus increasing the level of complexity of the learning process, and affecting the accuracy of the output.

Another key observation is that, while the proposed approach aims at supporting the conceptual modelers through the automatization of some steps of the engineering activities, humans still need to be in the loop of the process. Since the approach aims at making explicit unintended models, the only way to collect this information is, indeed, to leverage on the feedback of the modeler, and to manually annotate the simulations. The key aspect here is that we offer a facility to collect data about this (often tacit) information. Moreover, the output provided by the ILP algorithm still needs to be interpreted by the modeler. Depending on the applied set-up, different outputs can be provided, and each output can be used in different ways. Similarly, constraints with different levels of restriction can be learned, and the choice of what axiom to be selected depends on the modeler's goals. For instance, with the current set-up, instead of the constraint presented by formula (4), we can learn the following constraint:

$$\forall x.(Purchase(x) \rightarrow \neg \exists y.z.(involvesBuyer(x,y) \wedge Seller(y)$$
$$\wedge\, involvesSeller(x,z) \wedge Buyer(z)) \quad (5)$$

The above rule implies, indeed, a stronger restriction as it makes the roles 'Seller' and 'Buyer' disjoint (while formula (4) only requires that they are not played by the same person in the scope of the same Purchase). For this reason, for constraints that depart from DL expressivity such as (4) we consider the ILP output as "repair suggestions", i.e., the learned constraints must be checked and eventually adapted by the modeler. This strategy of providing partial solutions that are then adapted by the modeler was successfully employed for anti-pattern rectification in [31].

7   Conclusion and Perspectives

This paper makes a contribution to the theory and practice of (ontology-driven) conceptual modeling diagnosis and repair by: i) presenting a framework to combine model finding and ILP, in order to support model validation; ii) presenting a practical solution to generate and exploit multiple simulations for any given (Onto)UML conceptual model, thus allowing its analysis and annotation; iii) presenting a practical solution to learn constraints from the annotated simulations output. Adopted data and processes are available at /unibz-core/Mind-the-Gap and /unibz-core/gufo2alloy, respectively.

Based on the presented results, as future work, we plan to evaluate our approach over different OntoUML models, encoding errors with a higher level of complexity, thus uncovering also *recurrent* errors across models and related constraints. This involves both practical and theoretical research that examines the impact of various algorithms on the learning goal, as well as the generation of a data set of annotated simulations coming from different OntoUML models.

References

1. Benevides, A.B., et al.: Validating modal aspects of OntoUML conceptual models using automatically generated visual world structures. J. Univ. Comput. Sci. **16**(20), 2904–2933 (2010)
2. Bühmann, L., et al.: DL-Learner-a framework for inductive learning on the semantic web. J. Web Semant. **39**, 15–24 (2016)
3. Cairns-Smith, G.: The Life Puzzle: On Crystals and Organisms and on the Possibility of a Crystal as an Ancestor. University of Toronto Press, Toronto (1971)
4. Clarke, E.M., Jr., et al.: Model Checking. MIT press, Cambridge (2018)
5. Collins: Litmus test. In: Collins Dictionary. https://www.collinsdictionary.com/dictionary/english/litmus-test, Accessed 02 Apr 2021
6. Dang, D.-H., Cabot, J.: On automating inference of OCL constraints from counterexamples and examples. In: Nguyen, V.-H., Le, A.-C., Huynh, V.-N. (eds.) Knowledge and Systems Engineering. AISC, vol. 326, pp. 219–231. Springer, Cham (2015). https://doi.org/10.1007/978-3-319-11680-8_18
7. De Nicola, A., Missikoff, M., Navigli, R.: A software engineering approach to ontology building. Inf. Syst. **34**(2), 258–275 (2009)
8. De Raedt, L., Dries, A., Guns, T., Bessiere, C.: Learning constraint satisfaction problems: an ILP perspective. In: Bessiere, C., De Raedt, L., Kotthoff, L., Nijssen, S., O'Sullivan, B., Pedreschi, D. (eds.) Data Mining and Constraint Programming. LNCS (LNAI), vol. 10101, pp. 96–112. Springer, Cham (2016). https://doi.org/10.1007/978-3-319-50137-6_5

9. Faunes, M., et al.: Automatically searching for metamodel well-formedness rules in examples and counter-examples. In: Proceedings MODELS 2013, pp. 187–202 (2013)

10. Fonseca, C.M., Sales, T.P., Viola, V., Fonseca, L.B.R., Guizzardi, G., Almeida, J.P.A.: Ontology-driven conceptual modeling as a service. In: 11th International Workshop on Formal Ontologies Meet Industry (FOMI'21). CEUR-WS (2021)

11. Fumagalli, M., Sales, T.P., Guizzardi, G.: Towards automated support for conceptual model diagnosis and repair. In: 1st Workshop on Conceptual Modeling Meets Artificial Intelligence and Data-Driven Decision Making (2020)

12. Gogolla, M., Büttner, F., Richters, M.: A UML-based specification environment for validating UML and OCL. Science of Computer Programming (2005)

13. Gogolla, M., et al.: USE: A UML-based specification environment for validating UML and OCL. Sci. Comput. Program. **69**(1–3), 27–34 (2007)

14. Grüninger, M.: Ontology validation as dialogue (2019)

15. Guizzardi, G.: Ontological foundations for structural conceptual models. Telematica Instituut/CTIT (2005)

16. Guizzardi, G.: Theoretical foundations and engineering tools for building ontologies as reference conceptual models. Semant. Web **1**(1,2), 3–10 (2010)

17. Guizzardi, G., Fonseca, C.M., Almeida, J.P.A., Sales, T.P., Benevides, A.B., Porello, D.: Types and taxonomic structures in conceptual modeling: a novel ontological theory and engineering support. Data Knowl. Eng. **134** (2021). https://doi.org/10.1016/j.datak.2021.101891

18. Guizzardi, G., Sales, T.P.: Detection, simulation and elimination of semantic anti-patterns in ontology-driven conceptual models. In: Yu, E., Dobbie, G., Jarke, M., Purao, S. (eds.) ER 2014. LNCS, vol. 8824, pp. 363–376. Springer, Cham (2014). https://doi.org/10.1007/978-3-319-12206-9_30

19. van Harmelen, F., ten Teije, A.: Validation and verification of conceptual models of diagnosis. In: Proceedings EUROVAV 1997, pp. 117–128 (1997)

20. Huth, M., Ryan, M.: Logic in Computer Science: Modelling and Reasoning About Systems. Cambridge University Press, Cambridge (2004)

21. Jackson, D.: Software Abstractions: Logic, Language, and Analysis. MIT press, Cambridge (2012)

22. Jaffar, J., Maher, M.J.: Constraint logic programming: a survey. J. Logic Program. **19**, 503–581 (1994)

23. Janzen, D., Saiedian, H.: Test-driven development concepts, taxonomy, and future direction. Computer **38**(9), 43–50 (2005)

24. Kayama, M., et al.: A practical conceptual modeling teaching method based on quantitative error analyses for novices learning to create error-free simple class diagrams. In: Proceedings IIAI, pp. 616–622. IEEE (2014)

25. Lehmann, J., et al.: Class expression learning for ontology engineering. J. Web Semant. **9**(1), 71–81 (2011)

26. Leung, F., Bolloju, N.: Analyzing the quality of domain models developed by novice systems analysts. In: Proceedings HICSS, p. 188b. IEEE (2005)

27. Mirjalili, S.: Genetic algorithm. In: Evolutionary Algorithms and Neural Networks. SCI, vol. 780, pp. 43–55. Springer, Cham (2019). https://doi.org/10.1007/978-3-319-93025-1_4

28. Muggleton, S., De Raedt, L.: Inductive logic programming: theory and methods. J. Logic Program. **19**, 629–679 (1994)

29. Pérez, B., Porres, I.: Reasoning about UML/OCL class diagrams using constraint logic programming and formula. Inf. Syst. **81**, 152–177 (2019)

30. Roussey, C., et al.: A catalogue of OWL ontology antipatterns. In: Proceedings of the Fifth International Conference on Knowledge Capture, pp. 205–206 (2009)
31. Sales, T.P., Guizzardi, G.: Ontological anti-patterns: empirically uncovered error-prone structures in ontology-driven conceptual models. Data Knowl. Eng. **99**, 72–104 (2015)
32. Tort, A., Olivé, A., Sancho, M.R.: An approach to test-driven development of conceptual schemas. Data Knowl. Eng. **70**(12), 1088–1111 (2011)
33. Troquard N., et al.: Repairing ontologies via axiom weakening. In: McIlraith, S.A., Weinberger, K.Q. (eds.) 32nd AAAI Conference on Artificial Intelligence. AAAI Press (2018)

Detecting Value Capture Processes Using Fractal Enterprise Model (FEM)

Victoria Klyukina[✉]

DSV, Stockholm University, Stockholm, Sweden
victoria.klyukina@dsv.su.se

Abstract. Value creation and value capture are the two main concepts within strategic management. This because of firm's revenue depends on how these processes are managed. Value creation are associated with value chain processes that generate costs in a balance sheet. Thus, these are mostly tangible. Whereas, the value capture processes are associated with the processes intended to create any type of competitive advantage. Such advantage might be hidden in firm-specific routines or resources. Thus, value capture processes are ambiguous and often intangible. Practically, it is a challenging task to identify and manage them. This paper discusses how Enterprise Modelling (EM) may assist in detecting of this type of processes, particularly, Fractal Enterprise Model (FEM) is used for the challenge. A hypothetical example for detecting value capture processes is given using FEM technique.

Keywords: Value capture processes · FEM · Enterprise modelling ·
Firm-specific assets and resources · Strategic management

1 Introduction

Value creation and value capture are the two main concepts within strategic management. Value creation refers to the processes representing the core competence of the firm. These processes exist to produce and deliver products/services to the customers or society. Thus, this type of processes belongs to a value chain processes that are associated with the costs. Whereas, value capture processes are those that are designed for strategy implementation and building of a competitive advantage. Such advantage might be realised through a control over scarce tangible and intangible resources. The resources that might be evaluated as being Valuable, Rare, Inimitable and Specific (VRIS) [1] might be classified as unique. Through effective application of such resources the firm may achieve the distinctiveness that represents a competitive advantage [2]. Although, unlike the value creation elements that are mostly tangible, the value capture elements are firm-specific and are rooted in mostly intangible elements, e.g. organisational competences, managerial know-how, learning, sensing, etc. Hence, in practice such elements are hidden in firm's routines or resources. The firm-specific routines and resources are acquired

© IFIP International Federation for Information Processing 2021
Published by Springer Nature Switzerland AG 2021
E. Serral et al. (Eds.): PoEM 2021, LNBIP 432, pp. 80–89, 2021.
https://doi.org/10.1007/978-3-030-91279-6_6

through a configuration of assets available to a firm and the processes managing these assets. Thus, the value capture processes might be identified through interconnections of business elements, i.e. a chain leading to the sources (roots) for building the strategically important and firm-specific assets. However, due to the ambiguity and intangible nature of the elements it is a challenging task. This paper discusses the ways enterprise modelling may assist in detecting value capture processes. Particularly, Fractal Enterprise Model (FEM) is applied in the trial. FEM is based on the interconnections between processes and assets and, therefore, is considered being promising in addressing such challenge.

2 Methodology

The presented paper is a part of a broad research belonging to the Design Science (DS) paradigm [3]. This overarching research is related to the Fractal Enterprise Model (FEM) development. DS is concerned with finding a solution [4] or artefact [3] to joint Problem space and Solution space in terminology of [5, 6] (see Fig. 1). The presented research is placed in Evaluation space depicted in the Fig. 1 in iteration between Problem and Solution spaces.

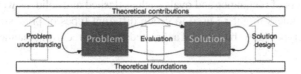

Fig. 1. Design science framework [7].

The motivation for this study comes from the results and analyses of the preceded case studies. In particular, the background of the empirical research where FEM was applied in operational decision making [8] spawned the idea of FEM potential usefulness in detecting value capture processes. During the work on this case the issue of a holistic approach become apparent when producing practical recommendations for efficiency improvement in operations. Particularly, the work encountered into the need to understand the nature and the role of the processes when dealing with the issue of cost reduction or increase of the revenue. Thus, our research group has realised the importance of managing not only value creating processes but also value capture processes in such task. But the identification of the value capture processes is not a straight forward task in practice. Hence, the research has fallen into the 'problem space' again (Fig. 1). Thence, the presented paper is the first attempt to discover whether FEM can be useful in addressing this challenge to some extent.

However, due to the limitations of time and space the hypothetical example used in the presented paper is taken from the another study of Bider and Perjons [9]. The matter of modelling for value-based organizational design has been already tackled by the authors. Hence, the presented illustration extends the authors' previous idea.

3   Short Overview of FEM

The development of Fractal Enterprise Model (FEM) was inspired by a fractal view on the organisation proposed by [18]. The approach is distinctive by its inherited emphases on the recurring patterns at the progressively smaller scale when constructing an artefact of organisational instances. Fractal view on the organisation also tackles the concause and multiple effects phenomenon providing guidance for decision making.

FEM consists of three types of the elements in building archetypes, so-called fractals: business processes, assets, and relationships between them. Graphically, a process is represented by an oval, asset by a rectangle and the relationships between them by the arrows (see Fig. 2). The names of the processes are labelled inside the oval, and the name of the assets are labelled inside the rectangles respectively. A solid arrow pointing from the asset to the process represents a relationship of a process using an asset. This pattern constructs a process-asset archetype (fractal). A dashed arrow pointing from an asset to the process represents a relationship of a process changing the asset. This pattern constructs an asset-process archetype (fractal). The arrows are also labelled showing the type of relationships between processes and assets. In process-asset archetype the relationships identify the role an asset plays in the process, e.g. workforce, equipment, etc. In the asset-process archetype the relationships identify the way a process affects the volume and the characteristics of an asset, e.g. acquire, maintain, retire. Also, different styles for boarders of rectangles and ovals such as dashed and solid, as well as different colours and thickness might be used to group different types of processes and assets. These two archetypes allow building of a directed graph in recurring manner to represent organizational instances.

4   Use of FEM for Value-Based Organisational Design (Hypothetical Example Borrowed from [9])

In the previous study [9] FEM was used for a firm design taking value-based organisational perspective. The hypothetical example was given in a hypothetical consultant company. The prime value creating process was defined as "Providing solutions for customers" (see in Fig. 2). Three main strategic choices in a way the value might be delivered to the customer were also determined. These choices were: developing firm's competence in management consultants, competence in procedures or competence in IT support/tools. It has been noted that the firm need all of these three assets for value creation but for successful strategy implementation the focus should be only on developing a competence that will define a firm's unambiguous distinctiveness. Below is presented a fragment of the original model from [9] where these three assets are represented by blue rectangles with relationships "Workforce,", "EXT", "Tech & Info Infrastructure".

Building up on this model and to detect value capture processes using FEM, there is a need to understand the representation of value creation and value capture within fractal modelling. In presented hypothetical example the main process "Providing solution for customers" represents the prime process according to value chain concept [10]. It is also a part of a business model (BM) design describing w*hat*, thus is a value creating process. While to depict value capture processes, one need to look beyond BM design.

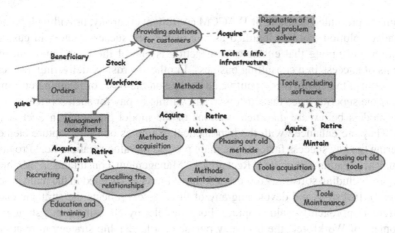

Fig. 2. A fragment of FEM representing JYAMCC [9].

It is necessary to analyse the ways of value creation in such a manner that allows the firm to retain a share of value it creates. Managerial processes are used for this purpose. However, the choice of strategies for value creation and its successful implementation is determined by the external factors and the assets available to a firm [2]. Since the resources are scarce, the configuration and management of available assets in a way that makes them firm-specific play a significant role in success. It follows, managerial processes are the once to look after in search for the value capture. In FEM the processes that mange an asset might be associated with the managerial processes. These are noted with relationships *Acquire, Maintain, Retire* in the Fig. 2. Hence, these are the processes that need to be evaluated and analysed when modelling for value capture.

5   Use of FEM for Detecting Value Capture Processes (Build on Hypothetical Example)

To enable value capture modelling with FEM in the example above, it is important to consider external environment. Particularly, to identify the key success factors in the industry that drive profit and is a base for competitive advantage. Then, the internal chain of interconnected elements leading to addressing the key success factors might be identified. This chain is constructed with recurring asset-process and process-asset archetypes including routinised processes (known as competences [11]), and firm-specific assets and processes whose services are difficult to buy or imitate (known as resources [11]–[14]). This type of assets may not be directly used in value creating process but is critical to linkage between processes that create value and capture it (building of competitive advantage).

Hence, the modelling for detecting of value capture processes starts with identification of the key success factors and the assets needed to deliver on these factors. The identification of the firm's key success factors might be done by either industry analysis, firm's external environment or from the interviews with the management.

From the presented example of JYACCM consultant company, providing high quality, creative solution can be identified as one of the key success factors in customer satisfaction; presuming that customer satisfaction is one of the most important measurements of success in a consulting business. In other words, by delivering a superior service the firm may build a competitive advantage on the basis of retaining customers and enjoy the superior price that customers are willing to pay for such service.

The models below are modified versions of the model presented in Sect. 4 (see Fig. 2). They are enhanced with the hypothetical examples of value capture elements considering the key success factor in the main process of value creation, i.e. "Providing high quality, creating solutions". Rectangles "Management consultants", "Methods" and "Tools, Including software" represent some of the assets needed in the main process (see Fig. 2). Investing and developing any of these assets reflects the strategic choice and different approach to value capture. For example, by choosing focus strategy on development of Workforce, the firm may pursue cost leadership strategy in relation to Methods and Tools. Meaning that by capturing value through development of Workforce the firm may need to abandon competence/capability development in Methods and Tools; perhaps, to outsource these functions or enter the alliance. Hence, in each case the main value capture processes may vary.

The following models illustrate three versions of organisational focus in respect to the chosen strategy. The main process of desired value creation is represented by the pink oval with the red-coloured boarder in the models. The value capture mechanisms are identified through the firm-specific assets and the processes managing such assets; these are marked with the blue borders. The connectivity chain of value capture mechanisms is highlighted through the colouring of the elements, whereas the hidden processes, i.e. the sources of such mechanisms are shown in dark-red. Note, that the ideas presented in this paper is a first attempt in addressing the challenge of modelling for value capture processes using FEM, particularly, use of intangible elements. Therefore, the results are yet the subject for discussion.

Expert-Oriented Value Creation

The first example refers to the firm's strategic choice of focusing on the Workforce while creating value for the customers. Figure 3 depicts the value capture mechanism in this case. The process "Providing high quality, creative solutions" on the top in pink with red boarder represents a firm's core capability that addresses the key success factor. If the firm chooses to deliver value through a high quality and creative solutions it may focus on HR skills and capabilities. In the graph it corresponds to managing "Top experts management consultants" asset in light-blue colour. Thus, processes that manage this asset (represented by pink ovals with connections *Acquire, Maintain, Retire*) are critical to deliver on the key success factor. However, these processes are routinised whereas the routine is characterised by the configuration of assets used in it; hence they are not value capture but may be capability building. If the asset used in such processes is firm-specific, it creates a firm-specific routine (key competence); the basis for capability building according to resource-based perspective [11]. In the dark-blue colour is shown the firm-specific asset "HR and career path polices". This asset is used in the routinised processes *Recruiting, Education and training, Cancelling the relationships* (management of "Management consultants" asset) and represent the strategically important assets that the competitive advantage might be built on. In building this type of competence the resources such as time and investments are needed. That is why this type of assets are difficult to imitate or buy. Hence, they become distinctive and specific to a firm. Hence, "HR and career management" (in red) is one of the managerial processes that builds and maintains these firm's specific assets (in dark-blue). Thus, this process is defined as one of the value capture processes. Note that the "Top experts management consultants" asset is not indicated as a firm's specific in this case. This matter will be discussed in the Sect. 6 'Discussion'.

Fig. 3. Value capture mechanisms in FEM. Red boarder - value creation, blue boarder - value capture, coloured elements – chain mechanism (enhancement of Fig. 2) (Color figure online).

Method-Oriented Value

The second example refers to the firm's strategic choice of focusing on the Methods while creating value for the customers (see initial Fig. 2). Figure 4 below depicts the value capture mechanism in this case.

Figure 4 depicts value creating process represented by the pink oval with red boarder "Providing high quality, creative solutions". If the firm chooses to focus on the Methods in value creation it has to be very innovative in developing methods that can be considered as firm-specific to capture some of the value it creates. This type of methods might be classified as Know-how, represented by dark-blue-border rectangle in Fig. 4. Know-how helps the firm to create value for the customers in a way that none of the competitors does. Thus, know-how method is a firm's specific asset. But for development of unique methods having simply human resources for the task does not guarantee the creation of know-how. Humans need to be motivated and encouraged in a way that enables them to think creatively and openly to deliver on such task. Thus, management of this asset must be supported by innovative environment, e.g. "Cross-functional team projects" (dark-blue rectangle Fig. 4)) might be a firm-specific organisational design promoting creative culture. Hence, the process of "Coordination of HR strategies and Business strategies" to achieve a success is the value capture process (in red oval). It supports both firm's unique resources, "Cross-functional team projects" directly and "Know-how methods" indirectly (in dark-blue rectangles Fig. 4).

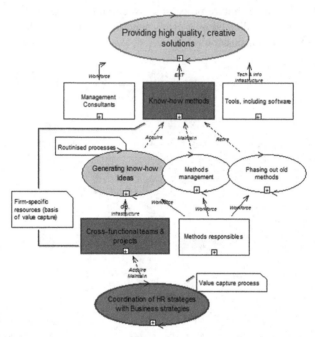

Fig. 4. Value capture mechanisms in FEM. Red boarder - value creation, blue boarder - value capture, coloured elements – chain mechanism (enhancement of Fig. 2) (Color figure online).

Tools-Oriented Value

The third example refers to the firm's strategic choice of focusing on the asset "Tools, Including software" while creating value for the customers (see initial Fig. 2). Figure 5 below depicts the value capture mechanism in this case.

Even in this case, Fig. 5 depicts the same value creating process "Providing high quality, creative solutions" in the pink oval on the top. If the firm chooses to focus on the asset "Tools, Including infrastructure", it has to develop tools that can be considered as unique and firm-specific. Such tool might be represented by the database of cases that can provide consultants with the instant access to the information necessary to create high quality, rapid solutions to the customers. Such information might be represented by previous experience of different consultants, description of the case, the solutions found in each instance, etc. However, to create such unique tool, the consultants must have incentives that encourage them to share personal, tacit knowledge acquired in the field. Hence, the process "Management of incentives & reward for knowledge share and cooperation" is a value capture process that manages database maintenance.

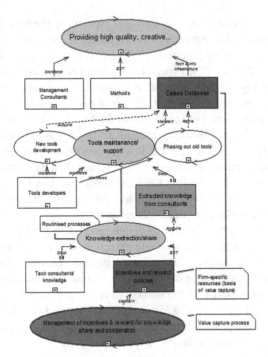

Fig. 5. Value capture mechanisms in FEM.. Red boarder - value creation, blue boarder - value capture, coloured elements – chain mechanism (enhancement of Fig. 2) (Color figure online).

6 Discussion

As mentioned in Introduction (see Sect. 1) value capture processes are the processes that manage building of competitive advantages on the basis of firm-specific assets and capabilities. The experience showed that such processes might be hidden in the process-asset archetype. This archetype assigns processes directly managing an asset with notation *Acquire, Maintain, Retire*. However, the linkage between value capture processes and specific asset are complex and may not be direct. The assets whose services is difficult to buy or imitate are developed in a chain of interconnected elements that may be hidden within the system. Note that modelling with FEM emphasising indirect interconnectivities to represent complex intangible elements is not a task FEM was developed for. Using FEM in such way might be seeing as finding the limits of FEM possibilities or opportunities for its development. Therefore, the results of this study are highly subjective.

In the presented hypothetical examples of FEM models the unique assets have been identified using VRIS model. But it has to be noted that this process is the matter of subjectivity and may influence the outcomes. Therefore, below follows the explanation of VRIS logic applied in the hypothetical examples.

Different HRM policies and strategies have been considered as firm-specific assets (see Fig. 3, Fig. 4 and Fig. 5) because of they are managerial know-how and is a part of the system that has no value when dispatched from the organisation. They are difficult to imitate due to ambiguity and, therefore, are highly specific to the firm. Besides, it is rare because of it takes time to develop and involves innovation and creativity. Thus, this asset is critical to building an internal expertise and attract the best specialists when focusing on Workforce. Note that the asset "Top experts management consultants" itself is not marked as firm-specific (see Fig. 3). This because of human resources rarely may be classified as firm-specific since the organisation does not own people or their knowledge. Human resources are not valuable, rare or inimitable to the firm but rather to the person itself; the person may leave the organisation taking all knowledge and experience away from the firm (probably to competitor). Hence, it is the processes of anchoring the resource that enables more value creation within the organisation than it could do outside makes the resource valuable to the firm. It is the identification of this type of processes that the modelling is concerned in the presented paper. In contrast, "Recruiting"," Education and training" and "Cancelling the relationship" processes maybe highly unambiguous and, therefore, neither may be identified as unique unless they are based on firm-specific assets. For example, to achieve the strategic objectives it is not enough simply to hire skilled people. The firm must provide motivation, desired behaviour, right attitudes, and certain cultural values. There might be many ways of managing these variables, whereas some will be more successful than the others. Thus, the HR processes presented in the examples (see Fig. 3, Fig. 4 and Fig. 5) are the managerial know-how and unique to the firm. Therefore, these processes represent the sources of value capture processes on which the competitive advantage might be maintained.

6.1 Lessons Learned

The experience of modelling with FEM for detecting value capture processes showed that:

- it is useful to define the main process in terms of capability to guide the modelling, e.g. "Providing solutions for customer" (see Fig. 2) vs "Providing high quality, creative solutions" (see Fig. 3, 4, 5);
- the result implies on that the asset-process archetype in FEM may contains value capture processes if the asset is firm-specific;
- a value capture processes may not directly manage a firm-specific asset. It is important to distinct between routinised processes that directly affect value creation and the processes without which firm-specific assets will be lost;
- the identification of the firm-specific assets is a subjective matter where other techniques should be used for resource appraisal, e.g. VRIS model.

7 Conclusion, Implications and Limitations

The trial of extending FEM application for detecting value capture processes has resulted in promising outcomes, however, the results are the matter for discussion. The value capture processes in FEM might be part of an asset-process archetype. If the asset that a process manages is firm-specific, i.e. corresponds to VRIS characteristics, then the process manages this asset might be a value capture process or a part of a value capture chain mechanism. The latter means that the value capture process may not manage a specific asset directly, rather through a complex coordination of interconnected elements leading to the process representing the root/source of value capture mechanism.

This study is limited to a hypothetical example to illustrate how FEM might be used for detecting of value capture processes. Hence, to strengthen the implications, there is a need to test this approach empirically, in the real case examples.

References

1. Barney, J.: Firm resources and sustained competitive advantage. J. Manag. **17**, 99–120 (1991)
2. Grant, R.M.: Contemporary strategy analysis: text and cases, 9th edn. Wiley, Chichester, West Sussex, United Kingdom (2016)
3. Hevner, M., Park, R.: Design science in information systems research. MIS Q. **28**(1), 75 (2004). https://doi.org/10.2307/25148625
4. Bider, I., Johannesson, P., Perjons, E.: Using empirical knowledge and studies in the frame of design science research. In: vom Brocke, J., Hekkala, R., Ram, S., Rossi, M. (eds.) DESRIST 2013. LNCS, vol. 7939, pp. 463–470. Springer, Heidelberg (2013). https://doi.org/10.1007/978-3-642-38827-9_38
5. Olsen, D.: The lean product playbook: how to innovate with minimum viable products and rapid customer feedback. Wiley, Hoboken (2015)
6. Reed, S.K.: The structure of ill-structured (and well-structured) problems revisited. Educ. Psychol. Rev. **28**(4), 691–716 (2015). https://doi.org/10.1007/s10648-015-9343-1
7. Is empirical enough?,Slidesshare, 28 May 2019. https://www.slideshare.net/PerRuneson/is-empirical-enough
8. Klyukina, V., Bider, I., Perjons, E.: Does fractal enterprise model fit operational decision making?. In: Proceedings of the 23rd International Conference on Enterprise Information Systems, Online Streaming, Select a Country, pp. 613–624 (2021). https://doi.org/10.5220/0010407306130624
9. Bider Ilia, I., Perjons, E.: Value-Based Organisational Design **8** (2019)
10. Porter, M.E.: Competitive strategy: techniques for analyzing industries and competitors: with a new introduction, 1st Free, Press Free Press, New York (1998)
11. Teece, D.J., Pisano, G., Shuen, A.: Dynamic capabilities and strategic management. Strateg. Manag. J. **18**(7), 509–533 (1997)
12. Penrose, E.T.: The theory of the growth of the firm, 4th ed., Rev. ed. Oxford, New York, Oxford University Press (2009)
13. Williamson, O.: Markets and hierarchies: analysis and antitrust implications: a study in the economics of internal organization. University of Illinois at Urbana-Champaign's Academy for Entrepreneurial Leadership (1975)
14. Wernerfelt, B.: A resource-based view of the firm. Strat. Mgmt. J. **5**(2), 171–180 (1984). https://doi.org/10.1002/smj.4250050207

OLIVE, a Model-Aware Microservice Framework

Damiano Falcioni[✉] and Robert Woitsch

BOC GmbH, Operngasse 20b, 1040 Vienna, Austria
{damiano.falcioni,robert.woitsch}@boc-eu.com

Abstract. In this paper we want to introduce OLIVE, a model-centric and low-code microservice framework, resulting from the lessons learned in five years of European projects. The requirements on those projects are summarized and used to extract the characteristics that a microservice framework should support in order to be aware of models. An implementation of the OLIVE framework has been proposed, focusing more on the concepts, and required models, instead that on the technical details and has been evaluated in each project with definition of the needed microservices. Microservice development using a low code approach is still an open research field and with OLIVE we want to provide an initial contribution relative to the dependencies between microservices and models, using ADOxx as reference meta-modelling platform, and proposing an initial modelling method for the definition of OLIVE microservices.

Keywords: Model-centric microservices · Low-code platform · OLIVE framework

1 Introduction

Models are an abstract way to represent relevant knowledge about a specific domain. The advantages of having such knowledge in a structured model, in addition to help reasoning about a specific problem, concern mainly the following purposes: documentation for the analysed problem/situation, configuration for model dependents functionalities, and data source for processing mechanisms [1]. In this paper we focus on the latter two cases, analysing their requirements and defining a framework for their management. Usually, model dependents functionalities and mechanisms do not have direct access to the model information, except when they are integrated in the modelling platform. In this case they can retrieve the model details directly from the platform, but in the majority of situations, they are implemented in external components and services that must implement the logic to parse and understand the model.

In this paper we identified different modalities in which a model can be used and required by a service, based on the experience in past European projects, and we defined a framework named OLIVE, addressing such requirements for the definition of services.

© IFIP International Federation for Information Processing 2021
Published by Springer Nature Switzerland AG 2021
E. Serral et al. (Eds.): PoEM 2021, LNBIP 432, pp. 90–99, 2021.
https://doi.org/10.1007/978-3-030-91279-6_7

With OLIVE we focus in particular on definition of microservices and their relations with the ADOxx meta-modelling platform, following a low-code approach.

Microservice is an architectural style increasing in popularity. A microservice is a small, autonomous, and isolated service, with a single and clearly defined purpose [2]. The focus of a microservice logic on the specific business task in particular, makes this architecture an ideal candidate for the abstraction in a model type enabling a low-code development [3].

The low-code approach [4] is a visual programming style that minimize the need of coding, abstracting the business logic in graphical form and favouring the configuration of existing components provided by the low-code platform. This approach has been chosen because, according to [5], low-code platforms will be used in 65% of application development work by 2024 and the ADOxx meta-model platform enable such business logic abstraction using a specific modelling method.

An implementation of this framework is provided, focusing more on the motivation and concepts behind the OLIVE framework instead then on its technical details. The proposed implementation has been evaluated in the context of each project and, at the end, the strengths and weaknesses of the approach have been reported.

2 Methodology

The model-aware characteristics of a microservice framework have been extracted in the last five years of involvements in European projects, from the requirements related to the meta-modelling platform ADOxx, used to create the domain specific model types for each project, in terms of both modelling methods and mechanisms [1]. In the following, such requirements have been briefly introduced for each EU project.

The **GO0D-MAN (H2020-723764)** project [6] constitutes a real-world implementation of the Industry 4.0 paradigm, through the integration and convergence of technologies for measurement and quality control, for data analysis and management, at single process and at factory level. The ultimate goal is to develop a production strategy that can guarantee high quality of products without interfering, actually improving, the production efficiency of the entire system. The ADOxx platform was used to develop a model-based tool for Industry 4.0 that supports multi-agent systems, smart on-line inspection tools and data analytics, for implementing a Zero-Defect Manufacturing (ZDM) strategy. A KPI meta-model has been created in this context in order to describe how to combine sensors data in order to calculate a KPI. Such modelling method had to be enriched with a mechanism to perform the effective KPI calculation based on the information in the model. One requirement here was to have such mechanism as a set services, one for each KPI model, where the user specify a KPI, and the service calculate and return the value. This imply that such services must (a) be able to be configured with the specific KPI model and (b) understand the KPI concepts.

DISRUPT (H2020-691436) [7] supports the digital twin of European manufacturer enterprises to Industry 4.0 by utilising the ICT capabilities to facilitate in-depth (self-) monitoring of machines and processes, provide decision support and decentralised (self-) adjustment of production, and foster the effective collaboration of the different IoT-connected machines with tools, services, and actors. The IoT devices, that create virtual counterpart of each element in the production line, provide data that will be analysed using models in the ADOxx platform, to detect complex events that will trigger automated actions. A modelling method for the DMN standard [8] have been implemented in ADOxx for modelling the rules to apply on each event as well as the mechanism to evaluate the rule, integrating an existing DMN evaluation engine, and to listen for events, integrating a connection with a message bus system. Such requirements, in order to be fulfilled, needed a system that (a) allows to integrate the ADOxx platform with external systems, (b) access the DMN meta-model concepts and (c) be generic enough to work in different scenarios (different event topics to listen on the message bus, each one with a specific DMN model to use for the evaluation) and to develop the services performing the triggered actions.

In **BIMERR (H2020 820621)** [9] have been designed and developed a Renovation 4.0 toolkit to support renovation stakeholders throughout the renovation process of existing buildings, from project conception to delivery. It comprises tools for the automated creation of enhanced building information models, a renovation decision support system to aid the designer in exploring available renovation options through an accurate estimation of renovation impact on building performance, as well as a process management tool based on the ADOxx platform that will optimize the design and on-site construction process toward optimal coordination and minimization of renovation time and cost. This have been done enriching the renovation process meta-model with a simulation mechanism that, taking as input some influencing factors for a specific process model like the expectation of supply chain delay or the weather conditions, will estimate the values of some time and cost related KPIs. The simulation mechanism had to be (a) a service (b) integrated into the meta-modelling platform in order to (c) recognize the concepts in the process to simulate and in the KPIs to estimate. Additionally, the renovation process, in order to be executed as workflow, needed a system that (a) connect all the workflows' automated tasks with appropriate services, (b) implementing the task logic.

With **Change2Twin (H2020 951956)** [10] the manufacturing small-medium enterprises (SMEs) where supported in their digitalization process by providing digital twin solutions through trusted local innovation hubs. Such digital innovation hubs (DIHs) analyse the digitalization potential and propose the best ready-to-use recipe for the use case from a technology marketplace, using dedicated knowledge models created with the ADOxx platform, to prepare the recipe for a complete solution, including the best components for the SME. One of the available receipts include a KPI dashboard, delivered as a service and configured through a specific KPI model that details not only how to calculate each KPI but also how to extract the required metrics from Internet of Things (IoT) sensors. This enhancement of the KPI model and dashboard respect to the ones in the GO0D-MAN project, required (a) a configurable system able to (b) connect with different IoT sensors and (c) integrate with the meta-modelling platform ADOxx. A specific meta-model has been created also to support the definition of marketplace items and the automatic generation of the marketplace portal using (a) a microservice that (b) interpretate the marketplace model and generate the portal pages.

Analysing the requirements pointed out in the above projects, we can identify some common characteristics. First, all the cases require the implementation of the functionalities in form of dedicated services. Service Oriented Architecture (SOA) and in particular Microservice Architecture (MSA) are well known styles that can be used for such purposes due to the focus on the business concepts, isolation, decentralization, and culture of automation [11]. Another recurring requirement is that such services must be configurable using models. Configurability is a characteristic that allows services to be reused in different contexts and we can see the needs to have multiple instances of the same service running in parallel, each one configured with a different model. The configurability of services using models rise the problem of understanding the semantic and the concepts in the model. Accessing the meta-model information is a requirement in order to avoid that the logic to interpretate the model as a configuration file will be hardcoded in the service. Accessing instead the meta-model information, like hierarchies and dependencies between concepts in the model, allows us to generalize and centralize the model interpretation in a framework instead that inside the service. The ADOxx meta-modelling platform used to create the model type for each project, provide the possibility to access such meta-model information, so an integration is required. This integration is used also to solve a last requirement that we can spot in the above projects: the need to extend the modelling methods of some project dependent model types, with mechanisms that provide a model specific feature directly inside the modelling platform. The ADOxx platform already allows to define custom mechanisms in form of algorithms, for a specific model type, but miss the possibility to use external and existing services as mechanisms and therefore communicate with the external world.

From this analysis we defined a framework, named OLIVE, for the definition of microservices with strong (meta-)model dependencies. Such framework highlights the following characteristics related to the model-awareness:

- Model-based Configurability: The framework gives the possibility to use models for the configuration of services. Additionally, the framework abstracts the services enough to automatically generate running service instances using only models. The microservice is created reflecting the concepts in the meta-model and is instantiated by the single model.
- Model Understandability: The framework allows to use models as input data for a service, giving the possibility to understand the concepts in a model, accessing the meta-model information.
- Meta-Model Enrichment: The framework expands the functionalities of the connected meta-modelling platform, providing a way to use services to enrich the mechanisms associated to a model type.

The OLIVE framework has been implemented as a microservice management system connected to the ADOxx meta-modelling platform. The proposed implementation has been successfully validated over the previously introduced European projects as described in the Sect. 5.

3 Related Works

Microservice Architecture is a recent style in software engineering and there are not so many papers addressing the application of a model-based approach for their defini-tion. Proposals have been made for model-based microservice frameworks but mainly to solve specific microservice issues, like self-adaptability, and scalability in multi-cloud environments, with the help of specific models containing dynamic requirements and adaptation rules [12], or to define the microservice logical architecture and its implementation skeleton from models describing functional requirements [13]. The OLIVE framework instead, want to address the complete generation of running microservice instances, starting from a model, used as configuration.

The approach followed share similarities with concepts in low-code/no-code frameworks [4]. Indeed, in the OLIVE framework, the user will not code a microservice, but will configure existing generic components provided by the platform, using specific models, in order to generate running microservices instances.

The authors in [14] use models to create self-configuring microservices based on TOSCA [15] standard in order to avoid a centralized orchestration. Microservices require indeed decentralized management and prefer choreography over orchestration [16]. The authors of [17] state that more research on choreography rather than orchestration is required. In the past, model-based orchestration has been used in the BPEL standard [18] that define a model-driven SOA architecture to address a specific business need, combining existing SOAP services. Within OLIVE we tried to be general enough to support both choreography and orchestration patterns, with the possibility to define dependencies between running microservices instances as well as generate REST microservices that act as orchestrators of other services.

The enhancement of a modelling method with mechanisms is a concept seen in [1] and supported in the ADOxx meta-modelling platform by a scripting language named ADOScript that only provide a limited set of features and do not allows complex interactions with external services. Other meta-modelling platforms like Eclipse EMF [19] do not permit to integrate mechanisms in the defined domain specific language (DSL) but allows only to use separate plugins to extend the DSL modelling environment with the needed features. The only attempt to extend a meta-modelling environment with microservices is in [3], where the authors provided an approach to integrate microservices as components of the DIME modelling environment. With the OLIVE framework we want to extend the ADOxx meta-modelling platform to use microservices as mechanisms for specific modelling methods.

4 Olive

OLIVE is a low-code framework to create model aware microservices through configuration of existing components, named Connectors resulting in ready to use REST microservices. The configuration of such Connectors can be performed using specific models, reflecting the framework concepts, created using the ADOxx graphical modelling environment. The connectors are part of the OLIVE platform but can be extended in case of needs, using plug-ins and provide the atomic functionality of a microservice. The created microservices can be combined together using a choreography or orchestration approach for the definition of your specific business logic.

The strength point of OLIVE is its model-awareness in the sense that the configurations of connectors are abstract enough that can be represented as models, and the out-of-the-box integration with the ADOxx meta-modelling environment allows to create the whole behaviour of a service, using models. This integration allows also ADOxx to communicate with the external world through a common interface, in a bi-directional way, using the microservices as mechanisms to enrich the modelling methods and using models as data for microservices. The OLIVE platform provides such features as a cloud environment where the user, instantiating existing components with specific configuration, can define the microservices, that can use and be used by ADOxx, and control their lifecycle. The Fig. 1 provide an overview of all the components involved in the framework.

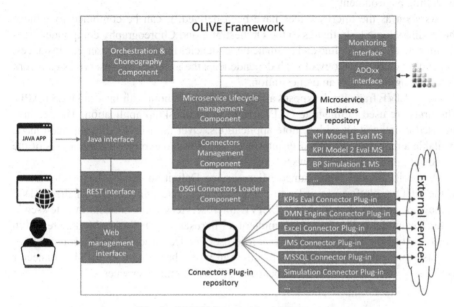

Fig. 1. OLIVE framework architecture

A Connector is a component developed in form of OSGi plug-in [20] that provide a specific functionality, like perform a query on a specific database or evaluate a DMN model. The name Connector derive from the fact that, usually (but not always), the main functionality is provided by an external system (like a database system or DMN engine) and the Connector is responsible to connect to such system to exploit its features. Each connector has its specific set of parameters that must be configured to generate a microservice instance (i.e., a database connector is configured with the endpoint and the query to perform). Olive integrates out-of-the-box 24 connectors. Custom connectors can be added to the platform and their OSGi standard format allows to reuse as connectors existing OSGi bundles, like all the one provided by the Apache Camel [20] project.

OLIVE allows to manage the configuration of such Connectors, giving the possibility to create microservices and control their whole lifecycle. Is responsibility of the Lifecycle Management component to (1) generate an instance of the REST microservice from the configuration of a Connector, (2) start the microservice, (3) keep the microservice running in an isolated environment, (4) stop the microservice and (5) dismiss it.

Each instantiated connector is exposed through a common REST interface with a standardized inputs and output formats, managed by the OLIVE platform.

The OSGi Connectors Loader component is responsible to load all the Connectors and make them available to the platform. It is built on the OSGi framework Apache Felix [21] and will dynamically check the presence of the OSGi bundles (plug-ins) defining Connectors, loading, and unloading them on request.

The ADOxx interface is creates as a special type of Connector, managing the bi-directional communication with the ADOxx platform. This component allows to retrieve models or concepts and use the available microservice instances from inside the ADOxx modelling environment.

As soon as the microservices have been defined, it can be combined to achieve the business logic task, thanks to the Orchestrator and Choreography component. This component allows to define and evaluate dependencies between microservice instances. Depending on the topology of such dependencies the group of microservices can work as a choreography or as an orchestration.

The OLIVE framework exposes all this functionality both with Java and REST APIs. The firsts are used to integrate OLIVE in local and desktop application. The seconds are used to integrate it with remote applications. Over the REST APIs has been made available a management web user interface that allows to exploit all the features of the framework through a web browser.

A specific model type, named Microservice Definition Model, has been created in the ADOxx platform in order to collect the most relevant concepts of the OLIVE framework and be able to define OLIVE microservices using models in a low-code style. The model in Fig. 2 is an example of a Microservice Definition Model created in the context of the BIMERR project. A Microservice Definition Model is composed of objects representing microservices of different types, based on the OLIVE Connector used, and relations representing dependencies between microservices.

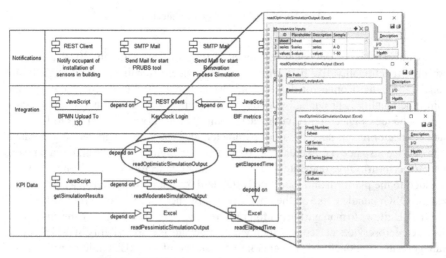

Fig. 2. OLIVE microservice definition model sample

Each of the specific microservice type objects has a set of common and specific attributes. Common attributes represent general microservice concepts like all the attributes related to the input parameters and the output of the microservice or about its health status. Specific attributes dependent instead on the Connector selected to provide the specific functionality for the microservice and are the parameters that this connector needs in order to work correctly. As a sample, in the case of the Excel connector used in the "ReadOptimisticSimulationOutput" microservice in Fig. 2, that read a simulation output from an Excel file, such attributes involve the path of the Excel file to open and the cells value to read, specified by sheet, rows and columns IDs. The microservice input parameters are then mapped and forwarded to the specific connector attributes values.

The Microservice Definition Model type also contains a mechanism to automatically push the modelled microservice to the OLIVE platform for their execution and lifecycle management.

More detailed documentation on the OLIVE platform involving technical concepts and APIs, as wells as its open-source code and binaries for download and test, can be found in the OLIVE webpage [22].

5 Evaluation

In the context of the GO0D-MAN project a specific connector for the OLIVE framework, named KPIs dashboard, has been created in order to calculate the value of a KPI in a model. This connector is configurable with the model id, used to retrieve the model directly form the ADOxx platform, and with the KPI name to find the KPI object. Seven KPI models have been created for the different use cases in the project and the new connector has been configured with each model, resulting in seven running microservices instances.

In DISRUPT the OLIVE framework has been extended with a connector to an external DMN engine and with two Java Messaging Systems (JMS) [23] compliant message bus connectors, one for subscribing and another for publishing on specific channels. The JMS connectors have been used in the configuration of four microservices, three for receiving events, actions, and data, subscribing to the respective topics, and one for publishing the actions handling the received events. Another microservice is created configuring the DMN engine connector, configured with the specific DMN model obtained from the ADOxx platform. This microservice is called by the event subscription microservice each time an event is received, then it evaluates the DMN to find the appropriate action for the event, and finally send it to the publishing microservice. With the OLIVE framework a microservice for each action has been configured and instantiate. Such microservices involve sending SMS and e-mail notifications, reset a device in critical status, etc.

For the BIMERR project, a microservice for simulating specific renovation process KPIs, has been defined and integrated in the ADOxx platform as a feature specific for the renovation process and KPI models. Thanks to the OLIVE framework the models required for the simulation, are extracted from the ADOxx platforms and the process concepts are mapped to a petri-net semantic that enable a token-based simulation. Also in this project, like in DISRUPT, the OLIVE framework has been used to generate notification services that, in this case, are referenced into renovation process workflows and called during their execution. In BIMERR, a modelling environment based on ADOxx for the definition of OLIVE microservices has been first released and used to model all the project specific OLIVE microservices. In this context, specific mechanisms for this microservice modelling environment have been created, in order to automatically generate the microservices documentation and to import the microservice definition in the OLIVE framework for their instantiation.

With Change2Twin the KPI model type defined in GO0D-MAN has been improved with information about how to obtain metrics values, referring the appropriate OLIVE microservice, responsible for the retrieval of specific IoT sensor data. The involved IoT sensors pushed data to different relational and time-series databases and connectors for each specific database have been created in OLIVE and configured to instantiate one microservice for each metric. Such microservices, referenced in the KPI model, are used, and called by the microservices responsible for the evaluation of each KPI model like in the GO0D-MAN use case. Finally, the modelling method created in ADOxx to describe the marketplace items, has been enriched with a mechanism, expressed as microservice in OLIVE, to generate the marketplace web pages for each item.

6 Conclusions

In this paper we presented our experience in different EU projects resulting on the definition of the relevant characteristics of a model centered microservice framework. An implementation has been proposed and evaluated over the projects. In particular in GO0D-MAN we evaluated the model-based configurability and model understandability characteristics of the framework with microservices for the evaluation of each KPI model. In DISRUPT, the meta-model enrichment and model understandability has been evaluated for the integration of ADOxx with microservices, handling the communication with a message bus and with a DMN evaluation engine. With BIMERR the model understandability has been exploited in a renovation process simulation microservice, while the model-based configurability enabled the definition of specific microservices for workflow automatic activities. In Change2Twin the meta-model enrichment characteristic of the framework has been exploited to integrate a marketplace generation microservice for a defined marketplace model while the model-based configurability, to generate microservices for retrieving the metric value of each IoT sensor.

Based on the experience in the above projects we have seen that the OLIVE framework enabled the integration of services in the ADOxx platform and improved the reuse of previously created logic, in particular about the extraction of information from models, speeding-up the release of microservices by reusing and adapting existing OLIVE connectors. Despite the big potential, the OLIVE framework still lacks some features in order to be extensively used as a low-code platform, in particular related to the logic abstraction. This is why we are planning to extend it with support for the Enterprise Integration Pattern (EIP) [24] notation and continue its evaluation in future projects.

References

1. Karagiannis, D., Kühn, H.: Metamodelling platforms. In: Bauknecht, K., Tjoa, A.M., Quirchmayr, G. (eds.) EC-Web 2002. LNCS, vol. 2455, pp. 182–182. Springer, Heidelberg (2002). https://doi.org/10.1007/3-540-45705-4_19
2. Lewis, J., Fowler, M.: Microservices (2014). http://martinfowler.com/articles/microservices.html. Accessed 20 July 2021
3. Chauhary, H, Margaria, T.: Integration of microservices as components in modelling environments for low code development. Syrcose (2021)
4. Woo, M.: The rise of no/low code software development—no experience needed? Eng. (Beijing, China) **6.9**, 960 (2020)
5. Wong, J., Driver, M., Vincent, P.: Lowcode development technologies evaluation guide. Gartner, Inc (2019). https://www.gartner.com/en/documents/3902331
6. GO0D MAN: Agent oriented zero defect multi-stage manufacturing. http://go0dman-project.eu/. Accessed 20 July 2021
7. DISRUPT: Transform manufacturing for Industrie 4.0. http://www.disrupt-project.eu/. Accessed 20 July 2021
8. OMG DMN: https://www.omg.org/dmn/. 20 July 2021
9. BIMERR: BIM-based holistic tools for energy-driven renovation of existing residences. https://bimerr.eu/. Accessed 20 July 2021
10. Change2Twin: Bringing digital twins to manufacturing SMEs. https://www.change2twin.eu/. Accessed 20 July 2021
11. Newman, S.: Building microservices: designing fine-grained systems. O'Reilly Media, Inc. (2015)
12. Pahl, C., Jamshidi, P.: Software architecture for the cloud – a roadmap towards control-theoretic, model-based cloud architecture. In: Weyns, D., Mirandola, R., Crnkovic, I. (eds.) ECSA 2015. LNCS, vol. 9278, pp. 212–220. Springer, Cham (2015). https://doi.org/10.1007/978-3-319-23727-5_17
13. Santos, N., Rodrigues, H., Ferreira, N., Machado, R.: Inputs from a model-based approach towards the specification of microservices logical architectures: an experience report. In: Franch, X., Männistö, T., Martínez-Fernández, S. (eds.) PROFES 2019. LNCS, vol. 11915, pp. 473–488. Springer, Cham (2019). https://doi.org/10.1007/978-3-030-35333-9_33
14. Kehrer, S.; Blochinger, W. AUTOGENIC: Automated Generation of Self-configuring microservices. In: CLOSER, pp. 35–46 (2018)
15. OASIS TOSCA: http://docs.oasisopen.org/tosca/TOSCA/v1.0/cs01/TOSCA-v1.0-cs01.html. 20 July 2021
16. Zimmermann, O.: Microservices tenets. Comput. Sci. Res. Dev. **32**(3–4), 301–310 (2016). https://doi.org/10.1007/s00450-016-0337-0
17. Schermann, G., Cito, Jürgen., Leitner, P.: All the services large and micro: revisiting industrial practice in services computing. In: Norta, A., Gaaloul, W., Gangadharan, G.R., Dam, H.K. (eds.) ICSOC 2015. LNCS, vol. 9586, pp. 36–47. Springer, Heidelberg (2016). https://doi.org/10.1007/978-3-662-50539-7_4
18. Pasley, J.: How BPEL and SOA are changing web services development. IEEE Internet Comput. **9**(3), 60–67 (2005)
19. Steinberg, D. et al.: EMF: Eclipse Modelling Framework. Pearson Education (2008)
20. Apache CAMEL: https://camel.apache.org. Accessed 20 July 2021
21. Apache FELIX: https://felix.apache.org/. Accessed 20 July 2021
22. OLIVE Homepage: https://www.adoxx.org/live/olive. Accessed 20 July 2021
23. JMS: https://en.wikipedia.org/wiki/Jakarta_Messaging. Accessed 20 July 2021
24. EIP: https://www.enterpriseintegrationpatterns.com/. Accessed 20 July 2021

Enterprise Modeling Methods and Method Engineering

An Experience Report on the Implementation of the KYKLOS Modeling Method

Georgios Koutsopoulos$^{(\boxtimes)}$ ⓘ and Martin Henkel ⓘ

Department of Computer and Systems Sciences, Stockholm University, Stockholm, Sweden
{georgios,martinh}@dsv.su.se

Abstract. Several types of enterprise models and methods have been developed that may help an organization to describe and improve its business. A common practice is also the development of tool support to complement an enterprise modeling method's application. The development of tool support for a modeling method includes creating a representation of the modeling concepts, but also designing how the user should interact with the tool. This paper reports on the challenges and opportunities encountered during the process of implementing the KYKLOS modeling method in a modeling tool. The KYKLOS method, which is an enterprise modeling method, is specialized in supporting the design and analysis of changing capabilities. Using as input an initial meta-model of capability change, all the necessary tasks are performed to elicit a language model, which is required for the implementation of the method in a tool.

Keywords: Enterprise modeling · Meta-modeling · Implementation · Capability · Business transformation

1 Introduction

Enterprise Modeling (EM), which is a subset of conceptual modeling, is focused on capturing organizational knowledge and providing input and motivation for the design of Information Systems (IS) for an organization [1]. The complexity of developing IS and other business solutions is on the rise because of rapidly changing business requirements [2]. The development and operation of an IS can be considered as a knowledge-based activity which is continuous and utilizes conceptual modeling in order to bridge the understanding of complex organizational phenomena and the effort to design IS which can support dynamic change and agility [3]. This usually involves employing modeling methods which have been implemented in supporting modeling tools. Using modeling tools to handle a method successfully is considered state-of-the-art, because they do not only support defining modeling languages and facilitate the creation of model representations that can be processed, but also enable accessing, storing and exchanging models and specifying functionalities for improved user experience [4]. A specialization of EM is capability modeling, which uses capability as its focal point. Several capability modeling methods exist and the majority also includes capability modeling languages and

© IFIP International Federation for Information Processing 2021
Published by Springer Nature Switzerland AG 2021
E. Serral et al. (Eds.): PoEM 2021, LNBIP 432, pp. 103–118, 2021.
https://doi.org/10.1007/978-3-030-91279-6_8

notations. They usually employ different meta-models which consist of different sets of concepts to capture the nature of capabilities.

KYKLOS is one such method [5], designed specifically for designing and analyzing changing organizational capabilities. In order to capture the relevant characteristics, the phenomenon of capability change has been explored and conceptualized in the earlier steps of our study. Starting with identifying the relevant concepts already existing in the literature [6, 7], requirements were elicited [8] and the phenomenon of capability change was conceptualized in the form of an initial meta-model [9, 10].

To be readily useable for a modeler, the KYKLOS method was in need of tool support to aid the user in creating models of capability change. The implementation of the method required a modeling language meta-model, which used as input the initial meta-model. Therefore, during the implementation, several transformations were made to the initial meta-model. These transformations were done to make use of the tool platform, and to make the implemented language less complex. For example, several classes in the initial meta-model were implemented as attributes of other classes in the final tool implementation. Thus, the initial detailed conceptualization of the phenomenon of capability change and the conceptualization of the method bear significant differences, mainly because of different degrees of operationalization potentials existing among the meta-model's concepts.

The aim of this paper is to share the KYKLOS implementation experience with the Enterprise Modeling community by reporting the opportunities, challenges and lessons learned that have been encountered during the implementation of the method in a tool.

The rest of the paper is structured as follows. Section 2 briefly presents the related background. Section 3 provides an overview of the KYKLOS method's state before the implementation. Sections 4 reports on the implementation procedure and the included activities. Section 5 discusses the procedure and its results. Finally, Sect. 6 provides concluding remarks.

2   Background

The primary aim of conceptual modeling is the description of specific aspects of the physical and social world for understanding and communicating. An abstract representation of specific aspects of entities that exist within a specific domain is called a conceptualization, e.g. a meta-model, while an abstraction of the domain's state of affairs that is expressed via a conceptualization is called a model [11]. Since models are abstract entities, they must be represented using an artifact, for documentation, communication and analysis purposes, and this indicates the need for a highly expressive modeling language, the focus of which should be on representation adequacy [11].

Furthermore, to construct a model, guidance is needed in the form of a modeling method. As defined in [2], the components of a modeling method are a modeling technique, which consists of a modeling language and a modeling procedure, and mechanisms and algorithms working on the models that the language describes. A modeling procedure describes the required steps to apply the method to create the resulting model.

The modeling language consists of its syntax, semantics and notation. The *syntax* includes the description of rules and elements for the creation of models and is described by a grammar. The two major approaches for modeling language grammars are graph grammars and meta-models [2]. A common means to describe the meta-model of the syntax is by using UML class diagrams [12]. The *semantics* describe a modeling language's meaning, often using informal textual descriptions for semantic definition. The visualization of a modeling language is described by the *notation*. There are static approaches that define symbols for the visualization of the syntactical constructs, like pixel-based or vector graphics, yet these do not take into consideration the model's state. Dynamic approaches consider this state and usually split the notation in two parts; representation, which maps to the static approach, and control, which defines rules that influence the visualization according to the model's state [2].

An important factor for a successful modeling method and language is the provision of a set of modeling elements that can express the given domain abstraction, and this benefits from complementing efficient tool support [11]. Thus, there are specialized modeling tools that support the user in creating models that follow a certain syntax.

The domain specificity [13] of KYKLOS is organizational capability change. Since there is no consensus in the literature, the concept of capability is defined in this project as a set of resources and behaviors, with a configuration that bears the ability and capacity to enable the potential to create value by fulfilling a goal within a context [14]. Often considered as the missing link in business/IT transformation, it is associated to core business concepts like goal, resource, actor, process [15] and serves as the basis for change management, impact analysis and strategic planning [16]. A detailed review of the concept, and the variety of capability modeling approaches that exists in the literature has been explored and reported in an earlier step of this project [6].

3   Overview of KYKLOS Before the Implementation

KYKLOS, which has been introduced in [5], is a capability modeling method that focuses on capturing the concepts that are relevant to the phenomenon of capability change, aiming to support organizational change. This section describes the initial meta-model, and the modeling procedure, which consists of the required steps for applying the method.

Figure 1 shows the initial meta-model. Using the meta-model enables capturing changes in a given capability. The meta-model is based on a previously published framework [6], which includes the functions of change, in particular, observation, decision and delivery. Observation is captured using the concepts of context, which consists of monitored factors that are expressed as Key Performance Indicators (KPIs), and Intention elements. The model describes that a *capability* has at least one *configuration* that leads to the realization of the capability. *Resources* are allocated to a configuration which also consists of *behavior elements*. Realizing the capability produces at least one outcome, which can be measured to serve as criterion for a decision to change, along with the capability's assessment via contextual factors. Regarding delivery, it concerns the transition from a configuration to another. The meta-model also includes elements of ownership in order to capture the owners of the capability, the change and the resources. When more than one owners exist, their interaction and boundaries are captured. One last part that is included in the meta-model is the description of the states of the capability and change in the form of their traits which have been identified in [7].

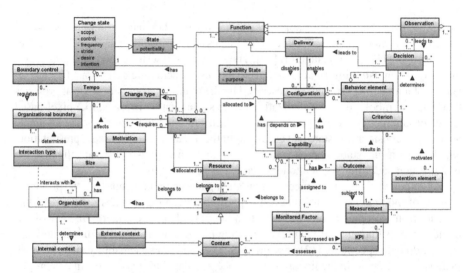

Fig. 1. The conceptualization of capability change, adapted from [10].

Concerning the modeling procedure, KYKLOS consists of four phases [5], namely (i) foundation, (ii) observation of context and intentions, (iii) decision alternatives, and (iv) delivery of change. Foundation is the initial phase and describes the base of the analysis, in terms of identifying the changing capability and its outcomes. The observation phase follows up and concerns capturing the need for change, in terms of context elements, with their associated monitored factors which are deemed relevant to the capability and are expressed as measurable KPIs. The organization's intentions are also captured in the form of goals, problems or any other element that motivates a change to the capability. The phase that follows is related to the analysis of alternative capability configurations that tackle the identified need to change. Different configurations can fulfill the same set of goals. A part of this phase is identifying the resources that need to be allocated to each alternative configuration and the behavior elements that are necessary for realizing the capability per configuration. Resources can be both material and immaterial. Capturing the ownership of the capability, the resources and change enables capturing potential organizational collaboration elements and the respective boundary controls. The final phase of the modeling procedure is the delivery of change. The focus of this phase is on understanding what is necessary to deliver the change. The change takes the form of a transition from one configuration to another. The delivery of change enables an inactive configuration while disabling an active one, or in the case of introducing a new capability or retiring an old one, there is a single enablement or disablement respectively. Describing how the change needs to be delivered includes capturing how the change is performed, in terms of identifying the attributes of change. These have been published in [7] and are (i) control, (ii) scope, (iii) frequency, (iv) stride, (v) time, (vi) tempo, (vii) desire, and (viii) intention. The process can be iterative, if, for example, the delivery has an impact on the context or outcome of the capability, the initial phases can initiate again.

4   The KYKLOS Implementation

The implementation of the KYKLOS method in a tool requires using the initial meta-model to develop a language meta-model, developing a graphical notation and facilitating the user's interaction with the tool. The implementation has taken place using the ADOxx meta-modeling platform [17], which is provided by the Open Models Laboratory (OMiLAB). The use of a platform also meant that the implementation needed to use the ADOxx platform's concepts for model implementation. The implementation was done iteratively and involved the following steps:

- Conversion of the initial meta-model concepts to a language meta-model that could be implemented. This step included the decision if a concept should be represented as a concept, attribute, or relationship in the language meta-model. Moreover, several concepts were removed.
- Creating a syntax for the concepts in the tool meta-model. This included creating the graphical representation using the ADOxx GraphRep language.
- Creating tool behavior to facilitate user interaction. ADOxx is quite flexible, so it was possible to add several dynamic aspects to the model.

4.1   Initial Meta-model to Language Meta-model Conversion

A color-coded version of the initial meta-model is depicted in Fig. 2. The colors depict how they have been handled during the transition to the language meta-model. A detailed description of the process follows in the current section.

Conversion of Classes

Transitioning from the initial meta-model to the language model provided the opportunity to reduce the number of included concepts. This contributes to reducing the complexity and clutter that has been identified to exist in the models derived from applying the initial meta-model [9]. The transition was done by converting initial classes to *attributes*, *association classes* or tool *functionalities*.

Conversion to Attribute.

- Owner: The Owner concept has been included in the initial meta-model to capture the ownership of capabilities, components and change. It has been modeled as a class as good modeling practice to avoid duplicate data. In the language model, it has been converted to an attribute with added functionality in the tool, which is better explained in Sect. 4.3. The introduced tool functionality makes it easier for the user to keep track of ownership, without the need to have it as a separate class.
- Tempo: This concept is a trait of change that has initially been modeled as a class because of its identified association to the Size class. Size is removed from the language meta-model (see below), and Tempo is converted to an attribute of Change.

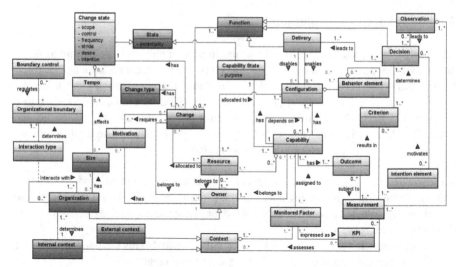

Fig. 2. A color-coded version of the meta-model, showing, remaining (orange) and removed (red) classes, along with classes converted to attributes (light blue), functionalities (grey) and association classes (purple). (Color figure online)

Conversion to Association Class.

– Change: The concept of Change has been essential in the conceptualization and has been associated to various concepts, the majority of which do not exist as classes in the language meta-model. It was initially decomposed in three functions, observation, decision and delivery, but, since these are removed from the language meta-model and are implemented as method phases and tool functions, Change gains a link to the transitioning Configurations. Additionally, there are specific attributes of Change that need to be captured, therefore, it has been converted to an association class that describes how a configuration transitions to another, also gaining the Change State attributes.

Conversion to Tool Functionalities.

– Capability state: The concept of capability state is meant to capture whether a capability is active or not. This is captured in the tool by associating the capability to an active configuration. Therefore, the class can be omitted from the language model since the functionality of the tool will keep track of the active configuration.
– Change state: The class Change state existed to capture if a change is active or not. The tool version of KYKLOS can depict this via the existence of an active configuration element that is the target of change. The temporal attributes of Change can also assist. So, it can be omitted as well. Its attributes have moved to class Change.
– Observation: It is one of the three functions of capability change that has been modeled as a class in the initial conceptualization. Naturally, including a class that captures an activity bears value in a conceptualization but has limited utility in an implemented

method and tool. As mentioned earlier, the KYKLOS method uses observation as its phase where the context factors and intentions whose fulfillment status motivates a potential change in the capability. All the necessary elements to perform this phase exist in the language meta-model, therefore, Observation can be omitted as a class.

- Decision: In a similar way to observation, the decision phase has been associated to a set of concepts that have been removed from the language meta-model, like criterion and configuration (as decision alternative), and replaced with tool mechanisms. The details on the specific related concepts follow.
- Delivery: The Delivery class captures the transition between capability configurations by enabling one and disabling another. In the method and tool implementation only one configuration is active at any time. This functionality captures the transition without a need to have the specific Delivery class.
- Criterion: This class refers to capturing how a decision is made, in terms of changing or not, and what to decide when changing. The tool design allows both these aspects to be addressed without including a specific Criterion class. Changing or not is motivated by the dynamic association elements between capability and contextual and intentional elements. In practice, a KPI or intention that is not fulfilled, is a criterion to change. What to decide refers to selecting a configuration among potentials. The tool allows a configuration to be active only when its required components are properly allocated. In this way, the decision is supported dynamically without needing the Criterion class, so, it is omitted.
- Measurement: In the initial meta-model, this class captured the act of comparing the target context and intention elements to reality. The functionalities described in the previous paragraphs also explain why this class has been omitted.
- Motivation: Same as Criterion, even though it can be included as an attribute to improve the descriptive ability of the tool. Moreover, in the implemented tool the motivation for performing a change can be implicitly shown by referring to one or several intention elements.
- Interaction type: This class captured the way two owning organizations interact with each other. The class requires a detailed understanding of the capability business ecosystem [18], which is not the primary goal of this project. The class has been converted to a high level tool functionality. The owners of the capability and the configuration components are captured in a control element of the notation that colors the borders of the components according to same or different ownership.
- Organizational boundary: Using the functionality that was introduced for different owners' interaction, the tool calculates the amount of externally owned required components and their owners and provides a decision-supporting suggestion to the user to take into consideration the reported results. In this way, the class is omitted from the language meta-model.
- Boundary control: Same as Organizational boundary.

Removal of Existing Classes.

- Size: It has been completely removed from the language meta-model. It refers to the size of an organization and has been introduced in [10], as a factor affecting the tempo of change. Even if an association between Size and Tempo has been strongly indicated, there was no clear and operational formula identified to provide utility in the tool. Thus, capturing the size of an organization without a clear effect on the tempo of change would have questionable value, therefore, Size was removed.

– Organization: As a specialization of Owner, the Organization class does not need to exist as a class since the parent class has been converted to an attribute.
– State: State existed in the phenomenon's conceptualization as a superclass of Capability state and Change state. There is no value in the existence of the superclass without its specializations, thus it is removed.
– Function: This class is the generalization of the three functions. Converting the specializations allows the removal of the superclass as well.
– Change type: This class captures if the change is an introduction of a new capability or the modification or retirement of an existing one. The model that is produced by the tool can capture this information by checking the activity states of configurations. If an active configuration has no prior alternative, it is an introduction, if it has transitioned from an alternative it is a modification and if it is deactivated without transitioning to an active configuration, it is retired.
– External context: The external context is a specialization of the Context class. The implementation can have a Context element described in terms of externality without a need for the specific subclass.
– Internal context: Same as External context.

Remaining Classes

The remaining concepts of the conceptualization are the core elements and focal points not only of the KYKLOS method but also of the tool. They cannot be absent the language meta-model and they also retain their class status. The concepts included in define the fragment of the conceptualization that comprises the language meta-model are:

- Capability
- Configuration
- Outcome
- Resource
- Intention element
- Context
- Monitored factor
- Behavior element
- KPI

Introduction of New Classes

The implementation provided the opportunity to introduce new classes to the language meta-model, as a means to improve the utility of the method via the tool. Three types of additions were performed to the KYKLOS meta-model in this step, in particular:

– Specializations of elements

  • The Behavior element, which is a meta-element, got a specialization class, in particular:

    ○ Process

The Process concept has been previously identified as the most common and popular concept [6] in the literature, regarding the behavioral aspect of capabilities. Other concepts like Activity, which are also popular, did not get included because a process consists of tasks and activities, and capturing the lower levels of a capability's behavior is beyond the scope of KYKLOS. In this way, Behavior element was implemented as an abstract class, which means that it is not usable in the tool. Only the specializations are visible and usable by the users.

- The Intention element, which is another of the meta-elements of the meta-model, has been complemented with three specialization classes, to improve the tool's descriptive capability. The specializations are:

  ○ Goal   ○ Problem   ○ Requirement

In addition, the specializations allow to capture the "purpose" attribute of the previously existing Capability State element, via their direct association to a capability. The Capability State captured what is the purpose of a capability, in terms of achieving a goal, avoiding a problem, or meeting a requirement, and if it actually succeeded in the fulfillment of the Intention element.

– Generalization of elements

  - Component was introduced; Process, as a Behavior element, and Resource, are both components of the Configuration class. This fact allowed the introduction of the Component abstract class, which is not visible and usable in the tool, but is the parent of both Component types and also gains their common Owner attribute.

– Utility addition

  - Resource pool, is a class that has no direct association to the phenomenon of capability change, however, its utility lies in the fact that the configuration components have been designed in a way that does not allow them to exist independently of a container. For this reason, the Resource pool element acts as a repository for the entire set of organizational resources that have not been allocated to a capability's configuration and improve partitioning potentials of a model.

Final Implemented Language Meta-model
The outcome of applying these changes to the initial meta-model is depicted in Fig. 3, while the complete set of language concepts and their definitions are shown in Table 1.

Table 1. The complete set of language concepts and their definitions, from [5].

Concept	Description
Capability	A set of resources and behaviors, whose configuration bears the ability and capacity to enable the potential to create value by fulfilling a goal within a context
Configuration	The set of resources that comprise the capability along with the behavior elements that deliver it. A capability may have several different configurations but only one may be active at any given moment in time
Resource	Any human, infrastructure, knowledge, equipment, financial or reputation asset that can be used by an organization to enable the capability's realization. It can be allocated to one or more capability configurations, based on its capacity
Resource pool	The complete set of an organization's available resources
Context	All the factors that form the setting in which a capability exists, are relevant to its performance and within which the capability is perceived
Outcome	The result of the capability's realization. Comparing it to KPIs and Intention elements can provide insight on whether a capability change is necessary or not
KPI	A preset measurable value that expresses an important aspect of the context that a capability depends on to reach the desired outcome. Used to assess the efficiency of the capability's realization when compared with outcome values
Monitored Factor	A context factor that has been identified and associated to a capability's performance and is being observed in relation to the capability. It is usually expressed as a KPI
Intention Element	An abstract element that includes all the concepts that refer to the intentions governing the capability, for example, goals, problems or requirements
Goal	A desirable state that an organization aims to achieve. It is a type of Intention element
Problem	An undesirable condition that an organization aims to avoid or tackle. It is a type of Intention element
Requirement	A necessary state that an organization has to fulfill. It is a type of Intention element
Behavior Element	An abstract element that describes a structured set of activities whose execution delivers the value of the capability, for example, a process, service, activity or task
Process	A behavior element that consists of activities aiming to fulfill a certain goal
Change	Change represents the transition from one configuration to another. It can be described using several change properties. A capability change is finalized when a configuration's activity state is modified

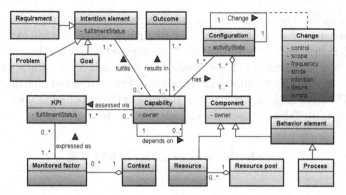

Fig. 3. The language meta-model, with the remaining (orange), converted (purple) and new (light green) classes. (Color figure online)

4.2 Graphical Notation

As mentioned earlier, an essential part of a modeling language is its notation. While the initial meta-model has been created using UML, for KYKLOS we introduced a new notation that combines both symbols and shapes. Symbols and shapes comprise the primary and secondary notation respectively. For the primary notation every concept of the language meta-model has been assigned a unique symbol, as shown in Table 2.

Table 2. The primary notation of KYKLOS.

Capability	Configuration	Resource	Outcome	KPI
Goal	Problem	Requirement	Process	Change
Monitored Factor	Intention element	Resource pool	Context	Behavior element
		Container	Container	N/A

Effort has been put to ensure the notation's short learning curve. This is achieved by a symbol set consisting of items that are consistent in terms of size, visual appearance and maximized simplicity, while in parallel preserving a clear distinction among them. The symbol color is black, to facilitate users with color deficiencies [19]. The secondary notation includes colored shapes but relying on color alone to distinguish image content is ineffective. The black symbols ensure that potential problems regarding compatibility with monochrome displays are avoided. Using color is not only for coding information but also for aiding visual search as the items become easily discriminable [19]. The secondary notation consists of standard shapes, i.e. polygons, ellipses and rectangles, and a set of colors that remain discriminable if superimposed on one another or juxtaposed [19], to improve memorability. The secondary notation includes the primary one and is complemented with text. Minimum elements have been used in both notations to avoid cluttered KYKLOS models, which has been a problem in earlier applications using the UML notation [9]. Table 3 depicts the secondary notation.

Table 3. The secondary notation of KYKLOS.

Capability	Configuration	Resource	Outcome	KPI
Capability New configuration	Configuration 1 Inactive	Human Resource	Outcome	KPI
Goal	*Problem*	*Requirement*	*Process*	*Change*
Goal	Problem	Requirement	Process	Change details
Monitored Factor	*Intention element*	*Resource pool*	*Context*	*Behavior element*
Monitored factor Type: Undetermined	Intention element	Resource pool Check component ownership	Context	N/A

4.3 User Interaction

The last part of the implementation consists of technical additions provided using the ADOxx platform. These additions are implemented using the AdoScript language and provide automation that facilitates modeling in the tool and improves empirical quality of the model in terms of graph aesthetics [20]. Figure 4 depicts these functionalities in an example KYKLOS model.

New configuration. Creating a new configuration is facilitated by a button existing on Capability objects. The tool creates and automatically connects a new Configuration, taking into consideration the spatial alignment of the object for increased visual quality.

Containment: This functionality uses the core ADOxx relationship "Is Inside". Having a model element graphically put inside another allows them to be related in an invisible way (no connecting lines required), which improves the model in terms of complexity by reducing crossing lines.

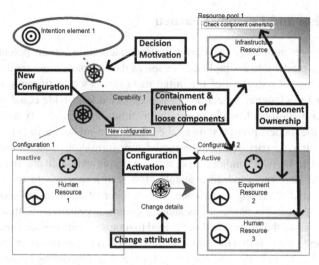

Fig. 4. User interaction facilities in the KYKLOS tool.

Configuration activation. Whether a configuration is active depends on whether the required components are allocated to it. In the tool, the required components are listed in a "Notebook" area. The tool checks on this list and calculates whether the components that are contained in a configuration match the list or not and activate or deactivate the configuration accordingly.

Component ownership. The ownership attribute captures if a component is owned by the same organization as the capability (internally) or not (externally). A button existing on Resource pool objects automatically calculates the ownership type and, changes the visualization of the component's right side border to blue (internal ownership) or red (external ownership) for improved comprehensibility. Similarly, it calculates and reports the externally owned components for consideration of organizational boundaries.

Prevention of loose components. Resources are components, so, they are not supposed to exist outside a container. For this reason, the tool does not allow the creation or movement of components if they are not contained.

Change attributes. An association exists between configurations that includes visually the attributes of change. This association class change includes a button that shows or hides the attributes of change in order to avoid clutter and complexity in larger models.

Decision motivation. KPIs and all Intention elements are connected to Capability with a special association called Status that is a control graphic element. Dependent on whether the object's content is fulfilled or not by the given capability, the visualization changes to facilitate identifying a reason for change, e.g. an unfulfilled goal.

Relationship grouping. Towards avoiding a large number of different association types, as in the language meta-model, all the associations except Status and Transition/Change are using the same visualization. However, strict rules have been coded to prevent using wrong association types in a produced model. This mitigates the risk of mistakes.

5   Discussion and Lessons Learned

The greatest opportunity addressed during the implementation was the potential to refine the initial meta-model into a simplified version in the language meta-model. This does not imply the loss or reduction of the initial meta-model's effectiveness. On the contrary, the KYKLOS language meta-model was expected to provide equal effectiveness with the initial meta-model, while in parallel avoiding the complexity and clutter that characterized the models produced using the initial meta-model, as in [9].

The most striking part of the meta-model transformation is the *reduction of the classes*, from 30 to 16, which indicates a significant simplification. In practice, a modeling tool that would have provided 30 available classes to a user would require a longer learning curve and modeling experience. The number of relationships has also been significantly reduced. Six associations share a common visualization that depicts the relationship status of the objects without a need to require additional learning steps from the user. Our lesson here is that the initial meta-model was created to cover "all" concepts of capability change and thus was not suited for creating a modeling language.

All the implementation activities bear their own advantages and disadvantages, often achieving a *balance between simplicity/utility and descriptive power*. Every intervention has been driven by advantages preponderating disadvantages. Introducing new classes increases the language meta-model's degree of complexity. However, all the introduced classes have provided either improved user experience, as for example, with the Resource pool class, or specified the more abstract concepts of the initial meta-model, as for example the Process and Goal classes specifying Behavior element and Intention element respectively. Similarly, it has been ensured that the removed classes have a minimal cost on the tool's descriptive power, for example, removing the Function class heavily simplified the model, and if desired, Functions can be described by other means such as creating separate models for each function. In both cases, we conclude that preponderance of simplicity or descriptive power has been the driver.

During the implementation it became clear that *the tool is more than the language meta-model*. The tool allows for more than just adding static concepts to a model, since it is possible to add functionalities too. For example, even if converting the Owner class to an attribute of two separate classes is considered a bad modeling practice in UML, adding the component ownership functionality enables the tool to compare attributes of different classes to see if they are "owned" by the same organization. Converting classes to functionalities like this does not reduce descriptive potential, but it improves the user's interactivity combined with reduced complexity, making the change worthwhile.

The greatest challenge has been to *retain an operational and semantic consistency* between the initial and the language meta-model. The tool also needed to be operationally aligned with the modeling procedure, that is, to provide an adequate set of primitives for capturing the required elements for documenting, analyzing and communicating the phenomenon of capability change during the different KYKLOS method phases. This has been theoretically addressed, yet, a practical evaluation of the implementation by the actual users is required. KYKLOS is meant to be used both by technical and business people, therefore, the implementation needs to be evaluated both by users with modeling experience and those without any, a step which is already planned as a future step of the project.

Implementing the method with a variety of functionalities can *facilitate the user following a modeling process*. The dynamic automated aspects of the KYKLOS tool make steps towards an evolved version of modeling software that can guide the user's actions, as for example with the automatic capability configuration design, and mitigate the risk of syntactic mistakes, as for example with the restrictions applied on the association selection in the KYKLOS tool. These functionalities have been possible because of the ADOxx environment whose core platform enables different levels of automation.

Regarding ADOxx as the selected platform for the implementation of the KYKLOS method, its advantages as a specialized meta-modeling platform can be summarized in the pre-existing functions and meta-modeling structure that saves a significant amount of time and effort for the developer. In theory, taking into consideration that the tool's requirements are not platform-dependent, platforms like Eclipse are equivalent, however, in practice, ADOxx's existing functions are valuable, especially when it concerns cases where a concept needs to be converted to a tool functionality and dynamic behavior is required, as encountered in the KYKLOS implementation.

We aspire that the reported remarks can also benefit any implementation initiative that encounters similar opportunities and challenges, especially when the addressed phenomenon is as complex and dynamic as capability change.

6   Conclusions

In this paper, the implementation of the KYKLOS modeling method, specifically designed for the phenomenon of capability change, has been reported along with the lessons learned from the procedure. The initial meta-model has been adjusted and simplified to improve the resulting tool models in terms of complexity and clutter. Converting the initial meta-model's classes to attributes, association classes and ADOxx functionalities, along with the removal and introduction of classes led to the language meta-model, which has been complemented with a graphical notation and additional UI functions that aim to facilitate the user's overall experience of the KYKLOS method, in terms of applicability, learning curve and operational alignment with the tool.

References

1. Persson, A., Stirna, J.: An explorative study into the influence of business goals on the practical use of enterprise modelling methods and tools. In: Harindranath, G., et al., (eds.) New Perspectives on Information Systems Development, pp. 275–287. Springer, Boston (2002). https://doi.org/10.1007/978-1-4615-0595-2_22
2. Karagiannis, D., Kühn, H.: Metamodelling Platforms. In: Bauknecht, K., Tjoa, A.M., Quirchmayr, G. (eds.) EC-Web 2002. LNCS, vol. 2455, pp. 182–182. Springer, Heidelberg (2002). https://doi.org/10.1007/3-540-45705-4_19
3. Fayoumi, A., Loucopoulos, P.: Conceptual modeling for the design of intelligent and emergent information systems. Expert Syst. Appl. **59**, 174–194 (2016)
4. Fill, H.-G., Karagiannis, D.: On the conceptualisation of modelling methods using the ADOxx meta modelling platform. EMISA **8**, 4–25 (2013)

5. Koutsopoulos, G., Henkel, M., Stirna, J.: Modeling the phenomenon of capability change: the KYKLOS Method. In: Karagiannis, D., Mayr, H.C., Mylopolos, J. (eds) Domain-Specific Conceptual Modeling: Concepts, Methods and Tools, vol. 2. Springer International Publishing, Cham (2021). https://doi.org/10.1007/978-3-319-39417-6

6. Koutsopoulos, G., Henkel, M., Stirna, J.: An analysis of capability meta-models for expressing dynamic business transformation. Softw. Syst. Model. **20**(1), 147–174 (2020). https://doi.org/10.1007/s10270-020-00843-0

7. Koutsopoulos, G., Henkel, M., Stirna, J.: Modeling the dichotomies of organizational change: a state-based capability typology. In: Feltus, C., Johannesson, P., Proper, H.A. (eds.) Proceedings of the PoEM 2019 Forum, pp. 26–39. Luxembourg (2020). CEUR-WS.org

8. Koutsopoulos, G., Henkel, M., Stirna, J.: Requirements for observing, deciding, and delivering capability change. In: Gordijn, J., Guédria, W., Proper, H.A. (eds.) PoEM 2019. LNBIP, vol. 369, pp. 20–35. Springer, Cham (2019). https://doi.org/10.1007/978-3-030-35151-9_2

9. Koutsopoulos, G., Henkel, M., Stirna, J.: Conceptualizing capability change. In: Nurcan, S., Reinhartz-Berger, I., Soffer, P., Zdravkovic, J. (eds.) BPMDS/EMMSAD -2020. LNBIP, vol. 387, pp. 269–283. Springer, Cham (2020). https://doi.org/10.1007/978-3-030-49418-6_18

10. Koutsopoulos, G., Henkel, M., Stirna, J.: Improvements on capability modeling by implementing expert knowledge about organizational change. In: Grabis, J., Bork, D. (eds.) PoEM 2020. LNBIP, vol. 400, pp. 171–185. Springer, Cham (2020). https://doi.org/10.1007/978-3-030-63479-7_12

11. Guizzardi, G.: Ontological foundations for structural conceptual models (2005)

12. Object Management Group (OMG): OMG® Unified Modeling Language® (2017). https://www.omg.org/spec/UML/2.5.1/PDF

13. Karagiannis, D., Mayr, H.C., Mylopoulos, J. (eds.): Domain-Specific Conceptual Modeling: Concepts, Methods and Tools. Springer, Cham (2016). https://doi.org/10.1007/978-3-319-39417-6

14. Koutsopoulos, G.: Managing capability change in organizations: foundations for a modeling approach (2020). http://urn.kb.se/resolve?urn=urn:nbn:se:su:diva-185231

15. Sandkuhl, K., Stirna, J. (eds.): Capability Management in Digital Enterprises. Springer, Heidelberg (2018). https://doi.org/10.1007/978-3-319-90424-5

16. Ulrich, W., Rosen, M.: The business capability map: the "Rosetta stone" of business/IT alignment. Cutter Consortium, Enterprise Architecture, p. 14, (2011)

17. OMiLAB: The ADOxx Metamodelling Platform. https://www.adoxx.org/live/home

18. Tsai, C.H., Zdravkovic, J., Stirna, J.: Capability management of digital business ecosystems – a case of resilience modeling in the healthcare domain. In: Herbaut, N., La Rosa, M. (eds.) CAiSE 2020. LNBIP, vol. 386, pp. 126–137. Springer, Cham (2020). https://doi.org/10.1007/978-3-030-58135-0_11

19. Post, D.L.: Color and Human-Computer Interaction. In: Handbook of Human-Computer Interaction, pp. 573–615. Elsevier (1997)

20. Krogstie, J.: Quality of conceptual models in model driven software engineering. In: Cabot, J., Gómez, C., Pastor, O., Sancho, M.R., Teniente, E. (eds.) Conceptual Modeling Perspectives, pp. 185–198. Springer International Publishing, Cham (2017)

Validation and Verification in Domain-Specific Modeling Method Engineering

Qin Ma[1]($\boxtimes$), Monika Kaczmarek-Heß[2], and Sybren de Kinderen[2]

[1] University of Luxembourg, 2 Avenue de l'Université,
4365 Esch-sur-Alzette, Luxembourg
qin.ma@uni.lu
[2] University of Duisburg-Essen, Universitätstrasse 9, 45141 Essen, Germany
{monika.kaczmarek-hess,sybren.dekinderen}@uni-due.de

Abstract. Enterprise models have the potential to constitute a valuable asset for organizations, e.g., in terms of enabling a variety of analyses. A prerequisite for realizing this potential is that an enterprise model is syntactically, semantically and pragmatically valid. To ensure these three types of validity, verification and validation (V&V) mechanisms are required to be in place while designing the enterprise modeling method, e.g., to validate identified requirements, to check created enterprise models against syntactic rules, or to ensure intra- and inter-model consistency. Therefore, the objective of this paper is to systematically embed verification and validation (V&V) techniques into the design of (enterprise) domain-specific modeling methods (DSMMs). To this end, we integrate steps and considerations of well-established DSMM engineering processes, and enrich them with V&V techniques based upon our earlier experiences and a literature analysis.

Keywords: DSMM design · Validation and verification · Design method

1 Introduction

Enterprise models have the potential to be of considerable value to organizations. In addition to facilitating communication, capturing and transferring knowledge, enterprise models also have the potential to enable a variety of analyses [1,45], which in turn may contribute to various organizational activities, such as enterprise transformation, IT-business alignment or business process management.

However, in order for an enterprise model to be valuable and worth the modeling effort, a pre-requisite is to ensure that the enterprise model is valid in the first place. Following [38,40,42], we consider validation and verification (V&V) of an enterprise model, and of an enterprise modeling method, from syntactic, semantic, and pragmatic perspectives. Firstly, an enterprise model must

© IFIP International Federation for Information Processing 2021
Published by Springer Nature Switzerland AG 2021
E. Serral et al. (Eds.): PoEM 2021, LNBIP 432, pp. 119–133, 2021.
https://doi.org/10.1007/978-3-030-91279-6_9

be syntactically valid, namely, it should adhere to all the syntactic rules specified for the modeling language in which the model is expressed. Briefly, for modeling languages, such syntactic rules include typing constraints, cardinality constraints, and additional well-formedness constraints. Secondly, the enterprise model should also be semantically valid, i.e., it should make sense in the context where the model is supposed to be used. Some example requirements for an enterprise model to be semantically valid include the model containing the necessary information [1,31], or statements from different parts of the enterprise model, which each capture a different perspective on the enterprise, being consistent [30, p. 32]. Thirdly, the enterprise model needs also to be pragmatically valid, i.e., as an enterprise model is considered to serve some purpose, therefore it should serve this purpose accordingly. For example, if the model is built for visualizing a business process, the choice of appropriate symbols and notations, in terms of a fit with the audience, plays a crucial role in a pragmatic validity check. In contrast, if the model is built for being input to a program to perform some analysis, it should at least be interpretable by the program, hence an exporting mechanism would be expected.

Although the perceived target of validation and verification are enterprise models, the validation and verification consideration should take place even before the existence of enterprise models, cf. [4,39,42]. Indeed, to ensure the three types of validity of enterprise models mentioned above, validation and verification techniques are required to be in place while designing the enterprise modeling method, e.g., to validate identified requirements, to check created enterprise models against syntactic rules, to ensure intra- and inter-model consistency, and to evaluate the effectiveness of the modeling method to solve its targeted purposes. Some V&V techniques are informal and rely mostly on human intervention. Others, in turn, are formalized and automated, which requires equipping associated meta modeling platforms with corresponding capabilities. For example, meta modeling platforms should allow for specification of syntactic rules (especially well-formedness constraints) of modeling languages, or provide reusable procedures and algorithms for the implementation of checking mechanisms in modeling methods.

As a response to the above, the objective of this paper is to systematically embed validation and verification techniques into typical activities of the lifecycle of domain-specific modeling methods (DSMMs). Particularly, we take two well-established DSMM development processes [18,32,33] as a point of departure, and extend them by explicitly including validation and verification techniques based on our earlier experiences, reported among others in [9,25,37], as well as experiences reported in the literature. Thereby, we add systemacy to enterprise modeling application scenarios wherein formalization plays a notable role, be it through formal analysis, simulation, or by means of model checking capabilities.

This paper is structured as follows. First the concept of validation and verification as applied to conceptual modeling is explained, and existing approaches to engineer domain-specific modeling methods are shortly introduced. Then, we present the merge of existing approaches with validation and verification being a first-class citizen, and discuss V&V mechanisms and capabilities in each stage of the process. The paper concludes with final remarks and an outlook on future work.

2   Background

2.1   Validation, Verification and Quality Assessment

Verification and validation are well-established techniques for ensuring the quality of a product within the overall software development life-cycle, and as such, are also important in the field of conceptual modeling, cf. [42]. There is no one commonly accepted definition of quality of a conceptual model, neither of the way how it may be exactly checked. Nevertheless, [42] already pointed to the need to account for syntactic quality (adhering to modeling language syntax), semantic quality (correct elements and relations of the domain), and pragmatic quality (the interpretation of the audience of the model) of conceptual models created, and thus, also on the need to be able to verify and validate those qualities. Others have extended this quality model by adding other quality goals [38], leading to the definition of the SEQUAL framework, cf. [40], being one currently well-established quality framework for conceptual modeling.

To assess model quality verification and validation techniques can play a useful role. An often used definition of verification and validation states that verification is "the process of determining that a model implementation and its associated data accurately represent the developer's conceptual description and specifications" and that validation is "the process of determining the degree to which a model and its associated data provide an accurate representation of the real world from the perspective of the model's intended use" [10, p. 2]. In the context of enterprise modeling, the goal of verification is usually defined as proving that enterprise models are correctly built [7,8], cf. syntactic quality. Such a verification is usually perceived to be an objective process conducted in a formal manner. Indeed, when it comes to syntactic and well-formedness analysis, there is a wide range of formal methods available, based on various mathematical foundations, such as first order logic, set theory, algebra, and process calculi [29]. In turn, validation usually aims at checking that the obtained result (an enterprise model) is an accurate representation of the domain under study, i.e., to check whether "it corresponds exactly to the expected needs by taking into account (and then limited to) the actor's viewpoint" [7]. Here informal, subjective validation strategies are usually followed such as interviews with domain stakeholders, interactive workshops, and scenario-based evaluation.

2.2   Approaches to Design Domain-Specific (Enterprise) Modeling Methods

According to [19, p. 40] a (domain-specific) modeling method "consists of at least one [domain-specific] modelling language [(DSML)] and at least one corresponding [domain-specific] process model which guides the construction and analysis of models." The process of engineering a modeling method is usually supported by different language workbenches and meta modeling platforms [5,15,28,44]. In the enterprise modeling community especially Eclipse EMF [50], ADOxx [16] and MetaEdit+ [51] gained popularity.

Different approaches have been proposed aiming at guiding the engineering of a modeling method. Based on our study, the two most commonly used in the enterprise modeling community seem to be: the Agile Modeling Method Engineering (AMME) approach, proposed by [32,33] and further extended, e.g., by [13,14], and the approach of Frank [18,20]. When it comes to the Frank's approach, the proposed method is meta modeling language and meta modeling platform independent, and encompasses seven main steps (including feedback-loops): (1) clarification of scope and purpose, (2) analysis of generic requirements, (3) analysis of specific requirements, (4) language specification, (5) design of graphical notation, (6) development of modeling tool, and (7) evaluation and refinement. In addition, for each step a corresponding micro-process and information on participants, input, risks and results are also provided. In turn, the AMME approach, often used together with the meta modeling environment ADOxx [16], as presented in [14] and based, among others, on [16,35], encompasses the following phases (also including feedback loops): (1) create, i.e., investigation of the system under study, scenarios and requirements, (2) design, i.e., specification of a modeling language and mechanisms/algorithms, (3) formalize, i.e., formalization of the specification of the modeling language for the needs of its implementation, (4) develop, i.e., implementation of the modeling method in a meta modeling environment, and (5) deploy, i.e., creation of a stand-alone application and its distribution.

Although both approaches focus on the full spectrum of a modeling method design, they seem to have different foci. While the AMME approach and its further extensions emphasize the need to be agile, as well as the formalize phase being supported by the proposed meta modeling environment, the distinguished phases have been defined predominantly on a high level, and some of the phases are only detailed in later publications (e.g., the create phase [34]). When it comes to the V&V mechanisms, evaluating acceptance and various quality criteria are explicitly mentioned in the deploy phase, as well as within produce-use cycles, cf. [33], however without providing additional details. Yet, additional mechanisms may be found in other works. For instance [14] focused on the create and design phases of AMME and proposed a modeling method called "Modeling Method Design Environment" (MMDE). The mechanisms and algorithms of MMDE include transformation of models in RDF format with the motivation, among others, to enable validation of meta models using semantic web technologies. In addition, in [34] a modeling method called CoChaCo (Concept-Characteristic-Connector) has been proposed, that among others ensures better traceability of the requirements and their validation in the create process.

Compared to AMME, Frank's approach is more detailed. Although Frank's method places less emphasis on formalization and the role of tooling, it offers an extensive set of guidelines and hints regarding the language design. Moreover, for

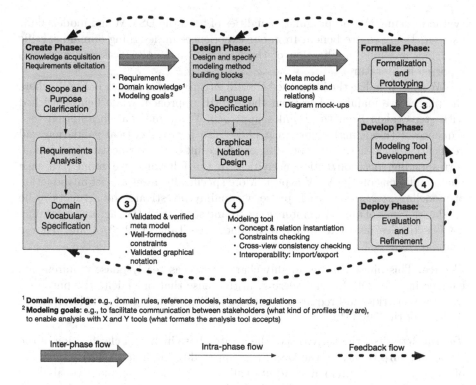

Fig. 1. A DSMM design approach with a focus on V&V techniques across the design life-cycle

all phases additional aspects are discussed like required inputs, involved stake-holders, and risks. The need for evaluation of developed artifacts is explicitly accounted for within micro-steps. Nevertheless, specific evaluation methods are only selectively described. For instance, Frank's method includes, on the one hand, activities such as creation of collection of test cases, checking the DSML against requirements, and an analysis of current practice or effects of the DSML's use. However, on the other hand, using formal methods to verify the correctness of a model, being of interest in this paper, are not considered in further detail.

3 Validation and Verification in Enterprise Modeling Method Life-Cycle

The different DSMM engineering approaches discussed in the previous section, do not consider validation and verification as first-class citizens in the engineer-ing process. Yet, as also argued by [4,39,42], a suitable modeling method is a prerequisite to ensuring V&V of enterprise models. Therefore, in the following we first integrate two well-established and still complementary approaches to DSMM engineering, namely the AMME approach and Frank's approach. There-after, we systematically embed validation and verification techniques to address syntactic, semantic and pragmatic qualities of both the DSMM and models built using it. Doing so, we benefit from our experiences in designing domain specific modeling methods, application of those, as well as experiences and examples reported in literature.

We conceptualize the integrated DSMM engineering approach in Fig. 1, where the phases are mainly taken from the AMME approach, while being enriched with steps taken from the Frank's approach. We argue that in addition to a sequence of (modeling) steps, each phase also involves critical validation and verification activities, and depending on the result of the verification/validation, corresponding decision/action activities. In the following, we zoom into each phase and focus on the V&V aspect. More specifically, after a brief introduction of modeling activities in each phase, we mainly investigate the artifacts to be validated, types of quality of interest, goals and scopes of V&V, actors performing V&V activities, and exemplary techniques (see Tables 1, 2, 3, 4 and 5 for a summary).

Create. This phase can be roughly characterized as "early-phase requirements engineering" for DSMM engineering, in the sense that one elicits the purposes, analysis scenarios, and requirements to be fulfilled, which guide the later design decision of the DSMM.

Typical Activities: the activities of the create phase include a clarification of the scope and purpose, which the DSMM is supposed to fulfill, as well as an analysis of the (specific) requirements. Additionally, one inventories domain vocabulary, in terms of a reconstruction of the professional terminology.

V&V Support: in the create phase, validation takes center stage. On the one hand, we need to ensure that the modeling method being engineered corresponds to the exact needs of actors. On the other hand, we also need to demonstrate that concepts in the modeling language constitute a reasonable representation of the domain at hand. Note that in this phase, validation mechanisms are mainly of an informal character, pertaining mostly to requirements elicitation techniques with stakeholder involvement.

To ensure a fit to *the needs* for the modeling method, there exist a variety of requirements engineering techniques, ranging from goal-oriented requirements engineering to scenario analysis [46]. Some of them have been employed in the context of DSML design. For example, [9] employed goal-oriented requirements engineering to ensure a fit between a DSML's expressiveness and the actor goals the DSML is supposed to achieve, while [49, pp. 36–37] and [20, pp. 11–12] proposed the use of domain scenarios and stating analysis questions in analyzing specific requirements for the DS(M)L at hand. Moreover, for DSMLs specifically, [20, pp. 11–12] also recommended the creation of mock-up diagrams to, already in an early phase, gain a further feedback on the language to be designed, based upon potential, drafty diagrams created with it. In this context, CoChaCo (Concept-Characteristic-Connector) and CoChaCo4ADOxx mentioned earlier may also be used to support requirements gathering, domain knowledge acquisition, concept identification and decomposition, concept selection and mapping, and for the definition of modeling method building blocks [34].

Table 1. V&V in the create phase

Artifact	Quality	Goals and scope	Actor	V& VApproach
Goals and main assumptions, application and use scenarios, mock-up diagrams, requirements, glossary of domain concepts	Semantic and pragmatic	Validation of the content of the artifacts developed and the extent to which their correspondent with the domain, expectation of clients and users etc.; Goal: Refining the created artifacts in-line with the feedback obtained	Domain experts, users, clients, business analysts	Workshops and interviews with the corresponding actors, interactive sessions, using techniques such as scenario analysis, repertory grid, and semantic differential. Validation against documents available or available domain description

To ensure that the concepts used in the DSMM constitute a *reasonable representation of the domain*, it is important to ensure validation of the domain vocabulary of the DSML. This validation includes a confrontation of the developed domain vocabulary against documents typical to the domain at hand, or generally speaking corpora of domain concepts [20, 41]. Moreover, it is also vital to receive a feedback on used domain concepts from the prospective end users themselves. Especially interesting in this regard, is to gain an insight into the "personal semantics" [41] of prospective end users, i.e., the semantics end users associate with a concept based upon their experiences with past instances of that concept [26]. Such personal semantics of end users can deviate from those specified in the domain vocabulary, and a lack of awareness of this may lead to considerable issues in the use of a DSML [41]. To gain an impression of such personal concept interpretations, [41] suggested the use of repertory grids and semantic differential studies to elicit the characteristics end users associated with concepts.

Design. In this phase, one specifies core constituents of the DSMM's language specification, in terms of its abstract syntax and corresponding semantics. Also, one specifies the visual notation.

Typical Activities: design a language specification (in terms of the abstract syntax and its associated semantics), design a draft visual notation.

V&V Support: like in the create phase, the design phase emphasizes validation, and it is likewise done mostly in an informal manner. In the design phase, validation concerns the shaping of the language specification, especially in terms of deciding what concepts and relations will be part of it. Also one can decide on the ontological foundation of DSML concepts. Finally, one should validate the visual notation.

Concerning *shaping of the language specification* one can employ guidelines for the design and assessment for both DSL design generally [36] and DSML design specifically [20, pp. 14–17]. Particularly, for the design phase such guidelines allow one to, for a given set of candidate concepts, decide upon its inclusion

Table 2. V&V in the design phase

Artifact	Quality	Goals and Scope	Actor	V&VApproach
Guidelines for abstract syntax design and assessment, foundational ontologies, guidelines for visual notation design and assessment, glossary of domain concepts	Syntactic, semantic and pragmatic	Ensure validation of the content of the key language specification constituencies in terms of it being a reasonable reflection of, both, the domain concepts at hand (when it comes to the abstract syntax), and the development of a suitable visual notation	Domain experts, language users, DSML designer	Workshops and interviews, in addition to conceptual-argumentative work (as it pertains to consistency checks, e.g., as with the use of foundational ontologies)

in the DSMM being engineered. To this end relevant guidelines include ensuring relevance, pertaining to what extent a candidate concept is relevant to the stated purpose of the DSML, and having invariant semantics (also termed "avoid conceptual redundancy" by [36]), pertaining to a candidate concept having its own essential meaning which sets it apart from other concepts.

It is also possible to validate a language specification against a foundational ontology, with the aim of assessing the semantics of the concepts standing behind a DSMM. Thus, one can address potential ambiguities of interpretations of these semantics. Foundational ontologies have for example been used for assessing several of the ArchiMate extensions [2,3], and the DEMO transaction patterns [47]. For example, [2, p. 29] pointed out that the "stakeholder" concept from the motivation extension of ArchiMate can have a manifold interpretations, encompassing both agent universals and roles, while one would ideally like to distinguish between these interpretations.

Concerning *validation of the (draft) visual notation*, a well-known means for validating the visual notation are the guidelines proposed in the Physics of Notation (PoN) [43]. PoN also has various adaptations. For example, building on PoN's notion of semantic transparency, i.e., the extent to which the visualization of a concept suggests its meaning, the work of [6] presented an approach for evaluating and improving the semantic transparency of concept notations.

Formalize. This phase concerns the application of formal methods to formalize the design of the DSMM in order to enable its formal verification and validation.

Typical Activities: language specification (which typically consists of a meta model specification and a set of well-formedness rules) is defined in terms of mathematical notations. Such mathematical notations include set theory, first-order logic, or algebra. In practice, this can be achieved by implementing a prototype of the language specification using a meta modeling platform that has a formal foundation. For example, the ADOxx platform is based on the FDMM formalism which describes the core constituents of ADOxx meta models in terms of set theory and first order logic statements [17]. The Lightning Language Work-bench [21,24] is another example of a DSML engineering platform with a formal foundation. In Lightning, language specification and concrete syntax design are both implemented as Alloy models [29], and their connection in terms of an F-Alloy model transformation [23]. The implementation is then executed by the Alloy Analyzer and the F-Alloy Interpreter to generate instance models of the language (as it is designed), and to render the generated models in a domain specific visualisation [22]. Here, the visualized models adhere to the design of the visual notation.

V&V Support: this phase is dedicated to the validation and verification of the DSMM. Firstly, mathematical proofs or verification can be run on the formal language specification, in order to analyze properties of the DSML, to detect errors in the language specification or inconsistency among well-formedness rules, or to simulate the formal semantics of the language. Taking the Alloy-based Lightning language workbench for example, the following two verification scenarios can be envisioned: (1) To check if the language (as it is designed) has a property P, we can wrap P in the form of an assertion and check it against the Alloy model, which is the formal counterpart of the language specification. In case a counter-example is found by the Alloy Analyzer, this counter-example constitutes an instance of the language for which the property is violated. The parts of the instance that violate the property are also indicated to make debugging easier; (2) Errors in the language specification, such as inconsistent type constraints, or a conflict between two well-formedness rules, will be signaled by the fact that no instances can be generated from the language specification (as it is designed currently). The first type of verification scenario can be exploited to ensure that semantic qualities are respected, such as the necessary amount of information (in terms of concepts and relations) is captured, and to ensure that domain rules or standards are respected. During the second type of verification scenario, we check the integrity of the DSML itself. Note that formal method based verification is often fully automated and offers more rigor and thorough checking of the language specification than any human checking could do.

Secondly, example instance models generated from the specification of the modeling language (as it is designed so far) enable validation of both semantic and pragmatic qualities. On the semantic side, these example models basically constitute the extensional definition of the language. Omissions (e.g., missing well-formedness rules), excess (e.g., unnecessary concepts), or mismatching (e.g., a relation between wrong types of concepts) can be detected by simply review-ing these example models. The reviewing activity is further enhanced when the example models are visualized in a domain specific notation, because exam-ple models foster understanding for domain experts and non-technical users. Hence, these stakeholders will be able to pinpoint errors. Moreover, the domain-specific notation used to visualize example models is indeed the notation which is required by users in the Create phase, and which has been defined and agreed upon among the stakeholders during the Design phase (using the discussed val-idation techniques of said phase). As such, seeing the visual notation applied to

Table 3. V&V in the formalize phase

Artifact	Quality	Goals and scope	Actor	V&VApproach
Formal language specification, generated instance models	Semantic quality and pragmatic quality	Ensuring semantic soundness and completeness; ensuring fitness of the concrete syntax	Domain expert, user, and language engineer	Formal verification, reviewing

concrete examples also allows the users validate the fitness of the notation itself, being one kind of pragmatic quality.

Develop. Based on the DSMM definition that has been designed, formalized, verified and validated in previous phases, this phase concerns the implementation of a modeling tool to enable modeling activities with the DSMM.

Typical Activities: Among others, the modeling tool typically consists of a graphical editor (to support different diagram types to model different subsets of concepts and relationships), validation mechanisms (to ensure syntactic validity of models and to ensure consistency across different diagrams), and provides import/export functions (to ensure interoperation with external tools). As a consequence, typical activities during this phase amount to realizing all these components of the modeling tool, manually, automatically, or in a hybrid manner.

V&V Support: After several iterations of the previous phases, we arrive at a formally verified and user validated specification of the DSMM, with the desired syntactic, semantic, and pragmatic qualities. It is thus crucial in this phase to preserve these qualities of the DSMM (and subsequently to ensure these qualities of models that can be built with the modeling method), by demonstrating that the modeling tool produced in this phase indeed respects the specification. Given that the modeling tool is a piece of software, one can leverage software verification techniques, such as software testing, formal verification [48] (i.e., to formally demonstrate that a program satisfies a formal specification), and program derivation [11,12,27][1].

The validation mechanisms implemented in the modeling tool ensure syntactic validity of models created using the modeling tool. This can be achieved either in a preventive manner or through checking. A preventive manner forbids syntactically incorrect models to be created at all in the first place. For example, prevention can be achieved by means of auto-completion of integral missing elements, or disallowing relating two type incompatible instances. Syntactic validity can also be achieved by checking the models against well-formedness constraints after models are created. Moreover, validation mechanisms should

---

[1] Program derivation means to derive an executable program from a formal specification through mathematical means. The program thus obtained is correct by construction.

Table 4. V&V in the develop phase

Artifact	Quality	Goals and Scope	Actor	V&VApproach
Modeling tool	Syntactic quality, semantic quality and pragmatic quality	To preserve the semantic and pragmatic qualities that have already been achieved in previous phases	Software developer, language engineer, user	Software testing, formal verification, program derivation

ensure coherence between (parts of) models that are obtained either by vertical refinement (e.g., decomposition of a business process into sub-processes, or the internal description of an organizational unit), or by horizontal refinement (e.g., two diagrams describing the same phenomenon but from different views, or the same organization but from different perspectives).

Many meta modeling platforms, such as ADOxx, MetaEdit+, or EMF+Sirius, come with generic configurable components ready to be reused for the implementation of the basic functions of the modeling tool, such as the graphical editor. However, when it comes to reusable algorithms or procedures for validation mechanisms, more support is still desired, for example by capitalising on formal methods, as suggested in [37].

Deploy. Within the deploy phase the systematic evaluation of the modeling tool, and thus, also the proposed modeling method takes place. If needed, the revision of the modeling tool, or parts of the modeling method follows, cf. Fig. 1.

Typical Activities: in this phase one evaluates the modeling tool supporting the designed domain-specific modeling method regarding, both, (1) its capabilities and extent to which the requirements formulated in the first phase are fulfilled, and (2) the contribution of the designed domain-specific modeling method, compared to the current situation, to improving productivity or quality of the targeted class of problems, [18, pp. 57–58], e.g., whether the domain-specific modeling method allows us to address the targeted problem/finding the solution by using less resources (such as requiring less time).

V&V Support: in this phase one focuses on the informal evaluation of the modeling tool and the modeling method, thus relying on subjective experience of modelers. By using the tool to solve targeted problems, i.e., using the tool in practice, the users evaluate mainly the pragmatic quality, nevertheless, they may also identify syntactic or semantic concerns. Apart from checking whether created models constitute a reasonable representation of the domain under study, and whether the requirements specified are accounted for, this phase enables also the detailed analysis of the modeling method using practical use scenarios. Following [18], this allows to compare current practice against the use of domain-specific modeling method in order to check, e.g., learning effort, productivity or quality of the solution and documentation. In addition, a comparative analysis of utility and costs can also be conducted in this phase [18, p. 58].

Table 5. V&V in the deploy phase

Artifact	Quality	Goals and scope	Actor	V&V Approach
Modeling method and supporting tool	Pragmatic, semantic and syntactic quality	A comparative assessment of current practice and effects of using the modeling method on problem solving/analysis	Domain Experts, Users	Informal evaluation using use scenarios, workshops with domain experts, controlled experiments and walk-through

4   Conclusions

To foster valid enterprise models, in this paper we promoted validation and verification to first-class citizens during the engineering of a domain-specific modeling method. To this end we synthesized existing approaches to engineer a domain-specific modeling method, and discussed the validation and verification mechanisms and their roles in different phases of DSMM engineering. In our discussion, we explicitly differentiated between the syntactic, semantic and pragmatic quality of DSMM's artifacts, as well as stress the role of meta modeling platforms and other language engineering workbenches in the validation and verification process.

Due to space restrictions, we do not provide a detailed discussion on the resulting requirements that meta modeling platforms or language engineering workbenches should fulfill, in order to provide a desired support to engineer domain-specific modeling methods in line with the validation and verification discussions presented in this paper. However, considering the arguments we have raised, availability of such requirements would be necessary in order to be able to answer the question: To what extent existing tools/platforms enable validation and verification in the domain of enterprise modeling? Our initial study clearly indicates that while support for the specification and checking of cardinality constraints and typing constraints is provided by most of the platforms, the support for other types of V&V varies substantially. For future work, it would thus be interesting to systematically derive requirements using this paper as a baseline, and to confront different meta modeling platforms against these.

References

1. Antunes, G., Barateiro, J., Caetano, A., Borbinha, J.: Analysis of federated enterprise architecture models. In: ECIS 2015 Completed Research Papers (2015), paper 10
2. Azevedo, C.L., Almeida, J.P.A., van Sinderen, M., Quartel, D., Guizzardi, G.: An ontology-based semantics for the motivation extension to ArchiMate. In: 2011 IEEE 15th International Enterprise Distributed Object Computing Conference, pp. 25–34. IEEE (2011)

3. Azevedo, C.L., Iacob, M.E., Almeida, J.P.A., van Sinderen, M., Pires, L.F., Guiz-zardi, G.: Modeling resources and capabilities in enterprise architecture: a well-founded ontology-based proposal for ArchiMate. Inf. Syst. **54**, 235–262 (2015)
4. Barjis, J.: Collaborative, participative and interactive enterprise modeling. In: Filipe, J., Cordeiro, J. (eds.) ICEIS 2009. LNBIP, vol. 24, pp. 651–662. Springer, Heidelberg (2009). https://doi.org/10.1007/978-3-642-01347-8_54
5. Bork, D.: Metamodel-based analysis of domain-specific conceptual modeling methods. In: Buchmann, R.A., Karagiannis, D., Kirikova, M. (eds.) PoEM 2018. LNBIP, vol. 335, pp. 172–187. Springer, Cham (2018). https://doi.org/10.1007/978-3-030-02302-7_11
6. Bork, D., Roelens, B.: A technique for evaluating and improving the semantic transparency of modeling language notations. Software and Systems Modeling, pp. 1–25 (2021)
7. Chapurlat, V., Braesch, C.: Verification, validation, qualification and certification of enterprise models: Statements and opportunities. Compu. Industry **59**(7), 711–721 (2008). enterprise Integration and Interoperability in Manufacturing Systems
8. Chapurlat, V., Kamsu-Foguem, B., Prunet, F.: A formal verification framework and associated tools for enterprise modeling: Application to ueml. Comput. Ind. **57**(2), 153–166 (2006)
9. De Kinderen, S., Ma, Q.: Requirements engineering for the design of conceptual modeling languages. Appl. Ontol. **10**(1), 7–24 (2015)
10. Department of Defense: Instruction 5000.61: Dod modeling and simulation (m&s) verification, validation and accreditation (vv&a). Technical report, Department of Defense (2003)
11. Dijkstra, E.W.: A Discipline of Programming. Pearson (1976)
12. Dijkstra, E.W., Feijen, W.: A Method of Programming. Addison Wesley Longman (1988)
13. Efendioglu, N., Woitsch, R.: Modelling method design: an ADOxx realisation. In: 2016 IEEE 20th International Enterprise Distributed Object Computing Workshop (EDOCW), pp. 1–8. IEEE Computer Society, Los Alamitos, CA, USA, September 2016
14. Efendioglu, N., Woitsch, R., Karagiannis, D.: Modelling method design: a model-driven approach. In: Anderst-Kotsis, G., Indrawan-Santiago, M. (eds.) Proceedings of the 17th International Conference on Information Integration and Web-based Applications & Services, iiWAS 2015, Brussels, Belgium, 11–13 December, 2015, pp. 59:1–59:10. ACM (2015)
15. Erdweg, S., van der Storm, T., Völter, M., Tratt, L., Bosman, R., Cook, W.R., Gerritsen, A., Hulshout, A., Kelly, S., Loh, A., Konat, G., Molina, P.J., Palatnik, M., Pohjonen, R., Schindler, E., Schindler, K., Solmi, R., Vergu, V., Visser, E., van der Vlist, K., Wachsmuth, G., van der Woning, J.: Evaluating and comparing language workbenches: Existing results and benchmarks for the future. Computer Languages, Systems & Structures 44, 24–47 (2015), special issue on the 6th and 7th International Conference on Software Language Engineering (SLE 2013 and SLE 2014)
16. Fill, H., Karagiannis, D.: On the conceptualisation of modelling methods using the ADOxx meta modelling platform. EMISA **8**(1), 4–25 (2013)
17. Fill, H.G., Redmond, T., Karagiannis, D.: Formalizing meta models with FDMM: the ADOxx case. In: Proceedings of the 14th International Conference on Enterprise Information Systems (ICEIS 2012). LNBIP, vol. 141, pp. 429–451 (2013)
18. Frank, U.: Outline of a method for designing domain-specific modelling languages. ICB Research Report 42, University of Duisburg-Essen, Essen (2010)

19. Frank, U.: Multi-perspective enterprise modelling: background and terminological foundation. ICB-Research Report 46, University of Duisburg-Essen, Essen (2011)
20. Frank, U.: Domain-specific modeling languages: Requirements analysis and design guidelines. In: Reinhartz-Berger, I., Sturm, A., Clark, T., Cohen, S., Bettin, J. (eds.) Domain Engineering, pp. 133–157. Springer, Berlin (2013)
21. Gammaitoni, L.: On the Use of Alloy in Engineering Domain Specific Modeling Languages. Ph.d. thesis, University of Luxembourg (2017)
22. Gammaitoni, L., Kelsen, P.: Domain-specific visualization of alloy instances. In: Proceedings of the 4th International ABZ Conference, ABZ 2014. LNCS, vol. 8477, pp. 324–327 (2014)
23. Gammaitoni, L., Kelsen, P.: F-alloy: a relational model transformation language based on alloy. Softw. Syst. Model. **18**(1), 213–247 (2019)
24. Gammaitoni, L., Kelsen, P., Glodt, C.: Designing languages using lightning. In: Proceedings of the 2015 ACM SIGPLAN International Conference on Software Language Engineering (SLE 2015), pp. 77–82 (2015)
25. Gammaitoni, L., Kelsen, P., Ma, Q.: Agile validation of model transformations using compound F-Alloy specifications. Sci. Comput. Program. **162**, 55–75 (2018)
26. Geeraerts, D.: Theories of Lexical Semantics. Oxford University Press, Oxford (2010)
27. Gries, D.: The Science of Programming. Springer, Cham (1981)
28. Iung, A., Carbonell, J., Marchezan, L., Rodrigues, E., Bernardino, M., Basso, F.P., Medeiros, B.: Systematic mapping study on domain-specific language development tools. Empir. Softw. Eng. **25**(5), 4205–4249 (2020)
29. Jackson, D.: Software Abstractions: Logic, Language, and Analysis. The MIT Press (2 2012), revised edition
30. Jeusfeld, M.A.: SemCheck: Checking Constraints for Multi-perspective Modeling Languages. In: Domain-Specific Conceptual Modeling, pp. 31–53. Springer, Cham (2016). https://doi.org/10.1007/978-3-319-39417-6_2
31. Johnson, P., Lagerström, R., Närman, P., Simonsson, M.: Enterprise architecture analysis with extended influence diagrams. Inf. Syst. Front. **9**(2–3), 163–180 (2007)
32. Karagiannis, D.: Agile modeling method engineering. In: Karanikolas, N.N., et al. (eds.) Proceedings of the 19th Panhellenic Conference on Informatics, PCI 2015, Athens, Greece, October 1–3, 2015, pp. 5–10. ACM (2015)
33. Karagiannis, D.: Conceptual modelling methods: the AMME agile engineering approach. In: Silaghi, G.C., Buchmann, R.A., Boja, C. (eds.) IE 2016. LNBIP, vol. 273, pp. 3–19. Springer, Cham (2018). https://doi.org/10.1007/978-3-319-73459-0_1
34. Karagiannis, D., Burzynski, P., Utz, W., Buchmann, R.A.: A metamodeling approach to support the engineering of modeling method requirements. In: Damian, D.E., Perini, A., Lee, S. (eds.) 27th IEEE International Requirements Engineering Conference, RE 2019, Jeju Island, Korea (South), 23–27 September, 2019, pp. 199–210. IEEE (2019)
35. Karagiannis, D., Kühn, H.: Metamodelling platforms. In: Bauknecht, K., Tjoa, A.M., Quirchmayr, G. (eds.) EC-Web 2002. LNCS, vol. 2455, pp. 182–182. Springer, Heidelberg (2002). https://doi.org/10.1007/3-540-45705-4_19
36. Karsai, G., Krahn, H., Pinkernell, C., Rumpe, B., Schindler, M., Völkel, S.: Design guidelines for domain specific languages. arXiv preprint arXiv:1409.2378 (2014)
37. de Kinderen, S., Ma, Q., Kaczmarek-Heß, M.: Towards extending the validation possibilities of ADOxx with alloy. In: Grabis, J., Bork, D. (eds.) PoEM 2020. LNBIP, vol. 400, pp. 138–152. Springer, Cham (2020). https://doi.org/10.1007/978-3-030-63479-7_10

38. Krogstie, J.: Evaluating UML Using a Generic Quality Framework, pp. 1–22. IGI Global, USA (2003)
39. Krogstie, J., Sindre, G., Jørgensen, H.: Process models representing knowledge for action: a revised quality framework. Eur. J. Inf. Syst. 15(1), 91–102 (2006)
40. Krogstie, J., Sindre, G., Lindland, O.I.: 20 years of quality of models. In: Seminal Contributions to Information Systems Engineering, pp. 103–107. Springer, Heidelberg (2013). https://doi.org/10.1007/978-3-642-36926-1_8
41. van der Linden, D., Hoppenbrouwers, S., Lartseva, A., Molnar, W.: Beyond terminologies: using psychometrics to validate shared ontologies. Appl. Ontol. 7(4), 471–487 (2012)
42. Lindland, O.I., Sindre, G., Sølvberg, A.: Understanding quality in conceptual modeling. IEEE Softw. 11(2), 42–49 (1994)
43. Moody, D.L.: The physics of notations: toward a scientific basis for constructing visual notations in software engineering. IEEE Trans. Software Eng. 35(6), 756–779 (2009)
44. Negm, E., Makady, S., Salah, A.: Survey on domain specific languages implementation aspects. Int. J. Adv. Comput. Sci. Appl. 10(11) (2019)
45. Niemann, K.D.: From enterprise architecture to IT governance, vol. 1. Springer (2006)
46. Pohl, K.: Requirements engineering: fundamentals, principles, and techniques. Springer Publishing Company, Incorporated (2010)
47. Poletaeva, T., Guizzardi, G., Almeida, J.P.A., Abdulrab, H.: Revisiting the DEMO transaction pattern with the Unified Foundational Ontology (UFO). In: Aveiro, D., Pergl, R., Guizzardi, G., Almeida, J.P., Magalhães, R., Lekkerkerk, H. (eds.) EEWC 2017. LNBIP, vol. 284, pp. 181–195. Springer, Cham (2017). https://doi.org/10.1007/978-3-319-57955-9_14
48. Seligman, E., Schubert, T., Kumar, M.V.A.K.: Formal Verification: An Essential Toolkit for Modern VLSI Design, 1st edn. Morgan Kaufmann (2015)
49. Vacchi, E., Cazzola, W., Pillay, S., Combemale, B.: Variability support in domain-specific language development. In: Erwig, M., Paige, R.F., Van Wyk, E. (eds.) SLE 2013. LNCS, vol. 8225, pp. 76–95. Springer, Cham (2013). https://doi.org/10.1007/978-3-319-02654-1_5
50. Steinberg, D., Budinsky, F., Merks, E., Paternostro, M.: EMF: eclipse modeling framework. Pearson Education (2008)
51. Tolvanen, J.P., Kelly, S.: Metaedit+ defining and using integrated domain-specific modeling languages. In: Proceedings of the 24th ACM SIGPLAN Conference Companion on Object Oriented Programming Systems Languages and Applications, pp. 819–820 (2009)

A Foundation for Design, Analysis, and Management of Digital Business Ecosystem through Situational Method Engineering

Chen Hsi Tsai(✉) and Jelena Zdravkovic

Department of Computer and Systems Sciences, Stockholm University, Stockholm, Sweden
{chenhsi.tsai,jelenaz}@dsv.su.se

Abstract. Digital Business Ecosystem (DBE) supports organizations to combine their expertise in a novel collaborative network through information and communications technology. Despite its beneficial aspects, a DBE is intricate and difficult to manage due to the dependent interactions and interrelationships among actors. Modelling, as a proven way to deal with complex problems in organisational settings, can support the capturing and documenting of a DBE. This can enhance the level of abstraction of the DBE to aid the analysis and decision-making. However, current scientific literature shows a lack of methodological guidance for modelling in support of the analysis, design, and management of DBEs. Hence, in this study, we have proposed a foundation for a DBE design, analysis, and management method based on Situational Method Engineering (SME). Using the requirements empirically collected from a number of industrial practitioners and experts, the main concepts and intentions relevant to DBE design, analysis and management were defined. Based on them, using the SME approach, we modelled and presented several method process parts that layout fulfilment of the intentions for the concepts' development using different, situation-related, strategies (i.e. method chunks).

Keywords: Digital Business Ecosystem · Method engineering · Method chunks

1 Introduction

Digital Business Ecosystem (DBE) is a notion based on Moore's concept of *Business ecosystem* which supports evolution and co-evolution in a complex system involving organisations and individuals of an economic community [1]. In the context of a DBE, as a new type of a collaborative network among organisations, the participating organisations and individual actors cooperate for product and service delivery or utilization through the support of information and communications technology (ICT).

A DBE, as compared to traditional multi-actor business models, possesses some unique characteristics, including heterogeneity, symbiosis, co-evolution, and self-organisation, which enables it to incorporate different business domains and diverse

© IFIP International Federation for Information Processing 2021
Published by Springer Nature Switzerland AG 2021
E. Serral et al. (Eds.): PoEM 2021, LNBIP 432, pp. 134–149, 2021.
https://doi.org/10.1007/978-3-030-91279-6_10

interests in its digital environment [2, 3]. These unique characteristics make DBE a highly-valued novel collaborative approach for organisations to, by engaging business capabilities across the involved actors, meet each of their goals and to leverage the offered and desired resources among the actors.

Despite the beneficial aspect of being part of a DBE, many correlated or dependent interactions and interrelationships among the involved actors often lead to complexity and, in turns, difficulties related to management [4]. Conceptual modelling and Enterprise Modelling allow capturing and documenting a specific domain and enhancing the level of abstraction of the domain for analysis and decision making. The modelling approach has proven to be useful in dealing with complex problems in organisational settings [5]. However, current scientific research suggested that there is a lack of means of model development, analysis, measurement, and management supporting DBEs [3, 6]. An ongoing systematic literature review, conducted by the authors, reveals also a need for a holistic modelling method which provides explicit guidance on the analysis, design, and management of DBEs. To address this need, an interview study [7]was conducted to understand DBEs from viewpoints of industrial practitioners and experts and elicit requirements for a DBE design and modelling method as a part of an ongoing design science research project.

In this study, to continue the line of work of our previous studies, and as a part of the design science research project, we aim to explore the possibility of classifying and aggregating the elicited requirements concerning DBE design [7] into a methodological approach, based on *Method Engineering* (ME) [8].

The rest of this paper is organized as follows. Section 2 gives background on the current research in DBE modelling, *Method Engineering* (ME) and *Situational Method Engineering* (SME), and DBE roles and responsibilities. In Sect. 3, results of the application of SME to the requirements are presented together with the examples of the DBE method process. Section 4 provides a discussion on the findings, while Sect. 5 briefly concludes the study and outlines future work.

2 Related Work

2.1 State of the Art – DBE Design and Modelling Method

Using a modelling method as an approach, which aims to reduce complex domains through abstraction, can be an appropriate way for describing DBEs and addressing their complexity. Nevertheless, the current state of the art suggests that the area of DBE design and modelling methods lacks holistic yet feasible solutions that address the multiple aspects of a DBE and support the design and management of a DBE throughout its lifecycle.

This topic has been investigated in an ongoing systematic literature review, where 3509 studies were screened and 63 included in the analysis. The review has, so far, revealed that few scientific studies proposed a comprehensive conceptual modelling method for DBEs, consisting of a modelling language and guidelines or procedures for modelling DBEs. Modelling procedures of the proposed methods suggested by the analysed studies were scarce. Moreover, many of the analysed studies did not include some important concepts concerning DBEs in their modelling language constructs; resources and capabilities are some of such examples. Aldea's [9] study successfully included more essential concepts (*actor, role, capability, relationship, and digital component*), but method for their design and analysis were not elaborated. A few examples of studies that suggested a more comprehensive method were the Methodology of Business Ecosystem Network Analysis (MOBENA) in [10], the methodology for modelling interdependencies between partners in a DBE in [4], and the approach for modelling and analysing DBEs from the value perspective in [9]; still, none of them have proposed a complete method encompassing all relevant concepts, nor the methods considered both design, analysis and management of DBE.

2.2 Situational Method Engineering

Method Engineering, and in particular *Situational Method Engineering* (SME) [8], provides theory and guidance to support the construction of methods that are situation-specific, adaptable, and configurable. A key feature of SME is the modularity of a method, which its definition varies from one SME approach to another in terms of method building blocks. As proposed in [11, 12], *method chunks* can be seen as method building blocks for a SME approach. A method chunk is an autonomous part of a method including its process and product elements. The process defines the activity of the method, whereas the product, with the help of a metamodel, formally defines the artefacts to be used and produced by the method chunk process. In addition, the method chunk user roles and supporting tools can be defined.

The composition of method chunks for the construction of a new method is based on the *Map* approach [7]. This approach is used to express the process model of the method in terms of engineering *intentions* (i.e., the engineering goal) and *strategies* to achieve the intentions. As one or more strategies can be defined to achieve an intention, the specification and implementation of the method are ensured to have a higher level of variability and flexibility. The process model takes the form of a labelled directed graph with intentions as nodes and strategies as edges between intentions. Each strategy in the map requires one or more method chunks specifying how to achieve the target intention by using the selected strategy. The Map approach provides method extension mechanisms as the adding of new strategies and new intentions leads to new method chunks.

In this study, we consider the SME approach using method chunks as method building blocks. Typically, SME relies on existing methods to facilitate design of situation-related method chunks when such a method does not exist, the focus is set on the product to be designed, i.e., DBE in this case. Main product elements are then used as the *concepts* for the method construction for guiding the Map in order to establish the method process [11]. Concerning the "situational" of the SME, we argue that the dynamics occurring in the context of a DBE are the situations being considered while applying the situational method. The contexts of DBEs concern specific domains, whereas the dynamic issues in the context of a DBE are situational.

2.3 Multi-view Modelling Methods

Multi-view or multi-perspective modelling approaches have had a long tradition in different application domains [13]. These approaches allow the representation of the different aspects or facets of a system through the use of different types of models or modelling languages. An example is the multi-perspective enterprise modelling (MEMO) [14], in which the author emphasised the different levels of perspectives and aspects being accounted for in an enterprise model while analysing and designing a system. In [15, 16], the authors looked further into the consistency between the different representations of models in multi-view modelling approaches and suggested a method for preserving consistency.

The idea of multi-view modelling approaches does not contradict the SME approach applied to the current study, where the method chunks support the modelling of different concepts in different situations concerning dynamic issues in DBEs and its process. In the concrete, the modelling views or perspectives known in multi-view modelling approaches could support the method chunks of SME, especially in structuring the product elements. Since the modelling views or perspectives are usually represented by different types of models, the approach could be jointly used in the situational method engineering process when defining the artefacts/modelling languages/types of models to be used, meaning the product elements of method chunks, during the creation of a new method.

2.4 DBE Roles and Responsibilities

Eight DBE roles and their corresponding responsibilities were proposed in [17] by synthesising existing scientific studies on the topic. A *Driver* has the characteristics of guiding and looking over all actors within an ecosystem, with responsibilities, such as setting up a common vision for all DBE actors, improving the overall health of a DBE, and collecting and raising end users' events and feedback. An *Aggregator* aggregates and combines multiple resources in a DBE into products and services without having the responsibility of leading a whole ecosystem and its involved actors. A *Modular Producer* pertains to the development of capabilities and offering of resources, such as products, services, technologies, knowledge, financial funding, etc., in a specialised domain within a DBE. A *Complementor* develops also capabilities and creates values in a specialised domain. However, its offerings are complements, often bundled by end users, that add extra value to the core resources of a DBE. A *Customer* is the beneficiary of a DBE's efforts and the sources of revenue as they pay for resources, whereas an *End User* consumes resources based on specific needs and provide feedback to other DBE actors. A *Governor* governs actors within a DBE by providing and/or defining normative contexts, such as standards, laws, policies, guidelines, norms, and ethics, related to the business concern of the DBE. A *Reputation Guardian* surveys and assesses DBE actors' trustworthiness, reliability, solvency, and worthiness.

These roles are of significance and serve as underlying knowledge for the method engineering process of the DBE method and starting points for some of the strategies in the DBE method application process (illustrated as examples in Sect. 3.3).

3 A Foundation for the Method Engineering Process for DBE Design, Analysis, and Management

3.1 Problem Context

The current study was based on the foundation of a previous study [7], where 11 industrial practitioners and experts from different business domains were interviewed to explore and understand DBEs, with the purpose of eliciting requirements for developing a holistic method for designing and modelling DBEs. The empirical data led to 30 requirements (as shown in Table 1) encompassing the essential concepts concerning DBEs.

Due to the lack of a holistic DBE design and modelling method, we applied SME with a product-driven approach [12] to identify intentions related to the product parts and thus construct the method process in the current study. This approach means that the essential concepts in the requirements for DBE design, analysis, and management from [7] were used as the main concepts or artefacts (i.e., product parts) in order to facilitate the intentions of the process (similar as the Map as mentioned in Sect. 2.2) of the DBE method that need to be constructed.

3.2 Identification of Main Concepts

In [7], we collected empirical data through interviews and conducted a thematic analysis on the data. Two themes, seven categories, and 25 codes emerged from the data analysis, which led to the elicitation of the requirements for a DBE design, analysis, and management method. Deriving from these requirements, 22 main concepts were used to drive the method engineering of the DBE method as products parts.

The 22 main concepts (shown in italic) correlated to the codes of the thematic analysis in [REF – accepted for a conference proceeding (BIR2021)] are described in the following. *Scope* of a DBE concerns business activities and value of the DBE based on its vision, whereas *boundaries* determine which actors are part of the DBE. *Vision* is a collection of *goals* on a strategic level. Based on this difference, both *goal* and *vision* are equally important artefacts in the context of DBE considering the multiple actors involved. *Actors* are organisations or individuals who take part in a DBE and establish *relationships* with each other. Each actor has specific *role*(s) and corresponding *responsibilities*. These DBE *roles* are defined in [17], including Driver, Aggregator, Modular Producer, Complementor, Customer, End User, Governor, and Reputation Guardian (c.f. [18] for the defined DBE roles and their responsibilities). Each actor has also its *domain specific focus area and interests, properties related to performance*, and *key performance indicators* (KPIs). Within a DBE, relevant *processes, capabilities, resources*, and *values* of participating actors are shared and exchanged, which contributes to the functioning and sustaining of the DBE. *Digital infrastructures* and *communication channels* shared and used between actors constitute the digital environment of a DBE, where *communication form(s)* agreed by the actors and *agreement(s)* about *exchanged information* between them are fundamental. *Policies* are usually rules that are made by companies, organizations, groups, or governments in order to carry out a plan and achieve certain aims and goals. In the context of a DBE, there could be external policies to which the DBE needs to adhere, but also but also internal policies in the DBE to which the actors need to adhere. *Regulations* are distinguishable from policy in a way that they are often made and imposed by public agencies as restrictions, with the effect of law, on activities within a community [19].

3.3 Identification of Intentions

Table 1 shows the 32 intentions relevant to the DBE method being identified based on the main concepts in the 30 requirements. These intentions, or so-called engineering intentions, according to ME, are used as the starting point for constructing process maps and as the composition of method chunks. Note that six requirements, R3, R4, R9, R12, R19, and R20, do not lead to identification of intentions but are considered constraints of the DBE method.

Table 1. Requirements and ME Intentions for the DBE method

Requirement	Intention
R1. The method shall aid the process of delimiting scope and boundaries of a DBE.	I1. Delimit scope and boundaries
R2. The method shall support assignment of DBE roles and responsibilities to actors.	I2. Identify actors
R5. The method shall support modelling of communication channels among actors.	I3. Identify communication channels used in DBE
R6. The method shall support modelling of commonly agreed form of communication among actors.	I4. Identify agreed communication forms in DBE
R7. The method shall support analysis of an actor's relevant part of a DBE.	I5. Analyse DBE's scope and boundaries from single actor's viewpoint
R8. The method shall support analysis of relationships and types of relationships among actors.	I6. Identify relationships (type) between actors
	I7. Analyse DBE's relationship network
R10. The method shall support modelling of actors' processes, capabilities, and resources on a DBE level.	I8. Identify processes of actors relevant for DBE
	I9. Identify capabilities of actors relevant for DBE
	I10. Identify resources of actors relevant for DBE
R11. The method shall be able to integrate actors' processes and streamline the overall process on a DBE level.	I11. Analyse possible integration of processes in DBE

(*continued*)

Table 1. (*continued*)

Requirement	Intention
R13. The method shall support modelling of values within a DBE.	I12. Identify relevant exchanged values in DBE
R14. The method shall support analysis of existing and future co-created values among actors.	I13. Analyse possible co-created values in future state of DBE
R15. The method shall support modelling of digital infrastructures within a DBE.	I14. Identify digital infrastructures shared in DBE
R16. The method shall support analysis of existing and future innovation created by shared infrastructures among actors.	I15. Analyse possible new innovation based on shared infrastructures in future state of DBE
R17. The method shall support modelling of policies and regulations within a DBE.	I16. Identify policies relevant for actors and DBE
	I17. Identify regulations relevant for actors and DBE
R18. The method shall support analysis of coverage of policies and regulations.	I18. Analyse coverage of policies and regulations on all actors
R21. The method should support identification of possible changes by obtaining relevant data.	I19. Identify possible changes occurring in and to DBE (by analyse external context data and relevant data of DBE actors)
R22. The method should support analysing of future state of a DBE when involving new actors.	I20. Analyse DBE's future state upon new actor join (concerning all other groups)
R23. The method shall support analysis of shareable and interchangeable capabilities and resources.	I21. Analyse properties of capabilities and their interchangeability
	I22. Analyse properties of resources and their interchangeability
R24. The method shall be able to show the agreement on what information and data are shared among actors.	I23. Identify information shared in DBE
R25. The method shall support modelling types of information exchanged and shared among actors.	
R26. The method shall support alignment of vision and goals among actors.	I24. Align actors' visions in DBE
	I25. Align actors' goals in DBE

(*continued*)

Table 1. (*continued*)

Requirement	Intention
R27. *The method shall support management based on actors' domain specific focus areas and interests.*	I26. Identify actors' domain specific activities, competences, and skills relevant for DBE
	I27. Manage DBE based on selected domain catalogues of actors' activities, competences, and skills
R28. *The method shall support management and monitoring of various levels of processes and monitoring of the overall process at a DBE level.*	I28. Monitor integrated DBE processes
R29. *The method shall support monitoring of actors' KPIs and indicators.*	I29. Identify KPIs and indicators of actors relevant for DBE
	I30. Monitor KPIs and indicators of DBE (based on goals and vision)
R30. *The method shall support analysis of various data concerning actors' properties and performance.*	I31. Identify relevant properties related to actors' performance in DBE
	I32. Analyse new actors' fitness and qualification in joining DBE based on properties (and performance)
R3. *The method shall support inclusion of actors regardless of geographical locations.*	n/a; *constraints*
R4. *The method shall support exposure of a DBE regardless of its geographical location.*	n/a; *constraints*
R9. *The method shall support the means and requirements for the accession to a DBE.*	n/a; *constraints*
R12. *The method shall support exposure of collaborating processes, capabilities, and resources among actors.*	n/a; *constraints*
R19. *The method shall be agile in order to support the dynamics of a DBE and fast decision-making withing the DBE.*	n/a; *constraints*
R20. *The method shall support an expandable knowledge base of the DBE framework and roles.*	n/a; *constraints*

3.4 Examples of the DBE Method Process

Using the Map approach (c.f. Sect. 2.2 and [7]), the process model of the DBE method, in terms of engineering intentions and different, situation-related, strategies to achieve the intentions, has been developed. Based on the entire set of intentions, a holistic process for the DBE method is aimed to be built. In this section, a few examples of parts of the process are defined and explained. The presented examples of the DBE method process, consisting of intentions and strategies, show also the dependencies between some of these intentions in different situations.

The green ellipses in the following figures represent the intentions and the arrows connecting them are the strategies used to achieve them. It is important to mention that the *Modelling (update, complement, modify)* strategy concerns the reuse of existing models of single actors, meaning that DBE actors' existing models shall be updated, complemented, and modified in line with the required information relevant in the DBE context.

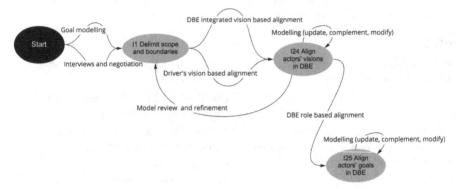

Fig. 1. DBE method process part (aka "map") for identifying the scope, boundaries, visions, and goals concepts of a DBE

Figure 1 shows the process of delimiting scope and boundaries and aligning actors' visions and goals in a DBE. The dependencies between *I1 Delimit scope and boundaries*, *I24 Align actors' visions in DBE*, and *I25 Align actors' goals in DBE* are established since the delimitation of the scope and boundaries of a DBE is often based on the overall vision of the DBE and the alignment of visions and goals should cohere with each other. To start with, two strategies can be used to achieve *I1*, either conducting a preliminary *goal modelling* or carrying out *interviews and negotiation* with the core actors of a DBE. After defining the scope and boundaries (moving from *I1* to *I24)*, two strategies can facilitate the alignment of actors' visions by basing on either the *integrated DBE vision* or the *DBE role Driver's vision*. The alignment is carried out using the *modelling* strategy, which could be supported by existing methods, such as 4EM [20] and i* [21]. By *reviewing the models*, mismatches can be identified and assist the *refinement* of the defined scope and boundaries of the DBE. Once the visions are aligned (moving from *I24* to *I25), DBE role-based alignment strategy* can be applied to align actors' goals. This is described preliminary in [22] on a Driver's viewpoint based on DBE resilience, but shall be applicable for all DBE roles. The alignment of goals is also carried out using the *modelling* strategy, which could be supported by similar methods as mentioned before.

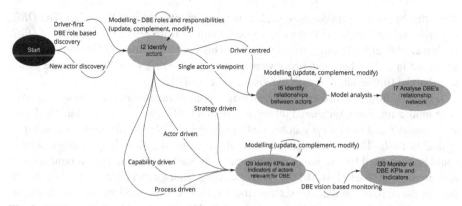

Fig. 2. DBE method process part for identifying the actor, relationship, and KPI concepts of a DBE

Figure 2 shows the process of identifying actors and their relationships and relevant KPIs. To start with, two strategies can be used to achieve *I2 Identify actors*. By a *Driver-first DBE role-based discovery* strategy, the actor(s) who has the DBE role *Driver* (c.f. Sect. 2.3) is first identified to facilitate the process of further actor identification as it is often easier to achieve this identification based on the revisiting of a DBE's scope, boundaries, and visions from the viewpoint of the central role – *Driver*. On the other hand, a *new actor discovery* strategy focuses on the condition when a new actor emerges or joins a DBE. The identification is carried out using the *modelling* strategy which should specifically focus on the roles and responsibilities suggested in Sect. 2.3 [17] and other studies [23–26].To move from *I2* to *I6 Identify relationships between actors*, either *Driver centred* or *single actor's viewpoint* strategy can be applied. By *Driver centred* strategy, the relationships between the *Driver(s)* and other DBE actors are identified, whereas *single actor's viewpoint* strategy aims to identify all relationships among all DBE actors from each and every actor's viewpoint. The identification is carried out using the *modelling* strategy, which could be supported by existing methods, such as the methodology for modelling interdependencies between partners in a DBE suggested in [4]. *Model analysis*, as a strategy, can be applied in order to move from *I6* to *I7 Analyses DBE's relationship network*. Several existing tools, such as [27–29], supports the visualisations and relationships of such networks in the context of a DBE. To move from *I2* to *I29 Identify KPIs and indicators of actors relevant for DBE*, different driven strategies can be applied, including *strategy driven, actor driven, capability driven,* and *process driven*. The identification is done by the *modelling* strategy, which could be

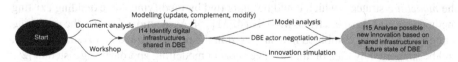

Fig. 3. DBE method process part for identifying the digital infrastructures and innovation concepts based on shared infrastructures in a DBE

supported by existing approaches, such as the ones mentioned in [18, 22, 30]. The *DBE vision-based monitoring* strategy can be used to move from *I29* to *I30 Monitor of DBE KPIs and indicators* in order to achieve *I30*. This could be supported by the approach described in [22], where examples were given based high-level DBE resilience goals that shall be further aligned with the vision(s) of the DBE.

Figure 3 shows the process of identifying digital infrastructures and analysing possible innovation based on shared infrastructure in a DBE. Two strategies, namely *document analysis* and *workshop*, can be used to achieve *I14 Identify digital infrastructures shared in DBE*. The identification is carried out using the *modelling* strategy, which could be supported by extending existing methods, such as Technical Components and Requirements Model of 4EM [20]. The *modelling* strategy can even be combined and used in the previous stage - *workshop* strategy, and be supported by the collaborative ecosystem modelling approach suggested in [29, 31]. After the identification of shared infrastructures (moving from *I14* to *I15 Analyse possible new innovation based on shared infrastructures in future state of DBE*), three strategies, *model analysis*, *DBE actor negotiation* (in terms of negotiation meetings among DBE actors), and *innovation simulation*, can facilitate the analysis of possible new innovation based on shared infrastructures, especially in the future state of a DBE, such as under the condition of new joining actors. The strategy *innovation simulation* could be supported by the many existing scientific research and approaches, such as in [32–34].

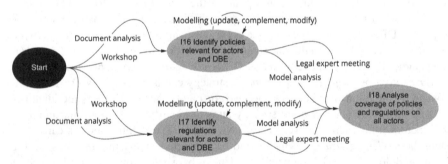

Fig. 4. DBE method process part for identifying the policies and regulations concepts, and their coverage analysis on all actors in a DBE

Figure 4 shows the process of identifying relevant policies and regulations and analysing coverage of them in a DBE. To achieve both *I16 Identify policies relevant for actors and DBE* and *I17 Identify regulations relevant for actors and DBE*, *document analysis* and *workshop* strategies can be used. The identification is carried out using the *modelling* strategy, which could be supported by modifying and extending existing methods, such as Business Rules Model of 4EM [20]. As mentioned above, the *modelling* strategy can also be combined here and used in the previous stage - *workshop* strategy, and be supported by the collaborative ecosystem modelling approach suggested in [29, 31]. After the identification (moving from *I16 and I17* to *I18 Analyse coverage of policies and regulations on all actors*), two strategies, *model analysis* and *legal expert meeting* can be used to achieve intention of the analysis of policy and regulation coverage.

Table 2. Example of method chunk for DBE actor modelling as shown in the process part in Fig. 2

Method chunk	Content
Name	Model the involving actors, their roles and responsibilities in a DBE
Intention	I2 Identify actors
Strategy	Modelling – DBE roles and responsibilities (update, complement, modify)
Goal	Create model(s) of the actors, their roles and responsibilities in a DBE from viewpoint of the DBE
Input	Lists of the involving actors, their DBE roles and responsibilities; existing models belonging to the actors based on viewpoint of a single organization (actor)
Activity	Update, complement, and modify the existing actor models; document, illustrate, and model the actors and their DBE roles and responsibilities
Output	DBE actor model(s) of the involving actors, their roles and responsibilities
Roles	--
Related chunk(s)	<<requires>> Identify actors by Driver-first DBE role-based discovery OR <<requires>> Identify actors by new actor discovery

Each of these strategies described in the four examples would require one or more method chunks specifying how to achieve the target intention. Due to the word limit, two examples based on the process part for identifying the actor and relationship concepts (as in Fig. 2) are given in the following Tables 2 and 3.

Table 3. Example of method chunk for relationship identification as shown in the process part in Fig. 2

Method chunk	Content
Name	Identify relationships of actors based on viewpoint of DBE Driver(s)
Intention	I6 Identify relationships between actors
Strategy	Driver centred
Goal	Establish a relationship network between the DBE Driver(s) and the DBE actors who have a relationship with the Driver(s)
Input	DBE actor model(s) of the involving actors, their roles and responsibilities
Activity	Associate and link the related DBE actors with the DBE Driver(s) in a relationship network
Output	Driver-centred relationship network of the DBE
Roles	--
Related chunk(s)	<<requires>> Model DBE actors – roles and responsibilities

4   Discussion

Considering the complexity of DBEs, the examples of the DBE method process parts and identification of the method chunks shown in Sect. 3 reflect a delicate work of applying such a method in practice. As the overall process of the method based on all the intentions is extensive and requires involvement of many different DBE roles, we envision that a catalogue should be used for documenting the modular parts of the overall process (as shown in the examples) and different user roles will either be responsible or participate in these parts. In practice, the organisations or actors playing specific DBE roles (c.f. Sect. 2.3) could be assigned to these parts as either the responsible or the participatory. For example, the actor(s) with the role *Governor* can be assigned as the responsible for the part of the DBE method process for the policies, regulations, and coverage analysis (Fig. 4). This assignment is based upon the responsibility for providing and/or defining normative contexts of a *Governor* in a DBE. At a more detailed level, various working roles (such as modeller, DBE analyst, legal content analyst, lawyer, etc.) can be assigned to the method chunks and strategies as parts of the overall DBE method process. For instance, the *legal expert meeting* strategy being used to achieve *I18 Analyse coverage of policies and regulations on all actors* in Fig. 4 can be assigned to working roles, e.g., legal content analyst and industrial lawyer.

Due to the complexity of the overall process of the DBE method, the application of the method to design, analyse, and manage a DBE is likely to be a compound and sizeable project. Whether the project should be a single one steered by one organisation or be divided into interconnected small projects steered by various organisations is uncertain. Future work should focus on practical applications of the method to industrial cases in order to validate the best practice.

We presented several elaborated parts of the overall DBE method process. Because of the complexity of DBEs, many of the main concepts related to DBE are interconnected. This means that the dependencies between the intentions are also highly intricate, which makes it difficult to illustrate an overall process of the method in a single Map concerning the word and space limit. Also, the listed strategies (in the examples) and intentions might not be a complete list, which is considered a limitation but also highlight the possibility and advantage of the Map approach as it provides extension mechanisms.

It the current study, we made a preliminary attempt to illustrate the possibility of supporting the modelling of various aspects of DBEs with the variety of method chunks under different situations. Further attempts should focus on the identification of how existing methods support each of the method chunks, especially the product elements. This will lead to a clearer picture of the method chunks not being supported sufficiently by existing methods and the inadequacy of these methods, which, in turns, felicitates creation of new methods using the DBE method process with the SME approach.

5   Conclusions

This study aimed to establish a methodological approach for development of DBE using the Situational Method Engineering methodology, based on a set of empirically elicited requirements from industry experts and practitioners. Using SME and its related Map approach, we have laid the foundations for the method process for the DBE design, analysis, and management method, especially in demonstrating some of the dependencies between the intentions and the possibility of compiling different parts of the overall process of the method. We further presented how each of the strategies for fulfilling the intentions described in the examples would require one or more method chunks specifying how to achieve the target intention. Aside from the ability of reusing method process parts for different DBE development, the method chunks may be reused within the single method process setting.

In the future work, we will continue designing and demonstrating the envisioned holistic process of the DBE method, by further exploring capabilities and fit of existing supporting methods and tools, and validating the method through the practical applications to industrial cases in order to elicit best practices.

References

1. Moore, J.F.: Predators and prey: a new ecology of competition. Harv. Bus. Rev. **71**, 75–86 (1993)
2. Nachira, F., Dini, P., Nicolai, A.: A network of digital business ecosystems for Europe: roots, processes and perspectives. In: Nachira, F., Nicolai, A., Dini, P., Le Louarn, M., Rivera Leon, L. (eds.) Digital Business Ecosystems, pp. 1–20. European Commission, Bruxelles (2007)
3. Senyo, P.K., Liu, K., Effah, J.: Digital business ecosystem: literature review and a framework for future research. Int. J. Inf. Manag. **47**, 52–64 (2019)
4. Senyo, P.K., Liu, K., Effah, J.: Towards a methodology for modelling interdependencies between partners in digital business ecosystems. In: IEEE international conference on logistics, informatics and service sciences (LISS 2017), pp. 1165–1170. IEEE (2017)
5. Persson, A., Stirna, J.: Why enterprise modelling? An explorative study into current practice. In: Dittrich, Klaus R., Geppert, Andreas, Norrie, Moira C. (eds.) CAiSE 2001. LNCS, vol. 2068, pp. 465–468. Springer, Heidelberg (2001). https://doi.org/10.1007/3-540-45341-5_31
6. Pittl, B., Bork, D.: Modeling digital enterprise ecosystems with ArchiMate: a mobility provision case study. In: 5th International Conference on Serviceology for Services, ICServ 2017, pp. 178–189 (2017)
7. Tsai, C., Zdravkovic, J., Stirna, J.: Requirements for a digital business ecosystem modelling method: an interview study with experts and practitioners. In: Buchmann, Robert Andrei, Polini, Andrea, Johansson, Björn., Karagiannis, Dimitris (eds.) BIR 2021. LNBIP, vol. 430, pp. 236–252. Springer, Cham (2021). https://doi.org/10.1007/978-3-030-87205-2_16
8. Henderson-Sellers, B., Ralyté, J., Ågerfalk, P.J., Rossi, M.: Situational Method Engineering. Springer, Heidelberg (2014). https://doi.org/10.1007/978-3-642-41467-1
9. Aldea, A., Kusumaningrum, M.C., Iacob, M.E., Daneva, M.: Modeling and analyzing digital business ecosystems: An approach and evaluation. In: 20th IEEE International Conference on Business Informatics, CBI 2018, pp. 156–163. Institute of Electrical and Electronics Engineers Inc. (2018)
10. Battistella, C., Colucci, K., Nonino, F.: Methodology of business ecosystems network analysis: A field study in telecom italia future centre. In: De Marco, M., Te'eni, D., Albano, V., Za, S. (eds.) Information Systems: Crossroads for Organization, Management, Accounting and Engineering: ItAIS: The Italian Association for Information Systems, pp. 239–249. Physica, Heidelberg (2012)
11. Mirbel, I., Ralyté, J.: Situational method engineering: combining assembly-based and roadmap-driven approaches. Requirements Eng. **11**, 58–78 (2006)

12. Ralyté, J., Rolland, C.: An approach for method reengineering. In: S.Kunii, Hideko, Jajodia, Sushil, Sølvberg, Arne (eds.) ER 2001. LNCS, vol. 2224, pp. 471–484. Springer, Heidelberg (2001). https://doi.org/10.1007/3-540-45581-7_35

13. Kheir, A., Naja, H., Oussalah, M., Tout, K.: Overview of an approach describing multi-views/multi-abstraction levels software architecture. In: ENASE 2013 - Proceedings of the 8th International Conference on Evaluation of Novel Approaches to Software Engineering (2013)

14. Frank, U.: Multi-perspective enterprise modeling: foundational concepts, prospects and future research challenges. Softw. Syst. Model. **13**(3), 941–962 (2012). https://doi.org/10.1007/s10 270-012-0273-9

15. Bork, D., Buchmann, R., Karagiannis, D.: Preserving multi-view consistency in diagrammatic knowledge representation. In: Zhang, Songmao, Wirsing, Martin, Zhang, Zili (eds.) KSEM 2015. LNCS (LNAI), vol. 9403, pp. 177–182. Springer, Cham (2015). https://doi.org/10. 1007/978-3-319-25159-2_16

16. Bork, D., Karagiannis, D.: Model-driven development of multi-view modelling tools the muviemot approach. In: 2014 9th International Conference on Software Paradigm Trends (ICSOFT-PT), pp. IS-11-IS-23. IEEE (2014)

17. Tsai, C.H., Zdravkovic, J.: A survey of roles and responsibilities in digital business ecosystems. In: Proceedings of the Forum at Practice of Enterprise Modeling 2020 co-located with the 13th IFIP WG Working Conference on the Practice of Enterprise Modeling (PoEM 2020) CEUR Workshop Proceedings, pp. 44–53 (2020)

18. del Rıo-Ortega, A., Resinas, M., Ruiz-Cortés, A.: Towards modelling and tracing key performance indicators in business processes. II Taller sobre Procesos de Negocio e Ingeniería de Servicios. PNIS (2009)

19. Selznick, P.: Focusing organisational research on regulation. In: Noll, R.G. (ed.) Regulatory Policy and the Social Sciences, pp. 363–364. University of California Press, Berkeley (1985)

20. Sandkuhl, K., Stirna, J., Persson, A., Wißotzki, M.: Enterprise Modeling [Elektronisk resurs] Tackling Business Challenges with the 4EM Method. Springer, Heidelberg (2014). https:// doi.org/10.1007/978-3-662-43725-4

21. Yu, E.S.K.: Towards modelling and reasoning support for early-phase requirements engineering. In: Proceedings of ISRE '97: 3rd IEEE International Symposium on Requirements Engineering, pp. 226–235 (1997)

22. Tsai, C., Zdravkovic, J., Stirna, J.: Capability management of digital business ecosystems – a case of resilience modeling in the healthcare domain. In: Herbaut, Nicolas, La Rosa, Marcello (eds.) CAiSE 2020. LNBIP, vol. 386, pp. 126–137. Springer, Cham (2020). https://doi.org/ 10.1007/978-3-030-58135-0_11

23. Giesecke, R.: The electric mobility business ecosystem. In: 2014 Ninth International Conference on Ecological Vehicles and Renewable Energies (EVER), pp. 1–13 (2014)

24. Senyo, P., Liu, K., Effah, J.: Understanding behaviour patterns of multi-agents in digital business ecosystems: an organisational semiotics inspired framework. In: Kantola, Jussi Ilari, Nazir, Salman, Barath, Tibor (eds.) AHFE 2018. AISC, vol. 783, pp. 206–217. Springer, Cham (2019). https://doi.org/10.1007/978-3-319-94709-9_21

25. Weill, P., Woerner, S.: What's Your Digital Business Model?: Six Questions to Help You Build the Next-Generation Enterprise. Harvard Business Press (2018)

26. Wieringa, R.J., Engelsman, W., Gordijn, J., Ionita, D.: A business ecosystem architecture modeling framework. In: 2019 IEEE 21st Conference on Business Informatics (CBI), pp. 147–156 (2019)

27. Basole, R.C., Srinivasan, A., Park, H., Patel, S.: ecoxight: discovery, exploration, and analysis of business ecosystems using interactive visualization. ACM Trans. Manage. Inf. Syst. **9**, Article 6 (2018)

28. Faber, A.: Towards a visual language approach for modeling business ecosystems. In: PoEM Doctoral Consortium, pp. 1–8 (2017)
29. Faber, A., Rehm, S.-V., Hernandez-Mendez, A., Matthes, F.: Modeling and visualizing smart city mobility business ecosystems: insights from a case study. Information 9, 270 (2018)
30. Zdravkovic, J., Stirna, J.: Towards data-driven capability interface. IFAC-PapersOnLine 52, 1126–1131 (2019)
31. Faber, A., Hernandez-Mendez, A., Rehm, S.-V., Matthes, F.: Visualizing business ecosystems: applying a collaborative modelling process in two case studies (2018)
32. Rehm, S.-V., Goel, L.: Using information systems to achieve complementarity in SME innovation networks. Inf. Manag. 54, 438–451 (2017)
33. Repenning, N.P.: A simulation-based approach to understanding the dynamics of innovation implementation. Organ. Sci 13, 109–127 (2002)
34. Windrum, P.: Simulation models of technological innovation. Am. Behav. Sci. 42, 1531–1550 (1999)

Business Process Modeling
and Management

Design Guidelines to Derive an e^3value Business Model from a BPMN Process Model in the Financial Securities Sector

Isaac da Silva Torres[1,3]($\boxtimes$), Marcelo Fantinato[2], Gabriela Musse Branco[3], and Jaap Gordijn[1]

[1] Vrije Universiteit, 1081 Amsterdam, HV, The Netherlands
{i.dasilvatorres,j.gordijn}@vu.nl
[2] Universidade de Sao Paulo, São Paulo, SP 03828-000, Brazil
m.fantinato@usp.br
[3] Universidade Federal do Rio Grande do Sul, Porto Alegre, RS 90040-060, Brazil
gabriela.branco@proplan.ufrgs.br

Abstract. Process models, e.g. BPMN models may represent how companies in an ecosystem interact with each other. However, the business model of the same ecosystem, e.g. expressed by an e^3value model, is often left implicit. This hinders the proper analysis of the ecosystem at the business level, and more specifically financial assessment, for which process models are less appropriate. Therefore, the question is if we can somehow derive e^3value models from BPMN models. This would not only allow for proper business model analysis but would also facilitate business model mining, similar to the success of process mining. However, although an e^3value model and BPMN model represent the same ecosystem, their perspectives differ significantly. Therefore an automated derivation of an e^3value model from a BPMN seems not to be feasible, but we can assist the e^3value model designer with practical guidelines. We illustrate our guidelines by means of a case study about financial securities trading.

Keywords: Ecosystems · Business model · Process model · e^3value · BPMN

1 Introduction

Trading of financial securities requires a complex ecosystem. Following Moore [10], we define an ecosystem as a collection of companies, institutions and end users that work cooperatively and competitively to satisfy customer needs. In the securities-trade ecosystem, investors, either as buyer or seller, play a role, as well as brokers, exchange markets, custodians, clearing houses, and the central clearing counterparts (CCPs).

To redesign the financial securities ecosystem, e.g. stimulated by disruptive technology such as blockchain, we argue that at least two perspectives of the

© IFIP International Federation for Information Processing 2021
Published by Springer Nature Switzerland AG 2021
E. Serral et al. (Eds.): PoEM 2021, LNBIP 432, pp. 153–167, 2021.
https://doi.org/10.1007/978-3-030-91279-6_11

ecosystem should be revisited: (1) the process perspective (e.g. represented by a BPMN model), and (2) the business perspective (e.g. depicted by an e^3value model). Although both perspectives differ significantly, and address different stakeholder concerns, there is also overlap between the two points of view. Often, in particular in case of redesign, there is already an understanding of the processes involved. However, the business model is in many cases left implicit.

The question is whether we can derive and/or redesign the business model based on a given process model. We argue that both models are too different to allow for such automatic translation (see e.g. [4] for important differences). Therefore, we propose a design-oriented approach, e.g. in [8], we have presented a method using intermediate models to derive a BMPN model from an e^3value model. This is useful for greenfield situations, that often start with the design of the business model, followed by a process model. In this paper, we are interested in the situation where the processes are already well known, but where the business model is not yet explicit. Such a business model is of use to analyse economic consequences changes in the ecosystem, e.g. as a result of a disruptive technology such as blockchain, and to pave the way for business model mining, similar to process mining.

In this paper, we propose a series of guidelines to derive an e^3value model from a given BPMN model. We test the guidelines by means of a case study in the financial securities trading sector. We develop a process model for the trade of securities, which serves as input, and by iterative application of our guidelines, we derive the corresponding e^3value model. For testing purposes, we also have constructed an e^3value model for the case at hand, just by interviewing the stakeholders, and not by using the guidelines. We then compare the e^3value model derived by solely applying the guidelines with the e^3value model created with the help of the stakeholders, to understand limitations and to improve our guidelines. Conclusions are presented in Sect. 4.

2 Related Work

The relation between process models and value models is the topic of ongoing research. We can characterize this research as *(1)* work investigating the links between process models and value models in general, and *(2)* how to derive a BPMN model from an e^3value model (or the other way around) specifically.

Although both e^3value and BPMN models try to capture an artefact in the real world (e.g. an ecosystem), they do so very differently. In [4], we identified that a BPMN model and e^3value model have very different ontological foundations. To mention a few, actors (in e^3value model) and resource lanes (in BPMN model) might look the same at first sight but are not. Actors are (legal) profit-and-loss responsible entities, whereas resource lanes are parties that execute work. Similarly, a value activity is something an actor executes to create a positive economic value flow (e.g., the total value of the objects flowing out is higher than the value flowing out), whereas a BPMN activity specifies some work to be done, which might have costs only.

In [1], formal consistency rules between coordination models (a kind of process model) and e^3value models are defined. The idea is that value transfers can be matched with a (set of) message flow(s). An e^3value model is, if quantified, an engine that calculates the net value flows based on the number of needs, the number of actors in a market segment, and dependency elements. This gives an indication of whether the e^3value model can be executed in an economically sustainable way by all the actors. As [1] assumes that a value transfer always matches with a (set of) message flow(s), the number of message flows can also be found, e.g., by means of simulation. An e^3value model is then consistent with a process model is the number of times a transfer occurs, corresponds to the occurrence of (a set of) message flows.

In addition to consistency checking, the e^3value model is used to derive other models. Zlatko uses e^3value models to elicit goal models [18]. In [14], the e^3value model is used to find Resource Agent Event (REA) models [9], and later also coordination models, e.g., cf. UN/CEFACT'S Modeling Methodology (UMM) [7] models [13]. Also, [2] examined conceptual representations (e^3value, UML class diagram) in context of value models and their impact to business processes while analyzing and evaluating the expressiveness in terms of ontologic coverage and overlap. The authors refer to the ability to transform the concepts of value models to the process level, not as an overall evaluation, but the proof of appropriateness of value modelling grammars to their potential of an enhanced user understanding. With that in mind, we call attention to the value object, a distinction should be made between the *ownership* of the product and the logistic transfer [12]. For e^3value model, the transfer of ownership is of interest (or the right to enjoy the outcome of a service), whereas the process model focuses on the flow of possession. Possession means physical access to the object (e.g., to transport it), but not ownership. In [16], this is generalized as a right on a certain resource, e.g., lending a book in a library. We tried to integrate all recent work on how to derive a process model based on an e^3value model in [8]. In brief, the proposed method distinguishes the two important design decisions: *(1)* trust, and *(2)* possession. Trust implies a particular flow, so time ordering of value transfers and the corresponding message flows, for example, whether a buyer has to pay first and then obtains his product, or the other way around. The notion of 'physical possession' is important, e.g., because a logistic provider needs to possess an object for a while in order to physically deliver a product to the customer.

As can be observed, quite some work was done on how to derive a process model given a value model, the opposite is not the case. As many (larger) companies have explicit process models, deriving value models from them is a logical next step, e.g., to do 'value-mining', as opposed to process mining. In this paper, we propose a set of guidelines how to do so. For this paper, we assume that the reader is familiar with both BPMN and e^3value. In [3] and [5], tutorials can be found on BPMN and e^3value respectively.

3   Technical Action Research: A Research Instrument for Design Science

Our research goal is to support the derivation of an $e^3 value$ model from a given BPMN model using *design guidelines*. We consider the development of a business model as a design problem, and hence we consider our research as an instance of Design Science [6]. More specifically, we want to learn how, and if, our guidelines work in practice, which is specific for Technical Action Research (TAR) (see e.g. [17]) which we apply (see Fig. 1). The specific case we consider is about trade of financial securities. To understand the problem domain, we have worked with persons affiliated with the Dutch National Bank (De Nederlandsche Bank - DNB).

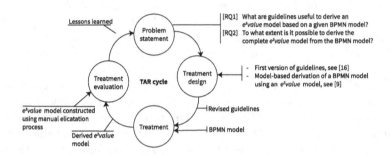

Fig. 1. Research design

We start the TAR cycle with articulating two research questions, which are about guidelines to derive an $e^3 value$ model from a BPMN model. We redesign an earlier developed treatment [15] that results in a set of revised guidelines. The revised guidelines are based on guidelines we have found as a result of an earlier TAR cycle (see [15]) and on work to derive a BPMN model from an $e^3 value$ model [8]; precisely the other way around. After treatment design, we design a BPMN process for the trade of securities using the standard practices for process model design. This process design is not part of the TAR cycle; how to design the BPMN model is not part of our research question, but serves as an input to derive an $e^3 value$ model from. This BPMN model is constructed in cooperation with domain experts. In the treatment step, we apply the revised guidelines on the found BPMN model. We also construct an $e^3 value$ model for the trade of financial securities using the normal practices to design an $e^3 value$ model for validation purposes. Again, the design of this $e^3 value$ model is not part of the TAR cycle. Finally, in the treatment evaluation step, we compare the *derived* $e^3 value$ model by using the guidelines, with the $e^3 value$ model we constructed using the *normal* method to design an $e^3 value$ model, and we compare them. Using differential analysis, we formulate lessons learned that can be used to improve the guidelines.

3.1 Problem Statement

Development of any ICT-enabled ecosystem requires many viewpoints. This also holds for the ecosystem of financial securities. Two of those viewpoints are the business model perspective and the cross-organizational business process, each with their own concerns. In this paper, we use for the business model the e^3 value language and for the process model BPMN. Although there is overlap between both languages, there are also substantial differences. To mention a few, e^3 value has the notion of *economic reciprocity* and supplier/customer side *bundling*. These concepts are not present in BPMN. Conversely, BPMN represents the time ordering in which activities take place, whereas e^3 value represents only causal dependencies. For ecosystem (re)design, both an e^3 value model and a BPMN model are useful. Since both models have some overlap, it is perhaps possible to derive the one model from the other. In [8], we derive a BPMN model from an e^3 value. This is useful in case of *new* ecosystem development, which often starts with the design of the e^3 value model.

In this paper, we propose to use *designed guidelines* to derive an e^3 value model based on a process model. This is particular useful in case of existing ecosystems, where (part of) the BPMN model is already available. This leads to the following research questions:

RQ1 What guidelines are useful to derive an e^3 value model based on a given BPMN model?

RQ2 To what extent is it possible to derive the complete e^3 value model from the BPMN model?

3.2 Treatment Design: From Process Model to Value Model

This research is based on our previous work [15], which resulted in a set of preliminary guidelines. We revised this set of guidelines, which is summarized in Table 1. Note that the guidelines indicate *conditional* correspondence between the BPMN- and e^3 value model by means of the verb 'may'. We explain these conditions per guideline explicitly.

G1 *BPMN start/end events may correspond to* e³value *consumer needs and boundary elements.*

  Description. A start event may result in a consumer need or boundary element in e^3 value. The same holds for the end event.

  Conditions. There are two conditions that should be satisfied for a correspondence.

  1. A customer need is a lack of something valuable that the actor wants to acquire [5]. A boundary element scopes an e^3 value model [5], e.g. the boundary of value transfers. Consequently, for correspondence, an event should either relate to something of value an actor wants, or should mark that no further value transfers occur. Many BPMN events are not related to customer value creation at all, but rather focus on operational aspects only (e.g. trigger an administrative process, such as sending a bill). Such events do not have a direct counterpart in e^3 value.

Table 1. Guidelines – from BPMN model to $e^3 value$ model

ID	BPMN element	$e^3 value$ element	Guideline description
G1	Start event End event	Consumer need Boundary element	BPMN start/end events may correspond to $e^3 value$ consumer needs and boundary elements.
G2	Pool	Actor Market segment	BPMN pools may correspond to $e^3 value$ actors or market segments.
G3	Lane 1 Lane 2	Value activity	BPMN lanes may correspond to $e^3 value$ value activities.
G4	Activity Subprocess	Value activity	BPMN activities and sub-processes may correspond to $e^3 value$ value activities.
G5	Message flow	Value transfer	BPMN message flows may correspond to $e^3 value$ value transfers.
G6	Activity Sequence flow Subprocess	Value transfer	BPMN activities and sub-processes and their sequence flows may correspond to $e^3 value$ value transfers.
G7	Message flow Sequence flow	Value interface	Following a BPMN sequence/message flow may lead to an $e^3 value$ value interface.
G8	Message flow Sequence flow	Value offering	Following a BPMN sequence/message flow may lead to an $e^3 value$ value offerings.
G9	Message flow Sequence flow	Dependency path	Following a BPMN sequence/message flow may lead to an $e^3 value$ dependency path.
G10	AND Gateway	AND dependency	BPMN AND gateways may correspond to $e^3 value$ AND dependencies.
G11	XOR Gateway	OR dependency	BPMN XOR gateways may correspond to $e^3 value$ OR dependencies.
G12	OR Gateway	AND dependency OR dependency	BPMN OR gateways may correspond to a combination of $e^3 value$ AND/OR dependencies.
G13	Loop	Cardinality dependency	BPMN loops may correspond to $e^3 value$ cardinality dependencies.

2. A start event may map onto a customer need *or* a boundary element. The same applies to the end event. A sequence flow in BPMN represents *time-ordering*, whereas in $e^3 value$ a dependency path represents *causal dependencies*. For example, a book store's start event may trigger ordering of a book at a publisher, followed by delivery, displaying the books, and finally selling the books, concluded by an end event. In $e^3 value$ however, the end event (representing the sale) would map onto a customer need, whereas the start event translates into an $e^3 value$ boundary element. Note that in case of an electronic book store (e.g. Amazon) the opposite happens in terms of BPMN: first selling, then printing, and finally distributing.

G2 *BPMN pools may correspond to* e³value *actors or market segments.*

Description. Pools in BPMN map one-to-one onto to actors or market segments in e^3*value*.

Conditions. There are two conditions that should be satisfied for a correspondence.

1. Following the definitions in e^3*value*, pools can only be mapped into actors if they are capable of taking their own economical and legal decisions. Sometimes, in BPMN pools are distinguished to represent resources capable of doing work but do not make their own economic and legal decisions. Then the pool can not be mapped, but perhaps the supervising agent for that pool can.

2. While considering a pool, one party (e.g. a single company) can be associated with the pool, or there can be more than one (possibly alternative) agent. In the first case, the pool results in an e^3*value* actor, in the second case the pool corresponds to a market segment.

G3 *BPMN lanes may correspond to* e³value *value activities.*

Description. Lanes in BPMN can model a role that a certain entity performs. The value activity construct in e^3*value* comes semantically closest to the notion of role.

Conditions. In e^3*value*, a value activity requires that at least one party should be able to generate a net cash flow by executing the activity. In BPMN, a lane represents a collection of activities and their sequence flow, which may result in a net cash flow. However, in BPMN a lane may only result in expenses. In such a case, a lane can not be mapped on a value activity.

G4 *BPMN activities and sub-processes may correspond to* e³value *value activities.*

Description. This guideline is actually a refinement of guideline G3. Rather than considering a full lane, now the focus on a subset of BMPN activities and/or activities (e.g. in a pool), and their sequence flow.

Conditions. Although one activity in BPMN may correspond to precisely one value activity in e^3*value*, the relation is often n-to-one. e.g. a combination of BPMN the activities result into one e^3*value* activity. Similarly, the condition of G3 applies.

G5 *BPMN message flow may correspond to* e³value *value transfers.*

Description. In BPMN, message flows between pools transfer 'content of communication' [11] (pg. 93). In e^3*value*, a value transfer is a transfer of ownership, the right to enjoy a service outcome, or even a valuable experience, collectively called value objects. So, ontologically, message flows in BPMN are very different from value transfers in e^3*value*.

Conditions. There are three conditions that should be satisfied for a correspondence.

1. In e^3*value*, a value object requires that it is (1) of economic value for at least one actor and (2) satisfies a need directly or indirectly (through another value object) [5]. For correspondence, the *object* transferred via a BMPN message flow in BPMN should qualify as an vlaue value object in

e^3 *value*. Often, this is not the situation, e.g. a 'bill' does not correspond to a value object directly (but the subject of the bill does).

2. There is correspondence if the message flow represents a transfer of *ownership* (see e.g. [8, 12]), or the right to enjoy the outcome of a service. In BPMN models, often the flow only transfers *possession*. We interpret 'possession' as the right to have physical *access* to an object, but not necessarily to *use* that object. E.g. a logistic provider needs to have access to book for transportation, but may not use/read the book. Ownership does not necessarily imply physical possession; e.g. oil is transferred many times to a new owner (while transported), without having the owner ever seen the oil physically.

3. A value transfer in e^3 *value* denotes the *willingness* of actors to transfer ownership [5]. Usually, an actor is only willing to transfer ownership (e.g. of a book) if there is a *reciprocal* transfer (e.g. of money). Message flows in a BPMN model corresponding to a reciprocal value transfer in e^3 *value* often can not be easily identified but are a required condition. See also guideline G7.

G6 *BPMN activities and sub-processes and their sequence flows may correspond to* e^3value *value transfers.*

Description. In some cases, a part of a BPMN model executed by a pool, e.g. a series of activities and sub-processes elements as well as their sequence flows, can be seen as a commercial service for which someone is willing to pay. This results in at least one value transfer representing the service outcome, and one reciprocal value transfer, e.g. a payment. Value transfers representing service outcomes by executing activities often do not have corresponding message flows, and only can be found by understanding the semantics of the activities and sequence flows in the BPMN model.

Conditions. The part of the BMPN model that may result in a value transfer should produce a service outcome for which at least one actor, market segment, or value activity wants to pay.

G7 *Following a BPMN sequence/message flow may lead to an* e^3value *value interface.*

Description. By following the sequence flow, and the associated message flow(s), a value interface can be found. In e^3 *value*, a value interface consists of value ports, and value offerings and are connected by means of value transfers. A value interface models *atomicity*: *all* value transfers connected to a value interface should transfer their corresponding value object or none at all. Also, the value interface models *economic reciprocity* as an interface should have at least one ingoing value transfer and at least one outgoing value transfer. BPMN does not have a construct to express economic reciprocity. However, the sequence flow can be followed and all resulting message flows can be listed. These flows are candidates for a (reciprocal) value transfers and hence value interfaces.

Conditions. There are two conditions that should be satisfied for a correspondence.

1. The found message flows that are candidate for triggering the creating of a value interface need to correspond to one or more value transfers (see guideline G5).

2. A value interface represents that an actor is *willing* to exchange an ingoing value object (e.g. a product) for an outgoing value object (e.g. a payment). Consequently, the transfers implied by the found message flows should be reciprocal, meaning that the object of the one transfers serves as an *economic compensation* for the object of the other transfer.

G8 *Following a BPMN sequence/message flow may lead to an* e^3value *value offerings.*

Description. By following the sequence flow, and the associated message flow(s), one or more value offerings can be found. In e^3value, a value offering groups all equally directed value ports in a value interface, and models *bundling*, e.g. a McDonalds Happy Meal consisting of various products. The sequence flow may indicate that multiple message flows should occur, for example by using an AND gateway.

Conditions. There are two conditions that should be satisfied for a correspondence.

1. The found message flows that are candidate for triggering the creation of a value offering need to correspond to one or more value transfers (see guideline G5).

2. A value offering represents *economic bundling*. The message flows corresponding to the transfers grouped into a value offering should *all* happen as a result of the execution of the sequence flow.

G9 *Following a BPMN sequence/message flow may lead to an* e^3value *dependency path.*

Description. By following the BPMN sequence flow, reciprocal value transfers can be found (see guideline G6), but also dependent value transfers and/or fragments of an e^3value dependency path. In e^3value, the dependency path relates dependency elements (customer need, boundary element, value interfaces, AND-, OR- and cardinality dependencies, leading to the more specific guidelines G9, G10, G11, G12 and G13 respectively)

Conditions. There are two conditions that should be satisfied for a correspondence.

1. The sequence flow should have as start point(s) a start event (guideline G1), or a message flow that results in value transfer (guideline G5), and should have as end point(s) an end event (guideline G1) or a message flow that results in value transfer (guideline G5).

2. Dependency paths are always restricted to a single actor, market segment or value activities.

G10 *BPMN AND gateway may lead to an* e^3value *AND dependency.*

Description. By following the BPMN sequence flow, AND gateways can be encountered. In e^3value, the AND dependency has similar semantics as the AND gateway in BPMN. An AND dependency *fork* spans off outgoing dependency paths that happen precisely the same number of times as the incoming dependency path. Similarly, an AND dependency *join* represents that the incoming paths to the AND dependency join should happen the same number of times.

Conditions. AND gateways result only in AND dependency elements if they influence the number of times the corresponding dependency path is executed. Often, a BPMN model contains more detail, needed to specify to process. Some of the AND gateways are part of the more detailed model and do not affect the number of times an e^3value path is executed.

G11 *BPMN XOR gateways may correspond to* e³value *OR dependencies.*

Description. By following the BPMN sequence flow, XOR gateways can be encountered. In e^3value, the OR dependency has similar semantics as the XOR gateway in BPMN. In e^3value, and OR dependency is evaluated per execution of the dependency path, and the selection of a particular disjunct is based on a (probability) distribution. This corresponds to the XOR gateway that makes a selection between disjuncts to decide which sequence flow to follow.

Conditions. See guideline G10.

G12 *BPMN OR gateways may correspond to a combination of* e³value *AND/OR dependencies.*

Description. By following the BPMN sequence flow, OR gateways can be encountered. In e^3value, there is not a direct related construct. Instead, the semantics of the OR gateway (one or more sequence flows connected to disjoints of the gateway continue) should be simulated. This is possible but does not lead to an elegant e^3value model. This should be solved by having an explicit OR and XOR dependency element in e^3value, which is subject of further research.

Conditions. See guideline G10.

G13 *BPMN loops may correspond to* e³value *cardinality dependencies.*

Description. A BPMN model may contain repetition (loops) in the sequence flow. Essentially, a BPMN model can be considered as a *cyclic* directed graph. An e^3value model however is an *acyclic* directed graph, e.g. it may not contain loops. Consequently, repetition in BPMN can not be mapped in e^3value directly. However, e^3value has the cardinality dependency, resulting in the execution of the dependee (dependency path) a number (n) of times, given the number of times (m) the dependent dependency path is executed. With the cardinality dependency element, the effect of a loop in BPMN can be simulated, e.g. by mapping out all loop executions explicitly. **Conditions.** See guideline G10.

3.3   Treatment: Trading of Financial Securities

Based on a BPMN model (Fig. 2), we derive an e^3value for the financial trade of securities in The Netherlands. To construct and validate the BPMN model, we have consulted experts affiliated with the Dutch National Bank (De Nederlandsche Bank - DNB). The construction of the BPMN model is outside the scope of the treatment, and is done via a normal knowledge acquisition process.

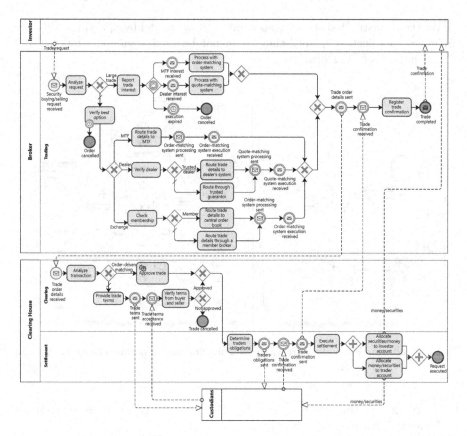

Fig. 2. BPMN model of securities trading

We briefly summarize the BPMN model. The process start with Investor(s) placing an order request (to buy/sell) for securities with brokers. Orders can be placed either as market orders (buy/sell at market price) or limit orders (buy/sell for a minimum/maximum price). For each case, the broker analyzes the best course of action, e.g. based on the size of the trade. After matching (left implicit in this model), the order details are sent for clearing and settlement. Every investor engages the services of a custodian to assist them in clearing and settlement activities. The Clearing House(CH)/Central Clearing Counterparty (CCP) is an entity that takes the credit risk between parties and provides clearing and settlement services for trades. CCPs calculates and informs the members of what their obligations are on the funds side (cash) and on the securities side. After the clearing corporation informs all members of their obligations, the clearing members should make available their securities (shares and money). Finally, settlement takes place. Payments are done and investors have their securities in their demat account.

We then constructed the corresponding e^3value model by applying solely the guidelines (see Sect. 3.2) until they could not be used anymore. The resulting e^3value model is in Fig. 3(a).

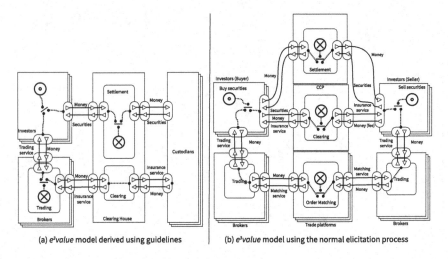

(a) e^3value model derived using guidelines   (b) e^3value model using the normal elicitation process

Fig. 3. e^3value models derived by using the guidelines and a normal elicitation process

1. G2 results in the actor - 'Clearing House', and the market segments - 'Investors', 'Brokers' and 'Custodians'.
2. G3 brings value activities with the same names as the lanes.
3. With guideline G4, we can not find additional value activities.
4. According to G1, the start event 'Request to buy/sell securities' represents a consumer need in the e^3value model. The second start event 'Trade Details', serves as an operational input to and does not satisfy condition 1 of guideline G1. Two of the five end events relate directly to economic effects: 'Trade completed' and 'Request executed' and result in boundary elements in their respective value activities ('trading' and 'settlement'). The other events indicate only non-approvals or dead-ends.
5. Guidelines G9, G10, G11, G12 and G13 discover dependency elements. The AND gateway after the activity 'Execute settlement' results in an AND dependency in the settlement value activity (G10). None of the other gateways influence the number of times a dependency path occurs and hence G11/G12/G13 do not apply.
6. With G9, the start event 'Request to buy/sell securities' has as an end event and a message flow that results in value transfer ('money/securities). This results in a dependency for the consumer need (buy securities). Also, because the BPMN model shows the custodians as a black pool, a lot of information is missed and some dependencies are disconnected.

7. G5, G6, G7 and G8 are used to discover value transfers, value interfaces and value offerings. G5 checks all the message flows in the BPMN for potential value object transfers. In BPMN, economic reciprocity is not a concept present and so what comes back of economic value is usually hidden. e.g. to satisfy the 'trade request', the investor likely has to pay a fee (money) (G6). There are explicit value transfers between the 'custodians' and 'investors' with the 'clearing house' (via the value activity 'settlement'). Unfortunately with G8, the relation was not found.

3.4   Treatment Evaluation

Observations Extracted from the Case. For validation purposes, we construct the e^3value model, called the normative model (Fig. 3(b)), using the normal e^3value elicitation process, so without taking the BPMN model into consideration. Again, the model is validated by experts from the DNB, and is briefly explained below. There are two 'Investors' market segments with the consumer need 'Buy securities' (Buyer) and 'Sell Securities' (Seller). Both 'Investors' market segment use (optionally) 'Brokers' for trading service and they use also a custodian (bank) to real-time check their valuables (optionality is not represented). The 'custodians' are also removed since investors do have a bank to store their financial means. The trade is then submitted to a 'Trade Platform' who performs 'Order Matching' of buyers and sellers. The 'Trade Platforms' are e.g. a Multilateral trading facility (MTF), an Exchange, etc. The 'Clearing' is performed by the CCP to protect against a defaulting buyer or seller. 'Settlement' is done to make the trading executable, which is performed by the Central Security Depository (CSD).

After a differential analysis between both e^3value models (Fig. 3(a) and (b)), we observe the following.

1. In Fig. 3, the 'Clearing House' actor (a) in reality are two parties: CCP and CSD (b). Still the same value activities (clearing and settlement) are performed. This is not due to the guidelines, but a result of the granularity of the earlier made BPMN model.
2. The market segment 'Trade Platforms' is according to the experts important and was not found in the BPMN model, but not considered relevant at that time. Perhaps taking a business model perspective stimulates experts to bring up the platforms. Again, omission in the derived e^3value model is not caused by the guidelines.
3. The market segment 'Custodians' is present in the derived model, but not in the model constructed in a session with the experts. The experts put forward that in traditional process descriptions, the custodian is still mentioned due to historic reasons but in practice they do not play a significant role anymore.
4. The AND dependency and boundary element in 'Trading' is moved to 'Order matching' to represent matching, which is a best practice in e^3value.
5. Both e^3value models are semantically correct and illustrate properly the real-world scenario of the case. However, the model based only on the guidelines

missed some important information due to the fact that the BPMN model failed to report it.

Limitations. The differential analysis has some limitations: Both the e^3value model as derived by the guidelines and the normative e^3value as elicited by using the conventional model elicitation process are executed by ourselves. By doing the model elicitation process, we obtained knowledge about the e^3value model which may influence the application of the guidelines to find the e^3value model using the set of guidelines. We tried to mitigate this bias by strictly applying the guidelines only. In follow up research, we want to separate the construction of the normative e^3value model and the construction of the e^3value model based on the guidelines by using a separate group of persons applying the guidelines. Also, our evaluation did not consider the time and cognitive load needed, which would show the practicability and usability of the method in real-world settings.

4   Conclusion

Revisiting our research questions, we have presented and used guidelines to derive an e^3value model from a BPMN model (RQ1). The model constructed using the normal e^3value process however shows some important differences from the developed by using only the guidelines, most notably the introduction of a new market segment 'Trade platforms'. Although different time frames and researchers were used while constructing both models, this acts as a limitation of our research, which leads to the observation that, before applying the guidelines, it is important to understand the bias taken on, and completeness of the BPMN model itself. All differences can be explained by missing elements in the BPMN model (e.g. to different perspectives taken by the experts, not asking the right questions, etc.) and not by the guidelines themselves. How to test properly the BMPN model for suitability to apply the guidelines is subject of further research. Once solved, more can be said about the completeness of the guidelines (RQ2).

Acknowledgements. The authors are thankful to Menno Broos, Ellen Naudts and Timothy Aerts, affiliated with the De Nederlandsche Bank (DNB), for explaining us how financial securities trading works, and for validating the models we have created. We also extend our thanks to Felix Fueyo for his help with the designed BPMN model.

References

1. Bodenstaff, L.: Managing dependency relations in inter-organizational models. Ph.D. thesis, University of Twente (2010)
2. Buder, J., Felden, C.: Ontological analysis of value models. In: 19th European Conference on Information Systems, ECIS 2011, Helsinki, Finland, 9–11 June 2011, p. 22 (2011)

3. Dumas, M., Rosa, M.L., Mendling, J., Reijers, H.A.: Fundamentals of Business Process Management, 2nd edn. Springer, Heidelberg (2018). https://doi.org/10.1007/978-3-662-56509-4
4. Gordijn, J., Akkermans, H., van Vliet, H.: Business modelling is not process modelling. In: Liddle, S.W., Mayr, H.C., Thalheim, B. (eds.) ER 2000. LNCS, vol. 1921, pp. 40–51. Springer, Heidelberg (2000). https://doi.org/10.1007/3-540-45394-6_5
5. Gordijn, J., Wieringa, R.: E3value User Guide - Designing Your Ecosystem in a Digital World. The Value Engineers, 1st edn. (2021)
6. Hevner, A., March, S., Park, J., Ram, S.: Design science in information systems research. MIS Q. Manag. Inf. Syst. **28**(1), 75–105 (2004)
7. Hofreiter, B., Huemer, C., Liegl, P., Schuster, R., Zapletal, M., et al.: UN/CEFACT'S modeling methodology (UMM): a UML profile for B2B e-commerce. In: Roddick, J.F. (ed.) ER 2006. LNCS, vol. 4231, pp. 19–31. Springer, Heidelberg (2006). https://doi.org/10.1007/11908883_5
8. Hotie, F., Gordijn, J.: Value-based process model design. Bus. Inf. Syst. Eng. **61**(2), 163–180 (2019)
9. McCarthy, W.E.: The REA accounting model: a generalized framework for accounting systems in a shared data environment. Account. Rev. **58**(3), 554–578 (1982)
10. Moore, J.F.: The Death of Competition: Leadership and Strategy in the Age of Business Ecosystems. HarperBusiness, New York (1996)
11. OMG: Business process model and notation, version 2.0 (2011). https://www.omg.org/spec/BPMN/2.0, Object Management Group (OMG)
12. Pijpers, V., Gordijn, J.: Bridging business value models and business process models in aviation value webs via possession rights. In: 20th Annual Hawaii International Conference on System Sciences (2007)
13. Schuster, R.: Requirements management for B2B processes: a worksheet driven approach from e3-value and REA to UMM. Ph.D. thesis, Vienna University of Technology (2010)
14. Schuster, R., Motal, T.: From e3-value to REA: modeling multi-party E-business collaborations. In: IEEE Conference on Commerce and Enterprise Computing, pp. 202–208 (2009)
15. Torres, I.S., Gordijn, J., Fantinato, M., Vieira, J.F.F.: Designing an ecosystem value model based on a process model – an empirical approach. In: Grabis, J., Bork, D. (eds.) PoEM 2020. LNBIP, vol. 400, pp. 293–303. Springer, Cham (2020). https://doi.org/10.1007/978-3-030-63479-7_20
16. Weigand, H., Johannesson, P., Andersson, B., Bergholtz, M., Edirisuriya, A., Ilayperuma, T.: On the notion of value object. In: Dubois, E., Pohl, K. (eds.) CAiSE 2006. LNCS, vol. 4001, pp. 321–335. Springer, Heidelberg (2006). https://doi.org/10.1007/11767138_22
17. Wieringa, R.J.: Design Science Methodology for Information Systems and Software Engineering. Springer, Heidelberg (2014). https://doi.org/10.1007/978-3-662-43839-8
18. Zlatev, Z.V.: Goal-oriented design of value and process models from patterns. Ph.D. thesis, University of Twente (2007)

Context-Aware Process Modelling for Medicinal Product Development

Zeynep Ozturk Yurt[1]([⊠]), Rik Eshuis[1], Anna Wilbik[2],
and Irene Vanderfeesten[1,3]

[1] Eindhoven University of Technology, Eindhoven, The Netherlands
{z.ozturk.yurt,h.eshuis,i.t.p.vanderfeesten}@tue.nl
[2] Maastricht University, Maastricht, The Netherlands
a.wilbik@maastrichtuniversity.nl
[3] Open Universiteit, Heerlen, The Netherlands

Abstract. Advanced Therapy Medicinal Products (ATMPs) are highly innovative medicinal products that are based on biomedical technology. ATMP development processes need to comply with complex regulatory frameworks. Currently, biomedical scientists that develop ATMPs manage the regulatory aspects of the ATMP development processes in an ad-hoc fashion, resulting in inefficiencies such as rework, or even withdrawal of ATMPs from the market if the regulatory requirements are not adequately addressed. This paper presents an explorative case study in which we investigate enterprise modelling and context-aware business processes to support ATMP scientists in managing the regulatory aspects of ATMP development processes more efficiently and effectively. The main objective of this case study is to offer regulatory-based guidance to scientists. We use enterprise models (domain, goal and process models) to describe the important concepts and views in ATMP development processes. By introducing context-awareness to the models, we enable regulatory-based guidance that supports ATMP scientists in performing relevant tasks to address the regulatory requirements efficiently and effectively.

Keywords: Context-awareness · Enterprise modelling · Business process management · Conceptual modelling

1 Introduction

Advanced Therapy Medicinal products (ATMPs) are medicines for human use that are based on innovative biomedical technologies [1]. Being a medicinal product for human use, ATMPs need to comply with complex regulations about safety and efficacy. Therefore, the two most prominent views in ATMP development processes are scientific development and regulatory compliance. Currently, the ATMP scientists manage regulatory aspects of ATMP development processes in an ad-hoc fashion. Yet, ATMP development processes suffer from inefficiencies

© IFIP International Federation for Information Processing 2021
Published by Springer Nature Switzerland AG 2021
E. Serral et al. (Eds.): PoEM 2021, LNBIP 432, pp. 168–183, 2021.
https://doi.org/10.1007/978-3-030-91279-6_12

such as reworks and withdrawal of ATMPs from market, due to not being able to adequately demonstrate regulatory compliance [10,18].

The cause of this is the complexity of ATMP regulatory framework and scientists' lack of regulatory knowledge and its impact on the scientific development process. ATMP regulations describe high level goals to be achieved in order to make sure that the ATMP being developed is safe and effective. This is done by, for instance, demonstrating physiological and biochemical properties of the product. Also, ATMP regulations are flexible, depending on development setting different regulatory requirements apply. Here, the development setting covers a set of factors related to the ATMP, defined by the scientist e.g., type of materials used, regulatory classification of materials etc. These two factors make the management of regulatory aspects of ATMP development challenging for scientists. Therefore, there is a need to support ATMP scientists in managing the regulatory aspects more efficiently and effectively.

To enable this support, we first need to investigate the ATMP development setting. Enterprise Modelling is an effective approach to capture, understand and relate the elements of a complex setting [20]. Enterprise modelling can support many purposes, for example, strategy development [15], change management [11] or process improvement [14]. In this case study, we use enterprise modelling as the stepping stone to enable more efficient and effective management of ATMP development processes. Using enterprise models such as: domain, goal and process models, we capture, understand and relate the main elements in ATMP development processes in a structured way. Building upon these models, we focus more on process modelling, in order to investigate ways to provide regulatory-based guidance in the scientific development processes.

Context-aware BPM deals with identifying factors that drive flexibility and variability in business processes [19]. Several authors investigated the notion of context for business processes with an aim to identify factors that affect the design and execution of a business process and make business processes context-aware by integrating these factors and their effect to the process models [21]. In this paper, we use the notion of context-awareness in BPM to guide scientists in working more efficiently and effectively towards regulatory compliance.

This paper presents an explorative case study in which context-aware ATMP development processes are modelled. We use enterprise models to describe scientific and regulatory views in ATMP development. To describe the main concepts and their relations in ATMP development, we use a domain model. We represent the scientific development process in a flexible process model and regulatory requirements in a goal model. By introducing context-awareness, we make the link between different regulatory contexts, regulatory requirements and the scientific development process explicit, and guide scientists in performing relevant tasks to address the regulatory requirements. Thereby, this paper presents an exemplary case study for guiding users in flexible and knowledge-intensive processes towards regulatory compliance.

The object of the case study presented in this paper is the biomaterial development process, which is a part of ATMP development processes, from the Horizon2020 iPSpine project[1]. In iPSpine, an ATMP for lower back pain is being developed. As a part of this project, we develop a digital platform to enable efficient and effective management of ATMP development processes. Therefore, this case study is driven by the problems in iPSpine.

The remainder of this paper is organized as follows. Section 2 introduces ATMP development processes and the problem addressed in this case study, and presents the objectives of the case study. Section 3 discusses how the objectives of the case study are addressed. Section 4 presents the preliminary evaluation made with iPSpine stakeholders on the usefulness of models and ideas presented in this paper. Section 5 discusses the relevant work on Context-Aware BPM. Lastly, Sect. 6 concludes the paper.

2   ATMP Development: The Need for Guidance

In this section, we introduce the ATMP development processes and the problem we address in this case study.

2.1   ATMP Development Process

Development of ATMPs involves several stages and the overall aim in these stages is to develop a safe and effective medicinal product. This is accomplished by collaboration of many stakeholders, where scientists and regulatory consultants are the main ones. Figure 1, describes the main phases and stakeholders in ATMP development.

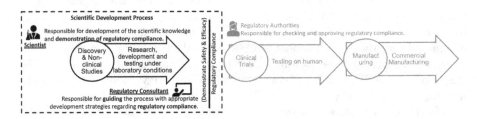

Fig. 1. ATMP development process & stakeholders (stakeholders and scope of this study in bold)

Research shows that ATMP development processes are associated with many hurdles such as reworks and even withdrawal of the ATMP due to shortcomings in providing adequate evidence for regulatory compliance [10]. This contributes to increased development costs and time-to market. Lack of regulatory knowledge among scientists is an important factor for these hurdles [10]. Being an expert, a scientist requires minimal guidance about the scientific aspects of ATMP development. However, establishing and maintaining the link between the scientific

---

[1] https://ipspine.eu/.

development process and the complex regulatory framework of the ATMP development is challenging for a scientist. In other words, there is a need to bridge the gap between the scientific and regulatory views on ATMP development processes. This requires identification and description of important concepts in an ATMP development setting. To do so, we use the conceptual enterprise models. The following section presents these models.

Note that, for demonstration purposes, we use models from a biomaterial development process, which is a part of the ATMP development studies. The models we use in this paper are simplified for readability and space considerations.

2.2   Modelling ATMP Development

Enterprise modelling covers several models [15,26]. Depending on the purpose of the enterprise modelling job, the models used and the level of detail included in the models should change [15].

For this case study, the purpose of modelling is to represent and relate the two most prominent views, regulatory and scientific views, of ATMP development processes. The regulatory view covers the reason or motivation behind performing ATMP development processes, i.e. the aim is to develop a safe and effective (in other words, regulatory compliant) product. The scientific view covers the activities to develop the product. Therefore, goal and process models are essential elements for our purpose. To understand and relate different concepts in these different views, a domain model is also essential.

There are other models used in enterprise modelling. For instance, actor/resource models and business rule models [15], organization and network models [26]. However, we haven't used such models since they do not provide considerable information for our modelling purpose. For example, modelling the different actors/resources and their relations do not provide any implications about the scientific and regulatory views in ATMP development, or modelling the business rules, e.g., some scientific procedures that constraint how experiments should be done, is not within the scope of our modelling purpose.

First, we built a domain model with domain experts, to structure the domain knowledge and understand complex concepts and the problems in the domain. Figure 2 shows the domain model we have created for this case study, using UML class diagrams.

ATMP regulations do not induce strict rules on how things should be done throughout the development process. Instead, they involve high-level goals that should be considered in order to demonstrate that the ATMP being developed is safe and effective. Therefore, we represent the regulatory requirements using goal models. Figure 3 shows an excerpt from the goal model of biomaterial development process in GRL notation [23].

Lastly, we model the scientific development process using flexible process models. ATMP development processes are knowledge-intensive processes. Traditional BPM focuses on managing routine and predictable work. Knowledge-intensive processes have different characteristics [9]. Traditional BPM is limited

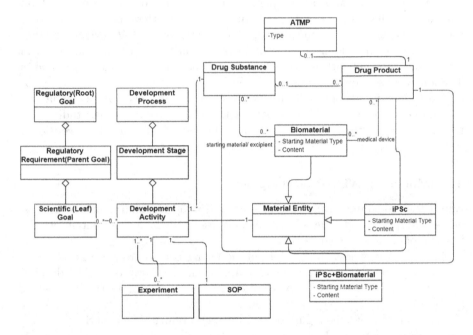

Fig. 2. Domain model of ATMP development

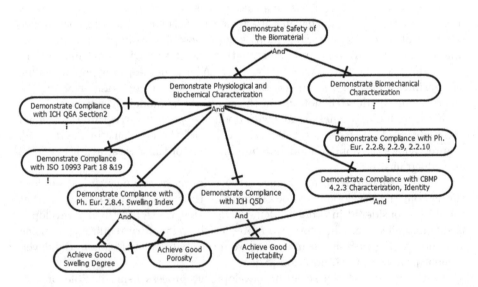

Fig. 3. Goal model of biomaterial development

when it comes to supporting flexible and unpredictable knowledge-intensive processes [9]. Case Management is an approach that recently emerged to overcome these limitations [2,22]. Therefore, we chose to support ATMP development processes with Case Management and, modelled the scientific development process using Case Management Model and Notation (CMMN) [6]. Figure 4 shows an excerpt from the biomaterial development process model.

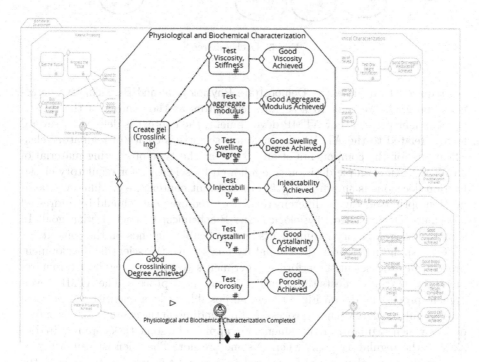

Fig. 4. Process model of biomaterial development

A top-down analysis of regulatory goals results in a goal model where the leaf goals are satisfiable by means of sub-processes or tasks in the process model. This way, we build a link between the regulatory goals and the scientific development process. Each leaf goal in the goal model corresponds to a milestone of a single task or sub-process in the process model. The milestones corresponding to the leaf goals have the same labels as the goals.

2.3 The Need for Guidance

Looking at the goal model in Fig. 3, we see that there is a set of sub-goals that are required to achieve Demonstrate Physiological and Biochemical Characterization goal.

Indeed, some factors related to the development process and the ATMP being developed determine which of the sub-goals (regulatory requirements)

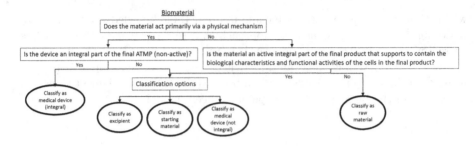

Fig. 5. Decision tree

are required to achieve the Demonstrate Physiological and Biochemical Characterization goal. We refer to a set of such factors as the context of the ATMP development process. For ATMP development, the context is defined by several factors related to the ATMP. For instance, scientist's choice of regulatory classifications for the components of an ATMP or the type of starting material of an ATMP. An example decision tree followed by scientists for regulatory classification decisions is shown in Fig. 5. For different contexts, e.g., different classification options in Fig. 5, different regulatory requirements should be addressed to achieve Demonstrate Physiological and Biochemical Characterization goal. In short, which regulatory requirements are applicable depends on the context.

Correspondingly, since the regulatory goals drive the scientific development process, i.e. the scientist performs experiments to address regulatory requirements, context also affects the scientific development process. The ATMP development process model on Fig. 4 covers all possible tasks a scientist can perform throughout the development process. Yet depending on the context, since context defines which regulatory requirements are applicable, some tasks are required to address the regulatory goals whereas some are not. The scientist can still perform other tasks that are not required to address the regulatory goals of the current context, for instance, out of scientific interest or to explore alternative contexts (See Fig. 5).

The scientist starts the process with an initial assumption on the context. However, the context is subject to changes throughout the development process. For example, different options (e.g., classifying the biomaterial as medical device or excipient) are investigated throughout the development. Depending on the results the scientist obtains throughout the process, she can decide to, for instance, classify the biomaterial as a medical device instead of as an excipient, following the decision tree in Fig. 5. This would change the context, regulatory goals to be addressed and hence the tasks to be executed to address relevant regulatory requirements. To ensure that the scientists performs the relevant tasks that addresses the relevant regulatory requirements, it is important to make explicit on the process model which tasks are required under which conditions (context).

In this case study, we intend to address the need of regulatory guidance in ATMP development processes. As a result of an analysis of literature on manag-

Table 1. Objectives of the case study

Main objective	Guide the scientists performing the scientific development process towards relevant regulatory goals
Sub-objective 1	Define and represent context for ATMP development processes
Sub-objective 2	Represent the variability of regulatory goals, depending on context
Sub-objective 3	Represent the effect of context on the scientific development process

ing ATMP development processes and our interviews with iPSPine stakeholders, we have identified the objectives in Table 1 for our case study.

3 Solution Design and Development

The need for regulatory guidance, as discussed in Sect. 2, motivated us to use the notion of context and context-awareness to guide ATMP scientists in working towards regulatory compliance. The following sections present how we address the objectives in Table 1.

3.1 Contextualizing the Domain Model

(Sub-objective 1). Every business process has a specific domain. Correspondingly, everything that influences a process is related to this domain [17]. Therefore, what constitutes context for a business process lies in the domain model. This motivates our choice of using domain models as a baseline to define context in ATMP development processes. For ATMP development, the experiments performed, results obtained, properties of the ATMP being developed or decisions taken throughout the process form the context of the development process. For instance, a decision, which is a part of the ATMP development process, about the regulatory classification of components of the ATMP is an important contextual element.

Below is an example (part of the) domain model and context definition. First, we created the domain model with experts. In the domain model, entities and their attributes are marked as contextual, shown in dashed boxes in Fig. 6, if they determine the regulatory goals to be addressed by the development process. For example, the decision about classification of biomaterial shown in Fig. 5, is represented as different roles that a biomaterial entity can take and marked as contextual element (See C1 and C2 in Fig. 6).

Instantiation of each contextual element is a partial context (C5, C6, C7, C1, C2 on Fig. 6). Also, combined instantiations of multiple contextual elements with different values is a partial context (C3, C4 on Fig. 6). Contexts which share the same contextual elements but with different values are mutually exclusive (C5, C6, C7 or C1, C2 or C3, C4 on Fig. 6). Contexts which include a combination of multiple contextual elements might imply contexts including less contextual elements (e.g., C4→C2, C3→C2, C4→C7 on Fig. 6). So they are not exclusive.

A set of non-exclusive partial contexts form the overall context in an ATMP development process (See context in Fig. 8).

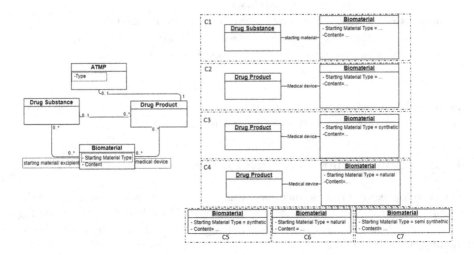

Fig. 6. Domain model (simplified) and example context definitions

3.2   Contextualizing the Goal Model

(Sub-objective 2). Having defined contexts, we annotate the root and the parent goals in the goal model with context labels, indicating which goal is adoptable under which conditions. The semantics of context annotations are provided by Ali et al. [3]. If a root goal, G, is annotated with a context label C_i, that means G is activated iff context C_i holds. If there is a goal G_i, that is decomposed into a sub-goal G_j with and *(or)* decomposition links then the link is annotated with a context label. This means, goal G_i, requires *(can be achieved)* via G_j iff context C_i hold.

These annotations enable us to derive the context for leaf goals. Figure 7 shows an example goal model for ATMP development processes where the context for leaf goals are derived using the contexts of goal model variants which includes these leaf goals (See Fig. 8).

The idea of using contextual goal models is inspired from [3]. In [3], authors use contextual goal models to model contextual requirements for an information system. Here, we use contextual goal models as a means to contextualize process models. In the following section, we describe how contextual goal models are used to contextualize ATMP development processes.

3.3   Contextuzalizing the Process Model

(Sub-objective 3). Our intention here is to contextualize the process model such that it guides scientists throughout the process execution. This is achieved by

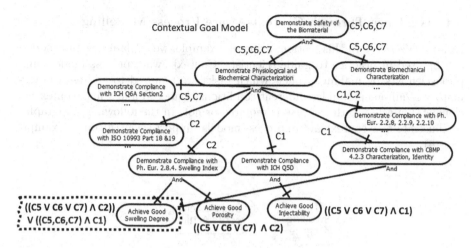

Fig. 7. Contextual goal model

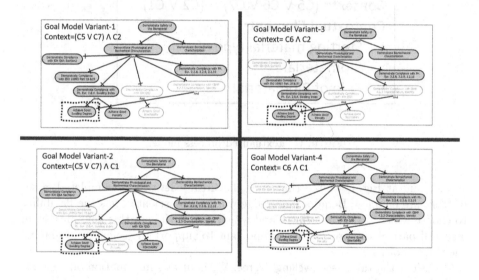

Fig. 8. Goal model variants

deriving the context of the leaf goals in the goal model. A leaf goal corresponds to a milestone of a single task or sub-process in the process model. Accordingly, once we derive the context of leaf goals, the corresponding task/sub-process is also implicitly contextualized. The elements in the domain model used to define the context of its goals are the contextual elements that affect the task or sub-process. The task or sub-process becomes relevant if its context holds.

3.4   Guidance Through Context-Aware Process Modelling

(Main Objective). In this section, using an example, we explain how our models can be used in practice to guide scientists. Context-aware process models support scientists by making explicit which tasks are required to address the regulatory requirements under different conditions(contexts) and what (contextual elements) affects whether a task is required or not. In the following paragraphs, we illustrate how context-aware process models support scientists on an example (Fig. 9).

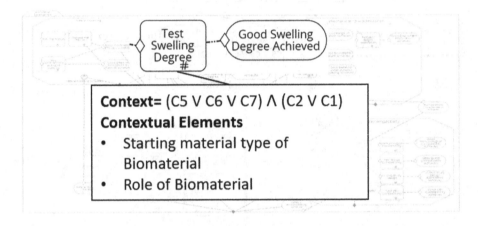

Fig. 9. Contextualized process model

Looking at Fig. 4, we see that once the Create Gel task is completed, a set of tasks are enabled. Being a knowledge-worker, the scientist has the flexibility to choose which tasks to perform and which not. Although this flexibility is an essential part of the process, it is important to support the scientist in making the these choices.

Consider the task Test swelling degree. Without any information on context, the scientist is free to skip this task. However, skipping this task would cause a problem if the biomaterial has a natural starting material and is classified as starting material in the drug substance (context C1 in Fig. 6 holds). Skipping the task will result in not being able to Demonstrate compliance with Ph.Eur. 2.8.4 Swelling Index, (See Fig. 7), and this will result in failing to get the authorizations for clinical trials. With the models in this paper, the scientist can choose a specific context and this way is able to see which goals and tasks are relevant. Thereby, the scientist ensures that the relevant regulatory requirements are addressed.

Additionally, it is important to explicitly show the factors (contextual elements) defining whether a task is relevant for the current context or not. For instance, knowing that the contextual elements related to Test swelling degree task are Starting material type and Role of biomaterial, the scientist sees how Role of the biomaterial affects the development process. This helps them define the right context, e.g., choosing the appropriate Role of the biomaterial in Fig. 5, that require fewer tests, which is more time and cost-efficient.

Lastly, since the context can change throughout the development, so do the regulatory goals to be addressed and the set of tasks to be executed to address those regulatory goals. Context-aware process models support scientists by making explicit which tasks are required for which contexts. Thereby, context-aware process models implicitly supports scientists in working more efficiently by helping them in prioritizing the tasks that are relevant for more contexts rather than performing redundant tasks that are only valid for a specific context, which is unlikely to occur.

4 Preliminary Evaluation

Initial feedback on the models and ideas presented in this paper has been gathered from senior iPSpine and regulatory experts. The stakeholders indicated that they are positive about the usefulness of models and ideas in practice.

Next, the usefulness of the main-objective of this case study was discussed with three junior scientists who are working on the biomaterial development studies, which is the part of ATMP development processes we focus in this case study. The scientists mentioned that the idea of linking the process model and the goal model is "definitely useful" when the scientific development is at the stage where different regulatory frameworks (different contexts, domain model) are investigated. They mentioned that they can use these models to justify what they have done (process) and identify what they need to do to better comply with the chosen regulatory framework (goals).

Further evaluation will follow when the models are implemented on the process management platform developed within the scope of iPSpine project. This implementation is currently under development. First, we plan to conduct semi-structured interviews with junior biomaterial development scientists who are actively using the platform. Then, further interviews will follow with senior scientists and other development cases will be implemented and tested in the platform.

5 Discussion

Our focus in this case study is to support scientists in working towards regulatory compliance. We do this by means of context-aware process models. In this regard, the notion of context in context-aware BPM is related to our purpose. Therefore, in this section, we discuss context-aware BPM papers that are highly relevant for our case study.

Context is not a new notion for BPM. Several authors investigated this notion with the aim of making the processes context-aware; responsive to the changes in its environment. Song et al. [21] present a comprehensive survey about various definitions of context in context-aware BPM. The authors conclude that there is still a lack of consensus in BPM on how context is defined, represented and integrated to the business processes [21].

A related work on contextualizing business processes is the paper by De La Vara et al. [7,8]. They use a context analysis method [3] to contextualize business processes. The context analysis method uses a set of expressions, so-called facts, to check if a particular context holds. A context analysis model defines alternative ways (or alternative combinations of facts) for checking a context, referred to as context variants. In our case, a context can not be verified by facts. Context is defined by different values taken by the contextual elements chosen by the scientist (user).

The importance of goals for investigating and integrating context for business processes is already discovered in context-aware BPM literature [12,17,19]. In these papers, goals are used to identify contextual elements, i.e., factors that have an impact on the achievement of business goals, and relate them to the business processes.

Similarly, in this case study, we use goals as a facilitator for identifying and relating context and contextual elements to business processes. However, different from existing approaches [12,17,19], we use contextual goal models for this purpose. In the existing approaches [17,19], analysis of process goals is only limited to identification of top level objectives and discovering factors (contextual elements) that have an effect on the achievement of those goals. Heravizadeh et al. [12], decomposes the process objectives into smaller objectives to discover contextual elements and to link them to the business process. However, in their case, context only affects how or how well the goals are achieved, but the goals are fixed. In our case, different contexts imply different goals.

Another related research area is guidance/recommendations for flexible, knowledge intensive processes. Supporting flexible and knowledge intensive processes is an emerging topic in BPM [9]. Providing guidance and recommendations for those processes has also drawn some attention [5,13,24,25]. These approaches provide guidance using historical knowledge about previous cases. ATMP development is a new field with a huge variability between different projects. Also, no historical data from previous projects is available for use. For this reason, existing process guidance approaches are not suitable for our case study. In this regard, this paper presents an exemplary case study for guiding flexible and knowledge-intensive processes where no historical data is available.

Lastly, although business process variability modelling [4,16] is a related research area, it is not the focus of this paper. The main problem we address in this paper was to bridge the gap between the regulatory and scientific views on an ATMP development process. So, our main focus was to identify and integrate the (regulatory related) factors that causes a variability in the scientific development process. Business process variability modelling approaches focus on the next step: deriving different process variants. They do not focus on identification and representation of the factors driving the variability. Also, deriving the process variant for a particular context is not intended in this case study. Alternative contexts are explored throughout an ATMP development study e.g., different classification decisions in Fig. 5. So, the process model should cover not only a single process variant of a particular context, but multiple process variants corresponding to alternative contexts that are explored in a single development process.

6   Conclusion

In this paper, we have presented a case study on modelling context-aware processes. The immediate contribution of this research are the models presented in Sect. 3 created and implemented for the iPSpine project. These models are used to guide ATMP development scientists work towards regulatory compliance in an efficient and effective manner. Furthermore, this case study presents an exemplary approach for guiding flexible and knowledge-intensive processes through context-awareness.

Contextualization of the existing process model provides a solution for guiding the scientists towards regulatory compliance in this case study. However, ATMP development processes are diverse. The process models we provide in this case study cover only a single ATMP development study in the iPSpine project. As future work, we plan to investigate creating process models, that cover the tasks for a set of contexts explored throughout an ATMP development study, using goal models.

Acknowledgements. The work presented in this paper is part of iPSpine project that has received funding from the European Union's Horizon 2020 research and innovation programme under grant agreement No. 825925.

References

1. Advanced Therapy Medicinal Products: Overview. www.ema.europa.eu/en/human-regulatory/overview/advanced-therapy-medicinal-products-overview. Accessed 05 Oct 2021
2. Aalst, W., Weske, M., Grünbauer, D.: Case handling: a new paradigm for business process support. Data Knowl. Eng. **53**, 129–162 (2005)
3. Ali, R., Dalpiaz, F., Giorgini, P.: A goal-based framework for contextual requirements modeling and analysis. Requirements Eng. **15**(4), 439–458 (2010)
4. Ayora, C., Torres, V., Weber, B., Reichert, M., Pelechano, V.: VIVACE: a framework for the systematic evaluation of variability support in process-aware information systems. Inf. Softw. Technol. **57**(1), 248–276 (2015)
5. Barba, I., Weber, B., Del Valle, C., Jiménez-Ramírez, A.: User recommendations for the optimized execution of business processes. Data Knowl. Eng. **86**, 61–84 (2013)
6. BizAgi, et al.: Case management model and notation (CMMN), v1.1, December 2016. OMG Document Number formal/16-12-01, Object Management Group
7. de la Vara, J.L., Ali, R., Dalpiaz, F., Sánchez, J., Giorgini, P.: Business processes contextualisation via context analysis. In: Parsons, J., Saeki, M., Shoval, P., Woo, C., Wand, Y. (eds.) ER 2010. LNCS, vol. 6412, pp. 471–476. Springer, Heidelberg (2010). https://doi.org/10.1007/978-3-642-16373-9_37

8. de la Vara, J.L., Ali, R., Dalpiaz, F., Sánchez, J., Giorgini, P.: COMPRO: a methodological approach for business process contextualisation. In: Meersman, R., Dillon, T., Herrero, P. (eds.) OTM 2010. LNCS, vol. 6426, pp. 132–149. Springer, Heidelberg (2010). https://doi.org/10.1007/978-3-642-16934-2_12

9. Di Ciccio, C., Marrella, A., Russo, A.: Knowledge-intensive processes: characteristics, requirements and analysis of contemporary approaches. J. Data Semant. 4(1), 29–57 (2014). https://doi.org/10.1007/s13740-014-0038-4

10. Elsallab, M., Bravery, C.A., Kurtz, A., Abou-El-Enein, M.: Mitigating deficiencies in evidence during regulatory assessments of advanced therapies: a comparative study with other biologicals. Mol. Therapy - Methods Clin. Dev. 18, 269–279 (2020)

11. van Gils, B., Proper, H.A.: Enterprise modelling in the age of digital transformation. In: Buchmann, R.A., Karagiannis, D., Kirikova, M. (eds.) PoEM 2018. LNBIP, vol. 335, pp. 257–273. Springer, Cham (2018). https://doi.org/10.1007/978-3-030-02302-7_16

12. Heravizadeh, M., Edmond, D.: Making workflows context-aware: a way to support knowledge-intensive tasks. In: Conference in Research and Practice in Information Technology Series, vol. 79 (2008)

13. Huber, S., Fietta, M., Hof, S.: Next step recommendation and prediction based on process mining in adaptive case management. In: Proceedings of the 7th International Conference on Subject-Oriented BPM. S-BPM ONE 2015. ACM (2015)

14. Koç, H., Sandkuhl, K.: Capability-driven digital service innovation: implications from business model and service process perspectives. In: Poels, G., Gailly, F., Serral Asensio, E., Snoeck, M. (eds.) PoEM 2017. LNBIP, vol. 305, pp. 126–140. Springer, Cham (2017). https://doi.org/10.1007/978-3-319-70241-4_9

15. Köhler, T., Alter, S., Cameron, B.H.: Enterprise modeling at the work system level: evidence from four cases at DHL express Europe. In: Buchmann, R.A., Karagiannis, D., Kirikova, M. (eds.) PoEM 2018. LNBIP, vol. 335, pp. 303–318. Springer, Cham (2018). https://doi.org/10.1007/978-3-030-02302-7_19

16. La Rosa, M., Van Der Aalst, W.M., Dumas, M., Milani, F.P.: Business process variability modeling: a survey. ACM Comput. Surv. 50(1), 1–45 (2017)

17. Mattos, T.D.C., Santoro, F.M., Revoredo, K., Nunes, V.T.: A formal representation for context-aware business processes. Comput. Ind. 65(8), 1193–1214 (2014)

18. Morrow, D., Ussi, A., Migliaccio, G.: Addressing pressing needs in the development of advanced therapies. Front. Bioeng. Biotechnol. 5, 55 (2017)

19. Rosemann, M., Recker, J., Flender, C.: Contextualisation of business processes. Int. J. Bus. Process. Integr. Manag. 3(1), 47–60 (2008)

20. Sandkuhl, K., Stirna, J., Persson, A., Wißotzki, M.: Enterprise Modeling: Tackling Business Challenges with the 4EM Method. Springer, Heidelberg (2014). https://doi.org/10.1007/978-3-662-43725-4

21. Song, R., Vanthienen, J., Cui, W., Wang, Y., Huang, L.: Towards a comprehensive understanding of the context concepts in context-aware business processes. In: Proceedings of the 11th International Conference on Subject-Oriented BPM, pp. 1–10. ACM (2019)

22. Swenson, K.: Mastering the Unpredictable: How Adaptive Case Management Will Revolutionize the Way That Knowledge Workers Get Things Done. Meghan-Kiffer, Tampa (2010)

23. International Telecommunication Union: Recommendation z.151 (10/12), user requirements notation (URN) - language definition (2012)

24. Voorberg, S., Eshuis, R., van Jaarsveld, W., van Houtum, G.: Decision support for declarative artifact-centric process models. In: Business Process Management Forum, pp. 36–52 (2019)
25. Weber, B., Wild, W., Breu, R.: CBRFlow: enabling adaptive workflow management through conversational case-based reasoning. In: Funk, P., González Calero, P.A. (eds.) ECCBR 2004. LNCS (LNAI), vol. 3155, pp. 434–448. Springer, Heidelberg (2004). https://doi.org/10.1007/978-3-540-28631-8_32
26. Zachman, J.: A framework for information systems architecture. IBM Syst. J. **26**(3), 276–292 (1987)

Process Model Repair Meets Theory Revision - Initial Ideas

Kate Revoredo$^{(\boxtimes)}$ (iD)

Vienna University of Economics and Business (WU), Vienna, Austria
`kate.revoredo@wu.ac.at`

Abstract. Process models are important artifacts to support organizations in documenting, understanding and monitoring their business. Over time, these process models may become outdated and need to be revised to again accurately describe the business, its culture and regulations. *Process model repair* techniques help at automatically revising the existing model from behavior traced in event logs. So far, such techniques have focused on identifying which parts of the model to change and how to change them, but they tend to overlook the potential of using knowledge from practitioners to inform the revision. *Theory revision* techniques are able to revise a logical theory using data. They allow the practitioner to specify which part of the theory is kept unchanged during the revision and which part of the data should or should not be explained by the theory. This paper dives into first ideas on how process model repair techniques can benefit from theory revision. In particular, it elaborates on the use of domain knowledge to identify which data are relevant to be considered and which parts of the model are indeed changeable. Finally, this paper analyzes existing process model repair techniques and discusses challenges that need to be addressed in order to exploit theory revision.

Keywords: Process model repair · Process mining · Theory revision

1 Introduction

Business Process Management (BPM) [9] relies on process models to support organizations in documenting, understanding and monitoring their processes. These models can be manually specified by stakeholders of the process or automatically discovered from process data using process discovery techniques [1]. Over time, with changes in the regulations, the business or the organization culture these models may become obsolete and less useful for monitoring. Thus, there is a need to revise these process models to meet the new understanding of the business.

In the BPM area, there are some initiatives on process model repair [2] to automatically revise the current model from observed behavior. They use event data collected from information systems to guide the necessary changes in the

E. Serral et al. (Eds.): PoEM 2021, LNBIP 432, pp. 184–194, 2021.
https://doi.org/10.1007/978-3-030-91279-6_13

model. This is typically done by applying conformance checking [6] techniques for identifying non conforming traces and applying local changes to the model to make it compliant to the analyzed traces. These techniques mainly focus on identifying where to apply the change and how to change the model. However, they overlook the importance of external knowledge in guiding the revisions. The necessary changes to the process model can have the goal to represent new behavior or to prevent undesired behavior. For instance, the organization may decide to switch to a more sustainable business and manage their internal projects digitally. In this scenario, it is important to distinguish in the data between desired and undesired behavior. That is, events from the previous physically managed cases should be marked as undesired while events from the digitally handled process should be marked as desired behavior. The process model repair technique should take these markings into account to guarantee that the final model accurately represents the current business process. Another benefit of considering domain knowledge concerns specific fragments of the process which represent normative work (e.g., safety fallback procedures in case of emergency, organization code of conduct). This kind of work is described by activities which must be done exactly as described in the model. Also, some parts of the model were derived from extensive discussions among the different stakeholders and they share a common understanding among the process participants. It is important that the model repair technique does not change these parts.

Theory revision [24, 25] is part of the *Inductive Logic Programming* [16] (ILP) area and it is motivated by concept drifts (i.e., the situation in which properties and relations of the studied data can change over time). It focuses on minimally changing a logical theory in the presence of positive and negative observations with the aim of finding a more accurate theory. Theory revision brings two advantages to the practitioner. First, it allows to distinguish between positive and negative observations (i.e., facts that must or must not be explained by the revised theory). Second, it allows to precisely specify parts of the model to be kept unchanged during the revision. This paper aims at bridging *process model repair* and *theory revision*. More specifically, it provides the first ideas on how to formulate a process model repair problem as a theory revision problem. To this end, it focuses on *i)* the distinction between desired (positive) and undesired (negative) behavior, and *ii)* changeable and unchangeable model fragments to be considered in the model repair. This paper analyzes existing techniques from a theory revision point of view and explores which concepts are already in use and which are further concepts that are useful for model repair.

The rest of the paper is structured as follows. Section 2 reviews preliminary concepts. Section 3 presents the proposal on how to frame process model repair based on theory revision. Section 4 presents an analysis of existing model repair techniques positioning them against derived concepts. Section 5 discusses related work. Section 6 concludes the paper and outlines future work.

2 Preliminaries

This section describes the two main concepts approached in this paper. Section 2.1 reviews the concept of process model repair. Section 2.2 describes the concept of theory revision.

2.1 Process Model Repair

A *process model* (M) is a description of the business process. It represents the sequence of process events (i.e., the activities and control-flow of the process). Usually, this is represented as a directed graph where the nodes represent the events and the edges represent the potential flow of control among the events. An *event log* (L) is a multi-set of traces and each trace (T) represents the execution of a process instance, (i.e., the sequence of process activities). Techniques for automatically discovering a process model from an event log were proposed in the literature [1]. The final process model is expected to conform with the event log (i.e., the model M is expected to replay all the traces T in L).

The event log represents the observed behavior while the model represents the expected behavior. Over time, the expected and the observed behavior may not align anymore, for instance because of concept drift. In this case *process model repair* [10] may be applied. Process model repair aims to improve the quality of a model through process data by applying minimal changes to the initial model. Existing methods take as input a model and an event log, and produce a new model that resembles the original one as much as possible while still guaranteeing that the new model is able to replay the traces in the log. More in detail, process model repair techniques need two inputs: a process model and an event log. A process model typically uses a graph-based notation to express the partial order relation of the activities within the different traces constituting the event log. Such model may have been designed manually by a person using a modeling tool or may have been generated by a process discovery tool. An event log typically comes from an information system (e.g., a BPMS, a database, etc.). The data presented in the event log may record events pertaining a large amount of time, including time periods in which the process is enacted differently (i.e., the actual process changed with respect to its model). This means that the initial model is no longer able to accurately describe the behavior recorded in the event log, especially when it comes to newer traces. Thus, the task of model repair is that to produce a new process model that is able to best describe all the facts and relations observed in the event log.

Process model repair can be positioned in between process discovery [1] and conformance checking [6] (i.e. taking a predefined model as the norm and checking whether the event log complies with it). The final model may reflect reality (i.e. observed behavior recorded in the event log) better than the initial model, but may also be very different from it, which can make the final model useless in practice. For instance, practitioners may heavily rely on the initial model to understand how a particular process functions. Presenting to them a model very different from the one they are accustomed with, may result in the final model being ignored by them. To address this issue, a minimality criterion is considered when repairing the initial model guaranteeing that the final model is as similar as possible to the initial one. However, the minimality criterion does not guarantee that still important parts (e.g., commonly agreed pieces of the process that represent a shared understanding of the work) are not changed by the technique. In this paper, I argue that the repair would be more useful to the practitioners if it takes into account predefined fragments of the model that they do not want to modify.

Furthermore, as stated in [3,4], existing approaches for process model repair are applied on whole event log. They apply the changes based on all the traces that did not comply with the model, thus including traces that the practitioners do not want to take into account for the repair. As a consequence, the final models is unnecessarily complex and harder to understand by the practitioners. In this paper, I also argue that the repair technique can benefit from a pre-processing step, in which the relevant traces for the repair are identified.

2.2 Theory Revision

A theory revision technique receives as input an initial logical theory (T_i) and a set of factual data (C) [24,25]. The theory is composed by a set of logic rules and can be either specified manually by domain analysts or automatically using an Inductive Logic Programming (ILP) system [16]. Furthermore, the initial theory is divided into two parts: unchangeable, which is assumed to be correct, and a changeable part that can be modified by the revision. The data are split into positive (C^+) and negative (C^-) observations. The final theory (T_f) should logically imply all the positive observations (completeness) $(\forall c^+ \in C^+, T_f \vDash c^+)$, none of the negative observations (consistency) $(\forall c^- \in C^-, T_f \nvDash c^-)$ and satisfy a criterion of minimality [25]. More in detail, theory revision needs two inputs: an initial theory and a dataset. The initial theory is a set of logical rules and it is divided into two parts: a changeable set of rules and an unchangeable one. Rules may be expressed in first-order logic notation (e.g., Horn clauses). These rule sets may have been specified manually by a person or may have been learned via a machine learning technique. A dataset is a collection of facts that may come from an information system (e.g., a database). The data presented in the dataset is divided into two sets: the positive and the negative sets. The positive set represents facts that must be explained by the theory whereas the negative set represent facts that must not be explained. The task of theory revision is to generate a final theory in which all the unchangeable rules of the initial theory are still present and some changeable rules have been replaced by new ones.

When applying theory revision three considerations must be made. First, it must be clear where the theory should be modified (*revision points*). Second, it must be clear how the theory should be revised (*revision operators*). Third, it must be clear what *evaluation function* is going to be considered in order to choose the best revision.

Revision points are defined through the data. Positive observations define *generalization revision points* while negative observations define *specialization revision points*. The first is the literal in a rule responsible for the failure of proving a positive example (failure point) and other antecedents (contributing points) that may have contributed to this failure. The second is defined by clauses used in successful proofs of negative examples. The specification of the revision point determines the type of revision operator that will be applied to make the theory consistent with the data. Generalization operators are used when a positive observation is not proved by the theory, i.e. the theory must be more generic in order to explain a positive observation. The second group is applied when a negative observation is proved by the theory, i.e. the theory should be more specific in order to not explain a negative observation.

Theory revision relies on operators that propose modifications at each revision point. Any operator used in machine learning (first-order) can be used in a theory revision system. For instance, the specialization operator *delete-rule*, that deletes the rule that is causing the proof of a negative observation and the operator *add-antecedent*, that adds antecedents to a rule in an attempt to make negative observations unprovable. As examples of generalization operators we can consider the *delete-antecedent* operator that deletes antecedents from a rule making this rule more generic and therefore allowing positive observations previously not proved by the theory to be proved. Another operator is the *add-rule* operator. This operator leaves the original rule in the theory and generates new ones based on the original. The process is made in two ways. First it copies the original rule and, using hill-climbing antecedent deletion, deletes antecedents without allowing any negative observation to be proven, and also those that allows one or more previously unprovable positive observation to be proven (even if doing so allows proofs of negatives). Then it creates one or more specializations of this core rule using the add-antecedents operator, to allow proofs of the desired positives while eliminating the negatives. An evaluation function such as accuracy is used to select the best proposed revision to be implemented.

3 Proposal

This section discuses how to frame the task of model repair as a theory revision task. Figure 1 introduces the overarching method.

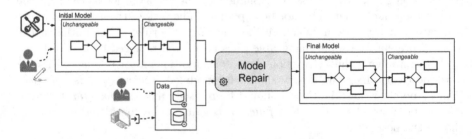

Fig. 1. Process model repair framed as a theory revision problem schema

As input, a model repair technique receives an initial model and an event log and outputs a revised model. The initial model is divided into two parts. The first one (BK) represents the part of the process model that should not be changed during the repair procedure. The specification of this part is done by the practitioners, based on their knowledge about the domain. For instance, it can represent some external or internal regulations that should be kept. Once the protected part of the process model is defined, all the rest is associated to the repairable part (M_i). For the repair to happen it is necessary that M_i is defined. The BK can be empty meaning that the practitioners chose to allow repair to be considered in the whole structure of the process model. The event log is also divided in two: positive (L^+) and negative (L^-) event logs. L^+ corresponds to the traces representing acceptable behavior while L^- corresponds to behavior that should be avoided. The model repair technique implements changes in the model (M_i) guided by the event logs generating a final model that includes the unchangeable part (BK) plus the repaired model (M_f). The choice of which change to implement follows a minimality criterion.

The changes are made in a batch mode, i.e. all the traces are received at once and the changes to the model are made considering all of them. There are some approaches for model repair that work in an incremental manner. In [13], an approach for incrementally learn declarative process models was proposed. The constrains are represented in a fragment of first-order logic consisting of Datalog Horn clauses. The approaches implements changes in the model based in one trace. It can learn from scratch as well as implementing modifications in an existing model. It does not required the definition of positive and negative observations implementing the modifications only based on positive observations. Incremental approaches are not in the scope of the present work.

4   Analysis of Existing Process Model Repair Techniques

This section reports the results of the analysis of the existing approaches for process model repair with respect to our proposal of framing the problem as a theory revision problem. All the approaches rely on using conformance checking techniques for identifying traces not conforming with the model and to guide the necessary repair in the model. They vary mainly on the alignment technique used and in the proposed repair. Therefore, revision points and revision operators are considered in an implicitly manner. This paper then focused the analysis on (i) specification of fragments of the initial model defining changeable and unchangeable fragments; (ii) partitioning of the event log into positive and negative traces; (iii) application of minimality criterion. This paper considered approaches where the revision procedure is fully automatized. Table 1 summarizes our findings.

In [5] the alignment of a trace and a process model is used to propose changes in the model. The approach uses a metric to calculate the alignment of the proposed repaired model with the initial one, aiming for repairs that provide minimal repair, thus a minimality criterion is used.

In [19] an impact-driven process model repair was proposed. The model repair problem was addressed as an optimization problem where each possible repair

Table 1. Summary of the model repair approaches

Approach	Model fragmentation	Event log partitioning	Minimality criterion
[5]			✓
[19]			✓
[20, 26, 27]			✓
[15]	✓		✓
[23]			✓
[22]			✓
[12]		✓	✓

had a cost and the task was to find the repaired model that maximize fitness constrained by the cost. A maximum degree change was considered, in this way minimality criterion is met.

In [26] an approach for repairing a process model described in logic Petri Net was proposed. It focuses on repairing a choice structure to make the model replay activities in different branches. Variations of the work considering non-free-choice structures [27] or process models with choice structures [20] were also considered. In all the approaches, a minimality criterion was considered.

In [15] the principle of divide and conquer was used to decompose the initial process model in several fragments. Then, each fragment is classified in good or bad fragment, depending whether they conform with the event log or not, respectively. For the bad fragments, repair operations are applied and the generated repair fragments are then composed with the good one generating a final repaired model. This work aligns partially with (i) decomposing the model in changeable and unchangeable fragments. However, the choice is based on conformance with the event log and not as a prior decision based on the understanding of the business and the needs of the practitioners as stated in this paper. Moreover, it can be the case that a part of the model that conforms with the data should not. By focusing on changing only the parts that did no conform with the event log keeping as much as possible the initial model, the minimality criterion is considered.

In [23], the process model as a workflow net and the event log are both represented as footprint matrix. The repair approach implements modification in the model based on differences found between the two footprint matrix. The approach searches for a minimal change in the model and consider all the event log as desirable traces.

In [22], the authors presented the task of generalized conformance checking. A level of quality trust is associated to the log and to the model and this quality is used to repair both the log and the model. Although the authors acknowledge the possibility of the event log not representing all the possible behaviors or representing undesirable behavior, the model repair does mot consider these issues in a different way, also because they are not distinguished in the event log. Therefore the consideration of positive and negative event logs is not take into account by this approach. The alignment between the original model and the final model is calculated, but the trust value associated to the model defines the amount of change accepted. If the trust on the model is high which cope with the idea of theory revision (i.e., the model is approximately correct), then the model will be changed minimally, therefore the approach follows a minimality criterion.

The approach proposed in [12] is the most related to the concepts presented in this paper. It uses conformance checking to find the sequence of the model most similar to the traces that did not conform. Then the parts that did not conform are separated and process discovery technique are used to learn the correspondent sub-process that are then included in the initial model repairing it. They separated in a different log traces that should not be replayed by the model. Therefore, they partially considered negative and positive traces. The approach satisfies a minimality criterion.

As a result of the analysis of the existing techniques for process model repair it is possible to observe that the techniques use a minimality criterion to guarantee that the final model resembles as much as possible the initial model. However, the techniques can be improved by the involvement of the practitioners for fragmentation of the initial model and partitioning of the event log. The approaches proposed in [15] and [12] partially fulfilled these two points, respectively.

5   Related Work

Given the analyzed sources of the literature, it can be observed that the concept of theory revision has not yet been considered for process model repair when the model follows an imperative paradigm. When the process model is represented with a declarative paradigm, work such as [7] can be mentioned. Theory revision concepts were used to improve DECLARE [18] rules, where a set of positive and negative event logs were built and used for the revision of the set of DECLARE rules. In the context of process discovery, the approach presented in [8] used a partitioning of the event log into positive and negative event logs to learn declarative process model.

The idea of framing an existing task as a theory revision task has been used in other areas such as learning game rules [17], updating social network in the presence of stream data [14] and discovering links in real biological networks [21]. This paper is a first attempt to provide formal foundations for process model repair. Especially, it sheds light on the necessity of the fragmentation of the initial process model and the partition of the event log involving practitioners' knowledge.

6   Conclusion

BPM relies on process models to support the practitioners in documenting, understanding and monitoring their processes. If these models become outdated over time, the monitoring of the process becomes inaccurate. Process model repair proposes to change the model in order to cope with the latest changes in the data recorded in event log. From the area of ILP, theory revision techniques allow the revision of a logical theory, i.e. a set of rules, guided by positive and negative observations. The logical theory is minimally changed in order to explain all the positive observations and none of the negative observations.

This paper explored the area of process model repair framing it as a theory revision problem. It identified two main points from theory revision that can contribute to process model repair, the fragmentation of the initial process model in a way that the practitioners may indicate fragments that should not be considered for repair and the definition of two event logs, namely positive and negative logs. The first one includes behavior that should be replayed by the model and the second includes behavior that should be avoided by the model. To use theory revision for process model repair, two main challenges should be addressed, namely the fragmentation of the initial process model and the partitioning of the event log.

As future work, I intend to i) delve deeper into formalizing other aspects of theory revision and ii) explore other facets of the broader area of *theory refinement* [25]. For what concerns i), as existing works are already implicitly using the concepts of revision points and revision operators, I plan to formally define them. For what concerns ii), the automatic improvement of logic knowledge bases, known as *theory refinement*, can be divided into two classes: *theory revision* and *theory restructuring*. Both aim at improving the quality of the logical theory. The revision task involves changing the answer set of the given theory, i.e., improving its inferential capabilities by adding previously missing answers (generalization) or by removing incorrect answers (specialization). On the other hand, the task of restructuring does not change the answer set of the given theory; its objective is to improve performance and/or user understandability of the theory. As a follow-up work, I intend to investigate how concepts of theory restructuring can support the task of process model repair, e.g. process simplification [11].

References

1. Aalst, W.: Data science in action. In: Process Mining, pp. 3–23. Springer, Heidelberg (2016). https://doi.org/10.1007/978-3-662-49851-4_1
2. Armas-Cervantes, A.: Process model repair. In: Encyclopedia of Big Data Technologies. Springer (2019). https://doi.org/10.1007/978-3-319-77525-8
3. Armas Cervantes, A., van Beest, N.R.T.P., La Rosa, M., Dumas, M., García-Bañuelos, L., et al.: Interactive and incremental business process model repair. In: Panetto, H. (ed.) OTM 2017. LNCS, vol. 10573, pp. 53–74. Springer, Cham (2017). https://doi.org/10.1007/978-3-319-69462-7_5
4. Armas-Cervantes, A., van Beest, N.R.T.P., Rosa, M.L., Dumas, M., Raboczi, S.: Incremental and interactive business process model repair in Apromore. In: BPM (Demos). CEUR Workshop Proceedings, vol. 1920. CEUR-WS.org (2017)

5. Buijs, J.C.A.M., La Rosa, M., Reijers, H.A., van Dongen, B.F., van der Aalst, W.M.P.: Improving business process models using observed behavior. In: Cudre-Mauroux, P., Ceravolo, P., Gašević, D. (eds.) SIMPDA 2012. LNBIP, vol. 162, pp. 44–59. Springer, Heidelberg (2013). https://doi.org/10.1007/978-3-642-40919-6_3
6. Carmona, J., van Dongen, B.F., Solti, A., Weidlich, M.: Conformance Checking - Relating Processes and Models. Springer (2018). https://doi.org/10.1007/978-3-319-99414-7
7. Cattafi, M., Lamma, E., Riguzzi, F., Storari, S.: Incremental declarative process mining. In: Smart Information and Knowledge Management, Studies in Computational Intelligence, vol. 260, pp. 103–127. Springer (2010). https://doi.org/10.1007/978-3-642-04584-4_5
8. Chesani, F., Lamma, E., Mello, P., Montali, M., Riguzzi, F., Storari, S.: Exploiting inductive logic programming techniques for declarative process mining. Trans. Petri Nets Other Model. Concurr. 2, 278–295 (2009)
9. Dumas, M., Rosa, M.L., Mendling, J., Reijers, H.A.: Fundamentals of Business Process Management, Second Edition. Springer (2018). https://doi.org/10.1007/978-3-642-33143-5
10. Fahland, D., van der Aalst, W.M.P.: Repairing process models to reflect reality. In: Barros, A., Gal, A., Kindler, E. (eds.) BPM 2012. LNCS, vol. 7481, pp. 229–245. Springer, Heidelberg (2012). https://doi.org/10.1007/978-3-642-32885-5_19
11. Fahland, D., van der Aalst, W.M.P.: Simplifying discovered process models in a controlled manner. Inf. Syst. 38(4), 585–605 (2013)
12. Fahland, D., van der Aalst, W.M.P.: Model repair - aligning process models to reality. Inf. Syst. 47, 220–243 (2015)
13. Ferilli, S.: Incremental declarative process mining with woman. In: EAIS, pp. 1–8. IEEE (2020)
14. Guimarães, V., Paes, A., Zaverucha, G.: Online probabilistic theory revision from examples with ProPPR. Mach. Learn. 108(7), 1165–1189 (2019)
15. Mitsyuk, A.A., Lomazova, I.A., Shugurov, I.S., van der Aalst, W.M.P.: Process model repair by detecting unfitting fragments. In: AIST (Supplement). CEUR Workshop Proceedings, vol. 1975, pp. 301–313. CEUR-WS.org (2017)
16. Muggleton, S.: Inductive logic programming. New Gener. Comput. 8(4), 295–318 (1991). https://doi.org/10.1007/BF03037089
17. Muggleton, S., Paes, A., Santos Costa, V., Zaverucha, G.: Chess revision: acquiring the rules of chess variants through FOL theory revision from examples. In: De Raedt, L. (ed.) ILP 2009. LNCS (LNAI), vol. 5989, pp. 123–130. Springer, Heidelberg (2010). https://doi.org/10.1007/978-3-642-13840-9_12
18. Pesic, M., Schonenberg, H., van der Aalst, W.M.P.: DECLARE: full support for loosely-structured processes. In: EDOC, pp. 287–300. IEEE Computer Society (2007)
19. Polyvyanyy, A., van der Aalst, W.M.P., ter Hofstede, A.H.M., Wynn, M.T.: Impact-driven process model repair. ACM Trans. Softw. Eng. Methodol. 25(4), 28:1–28:60 (2017)
20. Qi, H., Du, Y., Qi, L., Wang, L.: An approach to repair petri net-based process models with choice structures. Enterp. Inf. Syst. 12(8–9), 1149–1179 (2018)
21. Raedt, L.D., Kersting, K., Kimmig, A., Revoredo, K., Toivonen, H.: Compressing probabilistic prolog programs. Mach. Learn. 70(2–3), 151–168 (2008)

22. Rogge-Solti, A., Senderovich, A., Weidlich, M., Mendling, J., Gal, A.: In log and model we trust? A generalized conformance checking framework. In: La Rosa, M., Loos, P., Pastor, O. (eds.) BPM 2016. LNCS, vol. 9850, pp. 179–196. Springer, Cham (2016). https://doi.org/10.1007/978-3-319-45348-4_11

23. Sun, Y., Du, Y., Li, M.: A repair of workflow models based on mirroring matrices. Int. J. Parallel Program. **45**(4), 1001–1020 (2017)

24. Taylor, C., Nakhaeizadeh, G.: Learning in dynamically changing domains: theory revision and context dependence issues. In: van Someren, M., Widmer, G. (eds.) ECML 1997. LNCS, vol. 1224, pp. 353–360. Springer, Heidelberg (1997). https://doi.org/10.1007/3-540-62858-4_99

25. Wrobel, S.: First order theory refinement. In: De Raedt, L. (ed.) Advances in Inductive Logic Programming. IOS Press, Amsterdam (1996)

26. Xu, Y., Du, Y., Qi, L., Luan, W., Wang, L.: A logic petri net-based model repair approach by constructing choice bridges. IEEE Access **7**, 18531–18545 (2019). https://doi.org/10.1109/ACCESS.2019.2896079

27. Zheng, W., Du, Y., Wang, S., Qi, L.: Repair process models containing non-free-choice structures based on logic petri nets. IEEE Access **7**, 105132–105145 (2019)

Upper-Bounded Model Checking
for Declarative Process Models

Nicolai Schützenmeier[(✉)], Martin Käppel, Sebastian Petter,
and Stefan Jablonski

Institute for Computer Science, University of Bayreuth, Bayreuth, Germany
{nicolai.schuetzenmeier,martin.kaeppel,sebastian.petter,
stefan.jablonski}@uni-bayreuth.de

Abstract. Declarative process modelling languages like Declare focus
on describing a process by restrictions over the behaviour, which must be
satisfied throughout process execution. Although this paradigm allows
more flexibility, it has been shown that such models are often hard to
read and understand, which affects their modelling, execution and maintenance in a negative way. A larger degree of flexibility leads to a multitude of different process models that describe the same process. Often
it is difficult for the modeller to keep the model as simple as possible
without over- or underspecification. Hence, model checking, especially
comparing declarative process models on equality becomes an important
task. In this paper, we determine and prove a theoretical upper bound
for the trace length up to which the process executions of Declare models
must be compared, to decide with certainty whether two process models
are equal or not.

Keywords: Linear temporal logic · Model checking · Declarative
process management.

1 Introduction

In business process management (BPM) two opposing classes of business processes can be identified: routine processes and flexible processes (also called
knowledge-intensive, decision-intensive, or declarative processes) [9,10]. For the
latter, in the last years a couple of different process modelling languages such
as Declare [18], Multi-Perspective-Declare (MP-Declare) [5], DCR graphs [13],
and the Declarative Process Intermediate Language (DPIL) [19,25] emerged.
These languages describe a process by restrictions (so-called *constraints*) over
the behaviour, which must be satisfied throughout process execution. Especially
Declare has become a widespread and frequently used modelling language in the
research area of modelling single-perspective (i.e. focussing on the control-flow)
and flexible processes.

Although this paradigm guarantees more flexibility than the imperative one,
it turned out that declarative process models are for several reasons hard to

Published by Springer Nature Switzerland AG 2021
E. Serral et al. (Eds.): PoEM 2021, LNBIP 432, pp. 195–211, 2021.
https://doi.org/10.1007/978-3-030-91279-6_14

read and understand, which affects the execution, modelling, and maintenance of declarative process models in a negative way: the large degree of flexibility offers the modeller a multitude of options to express the same fact. Hence the same process can be described by very different declarative process models (cf. Sect. 2). In general, declarative process models possess a high risk for over- or underspecification, i.e. the process model forbids valid process executions or it allows process executions that do not correspond to reality, respectively. Often such a wrong specification is caused by hidden dependencies [2], i.e., implicit dependencies between activities that are not explicitly modelled but occur through the interaction of other dependencies. The Declare modelling language relies on linear temporal logic (LTL) [18]. Hence, constraints and process models, respectively, are represented as LTL formulas. Although there is a set of common Declare templates, this set is not exhaustive in the sense that sometimes plain LTL formulas are necessary to complete a process specification. Also for defining customized templates for reuse (i.e. if a dependency between more than two activities should be expressed) modellers are not aware of working with plain LTL. This deficiency increases since a canonical standard form for LTL formulas does not exist, so in general, these formulas are not unique. Mixing the predefined constraints with plain LTL exacerbates the problem of understanding such models.

Therefore there is a high interest to keep a process model as simple as possible without deteriorating conformance with reality. However, changing or simplifying such a process model bears the risks described above, i.e. over- and underspecification. Hence model checking, especially comparing models on equality, becomes an important task for modelling and verifying declarative process models. Most of the time this is achieved by simulating process executions of different length (so-called trace length) and by checking their validity. However, this is a very time-consuming and tedious task and can only be done for a limited number of traces and gives no guarantee that the considered process models are equal.

In this paper we determine and prove a theoretical upper bound for the trace length up to which the process executions must be compared to decide with certainty whether two process models are equal or not.

The rest of the paper is structured as follows: Sect. 2 recalls basic terminology and introduces a running example. In Sect. 3 we give an overview of related work and show how our work differs from existing work. In Sect. 4 we determine an upper bound, prove our claim, discuss existing limitations and the expandability to other declarative process modelling languages. Finally, Sect. 5 draws conclusions from the work and gives an outlook on future work.

2   Running Example and Basic Terminology

In this section we recall basic terminology and introduce a running example. Events, traces and logs are introduced to provide a common basis for the contents of both process models and process traces. Afterwards we give a short introduction of the Declare modelling language, since we focus on this modelling language in the rest of the paper.

2.1 Events, Traces and Logs

We briefly recall the standard definitions of events, traces and process logs as defined in [1]: An event is an occurence of an activity (i.e. a well-defined step in a business process) in a particular process instance. A trace is a time ordered sequence of events which belongs to the execution of the same process instance. Hence, a trace can be viewed as a record of a process execution. A (process) event log is a multiset of traces. We can now define these terms more formally:

Definition 1. *Let $\mathcal{E}$ be the universe of all events, i.e., the set of all possible events. A **trace** is a finite sequence $\sigma = \langle e_1, ..., e_n \rangle$ such that all events belong to the same process instance and are ordered by their execution time, where $n := |\sigma|$ denotes the **trace length** of σ. We use the notation $\sigma(i)$ to refer to the ith element in σ.*

We say a trace is completed if the process instance was successfully closed, i.e. the trace does not violate a constraint of the process model and no additional events related to this process instance will occur in future. Note that in case of declarative process modelling languages like Declare the user must stop working on the process instance to close them, whereas in imperative process models this is achieved automatically by reaching an end event [18]. However, a process instance can only be closed if and only if no constraint of the underlying process model is violated [18].

From the definitions above, we can derive the definition of an event log.

Definition 2. *An **event log** is a multiset $[\sigma_1^{w_1}, ..., \sigma_n^{w_n}]$ of completed traces with $w_i \in \mathbb{N}_+$.*

2.2 Declare and Declare Constraints

Declare is a single-perspective declarative process modelling language that was introduced in [18]. Instead of modelling all viable paths explicitly, Declare describes a set of constraints applied to activities that must be satisfied throughout process execution. Hereby, the control-flow and the ordering of the activities is implicitly specified. All process executions that do not violate a constraint are allowed. In Declare the constraints are instances of templates, i.e. patterns that define parameterized classes of properties [5]. Each template possesses a graphical representation in order to make the model more understandable to the user. Table 1 summarizes the common Declare templates. Although Declare provides a broad repertoire of different templates, which covers the most necessary scenarios, this set is non-exhaustive and can be arbitrarily extended by the modeller. Hence, the user is not aware of the underlying logic-based formalization that defines the semantic of the templates (respectively constraints). Declare relies on the linear temporal logic (LTL) over finite traces (LTL_f) [18]. Hence, we can define a Declare process model formally as follows:

Definition 3. *A **Declare process model** is a pair $(A, \mathcal{T})$ where A is a finite set of activities and $\mathcal{T}$ is a finite set of LTL constraints (i.e. instances of the predefined templates or LTL formulas).*

Table 1. Semantics for Declare constraints in LTL$_f$

Template	LTL$_f$ Semantics
existence(A)	$\mathbf{F}(A)$
absence(A)	$\neg\mathbf{F}(A)$
atLeast(A, n)	$\mathbf{F}(A \wedge \mathbf{X}(\text{atLeast}(A, n - 1)))$, atLeast$(A, 1) = \mathbf{F}(A)$
atMost(A, n)	$\mathbf{G}(\neg A \vee \mathbf{X}(\text{atMost}(A, n - 1)))$, atMost$(A, 0) = \mathbf{G}(\neg A)$
init(A)	A
last(A)	$\mathbf{G}(\neg A \rightarrow \mathbf{F}(A))$
respondedExistence(A, B)	$\mathbf{F}(A) \rightarrow \mathbf{F}(B)$
response(A, B)	$\mathbf{G}(A \rightarrow \mathbf{F}(B))$
alternateResponse(A, B)	$\mathbf{G}(A \rightarrow \mathbf{X}(\neg A U B))$
chainResponse(A, B)	$\mathbf{G}(A \rightarrow \mathbf{X}(B)) \wedge \text{response}(A, B)$
precedence(A, B)	$\mathbf{F}(B) \rightarrow ((\neg B) U A)$
alternatePrecedence(A, B)	precedence$(A, B) \wedge \mathbf{G}(B \rightarrow \mathbf{X}(\text{precedence}(A, B)))$
chainPrecedence(A, B)	precedence$(A, B) \wedge \mathbf{G}(\mathbf{X}(B) \rightarrow A)$
succession(A, B)	response$(A, B) \wedge$ precedence(A, B)
chainSuccession(A, B)	$\mathbf{G}(A \leftrightarrow \mathbf{X}(B))$
alternateSuccession(A, B)	alternateResponse$(A, B) \wedge$ alternatePrecedence(A, B)
notRespondedExistence(A, B)	$\mathbf{F}(A) \rightarrow \mathbf{F}(B)$
notResponse(A, B)	$\mathbf{G}(A \rightarrow \neg\mathbf{F}(B))$
notPrecedence(A, B)	$\mathbf{G}(F(B) \rightarrow \neg A)$
notChainResponse	$\mathbf{G}(A \rightarrow \neg\mathbf{X}(B))$
notChainPrecedence(A, B)	$\mathbf{G}(\mathbf{X}(B) \rightarrow \neg A)$
coExistence(A, B)	$\mathbf{F}(A) \leftrightarrow \mathbf{F}(B)$
notCoExistence(A, B)	$\neg(\mathbf{F}(A) \wedge \mathbf{F}(B))$
choice(A, B)	$\mathbf{F}(A) \vee \mathbf{F}(B)$
exclusiveChoice(A, B)	$(\mathbf{F}(A) \vee \mathbf{F}(B)) \wedge \neg(\mathbf{F}(A) \wedge \mathbf{F}(B))$

LTL makes statements about the future of a system possible. In addition to the common logical connectors ($\neg, \wedge, \vee, \rightarrow, \leftrightarrow$) and atomic propositions, LTL provides a set of temporal (future) operators. Let ϕ_1 and ϕ_2 be LTL formulas. The future operators $\mathbf{F}, \mathbf{X}, \mathbf{G}, \mathbf{U}$ and $\mathbf{W}$ have the following meaning: formula $\mathbf{F}\phi_1$ means that ϕ_1 sometimes holds in the future, $\mathbf{X}\phi_1$ means that ϕ_1 holds in the next position, $\mathbf{G}\phi_1$ means that ϕ_1 holds forever in the future and $\phi_1\mathbf{U}\phi_2$ means that sometimes in the future ϕ_2 will hold and until that moment ϕ_1 holds. The weaker form of the until operator ($\mathbf{U}$), the so-called weak until $\phi_1\mathbf{W}\phi_2$ has the same meaning as the until operator, whereby ϕ_2 is not required to hold. In this case, ϕ_1 must hold forever.

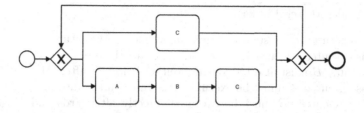

Fig. 1. Running example modelled with BPMN

For a more convenient specification, LTL is often extended to past linear temporal logic (PLTL) [26] by introducing so-called past operators, which makes statements on the past possible but does not increase the expressiveness of the formalism [17]. The past operators $\mathbf{O}, \mathbf{Y}$ and $\mathbf{S}$ have the following meaning: $\mathbf{O}\phi_1$ means that ϕ_1 sometimes holds in the past, $\mathbf{Y}\phi_1$ means that ϕ_1 holds in the previous position and $\phi_1 \mathbf{S} \phi_2$ means that ϕ_1 has held sometimes in the past and since that moment ϕ_2 holds.

For a better understanding, we exemplarily consider the response constraint $\mathbf{G}(A \rightarrow \mathbf{F}B)$. This template means that if A occurs, B must eventually follow sometimes in the future. We consider for example the following traces: $t_1 = \langle A, A, B, C \rangle, t_2 = \langle B, B, C, D \rangle, t_3 = \langle A, B, C, B \rangle$ and $t_4 = \langle A, B, A, C \rangle$. In traces t_1, t_2 and t_3 the response template is satisfied. Note that in t_2 this constraint is trivially fulfilled since A does not occur (so-called *vacuously satisfied*). However, t_4 violates the constraint, because after the second occurrence of A no execution of B follows.

We say that an event activates a constraint in a trace if its occurence imposes some obligations on other events in the same trace. Such an activation either leads to a fulfillment or to a violation of a constraint. Consider, for example, the response template. This constraint is activated by the execution of activity A. In t_4, for instance, the response template is activated twice. In case of the first activation, this leads to a fulfillment, because B occurs. However, the second activations leads to an violation, because B does not occur subsequently.

2.3 Running Example

In this paper we will refer to the following running example. Our sample process consists of three activities namely, A, B and C, with the following control-flow: Either the three activities are executed in sequence (i.e. ABC) or alternatively C is executed arbitrarily often but at least once. In other words, the process can be considered as a loop where in each pass you have the decision to execute activity C or the sequence ABC. For a better understanding, the process model is also shown as BPMN diagram in Fig. 1. This process can be modelled in Declare in different ways. Figure 2a shows a first option and Fig. 2b shows a second option. For representing the two models we use the common graphical Declare notation.

Process Model M_1 (cf. Fig. 2a):

1. If A is executed,B must be executed sometimes in the future.
2. If B is executed, A must be executed sometimes before.
3. If A occurs, B must also be executed (either before or after A).
4. If B is executed, C must be executed sometimes in the future.
5. If A is executed, B must be executed directly afterwards and C directly after B.

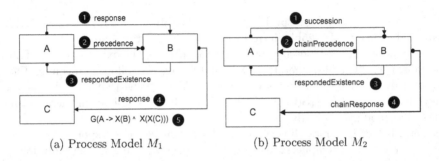

(a) Process Model M_1 (b) Process Model M_2

Fig. 2. Two different Declare process models, describing the same process.

Process Model M_2 (cf. Fig. 2b):

1. If A is executed, B must eventually be executed sometimes in the future and if B is executed, A must be executed sometimes before.
2. If B is executed, A must have been executed directly before.
3. If A occurs, B must also be executed (either before or after A).
4. If B is executed, C must be executed immediately afterwards.

Note that the two process models are made more complicated than necessary in order to demonstrate the difficulty of the comparing task. Apart from the *respondedExistence* template that occurs in both process models, they seem to be completely different with regard to both the applied Declare templates and the number of constraints. Note that in addition to these two variants there are several further options for modelling this process. In the rest of this paper we will explain all steps of this example and we will check whether the two process models are really the same.

3   Related Work

This work relates to the stream of research on modelling and checking declarative process models. Difficulties in understanding and modelling declarative processes are a well-known problem in current research. Nevertheless, there are only a handful of experimental studies that deal with the understandability of declarative process models. In [12] a study reveals that single constraints can be handled well by most individuals, whereas sets of constraints establish a serious challenge. Furthermore, it has been stated that individuals use the composition of the notation elements for interpreting Declare models. Similar studies [2,4] investigated the understandability of hybrid process representations which consist of graphical and text based specifications.

For different model checking tasks of both multi-perspective and single-perspective declarative process models there are different approaches. In [6] an automata based approach is presented for the detection of redundant constraints and contradictions between the constraints. In [8,23] the problem of the detection of hidden dependencies is addressed. In [23] the extracted hidden dependencies are added to the Declare models through visual and textual annotations to improve the understandability of the models. In [20] the authors transform the common Declare templates in a standardized form called positive normalform, with the aim of simplifying model comparisons. However, the proposed representation is not sufficient for a reliable identification of identical process models, since this normalform is not unique.

There is also some effort in transforming Declare process models into different representations for deeper analysis. In [21] formulas of linear temporal logic over finite traces are translated to both nondeterministic and deterministic finite automata. In [11] Büchi automata are generated from LTL formulas. In [24] Declare templates are translated into deterministic finite automata, that are used for implementing a declarative discovery algorithm for the Declare language.

The standard procedure for comparing the desired behaviour with the expected behaviour provided in a process model includes the generation of exemplary process executions, which are afterwards analyzed in detail with regard to undesired behaviour such as contradictions, deadlocks or deviations from the behaviour in reality. Often, for a better understanding of a model, also counterexamples are explicitly constructed to verify whether a model prevents a particular behaviour [16]. For generating exemplary process executions it is necessary to execute declarative process models. In [3] both MP-Declare templates and Declare templates are translated into the logic language Alloy[1] and the corresponding Alloy framework is used for the execution. For generating traces directly from a declarative process model (i.e. MP-Declare as well as Declare) the authors in [22] also use Alloy to generate event logs. In [16], based on a given process execution trace (that can also be empty), possible continuations of the process execution are simulated up to an a-priori defined length. The authors emphasize the usefulness of model checking of (multi-perspective) declarative processes by simulating different behaviours. However, the length of the look-ahead is chosen arbitrarily and, hence, can only guarantee the correctness of a model up to a certain trace length. In summary, the need for a generally applicable algorithm to determine the minimum trace lenth required to find out whether process models are equivalent is still there and this issue has not been solved so far.

---

[1] https://alloytools.org/.

4   Determining an Upper Bound for Model Checking

In this section we determine and prove an upper bound for the trace length to check two Declare models for equality. The main idea is to transform each of the process models to be compared into a deterministic finite state automaton. This automaton is constructed as a minimized product automaton of the corresponding automata representing the constraints of a process model. Hence, we transform the problem of checking two process models for equality into the language equivalence problem of deterministic finite state automata. This transformation allows us to give a mathematical proof that the trace length which must be considered depends on the product of the number of states of the corresponding product automata. In the following we first introduce deterministic finite state automata and explain the transformation of Declare templates into such automata (cf. Sect. 4.1). Afterwards we show the construction of the minimal product automaton for a process model (cf. Sect. 4.2). In Sect. 4.3 we prove our theorem and determine the theoretical upper bound for the trace length. In Sect. 4.4 based on this theorem, we formulate a general model checking algorithm and apply it to our running example. In Sect. 4.6 we discuss consequences of this theorem and the expandability to other declarative process modelling languages.

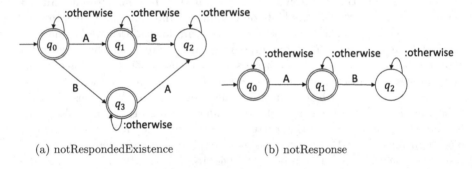

(a) notRespondedExistence   (b) notResponse

Fig. 3. FSA for additional Declare templates

4.1   Transformation of Declare Templates into Finite State Automata

The first step of our approach is to transform the Declare templates (cf. Sect. 2) into deterministic finite state automata (FSA) [14]. Therefore, we need some formal definitions:

Definition 4. *A **deterministic finite-state automaton (FSA)** is a quintuple* $M = (\Sigma, S, s_0, \delta, F)$ *where* Σ *is a finite (non-empty) set of symbols,* S *is a finite (non-empty) set of states,* $s_0 \in S$ *is an initial state,* $\delta : S \times \Sigma \to S$ *is the state-transition function, and* $F \subseteq S$ *is the set of final states.*

As we want to deal with words and not only single symbols, we have to expand the definition:

Definition 5. *Let Σ be a finite (non-empty) set of symbols. Then $\Sigma^* := \{a_1 a_2 \ldots a_n \mid n \in \mathbb{N}_0, a_i \in \Sigma\}$ is the **set of all words** over symbols in Σ. For each word $\omega \in \Sigma^*$ we define the **length of** ω as*

$$|\omega| := \begin{cases} 0 & \omega = \varepsilon \ (\varepsilon \text{ denotes the empty string}) \\ 1 & \omega \in \Sigma \\ |a| + |b| & \omega = ab \text{ with } a \in \Sigma \text{ and } b \in \Sigma^* \end{cases}$$

Definition 6. *For a FSA $M = (\Sigma, S, s_0, \delta, F)$ we define the **extended state-transition function** $\hat{\delta} : S \times \Sigma^* \to S$,*

$$(s, \omega) \mapsto \begin{cases} s & \omega = \varepsilon \\ \delta(s, \omega) & \omega \in \Sigma \\ \delta(\hat{\delta}(s, a), b) & \omega = ab \text{ with } a \in \Sigma \text{ and } b \in \Sigma^* \end{cases}$$

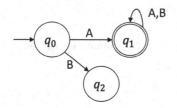

Fig. 4. Finite state automaton M with $\mathcal{L}(M) = \{A\omega \mid \omega \in \{A, B\}^*\}$

In the following, for the sake of simplicity, δ always denotes the extended state-transition function $\hat{\delta}$ for words $\omega \in \Sigma^*$.

Definition 7. *Let $M = (\Sigma, S, s_0, \delta, F)$ be a FSA. Then $\mathcal{L}(M) := \{\omega \in \Sigma^* \mid \delta(s_0, \omega) \in F\} \subseteq \Sigma^*$ is called the **language of** M.*

Example 1. Consider $\Sigma = \{A, B\}$. Then $\Sigma^* = \{\epsilon, A, B, AA, AB, BA, BB, \ldots\}$ consists of all strings including any number of A's and B's.
$L := \{A\omega \mid \omega \in \Sigma^*\} = \{A, AA, AB, AAA, \ldots\}$ is the language of all words with A at the beginning. The corresponding FSA is depicted in Fig. 4.

In [24], the authors present a transformation of most of the Declare templates into a FSA where Σ is the set of the occurring activities. We have determined the corresponding automata of the remaining Declare templates. The results are illustrated in Fig. 3.

The traces that fulfill a Declare template are exactly the elements of the language of the corresponding FSA. For example, the trace $t_1 = \langle A, A \rangle$ fulfills the *notResponse* template whereas the trace $t_2 = \langle A, A, B \rangle$ does not. The same thing holds for the automaton, too: t_1 is accepted and t_2 is not accepted (see Fig. 3).

The transitions labelled with *:otherwise* are needed because in general there are more than two activities in a process model. The other activities, that do not concern the corresponding template, do not influence the properties of the automata but must be included in the construction of the automata. Details will be described later.

4.2   Transformation of Declare Process Models to Finite State Automata

In this section we show how a Declare process model can be transformed into a finite state automaton. As a Declare process model M consists of a set of different Declare templates $\{T_1, \ldots, T_n\}$, a trace t that satisfies M is a trace, that satisfies all the templates:

$$t \text{ satisfies } M \iff t \text{ satisfies } T_1 \wedge \cdots \wedge T_n \tag{1}$$

In order to transform a Declare model into a FSA, we apply the concept of the *product automaton* [14]:

Table 2. Number of states of all automata for corresponding Declare templates.

Template	$|S|$	Template	$|S|$
existence(A)	2	alternatePrecedence(A, B)	3
absence(A)	2	chainPrecedence(A, B)	3
atLeast(A, n)	$n + 1$	succession(A, B)	3
atMost(A, n)	$n + 1$	chainSuccession(A, B)	3
init(A)	3	alternateSuccession(A, B)	3
last(A)	2	notPrecedence(A, B)	3
respondedExistence(A, B)	3	notRespondedExistence(A, B)	4
response(A, B)	2	notResponse(A, B)	3
alternateResponse(A, B)	3	notChainResponse(A, B)	3
chainResponse(A, B)	3	choice(A, B)	2
precedence(A, B)	3	exclusiveChoice(A, B)	4
coExistence(A, B)	4	notChainPrecedence(A, B)	3
notCoExistence(A, B)	4		

Definition 8. *Let* $M_1 = (\Sigma, S_1, s_{0_1}, \delta_1, F_1)$ *and* $M_2 = (\Sigma, S_2, s_{0_2}, \delta_2, F_2)$ *two deterministic finite-state automata over the same set of symbols* Σ*. The product automaton* $M = M_1 \times M_2$ *is defined as the quintuple* $M = (\Sigma, S_M, s_{0_M}, \delta_M, F_M)$

where $S_M = S_1 \times S_2$, $s_{0_M} = (s_{0_1}, s_{0_2})$, $\delta_M : S \times \Sigma \rightarrow S, ((s_1, s_2), a) \mapsto (\delta_1(s_1, a), \delta_2(s_2, a))$, *and* $F_M = F_1 \times F_2$.

From the definition of the product automaton $M = M_1 \times M_2$ of two deterministic finite-state automata M_1 and M_2 follows that M accepts exactly the section of $\mathcal{L}(M_1)$ and $\mathcal{L}(M_2)$ [14]:

Remark 1. Let $M_1 = (\Sigma, S_1, s_{0_1}, \delta_1, F_1)$ and $M_2 = (\Sigma, S_2, s_{0_2}, \delta_2, F_2)$ be two deterministic finite-state automata over the same set of symbols Σ. Then $\mathcal{L}(M) = \mathcal{L}(M_1) \cap \mathcal{L}(M_2)$.

Together with Eq. (1) follows: A trace t satisfies a Declare model $M = \{T_1, \ldots, T_n\}$ if and only if $t \in \mathcal{L}(M_1) \cap \cdots \cap \mathcal{L}(M_n) = \mathcal{L}(M_1 \times \cdots \times M_n)$ where M_i is the corresponding FSA of T_i.

4.3   Determining an Upper Bound

In this section we present a method for comparing two Declare process models. The essential part of our approach is the following theorem:

Theorem 1. *Let M_1 and M_2 be two FSA's with m states and n states. Then $\mathcal{L}(M_1) = \mathcal{L}(M_2)$ if and only if $\{\omega \in \mathcal{L}(M_1) \mid |\omega| < mn\} = \{\omega \in \mathcal{L}(M_2) \mid |\omega| < mn\}$*

Proof. We prove the two directions of the implication. As $\mathcal{L}(M_1) = \mathcal{L}(M_2)$, the equality holds for all subsets. That implies especially that $\{\omega \in \mathcal{L}(M_1) \mid |\omega| < mn\} = \{\omega \in \mathcal{L}(M_2) \mid |\omega| < mn\}$.

We prove the opposite direction by contrapositive. So suppose $\mathcal{L}(M_1) \neq \mathcal{L}(M_2)$ and let a be a word of minimal length with $a \notin \mathcal{L}(M_1) \cap \mathcal{L}(M_2) = \mathcal{L}(M_1 \times M_2)$. We further define $M := M_1 \times M_2$ as the product automaton of M_1 and M_2.

We assume by contradiction that $|a| \geq mn$. Regard $X := \{\delta(q_0, b) \mid b$ prefix of $a\}$. Since $|X| \geq mn + 1$ and $|S_M| = mn$, there exist two prefixes u and u' of a with $\delta_M(q_0, u) = \delta_M(q_0, u')$. We assume without any loss of generality that u is a prefix of u'. So there are two words v and z so that $uv = u'$ and $u'z = a$. It follows that $uvz = a$.

As $u \neq u'$, v is not empty. The equation $\delta_M(\delta_M(q_0, u), v) = \delta_M(q_0, u)$ says that v leads M through a loop from state $\delta_M(q_0, u)$ into itself. So we have found a word uz with $\delta_M(q_0, uz) = \delta_M(q_0, a)$ with $|uz| < |a|$. This is a contradiction to the minimality of a.

In order to compare Declare process models, we need to know the number of states S of the corresponding deterministic finite-state automaton of each Declare template. For example, the corresponding automaton of the *notRespondedExistence* template comprises four states ($|S| = 4$). The numbers of states of all Declare templates are shown in Table 2.

We now apply Theorem 1 to our running example. We first calculate the number of states of process model M_1. The corresponding FSA of the defined

---

Algorithm 1. Check the equality of two Declare models

Input: Declare Process Models $P_1 = (A_1, T_1)$ and $P_2 = (A_2, T_2)$
Output: True if the models are equal, otherwise False

```
 1  if A₁ ≠ A₂ then
 2  |    return False
 3  else
 4  |    A ← A₁
         /* Generate minimal FSA for P₁ and P₂                    */
 5  |    U₁ ← ∅
 6  |    for t ∈ T₁ do
 7  |    |    (A, Sₜ, s₀ₜ, δₜ, Fₜ) ← transform t to minimal FSA
 8  |    |    U₁ ← U₁.add((A, Sₜ, s₀ₜ, δₜ, Fₜ))
 9  |    end
10  |    (A, S_{U1}, s_{0U1}, δ_{U1}, F_{U1}) ← create minimal product automaton of U₁
11  |    n ← |S_{U1}|
12  |    U₂ ← ∅
13  |    for t ∈ T₂ do
14  |    |    (A, Sₜ, s₀ₜ, δₜ, Fₜ) ← transform t to minimal FSA
15  |    |    U₂ ← U₂.add((A, Sₜ, s₀ₜ, δₜ, Fₜ))
16  |    end
17  |    (A, S_{U2}, s_{0U2}, δ_{U2}, F_{U2}) ← create minimal product automaton of U₂
18  |    m ← |S_{U2}|
         /* Calculating upper bound −1 due to < in Theorem 1       */
19  |    upperBound ← m · n − 1
         /* Generate traces until upperBound                        */
20  |    tracesP₁ ← generate all traces for P₁ with length ≤ upperBound
21  |    tracesP₂ ← generate all traces for P₂ with length ≤ upperBound
         /* Comparing the generated traces                          */
22  |    if tracesP₁ ≠ tracesP₂ then
23  |    |    return False
24  |    else
25  |    |    return True
26  |    end
27  end
```

---

template $\mathbf{G}(A \rightarrow \mathbf{X}(B) \wedge \mathbf{X}(\mathbf{X}(C)))$ comprises 4 states. So for M_1 we get a total of $4 \cdot 3 \cdot 3 \cdot 2 = 72$ states. Analogously for M_2 we get $3 \cdot 3 \cdot 3 \cdot 3 = 81$ states. Our theorem says that we need to run all traces t with $|t| < 72 \cdot 81 = 5832$ in order to check the models M_1 and M_2 for equality.

4.4   Checking Declare Models for Equality

Based on the previous results it is now possible to describe an algorithm for checking equality of two Declare process models (cf. Algorithm 1). Therefore, we assume that in the two process models to be compared the activities are named identically, otherwise we consider the two models to be different. For both process models, we first transform the constraints of the process models into a minimal FSA and afterwards we construct the product automaton of these single FSAs. Hence, our process model is described by the product automaton. We use the Hopcroft Algorithm [15] for minimization of the product automaton, since this algorithm works very efficiently. To get a smaller upper bound, it is necessary to minimize this automaton. The product of the number of states of both automatons determines the upper bound. Note, that the explicit construction of the product automaton is only necessary if we want a smaller upper bound, otherwise it would be sufficient to multiply the number of states of the FSAs of the constraints to get an upper bound. Afterwards, the determined upper bound is used to configure trace generators for Declare process models, such as proposed in [16,22]. In the typical use cases of trace generators the generated traces possess a trace length that ranges between 0 and a few hundreds. However, from the technical perspective these tools are not limited with regard to the trace length. Hence, they are suited for this task but require more computational power. Eventually, the set of generated traces must be compared for equality. If the two sets are identical, we can say that the process models are equal, too. Otherwise the process models differ.

4.5   Evaluation and Runtime Analysis

We discuss the execution time of our algorithm by determining its asymptotic behaviour. For the construction of the non-mimized product automaton from the constraints of a process model we get an execution time of

$$\mathcal{O}\left(\prod_{t\in T_1}|S_t|\right).$$

The product automaton can be minimized in [15]:

$$\mathcal{O}\left(\prod_{t\in T_1}|S_t|\cdot\log\log\left(\prod_{t\in T_1}|S_t|\right)\right).$$

The most computational intensive task is the generation and checking of the traces. In dependency of the applied technique (i.e. SAT solving) the execution time differs. We denote this execution time in dependency of the considered process model $\mathcal{P}$ with $\gamma(\mathcal{P})$. SAT solving for propositional logic is known to be NP-complete (Cook-Levin theorem [7]). Hence, the execution time for generating and validating traces is exponential and also dominates the execution time of our algorithm. Note that measuring the execution time does not primarily evaluate the algorithm itself rather than the applied SAT solver. Hence, we have in summary the following asymptotic behaviour for our algorithm, where the first two terms describe the execution time of constructing the corresponding non minimal product automata, the third and fourth term the minimization of the two product automata, and the last two terms describe the execution time for generating and checking the traces until the upper bound:

$$\mathcal{O}\left(\prod_{t\in T_1}|S_t|\right) + \mathcal{O}\left(\prod_{t\in T_2}|S_t|\right) + \mathcal{O}\left(\prod_{t\in T_1}|S_t|\cdot\log\log\left(\prod_{t\in T_1}|S_t|\right)\right)$$

$$+ \mathcal{O}\left(\prod_{t\in T_2}|S_t|\cdot\log\log\left(\prod_{t\in T_2}|S_t|\right)\right) + \gamma(\mathcal{P}_1) + \gamma(\mathcal{P}_2).$$

Since the last terms are the predominately ones the execution time of our algorithm is exponential. However, if we are only interested in the upper bound, the execution time is constant, since both the explicit construction of the product automata as well as the trace generation is unnecessary. We evaluate the development of the upper bound in dependency of the number of constraints in the considered process models. Therefore, we assume the worst case, i.e. that each FSA of the corresponding templates has 4 states, since this is the maximal number of states, beside the recursive templates *atLeast* and *atMost*.

$$\left(\prod_{t\in T_1}|S_t|\right)\cdot\left(\prod_{t\in T_2}|S_t|\right) - 1 \le 4^{|T_1|}\cdot 4^{|T_2|} - 1$$

We observe that the upper bound grows also exponentially. In Fig. 5 we exemplarily depict the increase of the upper bound in dependency of the number of constraints of two process models.

4.6   Limitations and Expandability to Other Process Modelling Languages

Since our upper bound depends only on the ability to transform a process model into a FSA, this concept can be applied to any declarative modelling language whose expressiveness allows a mapping to a FSA. For example, in case of the multi-perspective extension of Declare, MP-Declare, that means that first the templates must be transformed into Colored-Petri-Nets. Afterwards, these Petri Nets can be transformed into a FSA. However, as the small running example already reveals, in general the upper bound is relative high. Hence, it needs a lot of computational power to check process models for equality in this way. However, since the statement of the theorem is an equivalence, this theorem can be used for searching a counterexample to prove the difference of the models. For this issue, in many cases it will not be necessary to simulate all traces to the upper bound to verify the difference of models.

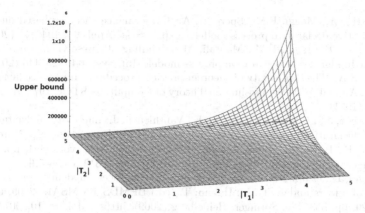

Fig. 5. Development of the upper bound in dependency of the number of constraints of the process models to be compared

5 Conclusion and Future Work

In this paper we determined and prove an upper bound for the trace length for comparing two Declare process models for equality by using FSA construction and minimization. We used this upper bound for formulating a model checking algorithm and analyzed its execution time in detail. The algorithm shows an exponential execution time. Also the upper bound increases exponentially in dependency of the number of constraints. In future work, it will be investigated whether a significant smaller upper bound can be found by considering the process specific characteristic of the Declare templates. It should be also investigated whether a probabilistic upper bound, that guarantees equality with a particular probability, can be found. An upper bound for further modelling languages, like MP-Declare, should also be determined.

References

1. van der Aalst, W.M.P.: Process Mining - Discovery, Conformance and Enhancement of Business Processes. Springer, Wiesbaden (2011). https://doi.org/10.1007/978-3-642-19345-3
2. Abbad Andaloussi, A., Burattin, A., Slaats, T., Petersen, A.C.M., Hildebrandt, T.T., Weber, B.: Exploring the understandability of a hybrid process design artifact based on DCR graphs. In: Reinhartz-Berger, I., Zdravkovic, J., Gulden, J., Schmidt, R. (eds.) BPMDS/EMMSAD -2019. LNBIP, vol. 352, pp. 69–84. Springer, Cham (2019). https://doi.org/10.1007/978-3-030-20618-5_5
3. Ackermann, L., Schönig, S., Petter, S., Schützenmeier, N., Jablonski, S.: Execution of multi-perspective declarative process models. In: OTM 2018 Conferences (2018)
4. Abbad Andaloussi, A., Buch-Lorentsen, J., López, H.A., Slaats, T., Weber, B.: Exploring the modeling of declarative processes using a hybrid approach. In: Laender, A.H.F., Pernici, B., Lim, E.-P., de Oliveira, J.P.M. (eds.) ER 2019. LNCS, vol. 11788, pp. 162–170. Springer, Cham (2019). https://doi.org/10.1007/978-3-030-33223-5_14

5. Burattin, A., Maggi, F.M., Sperduti, A.: Conformance checking based on multi-perspective declarative process models. Expert Syst. Appl. **65**, 194–211 (2016)
6. Ciccio, C.D., Maggi, F.M., Montali, M., Mendling, J.: Resolving inconsistencies and redundancies in declarative process models. Inf. Syst. **64**, 425–446 (2017)
7. Cook, S.A.: The complexity of theorem-proving procedures. In: Proceedings of the Third Annual ACM Symposium on Theory of Computing. STOC 1971, ACM, NY, USA (1971)
8. De Smedt, J., De Weerdt, J., Serral, E., Vanthienen, J.: Improving understandability of declarative process models by revealing hidden dependencies. In: Nurcan, S., Soffer, P., Bajec, M., Eder, J. (eds.) CAiSE 2016. LNCS, vol. 9694, pp. 83–98. Springer, Cham (2016). https://doi.org/10.1007/978-3-319-39696-5_6
9. Fahland, D., et al.: Declarative versus imperative process modeling languages: the issue of understandability. In: Halpin, T. (ed.) BPMDS/EMMSAD -2009. LNBIP, vol. 29, pp. 353–366. Springer, Heidelberg (2009). https://doi.org/10.1007/978-3-642-01862-6_29
10. Fahland, D., Mendling, J., Reijers, H.A., Weber, B., Weidlich, M., Zugal, S.: Declarative versus imperative process modeling languages: the issue of maintainability. In: Rinderle-Ma, S., Sadiq, S., Leymann, F. (eds.) BPM 2009. LNBIP, vol. 43, pp. 477–488. Springer, Heidelberg (2010). https://doi.org/10.1007/978-3-642-12186-9_45
11. Gastin, P., Oddoux, D.: Fast LTL to Büchi automata translation. In: Berry, G., Comon, H., Finkel, A. (eds.) CAV 2001. LNCS, vol. 2102, pp. 53–65. Springer, Heidelberg (2001). https://doi.org/10.1007/3-540-44585-4_6
12. Haisjackl, C., et al.: Understanding declare models: strategies, pitfalls, empirical results. Softw. Syst. Model. **15**(2), 325–352 (2016)
13. Hildebrandt, T.T., Mukkamala, R.R., Slaats, T., Zanitti, F.: Contracts for cross-organizational workflows as timed dynamic condition response graphs. J. Log. Algebr. Program. **82**(5–7), 164–185 (2013)
14. Hopcroft, J., Motwani, R., Ullman, J.: Introduction to Automata Theory, Languages, and Computation. Pearson/Addison Wesley, Boston (2007)
15. Hopcroft, J.E.: An n log n algorithm for minimizing states in a finite automaton. Technical report, Stanford, CA, USA (1971)
16. Käppel, M., Ackermann, L., Schönig, S., Jablonski, S.: Language-independent look-ahead for checking multi-perspective declarative process models. Softw. Syst. Model. **20**(5), 1379–1401 (2021). https://doi.org/10.1007/s10270-020-00857-8
17. Laroussinie, F., Markey, N., Schnoebelen, P.: Temporal logic with forgettable past. In: Proceedings of the 17th Annual IEEE Symposium on Logic in Computer Science (2002)
18. Pesic, M.: Constraint-based workflow management systems : shifting control to users. Ph.D. thesis, Industrial Engineering and Innovation Sciences (2008)
19. Schönig, S., Ackermann, L., Jablonski, S.: Towards an implementation of data and resource patterns in constraint-based process models. In: Modelsward (2018)
20. Schützenmeier, N., Käppel, M., Petter, S., Schönig, S., Jablonski, S.: Detection of declarative process constraints in LTL formulas. In: Pergl, R., Babkin, E., Lock, R., Malyzhenkov, P., Merunka, V. (eds.) EOMAS 2019. LNBIP, vol. 366, pp. 131–145. Springer, Cham (2019). https://doi.org/10.1007/978-3-030-35646-0_10
21. Shi, Y., Xiao, S., Li, J., Guo, J., Pu, G.: Sat-based automata construction for LTL over finite traces. In: 2020 27th Asia-Pacific Software Engineering Conference (APSEC) (2020)
22. Skydanienko, V., Francescomarino, C.D., Maggi, F.: A tool for generating event logs from multi-perspective declare models. In: BPM (Demos) (2018)

23. Smedt, J.D., Weerdt, J.D., Serral, E., Vanthienen, J.: Discovering hidden dependencies in constraint-based declarative process models for improving understandability. Inf. Syst. **74**(Part), 40–52 (2018)
24. Westergaard, M., Stahl, C., Reijers, H.: Unconstrainedminer: efficient discovery of generalized declarative process models. BPMcenter. org, BPM reports (2013)
25. Zeising, M., Schönig, S., Jablonski, S.: Towards a common platform for the support of routine and agile business processes. In: Collaborative Computing: Networking, Applications and Worksharing (2014)
26. Zuck, L.: Past temporal logic. Ph.D. thesis, Weizmann Institute, Israel (1986)

Requirements Engineering for Privacy, Security and Governance

On the Philosophical Foundations of Privacy: Five Theses

Mohamad Gharib[1,2(✉)] [iD] and John Mylopoulos[3]

[1] University of Tartu, Tartu, Estonia
mohamad.gharib@ut.ee
[2] University of Florence, Florence, Italy
mohamad.gharib@unifi.it
[3] University of Trento, Trento, Italy
john.mylopoulos@unitn.it

Abstract. Privacy has emerged as a key concern for companies that deal with Personal Information (PI) since they need to comply with certain privacy requirements. Unfortunately, these requirements are often incomplete or inaccurate due to the vagueness of the privacy concept. This paper tries to tackle this problem, contributing to the philosophical foundations of privacy by addressing several foundational questions such as What is privacy? What makes information a PI? Is PI a property? Do we own our PI? To what extent we are entitled to protect our PI? How do we protect our PI? After answering the aforementioned questions, we characterize the privacy concept that allows providing a more precise and meaningful conceptualization of privacy requirements, which may improve dealing with them during the design of privacy-aware systems.

Keywords: Privacy · Personal information · Philosophical foundations · Conceptual modeling · Requirements engineering

1 Introduction

Privacy has emerged as a key concern for companies that collect and manage PI since they need to comply with certain privacy requirements [1]. If such privacy requirements were captured and addressed appropriately during system design, most of the privacy concerns could be tackled. Unfortunately, privacy requirements are often inaccurate and incomplete, which is mainly due to the vagueness and complexity of the privacy concept [2]. More specifically, many requirements engineers limit the wide scope of privacy requirements to narrow perspectives (e.g., confidentiality, secrecy) [3].

Privacy is one of the few concepts that has been thoroughly studied across many disciplines for centuries, including Psychology [4], Philosophy [5,6], Sociology [7], Law [8–10], and Political Science [11] to mention a few. Despite this, it is still elusive and vague concept to grasp [3,12,13]. Moreover, there is no

© IFIP International Federation for Information Processing 2021
Published by Springer Nature Switzerland AG 2021
E. Serral et al. (Eds.): PoEM 2021, LNBIP 432, pp. 215–229, 2021.
https://doi.org/10.1007/978-3-030-91279-6_15

consensus on the definition of the privacy concept among these disciplines [3]. For instance, privacy has been defined as "the right to be left alone" [8], and "a state of limited access to self" as defined in [11]. Other scholars (e.g., [14]) defined privacy as a "control over when and by whom the various parts of us can be sensed by others". Several other scholars recognized that privacy cannot be limited to a single concept [3], and they consider integrating different conceptions (called "cluster formulations") to define privacy.

On the other hand, several researchers differentiate between what can be called *general privacy theories* [4,11,12] that considers both the *spatial* and *informational* perspectives, and *information privacy theories* that focuses mainly on the *informational* perspective [13], which is the main focus of this paper. All of this has led to confusion when dealing with privacy requirements either on the side of requirements engineers or on the side of individuals, who are expected to play an active role in specifying their privacy requirements.

In previous research [15,16], we proposed an ontology for privacy requirements that has been mined through a systematic literature review [2,17]. The ontology has been implemented, validated, and its completeness/coverage was evaluated with the help of privacy and security researchers. However, an ontology is concerned with answering questions like *what entities exist*, not *why they exist*, which can be answered relying on metaphysics that studies the very nature of an entity and explains why it exists [18].

This paper tries to tackle this problem contributing to the philosophical foundations of privacy by addressing several foundational questions related to the concept of privacy such as "What is privacy?", "What makes information a PI?", "To what extent we are entitled to protect our PI?" Answering these questions can widen our knowledge and understanding of the privacy concept allowing us to identify five key theses of privacy, which we use to characterize the privacy concept. This enables a more precise and meaningful conceptualization of privacy requirements, which may facilitate and improve dealing with them by increasing privacy awareness on the side of both requirements engineers and individuals during system design.

The rest of the paper is structured as follows; Sect. 2 presents a historical overview of the privacy concept. Section 3 discusses the philosophical foundation of privacy identifying five key theses of privacy, and Sect. 4 characterizes the privacy concept in light of the aforementioned theses. Section 5 proposes a new conceptualization of privacy. We discuss challenges and future work in Sect. 6, and we conclude the paper in Sect. 7.

2   The Concept of Privacy: A Historical Overview

The concept of "privacy" has historical origins that date back into antiquity, most notably in Aristotle's distinction between the public sphere and the private one that is associated with family and domestic life [19]. Similarly, the concept of privacy ("being private") was linked to the individuals' private properties (e.g., own house) in Roman times [6]. In fact, the Latin word "privatus" makes a legal distinction between what is "private" and what is "public" ("publicus") [20]. Hence, both of the Greeks and Romans have almost the same view concerning privacy, which was geared more toward the sense of property, i.e., what is private should belong to an individual's property, otherwise, it is public.

According to Holvast [21], this sense continues to exist during the *Early modern period (1450–1800)* as people went to court for eavesdropping or opening and reading personal letters. The same sense still survives today with the legal recognition of the individuals' right to property [6]. In particular, it has been grounded in Law when the "privacy as a right" was born, first defined by Warren and Brandeis [8] in 1890 as the "the right to be left alone", which became central to legal interpretations and court decisions [13].

Debates concerning privacy became prominent in the second half of the twentieth century. For instance, Prosser [9], in his highly influential paper that shaped the development of the American law of tort privacy, divided the "right to privacy" into four discrete torts: 1- an intrusion upon the plaintiff's seclusion, solitude, or private affairs; 2- public disclosure of embarrassing private facts about the plaintiff; 3- publicity that placed the plaintiff in a false light in the public eye; and 4- appropriation for the defendant's advantage of the plaintiff's name or likeness. Although Prosser gave tort privacy legitimacy, he also limited its ability to adapt to the problems of the Information Age [10]. In particular, privacy has been mainly understood in a narrow sense referring to physical privacy in the home or office, etc. [7], i.e., what happened behind "closed doors" stays there. This perspective "fail short" to deal with recent privacy concerns such as the extensive collection, use, and disclosure of PI [10].

Besides Law, other disciplines have their contributions to the concept of privacy. For example, privacy has been viewed as a feeling, an emotion, a desire that supports our social interaction with others in Psychology [13]. In Philosophy, privacy was defined as "a state of limited access or isolation" [5]. Economists have sketched the essential elements of privacy based on economic value [22]. In Political Science, privacy was defined in terms of self-determination, i.e., it provides individuals and groups with preservation of autonomy [11]. In Sociology, privacy was approached from the "power and influence" perspectives between individuals, groups, and institutions within society [7].

Each of these definitions carries a set of dimensions that point to the multidimensional nature of privacy [13], which motivated expanding the view on the privacy concept to include a number of so-called *privacy interests* [23] such as control [14], confidentiality [8], self-determination [11], solitude [9], anonymity [24], secrecy [12], etc. Such interests (concepts) can be considered as dimensions of privacy [13], which contributes to the confusion while dealing with privacy.

3   The Philosophical Foundation of Privacy

Privacy has received relatively little attention from philosophers compared to other important concepts, such as Freedom, Human rights, or Democracy [6]. Nonetheless, there are very interesting philosophical works related to privacy, and the main focus of this section is to review these works trying to contribute to our understanding of key philosophical aspects of privacy.

What Privacy is: the Five theses of Privacy. It is natural for a complex concept like privacy to have a variety of definitions [6]. As we saw earlier, philosophers, psychologists, sociologists, economists, and legal theorists have great difficulty in reaching consensus on a definition of privacy even in their respective domains [25]. Such diversity of definitions indicates uncertainty concerning what privacy is [14], which led some scholars to even renounce the idea of providing a precise definition of privacy [3,6]. However, the core aspects of privacy can be identified by comparing the commonalities in how scholars have approached this complex concept. Reviewing the existing definitions of privacy, it can be noted that most of them agree on most of the following five key aspects:

1. Privacy is centered around an *individual*, who can claim it;
2. The *private sphere* (not necessarily physical) entitles the individual to protect only a subset of her PI;
3. An individual should have *a right* to justify her claims concerning the protection of her PI, especially, outside of her *private sphere*;
4. An individual should have a "sort" of *ownership* over her PI; and
5. An individual should be entitled to *control* the "use" of her PI.

The thesis of this paper is considering these aspects as the five theses of privacy and discussed in the rest of this section.

3.1   Thesis One: Privacy as an Individual Right

The conceptual relationship between privacy and the individual has received vast attention in the philosophical discussions [6,26]. We have seen that privacy was linked to individuals and their private properties since Greek and Roman times, and the relation between privacy and individuals is clear in many definitions of privacy. For example, privacy has been also considered as an essential requirement for an individual's autonomy [27,28], her freedom of choice and actions [26], and her moral worth and dignity [5] to mention a few.

According to Hongladarom [6], privacy seems to be a quintessentially individual concept, and it is seen as something that only an individual enjoys [6,11]. Therefore, the individual is central in any definition of privacy, simply because without an individual, there is no need for privacy. In such a context, one main difference between information and PI is the individual that PI is related to. Moreover, most scholars consider that PI also covers some of the individual's activities/behavior, etc. [22]. However, do we consider any information that is related to an individual, her activities, etc. as her PI? Many relatively recent studies (e.g., [15,24]) highlighted that information should allow the identification of an individual to be considered her PI, i.e., it is not sufficient to be only related to an individual but it also should "sufficiently" identify her. To this end, the main objective of this thesis is answering *whether an information item can be considered PI, and if it is, identifying the individual it is related to.*

The question now is, are we entitled to protect (e.g., control the access and use of) all of our PI? Consider for example a manager who wrote a recommendation letter for one of his employees. Information in such a letter is surely related to the employee (an identified or identifiable natural person) as it describes some of her professional characteristics, her attitude towards work, activities she performed, etc. But why she cannot control the access and use of such information? Or even read the letter unless she was permitted by the manager who wrote it? We will elaborate on this issue while discussing the other theses of privacy.

3.2 Thesis Two: Privacy as Solitude in the Private Sphere

We have seen that an individual is essential for privacy, and we discussed when information can be considered PI. The question now, *How we can specify when an individual is entitled to protect her PI?* A good starting point could be the notion of private sphere [6,26]. As previously discussed, the sense of privacy that is related to a private sphere, separating what is private and what is public, has been grounded in Law when the "privacy as a right" was born in 1890 [8]. Although, this line is not clear as it used to be, the notion of separating what is private from what is public survived.

To understand the main purpose of such a sphere, we need to answer the question: *Why an individual needs a private sphere?* According to various researchers (e.g., [6,11]), individuals behave differently when they know they are being watched as they behave according to the wish of others rather than of their own free will [26]. Other scholars believe that such a sphere is necessary for an individual's autonomy [5,27]. Therefore, a main purpose of a private sphere is to allow an individual to maintain her autonomy and freedom of behavior by controlling when, and to what extent she can be accessed by others.

We know, by now, that a private sphere is related to an individual, and may represent a physical or a virtual area, where an individual may exist and perform her activities. What is not clear, *How can we specify such sphere?* Considering the letter example, if the employee exists and behaves within a private sphere that preserves her PI/privacy, how such letters can be written? We know that the letter contains information related to the employee's professional characteristics and activities. We also know that such a letter does (or should) not contain any information related to the employee's private life (e.g., religion, sexual orientation). Why it is ok for some PI to be used almost "freely" by others, while for other PI, it is forbidden?

Reviewing the PI included in the letter, it is easy to note that such PI describes employee's characteristics or activities that are "publicly" available or were performed, where she cannot control who has access to her PI/activities. While PI that has not been included in the letter can be considered private to the employee and she can control (or has the right to control) who has access to them. Thus, a main distinctive feature of the private sphere is the individual's right (and capability) to control who has access to it.

To this end, the private sphere can be described as any physical or virtual area, where an individual may exist (e.g., house) and/or perform activities (e.g., cellphone) and has the right and capability to control who has access to it. In this context, this privacy thesis aims at answering *whether a sphere can be considered private*, and if it is, the individual is entitled to control access to it by various means. Note that if the individual failed to properly control the access to such sphere, no one has the right to acquire, collect or use any PI enclosed in the private sphere. We will elaborate more on this issue while discussing thesis five.

3.3 Thesis Three: Privacy as Property and Legal Right

Almost half a century ago, Thomson [29], a notable philosopher who worked on Ethics and Metaphysics, stated that *the most striking thing about the right to privacy is that nobody seems to have any very clear idea what it is.* In what follows, we will discuss the different approaches that have been followed to interpret the right to privacy, and argue on which basis privacy claims can be justified.

One of the most legalistic approaches to safeguarding privacy that has been offered to information is the notion of treating PI as a property [30–32]. However, this notion has lost its momentum in the early 2000 s [30,31], since it mainly considers negative rights[1] whereas positive rights are also vital for PI protection and should be considered as well [33].

Other philosophers and scholars have come to doubt that there is anything distinctive about the right to privacy [34]. For instance, Thomson [29] stated that "there is no such thing as violating an individual's right to privacy by simply knowing something about him". She further argued that whatever rights to privacy a person has, such rights can be fully derived from property rights, and rights a person has over his own self [34]. In Thomson's view, privacy is a cluster of derivative rights. A similar view was adopted by Posner [22], who argued that a person's right to privacy is violated only if another, more basic, right has been violated [5].

On the other hand, several scholars have argued that there is something distinctive about the right to privacy but it cannot be captured relying only on property rights or rights over individual's herself [5,31,32,34]. In response to that, they propose to adopt a more novel paradigm. For example, Samuelson [31] suggested considering a moral rights-like approach. Other scholars debate that the law, in general, can grant individuals a protectable interest concerning their PI without grounding such interest on fundamental rights [35], personal rights [5] or even property rights [31,32,34]. Finally, several researchers argued that the propertisation of PI might be required but it is not sufficient, and regulation should be also considered [30,33].

As the principle aim of this thesis is answering the question *on which basis privacy claims can be justified?* We favor adopting the notion of a hybrid model of property and legal/regulation based rights that an individual can have, which she can employ to protect her PI. Such model justifies why some PI have been included or excluded from the letter, and why the employee cannot claim any

---

[1] A negative right exists unless someone acts to negate it, while a positive right is a right to be subjected to an action of another person or group.

right concerning the content of such letter since she "willingly" made such PI publicly available to others.

3.4 Thesis Four: Privacy as Ownership of PI

The concepts of ownership have been of interest throughout history, and some researchers suggest that advanced forms of ownership appeared more than 10000 years ago. In the late nineteenth century, the ownership concept was linked to the producing entity, i.e., the owner is the person who has "produced" (found and appropriated) the object [36]. Recently, Janeček [37] discussed three property-based ownership theories concerning information: 1- *first occupancy theories*, grants ownership rights to the producer of information; 2- *last occupancy theories*, grants ownership rights to those who get last to gain control of the information; and 3- *the Humean theories*, in which ownership rights are justified by common sense that is recognized by the community. Janeček stated that these theories are far from being perfect for allocating ownership concerning information since they are mostly inspired by the notion of property ownership.

Concerning the letter example, can we consider the employee as the owner since most information included in it describes activities that were performed by her (*first occupancy theory*)? Or the owner should be the manager who wrote the letter? Since the manager is the actual producer of the letter content. We may argue that the *last occupancy theory* might also apply to grant ownership to the manager since he was the last to gain control of information. Relying on the same theory, the recipient of the letter can also claim ownership. Finally, it is clear that we cannot rely on common sense to specify the owner.

To this end, relying on a pure property-based ownership right might not be adequate for specifying the owner of information. Yet, if ownership is also based on legal/regulation rights this issue might be solved [37]. In this context, and as the main objective of this thesis is answering *what "sort" of ownership an individual can have over her PI*. We believe that adopting property and legal/regulation based ownership approach, in which the individual is, usually, the owner of her PI is the best approach to solve this problem.

It is worth mentioning that providing ownership rights concerning novel "objects" is not a smooth process. For example, intellectual property represented a challenge when it was first introduced since rights in such case do not concern solely a tangible object, rather, the object is intangible [38]. Back to letter example, the employee cannot claim any property or legal/regulation-based ownership rights concerning the content of the letter as she made such information available to be used by others.

3.5 Thesis Five: Privacy as Control over PI

We saw that privacy is not an absence of information about us; rather it is having the capability to control our PI. The question now *Why does an individual wants to control the collection, disclosure, and usage of her PI?* The answer is quite simple, when privacy is invaded, breached or violated, it is lost, which may result in consequences of having an individual's information in "the wrong hands". Therefore, one of the most cited and notable reasons for controlling the collection, disclosure, and use of PI is concerns/risks of losing privacy (e.g., breaches, violations, misuse) [13]. But *How individuals, as owners, control the collection, disclosure and usage of our PI?* Massin [39] provides an extensive discussion on the metaphysics of ownership rights differentiating between the property, its possession, and the rights over it.

Although ownership of PI is not exactly as the ownership of a property as discussed earlier, the same notions can be applied to PI. To this end, we base our discussion while answering *what kind of control an individual is entitled to over the "use" of her PI*, the main objective of this thesis, on Massin's work. In short, PI is distinct from its possession and from rights over it. An individual is, usually, the original owner of her PI and holds absolute rights over it. Ownership over PI can be transferred by the owner. Similarly, rights over PI can be transferred/granted by the owner-temporarily or permanently, partly or wholly, conditionally or unconditionally, even without transferring ownership. An individual can transfer these rights in terms of permissions (e.g., possession, collect) to other legal entities. Finally, PI can be possessed and transferred/shared, yet possession of PI does not ground any right, i.e., it is possible to possess PI without having any right to use it.

4   Characterizing the Privacy Concept

After identifying and discussing the five theses of privacy, we can define privacy as the ability of an individual to express herself selectively to others by controlling the collection, use, share, etc. of her PI. A simplified representation of the concepts identified while discussing the five theses is shown in Fig. 1. We can identify an individual and her two spheres (e.g., private and non-private instead of public).

PI can be specialized into two sub-categories: 1- *private PI* represents any PI that has a private nature and the private sphere can be employed to protect it; and 2- *non-private PI* represents any PI that cannot be classified as a private PI. An individual has full ownership and control over her PI (private and non-private PI) unless she willingly made such PI public, thus, we can identify another category of PI that is *PI made public*. In this category, the individual does not have any ownership or right to control over PI concerning privacy as she loses them when such PI has been made public by her, i.e., *PI made public* can be collected, used, disclosed/shared without the individual permission. Despite this, it is assumed that such PI will be used in contexts compliant with the purposes for which it has been disclosed.

Concerning the collection of non-private PI, the individual should be notified about such collection and she can decide whether to allow it or not. For example, entering a supermarket or any other place, which clearly states that they are using surveillance cameras (notice) means that the individual implicitly consents (grant permission) for the collection of her non-private PI (e.g., shopping

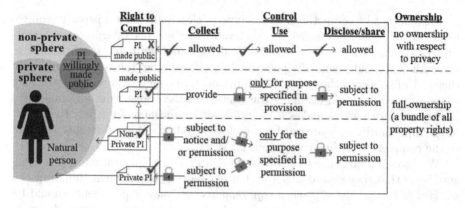

Fig. 1. An individual, her spheres, categories of PI, right to control, control and ownerships over such PI categories

activity). However, collected PI can be used only for the purposes specified in the collection and cannot be shared without the individual's permission.

As private PI are supposed to be protected within the private sphere, its collection is subject to permission. For example, various technologies exist these days for sensing/collecting the vital signs, location, and activities of elderly individuals and forward such PI to a medical authority, which allows for evaluating their health status remotely and continuously. The collection, usage, share, etc. of such PI is subject to the individual's permission.

5   Conceptualizing Privacy Requirements

Naturally, the concept of privacy requirement is centered on the five aforementioned privacy theses, and the main aim of this section is to crystallize the privacy requirement concept, exploring its underlying rationality by answering two questions: 1- *What are the main characteristics of privacy requirements? How are they different from other types of requirements?* and 2- *How can we qualify the quality of privacy requirements?* Then, we provide a more precise and meaningful conceptualization of privacy requirements.

5.1   The Underlying Rationality of Privacy Requirements

Privacy requirements are supposed to capture an individual's privacy needs concerning her PI. Therefore, a privacy requirement should be composed of an individual, PI she has a right to control as well as her privacy needs concerning such PI. Accordingly, any requirement that does not include any of these three elements cannot be considered a privacy requirement.

Like other types of requirements, privacy requirements should ideally be: "complete" (capture all relevant privacy needs of an individual), consistent (such that should not be conflicting), unambiguous/clear (such that a privacy requirement can be easily interpreted, i.e., preferably has only one interpretation), realistic (such that they can be actually realized), and verifiable (such that it is known how to, and practically possible, to verify whether the system can satisfy them). Unlike most other types of requirements, privacy requirements are very context-dependent, i.e., changing the context of the application may raise new privacy concerns, which makes it very difficult to continuously satisfy them [40]. More importantly, they are hard to be clearly and unambiguously specified due to the complexity of the privacy concept [1,41].

We know, by now, the basic elements of a privacy requirement, its key characteristics that they shared or not with other types of requirements but *How can we qualify the quality of privacy requirements?* Privacy requirements should be specified by an individual in response to her concerns/risks of losing privacy as discussed in Sect. 3 (Thesis five: Privacy as control over PI). However, as highlighted by many scholars (e.g., [10,13,41]), individuals fail short in clearly understanding related privacy risks. In turn, they may not have the ability to specify complete, consistent, unambiguous, realistic and verifiable privacy requirements. This leads to confusion not only concerning the specified privacy requirements but also how privacy concerns can be mitigated.

Based on [41], an individual can make an informed decision concerning her privacy requirements if she knows related laws and regulations concerning privacy protection (e.g., the General Data Protection Regulation (GDPR) [42]), strategies for privacy control, and most importantly, potential privacy threats and how such threats can be dealt with. In this context, it is crucial to make individuals aware of potential privacy threats, which allow them to frame their privacy concerns, and in turn, specify their privacy requirements in a realizable way that can tackle such concerns. To elaborate on this issue, we consider an individual called Lara that is planning to use a dating App on her cellphone. Then, we will list key privacy concerns that she became aware of, and discuss how various privacy requirements, we have mined through a systematic literature review [17][2], can be specified and realized to tackle such concerns.

Lara needs to provide some PI to the App to be used for delivering the dating service, yet she might be worried (a privacy concern) that her PI might be used for purposes rather than the dating service. To mitigate such concern, she might have a *confidentiality requirement* concerning the use of her PI, which guarantee that her PI: 1- will not be disclosed to/shared with another entity without her permission (non-disclosure), 2- will only be used if it is strictly necessary for a certain purpose, and 3- will only be used for specific and legitimate purposes (Purpose of Use (PoU)). Even with the confidentiality of her PI is assured, she might consider the risk that her PI might be leaked, breached, etc. due to a wrong practice on the service provider side. To hold them accountable for such breach, an *accountability requirement* might be specified at her side. Finally, if

---

[2] In [17], privacy requirements were further specialized into more refined concepts such as confidentiality, anonymity, unlinkability, unobservability, notice, minimization, transparency, accountability, and the right to erasure/ be forgotten.

she is no longer interested in using the App but she is worried that the service provider will not delete her PI when she uninstalls the App, she can rely on *the right to erasure/be forgotten* (a privacy requirement) to assure that her PI will not be kept by the service provider.

5.2   A New Conceptualization of Privacy Requirements

Following Solove [3], a bottom-up approach has been adopted, which starts conceptualizing privacy requirements within particular contexts focusing on concrete practices. Additionally, we adopted the three criteria for characterizing privacy proposed by Parker [14]. In which, a characterization of privacy requirements should 1- not be overbroad or too narrow; 2- be simple and easily understandable; and 3- be applicable, i.e., allows answering key questions like whether an individual is allowed to the right of privacy, whether she has lost privacy, whether she knows that she has lost privacy, how her privacy has been lost, etc. For example, if a privacy requirement is viewed as a feeling, an emotion, or a psychological state, it would be almost impossible to deal with it concretely.

Based on the previously presented notions, a conceptual model[3] (depicted in Fig. 2) that contains key privacy concepts and relationships for dealing with privacy requirements has been developed. The concepts of the model can be broadly organized into five subcategories of concepts corresponding to the five key theses of privacy. Concerning the first thesis of privacy, we can identify the *natural person* concept that is specialized from the *legal entity* concept, which can be an individual, a company, or an organization that has legal rights and obligations. The *Information* concept can be specialized into two concepts: *PI* and *non-PI*, where the first represents any information that can be *related* to an identified or identifiable legal entity while the last represents any information that cannot be *related* to an identified or identifiable legal entity.

Concerning the second thesis, we can identify the *Sphere of Action (SoA)* concept, which represents a physical or virtual operational environment that is a part of a *domain*. A *natural person* can *perform activities* in a *SoA*. An *activity* can be a *private* or *non-private*. The first can be *described* by *private PI* and must be performed in a *private sphere*, where the *natural person* have a right and can control access to it. While the last can be *described* by *non-private PI* and can be performed in a *non-private sphere*. For the third thesis, we can identify the *superior authority* that can *set governance rules*, which can be defined as a group of policies and decision-making criteria that *determine* the *authority*, which *empowers* the *natural person* to *control* her *PI subject to the right to privacy*. Such PI covers *private* and *non-private PI* that has not been made public by the *natural person*. Concerning thesis four, we can identify the *ownership* relationship between the *natural person* and her *PI* that has not been made public by her, i.e., *PI subject to the right to privacy*. Accordingly, *PI not subject to the right to privacy* covers any *PI* that has been made public by the natural person, and she does not have *control* nor *ownership* over such *PI*.

---

[3] For reasons of readability, multiplicity and other constraints have been left out.

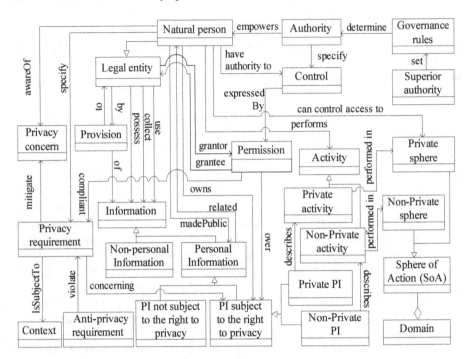

Fig. 2. The meta-model of the propose conceptual model

Concerning the fifth and final privacy thesis, a *natural person* may have or can become *aware of privacy concerns*, as a response, she *specifies* her *privacy requirements* (e.g., confidentiality, anonymity) to *mitigate* such *concerns*. A *privacy requirement* is subject to a *context* that identifies the state of affairs relevant to the *requirement*. A *privacy requirement* can be *violated* by what can be called an *anti-privacy requirement* that represents the requirement of a *legal entity* with malicious intent (e.g., misusing, breaching, spying) concerning privacy/PI.

A *natural person* have authority to *control* her *PI subject to the right to privacy*, where such *control* can be *expressed by permissions* that specify the type (e.g., possess, transfer) and the *purpose* of PI use. *Permissions* can be *granted/revoked*, initially, by the *natural person*. Granted *permissions* should be *compliant* with the *privacy requirements* that are *specified* by the *natural person* concerning her *PI subject to the right to privacy*. Finally, a *legal entity* may *possess, collect, transfer* and/or *use PI subject to the right to privacy*. However, possessing, collecting, transferring, the type and purpose of information usage is subject to having related *permissions*.

6   Challenges and Future Work

Having formulated a new conceptualization of privacy requirements, we list and discuss several significant challenges related to this track of research, which provide opportunities for future research:

A model for PI ownership: Many may agree that ownership of PI cannot be shared [39]. Yet, we have many examples, when this notion does not hold. For instance, do we own our DNA? given that we share a big portion of it with our relatives, ancestors, and offspring. Therefore, a model for PI ownership that is capable of answering this and similar questions should be developed.

Ownership of anonymized PI: It is arguable whether anonymized PI can be considered as PI. Thanks to the excessive availability of PI and profiling techniques, a small item of PI (e.g., IP address) that may identify a person can be combined with anonymized PI and violates her privacy. Thus, the relationship between a person and her anonymized PI needs to be revisited in light of the new advancement of technologies.

Collection of public PI: A deep investigation of the collection of PI that has been made public is required to better understand when such collection is "acceptable" or it can be considered as a type of invasion of privacy.

Usage of public PI: As previously mentioned, individuals may disclose some of their PI for public use with the assumption that such PI will be used in contexts compliant with the purposes for which PI has been disclosed. Analyzing whether the usage of such PI is compliant with disclosure purposes is challenging and requires concretely characterizing both contexts of usage as well as purposes of disclosure, which is on the list of future work.

7 Conclusions

Like architectural foundations that provide an underpinning for buildings, philosophical foundations for privacy provide basic concepts, relationships and assumptions that enable the definition and analysis of privacy requirements. This paper contributes to our understanding of privacy by investigating its philosophical foundations, identifying its core theses, and based on these, formulating a new conceptualization of privacy requirements. The proposed conceptualization of privacy requirements is expected to facilitate and improve dealing with privacy requirements by increasing awareness concerning such requirements on the side of requirements engineers as well as individuals who are expected to play an active role in specifying their privacy requirements.

In this paper, we provide a preliminary check for the validity of our proposed conceptualization of privacy requirements, which needs to be complemented in the future with empirical validation through controlled studies. The main aim of this track of research is proposing a well-defined privacy ontology, which when completed would constitute a great step forward in improving the quality of privacy-aware systems. Therefore, we plan to integrate the conceptual model developed in this paper into our ontology for privacy requirements that we have proposed earlier [15,16]. This will significantly improve the capability of the ontology for capturing more explicit knowledge concerning PI and, in turn, privacy requirements, which will allow a more comprehensive analysis concerning such requirements.

References

1. Gharib, M., et al.: Privacy requirements: findings and lessons learned in developing a privacy platform. In: the 24th International Requirements Engineering Conference, pp. 256–265. IEEE (2016) https://doi.org/10.1109/RE.2016.13
2. Gharib, M., Giorgini, P., Mylopoulos, J.: Towards an ontology for privacy requirements via a systematic literature review. In: Mayr, H.C., Guizzardi, G., Ma, H., Pastor, O. (eds.) ER 2017. LNCS, vol. 10650, pp. 193–208. Springer, Cham (2017). https://doi.org/10.1007/978-3-319-69904-2_16
3. Solove, D.J.: Conceptualizing privacy. Calif. Law Rev. **90**(4), 87–155 (2002). https://doi.org/10.2307/3481326
4. Altman, I.: Privacy: a conceptual analysis. Environ. Behav. **8**(1), 7–29 (1976)
5. Schoeman, F.D.: Privacy: philosophical dimensions. Am. Philos. Q. **21**(3), 199–213 (1984). https://doi.org/10.2307/20014049
6. Hongladarom, S.: Philosophical foundations of privacy. In: A Buddhist Theory of Privacy, pp. 9–35 (2016) https://doi.org/10.1007/978-981-10-0317-2_2
7. Waldo, J., Lin, H.S., Millett, L.I.: Engaging Privacy and Information Technology in a Digital Age. National Academies Press, Washington (2007). https://doi.org/10.17226/11896
8. Warren, S.D., Brandeis, L.D.: The right to privacy. Harvard Law Rev. **4**(5), 193 (1890). https://doi.org/10.2307/1321160
9. Poel, H.G.: Privacy. Tijdschrift voor Urologie **8**(5), 67–67 (2018). https://doi.org/10.1007/s13629-018-00219-6
10. Richards, N.M., Solove, D.J.: Prosser's privacy law: a mixed legacy. Calif. L. Rev. **98**, 1887 (2010)
11. Westin, A.F.: Privacy and freedom. Washington Lee Law Rev. **25**(1), 166 (1968)
12. Solove, D.J.: A taxonomy of privacy. Univ. Pennsylvania Law Rev. **154**(3), 477 (2006). https://doi.org/10.2307/40041279
13. Dinev, T., Xu, H., Smith, J.H., Hart, P.: Information privacy and correlates: an empirical attempt to bridge and distinguish privacy-related concepts. Eur. J. Inf. Syst. **22**(3), 295–316 (2013). https://doi.org/10.1057/ejis.2012.23
14. Parker, R.B.: A definition of privacy. Rutgers L. Rev. **27**, 83–104 (1973)
15. Gharib, M., Mylopoulos, J., Giorgini, P.: COPri - a core ontology for privacy requirements engineering. In: Dalpiaz, F., Zdravkovic, J., Loucopoulos, P. (eds.) RCIS 2020. LNBIP, vol. 385, pp. 472–489. Springer, Cham (2020). https://doi.org/10.1007/978-3-030-50316-1_28
16. Gharib, M., Giorgini, P., Mylopoulos, J.: COPri vol 2 - a core ontology for privacy requirements. Data Knowl. Eng. **133**, (2021). https://doi.org/10.1016/j.datak.2021.101888
17. Gharib, M., Giorgini, P., Mylopoulos, J.: An ontology for privacy requirements via a systematic literature review. J. Data Semant. **9**(4), 123–149 (2021). https://doi.org/10.1007/s13740-020-00116-5
18. Nodelman, U., Allen, C., Perry, J.: Stanford encyclopedia of philosophy. p. 380 (2002). https://doi.org/10.1145/544317.544327
19. Romano, N.C., Fjermestad, J.: Privacy and security in the age of electronic customer relationship management. Int. J. Inf. Secur. Priv. (IJISP) **1**(1), 65–86 (2007). https://doi.org/10.4018/jisp.2007010105
20. Richardson, J.S.: The ownership of roman land: Tiberius Gracchus and the Italians. J. Roman Stud. **70**, 1–11 (1980). https://doi.org/10.2307/299552

21. Holvast, J.: History of privacy. In The History of Information Security, pp. 737–769. Elsevier Science BV (2007) https://doi.org/10.1016/B978-044451608-4/50028-6
22. Posner, R.A.: The right of privacy. Ga. L. Rev. **12**, 393 (1977)
23. Milberg, S.J., Smith, H.J., Burke, S.J.: Information privacy: corporate management and national regulation. Organ. Sci. **11**(1), 35–57 (2000)
24. Pfitzmann, A., Hansen, M.: A terminology for talking about privacy by data minimization: Anonymity, Unlinkability, Undetectability, Unobservability, Pseudonymity, and Identity Management. Tech. University Dresden, pp. 1–98 (2010)
25. Gavison, R.: Privacy and the limits of law. Yale Law **89**(3), 421–471 (1980)
26. Introna, L.D.: Privacy and the computer: why we need privacy in the information society. Metaphilosophy **28**(3), 259–275 (1997). https://doi.org/10.1111/1467-9973.00055
27. Rossler, B.: The Value of Privacy. Wiley, Hoboken (2018)
28. Solove, D.: Understanding Privacy. Harvard University Press, Cambridge (2008)
29. Thomson, J.J.: The right to privacy. Philos. Public Aff. **4**(4), 295–314 (1975)
30. Schwartz, P.M.: Property, privacy, and personal data. Harvard Law Rev. **117**(7), 2055–2128 (2003)
31. Samuelson, P.: Privacy as intellectual property? Stanford Law Rev. **52**(5), 1125 (2000). https://doi.org/10.2307/1229511
32. Litman, J.: Information privacy/information property. Stanford Law Rev. **52**, 1283–1313 (2000)
33. Purtova, N.: Property in personal data: second life of an old idea in the age of cloud computing, chain informatisation, and ambient intelligence. In: Gutwirth, S., Poullet, Y., De Hert, P., Leenes, R. (eds.) Computers, Privacy and Data Protection: an Element of Choice, pp. 39–64. Springer, Dordrecht (2011). https://doi.org/10.1007/978-94-007-0641-5_3
34. Marmor, A.: What is the right to privacy? Philos. Public Aff. **43**(1), 3–26 (2015). https://doi.org/10.1111/papa.12040
35. Rotenberg, M., Jacobs, D.: Updating the law of information privacy: the new framework of the European union. Harvard J. Law Public Policy **36**(2), 605–652 (2013)
36. Veblen, T.: The beginnings of ownership. Am. J. Sociol. 4(3), 352–365 (1898). https://doi.org/10.4324/9781351311441-4
37. Janeček, V.: Ownership of personal data in the Internet of Things. Comput. Law Secur. Rev. **34**(5), 1039–1052 (2018). https://doi.org/10.1016/j.clsr.2018.04.007
38. Fairfield, J.A.: Virtual property. Boston Law Rev. **85**(4), 1048–1102 (2005)
39. Massin, O.: The metaphysics of ownership: a reinachian account. Axiomathes **27**(5), 577–600 (2017)
40. Omoronyia, I., Cavallaro, L., Salehie, M., Pasquale, L., Nuseibeh, B.: Engineering adaptive privacy: On the role of privacy awareness requirements. In: Proceedings - International Conference on Software Engineering, pp. 632–641 (2013)
41. Trepte, S., et al.: Do people know about privacy and data protection strategies? Towards the online privacy literacy scale (OPLIS). In: Reforming European Data Protection Law, pp. 333–365 (2015)
42. Parliament, E.: Regulation (EU) 2016/679 of the European parliament and of the council on the protection of natural persons with regard to the processing of personal data and on the free movement of such data, and repealing directive 95/46/EC. Official J. Eur. Commun. **59**, 1–88 (2016)

A Cyber Security Digital Twin for Critical Infrastructure Protection: The Intelligent Transport System Use Case

Giovanni Paolo Sellitto[1]([⊠])(iD), Massimiliano Masi[2]([⊠])(iD), Tanja Pavleska[3],
and Helder Aranha[4](iD)

[1] Independent Scholar, Rome, Italy
gogiampaolo@gmail.com
[2] Autostrade Per L'Italia SpA, Rome, Italy
mmasi@autostrade.it
http://www.autostrade.it
[3] Jozef Stefan Institute, Ljubljana, Slovenia
[4] Independent Scholar, Lisbon, Portugal
hmspider@gmail.com

Abstract. The problem of performing cybersecurity tests over existing industrial control systems is well-known. Once it is deployed, a critical system cannot be made unavailable for the purpose of simulating a cyber attack and thus it is hard to introduce corrective measures based on actual test outcomes. On the other hand, a high security posture is required for critical infrastructure and security by design is mandatory for new projects. Such requirements call for an architectural approach to introduce security straight from the early development phases. However, the adoption of a systematic design approach does not guarantee the cost-effectiveness of security countermeasures analysis, which is an extremely cumbersome task as the creation of a physical model is often costly or impossible.

To address these issues, we propose the introduction of a specific view in the system's architectural blueprint, called the Cybersecurity Digital Twin. It is an Enterprise Architecture model of the system specifically targeted at providing a sound base for simulations in order to devise proper countermeasures without any outage of the physical infrastructure. To provide a proof of concept and demonstrate the practical viability of the proposed solution, we apply the methodology to a Cooperative Intelligent Transport System use case, evaluating the system security of the obtained solution.

Keywords: Cyber security · Digital twin · Threat modeling · C-ITS

1 Introduction

Model-based approaches have been widely used for system design and testing (e.g. in digital circuits design, aviation, space technology, housing) and for gover-

© IFIP International Federation for Information Processing 2021
Published by Springer Nature Switzerland AG 2021
E. Serral et al. (Eds.): PoEM 2021, LNBIP 432, pp. 230–244, 2021.
https://doi.org/10.1007/978-3-030-91279-6_16

nance purposes in socio-technical systems, since the availability of digital models facilitates the use of simulations to forecast the system behavior under conditions and stresses that cannot be achieved on the real system without detrimental consequences.

One field of application for model based engineering is the design and testing of *industrial control systems* (ICS), which is a challenging task, since old ICS are usually based on the *Supervisory Control And Data Acquisition* (SCADA) architecture, where each plant (water pipes, intelligent electronic devices, or tunnels in motorways) is a complex system on its own. Moreover, ICS are usually custom-built and their blueprints do not follow an enterprise architecture approach. The simulation of Business Continuity Plans in ICS (required by international best practices such as in ISO 22301 and national regulations) and their assessment is usually restricted to the design/construction phases because halting a critical system to perform tests is not an option.

To mitigate this problem, recently the concept of *digital twin* (DT) emerged as a tool to perform analysis, testing, and simulation of aspects such as service interruption, lack of availability, or continuity in an ICS [2]. A Digital Twin is a digital representation (a model) of the real system that contains enough information to control specific operational parameters or aspects of the physical infrastructure. Digital twins are common in civil engineering industry, where the Building Information Model (BIM) is the de-facto standard to design and operate buildings. In the field of ICS, digital models could offer a viable solution to replace destructive tests and to simulate the effect of events like earthquakes and flooding, which would be impossible to test on the real infrastructure [23].

While in the EA field some authors have tackled the challenge of deriving a Digital Twin from an Enterprise Architecture (EA) model of the system, in the case of ICS the derivation of a digital twin aimed at performing simulations is usually considered as an infrastructure maintenance task instead of being part of the architectural design phases. This is due to the relative novelty of the concept of digital twin, the rapid development of commercial tools to perform visual simulations and also to the frequent lack of an EA model in the case of SCADA systems. The situation is even worse when we consider the specific application of a digital twin for a security assessment of an ICS as, firstly, the modeling languages used to describe a cyber security digital twin have little in common with usual EA modeling languages, like Archimate or UML and, secondly, the models used in Visual Threat Modeling have little resemblance with the Reference Architectures used in the field of IoT or Industry 4.0.

In this paper, we propose a methodology to derive a digital twin of a critical infrastructure, aimed at performing simulations for cyber security and visual threat modeling, starting from an architectural blueprint of the system. Following a common approach in architectural design, we refactor the system architecture[1] to derive a specific architectural view, which is used to produce a digital twin. In turn, the results of the simulations performed on the digital twin will be fed back into the EA, guiding the designers in the inclusion of the counter-

---

[1] Following IEC 62443-3-3.

measures foreseen by simulations. Given that usually there is no EA blueprint readily available for ICS systems based on SCADA, we propose a methodology that leverages a Reference Architecture (RAMI 4.0, in the specific case of this paper) to take stock of the assets that are relevant to build the digital twin (DT). This methodology takes an existing EA model or a blueprint as an input and categorizes the assets, bridging the gap towards their description in the specific architectural language used to describe the DT.

Our method builds upon the notions of architectural viewpoints and views [14]. The digital twin is obtained through a specific cybersecurity viewpoint of an ICS that can lead to multiple views, since cybersecurity is a cross-cutting concern.

To illustrate the application of the theory, we present a real world Use Case in the domain of *Cooperative Intelligent Transport System* (C-ITS), deriving the DT and performing simulations for a simple transport infrastructure. C-ITS is a networked system of devices aiming at increasing safety and sustainability levels through the application of the Internet of Things (IoT) in the sector of road transportation [11, 16, 30].

The availability of a DT enables the application of probabilistic risk analysis, reasoning on possible threats represented as attack trees. Based on the results, countermeasures are derived and the process is repeated until the overall risk of an attack that can compromise the critical infrastructure is lowered to an acceptable level. When a satisfactory solution is thus reached, the results are fed back into the architecture leading to an improved blueprint [27].

The product used to perform the visual threat analysis (SecuriCAD [24][2]) requires that the System Under Testing (SUT) is modeled using a specific Meta Attack Language (MAL). This is quite a common situation when dealing with digital models targeted at performing simulations or used to control SCADA infrastructures. To cater with this scenario we propose a separate step that translates the DT into MAL, making the procedure parametric with respect to the target language used to model the DT.

The rest of this paper is structured as follows: Sect. 2 presents some preliminary concepts. Section 3 describes the methodology, deriving a cybersecurity view and distilling a Digital Twin. Section 4 presents the application of the methodology to the C-ITS use case. In Sect. 5 we present related works, and, finally, in Sect. 6 we touch upon future work and conclude.

2   Theoretical Background

This section introduces some concepts that will be exploited throughout the rest of the paper. In Sect. 2.1, we introduce the concept of EA and show how the constellation of concepts introduced here are relevant for the design of digital twin, which is described in Sect. 2.2.

---

[2] SecuriCAD is a tool that adopts a probabilistic approach to *threat modeling*, based on the definition of Attack Trees, which are the set of steps that the attacker is likely to perform in order to reach our assets.

2.1   Enterprise Architecture, Viewpoints, Views

An architectural approach to system analysis and design defines rules for building a blueprint. Usually, it relies on some *Reference Architecture (RA)*, which is a generic conceptual model that provides a template to design an *Enterprise Architecture* in a particular domain.

Viewpoints define abstractions on the set of models representing the enterprise architecture, each aimed at a particular type of stakeholder and addressing a particular set of concerns. Viewpoints can be used to address specific concerns in isolation or to relate several concerns.

A Reference Architecture usually exploits some domain knowledge to define a set of architectural viewpoints, targeted to specific purposes and categories of stakeholders. In the case of the Internet of Things, a number of Reference Architecture models have emerged: the Reference Architecture for Industries 4.0 (RAMI 4.0) defines some viewpoints which are typical for the industrial automation, while the Internet of Things Reference Architecture (IoT RA) presents an integrated architectural model for IoT, whereas the Industrial Internet Reference Architecture (IIRA) is specially devised for industrial control systems. Some authors have pointed out the similarities between these reference architectures [29] with respect to the viewpoints, as shown in Table 1.

Table 1. Comparison between viewpoints in EAs

IoT RA	IIRA	RAMI 4.0
	Business	Business
Usage	Usage	
Functional	Functional	Functional
Information		Information
Communication		Communication
System	Implementation	Integration
		Asset

For the purpose of explaining our approach, we choose RAMI 4.0 as it can describe any IoT system and provides a built-in dimension to describe the system life cycle. However, the whole approach does not depend on the underlying Reference Architecture model.

RAMI 4.0: RAMI 4.0 model represents a consolidated architectural framework for the Industry 4.0 domain [21]. The conceptual space, depicted in Fig. 1, is structured along three axes. The first axis presents the six RAMI architectural layers. From top down, the *business layer* addresses the economic and regulatory aspects, the *functional layer* describes the functionality implemented by the various architectural assets and their run-time environment; the *information layer*

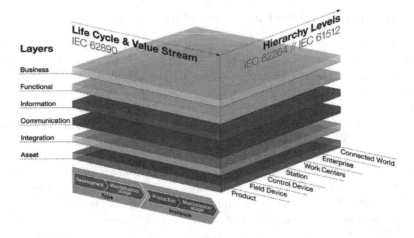

Fig. 1. The reference architectural model for Industrie 4.0

describes data and it is used to support the semantic interoperability aspects. The *communication layer* describes the access to information and the functions of a connected asset (e.g., REST, SOAP, DSRC, 5G). The *integration layer* represents the transition from physical to information world (e.g.man-machine interfaces) and finally the *asset layer* represents the assets that exist in the physical world (sensors, actuators, SCADA).

The second axis follows the *Life cycle* and *Value stream* and they represents the distinction between the instance and the type: the type represents the concept, while the instance, the object, represents the physical object in the system memory.

The third axis, the *Hierarchy*, consists of: the *Product*, describing the unit produced by a system/machine; the *Field Devices* and the *Control Devices*, i.e. the physical unit coordinating the other devices; *Stations* - systems grouped together into a *Work Center*; the *Enterprise*, which is the organization and the *Connected World*, the interface with external systems.

2.2   Digital Twin

There are multiple definitions of *digital twin*: we borrowed one that defines it as a "virtual description of a physical product that is accurate to both micro and macro level" [13]. Digital twins are expected to exhibit *fidelity*, i.e., a high number of parameters transferred between the physical and virtual entity, high accuracy and a satisfying level of abstraction [19]. In [7], digital twins are used to perform simulation of the security aspects of cyber and physical systems to enable security by design, whereas in [3] they are defined as "an evolving digital profile of the historical and current behaviour of a physical object or process". Following the reasoning of [7], the cybersecurity digital twin is defined as a "virtual replica of the system that accompanies its physical counterpart during its lifecycle, consumes real-time data if required, and has the sufficient fidelity to allow the implementation, testing, and simulation of desired security measures and business continuity plans".

However, these representations alone cannot show whether the system is secure or if a recovery plan is effective. Therefore, a cost-effectiveness analysis is usually performed to find the balance between security and usability, safety, functionality and financial impact. By creating a specific cybersecurity digital twin and applying a security by design approach, the verification of the desired security properties and the cost-effectiveness analyses have a measurable impact.

3 Methodology

In our work, we will introduce a *cybersecurity viewpoint* in the enterprise architecture, from which the *cybersecurity digital twin* is derived as a separate set of *views* in the EA blueprint. In new projects, it can facilitate architectural design, while for existing systems, it facilitates the evaluation of new countermeasures and the elimination of obsolete ones. In this section we show how to build the digital twin of an ICS from its architectural representation while ensuring fidelity, as depicted in Fig. 2. For a new ICS following the *security by design* approach, the starting point is the System Architecture, the *high level system blueprint*. For existing systems, a *reverse engineering from existing ICS* step is required, to derive the architecture by introspecting the system and mapping it onto a target EA conceptual space.

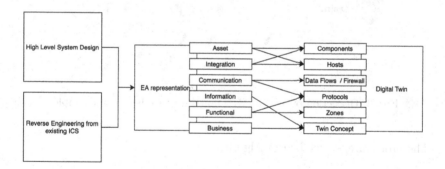

Fig. 2. Digital Twin design process

In the first phase, we derive a cybersecurity view from an existing EA blueprint and in the second phase we distill a digital twin to support cybersecurity simulations. We will include all of the relevant assets in a specific view that will pave the way for distilling a digital twin purposefully designed to perform cybersecurity simulations.

3.1   Phase 1: Derive a Cybersecurity View

The first step is to choose a reference EA model. In this paper, the methodology is explained referring to the RAMI 4.0 architectural model. Based on the reference architecture, a cybersecurity view is derived. The cybersecurity view contains all the assets that are relevant for security purposes. Some guidelines exist that can be adopted to perform this step. For ICS, it is recommended to define and map data flows[3]. To do that, the components of the system can be categorized as different views (e.g. architecture layers).

The assets to protect are selected and included in a specific view **dissecting** the EA blueprint over the RAMI 4.0 reference model. The **dissection** is an analytical process which maps each component of the EA onto a specific element of the RAMI 4.0 2.1. Figure 3 depicts a generic example of applying this process over a single layer.

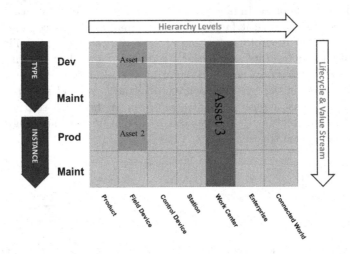

Fig. 3. Dissection over a RAMI 4.0 architecture layer: an example

The procedure is sketched in Algorithm 1.

3.2   Phase 2: Derive the Cyber Security Digital Twin from the Cybersecurity View

Different formal languages exist to represent the digital twin of a physical system [5,19,22]. For our purpose, the relevant architectural assets and its relationships are represented using the Meta Attack Language MAL [18], which is suited

---

[3] See, e.g., NIST cybersecurity framework for the protection of critical infrastructure [25] that has a specific control (ID.AM-3) requiring that *organizational communication and data flows are mapped* in order to segment and segregate network traffic, and identify firewall rules (the *zone and conduit* principle of IEC 62443).

Algorithm 1: From EA to Cybersecurity View

---

1 an EA blueprint (new systems) or a blueprint (for a legacy system) **Result:** A
     View containing $\mathcal{A}$, the assets to protect
2 Let $p = \emptyset$ be the set of assets to protect;
3 Let $i = Business$ layer in RAMI 4.0 model;
4 **foreach** *layer i in RAMI 4.0 model* **do**
5 | *dissect* blueprint over layer i
6 | *identify* assets to protect p using guidelines
7 | $\mathcal{A} = \mathcal{A} \cup (i,p)$
8 **end**

---

for security application and, more specifically, for attack simulation and threat modeling. To do that, MAL provides structures (graphs) to model the domain. To translate the Cybersecurity View into the cybersecurity Digital Twin, we can simply describe the relevant Architectural Assets and their relationships using the Meta Attack Language mentioned above. For this paper, we defined the target model using SecuriCAD, the visual editor for MAL. SecuriCAD comes with a set of pre-defined objects that can be used for the creation of a model of the ICS system:

- *components*, such as clients (ssh clients, generic in house-build, GPL, or COTS components);
- *keystore* to hold secrets;
- *access control systems*;
- *hosts*, grasping the peculiarities of Windows or Linux. Hosts can be considered patched and hardened, or unsupervised and unpatched. Typical unpatched hosts are CCTV cameras, while hardened systems could be workstations in a control room;
- *data flows*, *firewalls*, and *protocols* representing the details around the system communications. Data flows also represent *zones* and *conduits* or *protection rings* à la ISO 27002, that can be either physical or logical.

The graph represents the digital twin where the reasoning can start by applying business concepts. As part of the mapping, all assets and integration parts can be either components or hosts. This depends on their maturity model or their inherent characteristics: a device that has an off-the-shelf operating system is a host, while a PLC is a component. The communication entries are data flows and protocols, while the information components become part of the cyber security digital twin concept (since the information has to be protected). Functionalities are then related both to protocols and to zones according to IEC 62443, while business considerations tell us "what to model" and what goes into the digital twin.

4   The Cooperative-Intelligent Traffic Systems Use Case

This Section will introduce the C-ITS use case. Section 4.1 will set the context of C-ITS, and its architecture will be defined in Sect. 4.2. Section 4.3 will then use these definitions to build the C-ITS Cyber Security Digital Twin.

4.1   C-ITS Overview

Road transportation systems are one of the key factors for a thriving economy and sustainable development. Thus, their full functioning is critical for any community. However, the traffic volume in the roads is increasing, demanding deployment of specific equipment to enhance the travel experience of the road user, while increasing the safety of the road itself, lowering the carbon consumption and other factors. Similarly, vehicles are increasingly endowed with smart technology to increase the safety of the car's driver and passengers, by using sensors (e.g. tyre pressure, RADAR and Ultrasonic), and communications (e.g. infotainment, GPS, and Telematics). Those two aspects, the vehicle and the road infrastructure, and the messages exchanged between them, either from the vehicle to the road or vice versa, are part of a bigger ecosystem named Cooperative Intelligent Transport system, C-ITS.

Data in C-ITS is used by actuators (the Road Side Units) exchanging messages with the vehicles and, indirectly, with the rest of the C-ITS system. Hence, the application context we are accounting for is not one of a closed system, as data is not only exchanged within a single road transportation environment, but with other road operators and even other different critical infrastructures. Smart Cities, hospitals and fire brigades all consume traffic data, e.g., to define alternative traffic routes or other paths to be followed by the ambulances for carrying patients, or to arrive to a site in case of accidents. In that sense, the methodology presented here is also applicable for a setting where the inter-dependencies between the various critical infrastructures may lead to cascading effects, since the consequences from malfunctions or from a cyber-physical attack on one critical infrastructure have impact on all inter-connected ones.

4.2   Enterprise Architectures for C-ITS

The C-ITS architecture is mainly based on the hub-and-spoke paradigm [15, 30], where a central system carries the messages to the RSUs located on the motorway. The communication between the vehicle On Board Unit (OBU) and a Road Side Unit (RSU) is usually performed via radio waves [10]. A traffic control center (TCC) collects the events from the road that, in turn, are forwarded to an agent who knows for which specific subset of Road Side Units the event is relevant: an event about road works in 500 km will not be relevant. This agent, named *proxy*, plays the role of Central ITS-Station, while the RSU are named ITS-Stations. The high level architecture is shown in Fig. 4. Road Operators notify the TCC about the event (e.g., road works, slippery road) or a Radio Operator is notified by other sources (e.g., other road owners or infrastructure).

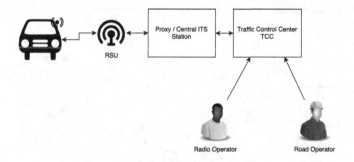

Fig. 4. C-ITS System Architecture for a road operator

Tt also notifies the TCC, who decides the relevance of the event and prepares the message to be propagated to the RSU network. The OBU and the vehicle cooperate with the ITS by acting upon the information received, via DENM[4] messages and by sending their sensed data back to the TCC.

The EA of the system can be represented as follows: according to the viewpoints defined for RAMI 4.0 in Table 1, the devices (RSU, Proxy, TCC) are grouped in the *asset* view, while the protocols (e.g., [1,10,17,26]) used to exchange data between those assets are logically grouped in the *communication* view. The syntax of the data exchanged (e.g., [9]) is in the *Information* view. The functionalities needed by the system and the objectives (and value assets) are then set in their respective views, *functional* and *business*.

4.3   Evaluating the C-ITS Cyber Security Properties

Here, we describe a practical application of the methodology to evaluate the Cybersecurity Digital Twin for C-ITS using MAL and the SecuriCAD tool.

The model is depicted in Fig. 5 and it has three logical zones. The first one is the Traffic Control Center (attached to the Corporate Network), represented by the host TCC. The host comes from the asset layer of the system's EA, that has a client named TCCBatch, which is responsible to forward the DENM to the Central ITS Station. Attached to the network is the Laptop Maintainer, which belongs to the system administrator connected to all other hosts via ssh. The second zone is the Proxy/Central ITS Station, represented by its host and two streams: the downstream from the TCC ProxyBatch, which is receiving the DENMs for processing, and the upstream to the RSU, composed by a client Proxy and a service, based on Apache Kafka technology, to receive the CAMs. The third zone, the Road Side Units, are placed on the motorway (represented by its Physical zone) where the RSU host (a Linux system) runs a BXC, an in-house software that processes the CAMs and DENMs. Finally, the communication and information aspects (protocols and data flows) are represented in the data flow section. The "star" present in some of the components represents the functional

---

[4] Decentralized Environmental Notification Message.

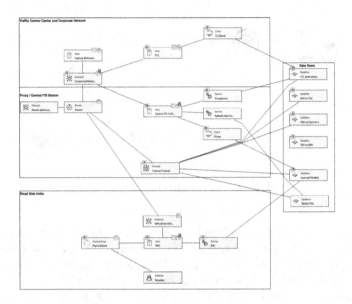

Fig. 5. The Cyber Security Digital Twin of the C-ITS

and business layers, e.g., the functionalities and the high value business objects that have to be protected. This model represents the EA as described in Sect. 4. The two other components shown in the Figure are the central firewall and the VPN of the RSU.

To perform the simulation, the attacker is placed in the physical zone. This is done in order to check the security of the EA by reasoning over the system representation. The countermeasures that will be used to protect the functionalities of the business objects are defined by discovering attack trees and the likelihood that a specific asset could be compromised.

In this case, the business reasoning identified three canonical attack scenarios that can be simulated (CITS1, CITS2, CITS3), in which the attacker compromises either the IT network or the RSU network or targets both the IT and the RSU services. Table 2 shows the reasoning used to lower an initial high risk (>60%) to a medium (30% ≤ risk < 59%) and then to low (<29%), which has previously been determined as an acceptable value. In scenario CITS1, the attacker connects to the Corporate Network as in Fig. 5. Without any countermeasures (as defined in the first version of the EA, column *Without Countermeasure (CM)*) the attacker can reach the IT services (TCC and Central ITS Station) with a very high probability. The addition of a central firewall, as shown in Fig. 5, would mitigate the reachability (column *with CM*) but the attack is still possible (with a medium risk), since the attacker can exploit a path compromising unpatched/zero day known protocols (ssh). The results of these simulations provide feedback to improve the EA, resulting in the addition of the Central Firewall among the EA's assets. This new version of the EA is used to simulate CITS2,

Table 2. Attack scenario

Attack ID	Description	Without CM	With CM	Mitigation
CITS1	The attacker is connected to the corporate network and compromise the Central ITS-S and the TCC	69%	46%	Adding a Firewall as countermeasure reduce the risk, since it attacks are possible only on allowed protocols and lateral movements are limited. Additional countermeasure: systems have to be patched continuously
CITS2	The attacker compromise the maintainer's laptop and then compromise the RSUs	50%	23%	Still with the Firewall, attacks are possible. Adding IDS, Privilege Access Management, the attack goes still through sshd and then needs to find an exploit to the in-house software BXC
CITS3	The attacker perform a physical access to the RSU and compromise other RSUs	30%	30%	With the same countermeasures as CITS1 and CITS 2, the mitigation are sufficient to have a low risk of compromise

positioning the attacker in the maintainer laptop, targeting at compromising the RSU. The result is again medium (comparable to the CITS1 with the firewall) as there is no additional countermeasure. By adding Intrusion Detection Systems (IDS), like an antivirus, and a Privilege Access Management (PAM) as a Secure Remote Access (thus monitoring and controlling all accesses) we lower the risk to an acceptable level (23%), leaving the attacker to compromise the in-house software with a very low likelihood. As previously, we provide feedback to the EA and start simulating CITS3. In this scenario, the attacker has physical access to the RSU and wants to compromise all other RSUs. We added to the model another copy of the RSU component and run the simulation. The countermeasures found for CITS2 are sufficient for CITS3, so there is no difference in the risk scoring by adding a local firewall on the RSU network. Through simulations and modifications, we were able to derive a new version of the EA for the system, to perform gap analysis and to prove the cost-effectiveness of adding some specific solutions (IDS, Firewall, PAM).[5]

5   Related Works

The concept of digital twin is introduced in many publications [19] and, although well understood by both academia and industry, several issues are still open. For instance, the *fidelity* of the digital twin with respect to the physical part, the physical-to-virtual connection, and its maintenance over the product life-cycle are points that require further analysis. In [28], authors define a method to build the digital twin. Furthermore, [7] lays down some concepts for the use of a digital twin for security in order to reduce the attack surface and to perform intrusion detection. A framework that, starting from system specifications, creates a model to be used for simulations is presented in [6], where the authors concentrate on ICS and build a digital twin by leveraging the data exchange

---

[5] See https://www.dropbox.com/s/0exeadyz6t2yzin/ModelForCRITIS.sCAD?dl=0.

format. Similar to these works, our approach is focused on the security aspects, but it is parametric to its EA (see Sect. 2), hence it can be applied to multiple systems and is independent of the reference architecture. Another difference is that our methodology not only encompasses the physical aspects of the system, but also its business objectives, tackling security as a *cross cutting concern*, spanning from cyberphysical components to data communication, data syntax, semantics, functionalities, and business models.

Using models for security evaluations is part of a research area named threat modeling. In [20] authors evaluate the extent to which countermeasures can improve the security posture of a power grid SCADA-based system. A work that comes close to ours has been carried out in the Energy Shield project [8]. There, authors derive a model for security simulations using System Theoretic Process Analysis (STPA). We generalise this approach through a formalisation by means of Enterprise Architecture. OWASP[6] defines threat modeling as a way to identify and understand threats, evaluate mitigation practices to protect a valuable asset and define best practices on how to protect it. Our digital representation of the system enables all of the above by performing threat modeling over a digital representation of the entire system, taking into account assets, data flows and messages, as well as functionalities and business objectives.

According to the EU NIS directive [12], operators of essential services are a subset of critical infrastructures. Among the essential services we find the *cooperative intelligent transport systems (C-ITS)*, a set of services implemented by motorways, smart cities, and vehicle manufacturers, that cooperate together for a safer and greener transportation. These systems are usually built and operated in a systematic manner, based on the design of an EA blueprint [15, 30]. In [4], a digital twin is built to demonstrate privacy enhancement mechanisms in the automotive industry, starting off by identifying the stakeholders. Our approach is systematic, implying that for new systems, the definition of an architectural model is part of the design, while for existing systems, architectural models are drawn by reverse engineering of the components and the connectors.

6   Conclusion and Future Work

In this paper, we defined a method to build a security-oriented Digital Twin of a cyber-physical system, starting from its architectural blueprint (EA). The EA can include security-by-design concerns for new projects or be obtained by performing architecture reconstruction and reverse engineering for existing projects. Either approach produces a catalogue of assets to protect, organized into views according to architecture viewpoints.

We then described how to map assets to components in the newly introduced Cyber Security view - the Digital Twin that will be used to perform cybersecurity simulations. For that, we employed the SecuriCAD tool, modeling the Digital Twin using a user interface front-end for the MAL language. The tool supports cyber-attack simulations based on MAL.

---

[6] See https://owasp.org/www-community/Application_Threat_Modeling.

Finally, we applied the methodology to a real use case of a critical infrastructure - the Cooperative Intelligent Transport System (C-ITS). We mapped the typical EA views used worldwide to represent such systems into a threat-oriented Digital Twin and performed security reasoning. We defined three typical cyber-attack scenarios for Operational Technology (attacker is in the IT network first, and then in the OT network) and applied countermeasures to mitigate the attack scenario. By incorporating feedback into the EA, we enabled the achievement of a desired fidelity level. In this way, we performed tasks such as Vulnerability Assessment and security testing without causing any service interruption in the running system.

Although MAL and SecuriCAD are powerful tools, they cannot capture a detailed-level system design. For instance, at this moment, protocol-specific risks and device peculiarities are not taken into account. Therefore, as a future work we aim to define a way of grouping architectural assets to automatically determine the specifications of digital twin components to be reused, for a more efficient modeling process. Moreover, we aim at making the target modeling language parametric as well, to avoid a vendor lock-in.

References

1. Apache kafka. https://kafka.apache.org. Accessed 6 Oct 2021
2. Augustine, P.: The industry use cases for the digital twin idea, Chap. 4. In: Raj, P., Evangeline, P. (eds.) The Digital Twin Paradigm for Smarter Systems and Environments: The Industry Use Cases. Advances in Computers, vol. 117, pp. 79–105. Elsevier (2020)
3. Bécue, A., et al.: Cyberfactory1 - securing the industry 4.0 with cyber-ranges and digital twins. In: 2018 14th IEEE International Workshop on Factory Communication Systems (WFCS), pp. 1–4 (2018)
4. Damjanovic-Behrendt, V.: A digital twin-based privacy enhancement mechanism for the automotive industry. In: 2018 International Conference on Intelligent Systems (IS), pp. 272–279 (2018)
5. Dietz, M., Vielberth, M., Pernul, G.: Integrating digital twin security simulations in the security operations center. In: Proceedings of the 15th International Conference on Availability, Reliability and Security, ARES 2020. Association for Computing Machinery, New York (2020)
6. Eckhart, M., Ekelhart, A.: Towards security-aware virtual environments for digital twins. In: Proceedings of the 4th ACM Workshop on Cyber-Physical System Security, CPSS 2018, pp. 61–72. Association for Computing Machinery, New York (2018)
7. Eckhart, M., Ekelhart, A.: Digital twins for cyber-physical systems security: state of the art and outlook. In: Security and Quality in Cyber-Physical Systems Engineering, pp. 383–412. Springer, Cham (2019). https://doi.org/10.1007/978-3-030-25312-7_14
8. Energy Shield: Developing the cyber toolkit that protects your energy grid (2021)
9. ETSI. EN 302 637-3: Intelligent Transport Systems (ITS); vehicular communications; basic set of applications; part 3: specifications of decentralized environmental notification basic service (2014)
10. ETSI. Intelligent Transport Systems (ITS): Mitigation techniques to avoid interference between European CEN Dedicated Short Range Communication (CEN DSRC) equipment and Intelligent Transport Systems (ITS) operating in the 5 GHz frequency range (2015)

11. European Commission: Cooperative, connected and automated mobility (CCAM) (2021)
12. European Parliament and the Council: Directive EU 2016/1148 (2016)
13. Grieves, M.: Digital twin: manufacturing excellence through virtual factory replication (March 2015)
14. The Open Group. Togaf 9.2 (2019)
15. ICT4CART: A connected future for automated driving (2021)
16. Intelligent Transport Systems Australia. ITS Australia (2021)
17. ISO. ISO/IEC 20922:2016: Information technology - Message Queuing Telemetry Transport (MQTT) v3.1.1 (2016)
18. Johnson, P., Lagerström, R., Ekstedt, M.: A meta language for threat modeling and attack simulations. In: Proceedings of the 13th International Conference on Availability, Reliability and Security, ARES 2018. Association for Computing Machinery, New York (2018)
19. Jones, D., Snider, C., Nassehi, A., Yon, J., Hicks, B.: Characterising the digital twin: a systematic literature review. CIRP J. Manuf. Sci. Technol. **29**, 36–52 (2020)
20. Korman, M., Välja, M., Björkman, G., Ekstedt, M., Vernotte, A., Lagerström, R.: Analyzing the effectiveness of attack countermeasures in a SCADA system. In: Proceedings of the 2nd Workshop on Cyber-Physical Security and Resilience in Smart Grids, SPSR-SG@CPSWeek 2017, Pittsburgh, PA, USA, 21 April 2017, pp. 73–78. ACM (2017)
21. Koschnick, G.: Industrie 4.0: the industrie 4.0 component (2015)
22. Lim, K.Y.H., Zheng, P., Chen, C.-H.: A state-of-the-art survey of Digital Twin: techniques, engineering product lifecycle management and business innovation perspectives. J. Intell. Manuf. **31**(6), 1313–1337 (2019). https://doi.org/10.1007/s10845-019-01512-w
23. Lu, Q., Xie, X., Heaton, J., Parlikad, A.K., Schooling, J.: From BIM towards digital twin: strategy and future development for smart asset management. In: Borangiu, T., Trentesaux, D., Leitão, P., Giret Boggino, A., Botti, V. (eds.) SOHOMA 2019. SCI, vol. 853, pp. 392–404. Springer, Cham (2020). https://doi.org/10.1007/978-3-030-27477-1_30
24. Mao, X., Ekstedt, M., Ling, E., Ringdahl, E., Lagerström, R.: Conceptual abstraction of attack graphs - a use case of securiCAD. In: Albanese, M., Horne, R., Probst, C.W. (eds.) GraMSec 2019. LNCS, vol. 11720, pp. 186–202. Springer, Cham (2019). https://doi.org/10.1007/978-3-030-36537-0_9
25. NIST: Cybersecurity framework (2021)
26. OASIS: Advanced message queuing protocol (AMQP) version 1.0 (2012)
27. Paskevicius, P., Damasevicius, R., Štuikys, V.: Change impact analysis of feature models. In: Skersys, T., Butleris, R., Butkiene, R. (eds.) ICIST 2012. CCIS, vol. 319, pp. 108–122. Springer, Heidelberg (2012). https://doi.org/10.1007/978-3-642-33308-8_10
28. Talkhestani, B.A., Jazdi, N., Schloegl, W., Weyrich, M.: Consistency check to synchronize the digital twin of manufacturing automation based on anchor points. Procedia CIRP **72**, 159–164 (2018). 51st CIRP Conference on Manufacturing Systems
29. The Open Group: Reference Architectures and Open Group Standards for the Internet of Things - Four Internet of Things Reference Architectures (2021)
30. United States Department of Transportation. Intelligent Transportation Systems, Joint Program Office (2021)

Expanding Data Governance Across Company Boundaries – An Inter-organizational Perspective of Roles and Responsibilities

Marvin Jagals(✉) (iD)

University of Duisburg-Essen, Essen, Germany
marvin.jagals@uni-due.de

Abstract. The exchange of data between participants within inter-organizational networks becomes a prominent field of action. However, intra-organizational data governance mechanisms reach their limits across company boundaries. Current research barely addresses the need to model organizational data governance roles for managing inter-organizational networks. Therefore, this contribution aims to identify existing data governance roles in an inter-organizational context. A literature review is conducted to provide a holistic overview of data governance roles. Then, these results are concatenated with network management requirements, gathered from inter-organizational management research, to take a first step in shaping an inter-organizational role model for data governance. Limitations include the lack of evidence on the practical applicability of the results and the lack of heterogeneity in the research background.

Keywords: Inter-organizational data governance · Inter-organizational networks · Data governance roles

1 Introduction

Organizations support more self-service analytics or even create requirements for a collective comprehension of data across companies. Efficient data governance frameworks support organizations to reach that aim [1]. Simultaneously, companies seek to get involved in complex inter-organizational network structures due to increased competition, higher customer expectations, or environmental conditions [2]. However, sources of inter-organizational uncertainty emerge within network coordination [3]. This uncertainty demands role-clarifying, inter-organizational data governance (IODG) concepts. Data governance should build the frame for decision rights and accountabilities for data management. Subsequently, organizations must determine the who and the what of data governance within an inter-organizational context [4]. However, this research stream is still underdeveloped. Previous investigations have mainly focused on modeling data governance structures within an intra-organizational environment [4, 5].

© IFIP International Federation for Information Processing 2021
Published by Springer Nature Switzerland AG 2021
E. Serral et al. (Eds.): PoEM 2021, LNBIP 432, pp. 245–254, 2021.
https://doi.org/10.1007/978-3-030-91279-6_17

Prior research on inter-organizational phenomena laid valuable groundwork, which also influenced this research project [6–9]. For instance, Tiwana et al. [8] introduce a framework for understanding platform-based ecosystems. Indeed, they deal with governance-related constructs within platforms, but their focus is not on data governance specifically. Oliveira et al. [9] provided a detailed study of structural research on data-related roles and responsibilities. Governance roles are also identified but are only partially defined precisely. Likewise, there is no link to intra-organizational data governance research, although a knowledge synthesis of intra-organizational data governance and inter-organizational information systems (IS) research could be fruitful for addressing upcoming IODG challenges.

The identified research gap leads to the following research question: *How to expand intra-organizational data governance roles towards an inter-organizational environment?*

In the following sections of the paper, the author gives an overview of data governance and inter-organizational networks, where after the research background is described to locate the study. After providing details about the research method, the author presents the findings. The actual body of knowledge of intra-organizational data governance roles and their relations is gathered to reach the present research goal. To accomplish that, a systematic literature review is conducted [10]. These preliminary results form the point of departure to develop data governance roles and responsibilities towards a network environment by establishing a bridge between intra-organizational and inter-organizational research. This concatenation consists of network management requirements, adopted from Knight and Harland's study on network management core roles and, therefore, outlines this contribution's research background [11]. Generally, the present work strives to contribute to one of the first research attempts dealing with inter-organizational design perspectives of IODG in IS research. Finally, the results are discussed and placed in the overall context of IODG research.

2 Related Work

2.1 Data Governance

IT governance has advanced from corporate governance to a distinct concept [12]. Subsequently, Khatri and Brown [5] differentiate between IT assets and data. Therefore, they recommend separate governance for data to address the upcoming importance of data assets. However, conceptually, data governance overlaps with IT governance since it generally frames IT strategy regulations and brings IT management in line with corporate goals [13].

Data governance defines and manages the implementation and performance of data management [14]. Weber and Otto endow data governance with a structural, organizational design which "specifies the framework for decision rights and accountabilities to encourage desirable behavior in the use of data" [4]. This contribution unemptied follows this definition since the concept of governance was initially developed to manage decision-making rights, which also emerges as a fundamental challenge within data governance [12].

2.2 Inter-organizational Networks

Many terms are used in the literature to describe the characteristics of cooperations. The most common are value networks or networked organizations [15]. Moreover, the term inter-organizational network refers to all structures, such as strategic alliances, joint ventures, or industrial cooperations [16].

Further, organizational roles perform the tasks within a network. Huckvale and Ould define a role as "a set of activities that an individual or group generally carries out with some organizationally relevant responsibility" [17]. These activities are pursued with presupposed qualities such as experience, qualifications, and personal or social attributes that the actors possess to fill a role [18]. Developing a role model can prevent companies from restricting their innovation within organizational frameworks [19].

3   Research Background: Network Management Requirements

Knight and Harland [11] identified six core roles for effectively managing a network by synthesizing both findings. The *Innovation Facilitator* deals with the development and facilitation of product development and innovations. This role also promotes higher spending on research and development. The *Coordinator* serves as supervisor of inter-organizational operations or as project manager. This role brings the members from around the network together and is interested in managing the partnerships. The *Policy Maker* is charged with determining policy for the network structure and is responsible for setting standards for purchasing the practice and providing support for developing purchasing staff. The *Advisor* is responsible for formal and informal consulting within the whole network. The *Information Broker* is entrusted with determining network policy and is responsible for setting criteria for all activities within the network. The *Network Structuring Agent* evaluates and impacts the whole structure of the network and seeks opportunities for improvement. Knight and Harland [11] based their study on the contribution of Snow et al. to dynamic networks [20] and Mintzberg's managers' role theory [21]. The author seeks to adopt these essential core roles within the results section to shape the shift between intra- and inter-organizational data governance. Therefore, these requirements serve as research background.

4   Research Method

A literature review seems feasible to synthesize existing data governance roles and their mutual dependencies [10].

The review is conducted through a keyword-based search [22]. After a few trial searches, "data governance" was identified as the search term in AISeL, ScienceDirect, ProQuest, ACM, IEEE, and Business Source Premier Database in EBSCOhost. Since they comprise almost the entire range of conference and journal publications, these databases are selected as they are most significant in IS research and computer science.

The review was conducted in March 2021. This step resulted in a total of 1007 hits across all databases. Next, a qualitative assessment is carried out consisting of two steps. First, papers are filtered based on their titles and abstracts and removed those which not deal with data governance roles in general or responsibility-related topics within data governance. One duplicate article was also removed. This step reduced the number of hits to 58. Second, those remaining articles were read, non-relevant papers were excluded. Then, the left 26 papers were included in the review.

Further, a backward and forward search was implemented. The backward search resulted in 12 relevant papers. For the forward search, Google Scholar was used. Additional four relevant papers were reviewed.

5   Results

5.1   Intra-organizational Data Governance Roles

In this section, all available data governance roles in IS and related literature will be synthesized. Mutual dependencies between individual roles are transferred to the entire construct (Fig. 1).

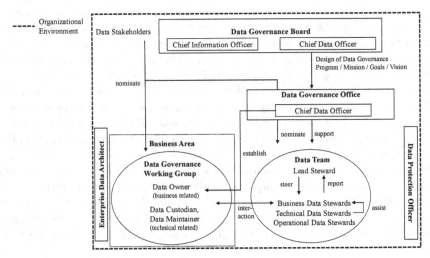

Fig. 1. Intra-organizational data governance role model

The Data Governance Board establishes a data governance system, including goals and roadmaps [23]. The literature similarly describes the Data Governance Council. The Data Governance Council monitors the mission goals, including current improvement projects [24–26]. In addition, it establishes guidelines and aligns its data governance program with its objectives [1]. In this context, other terms also refer to activities of the Data Governance Board, such as the Data Quality Board, the Data Governance Steering Committee, or the Executive Sponsor [24, 27].

The Chief Data Officer is the leading company-wide data manager and the responsible head of data governance processes. This role is responsible for the company-wide data preparation, use, and deletion cycle [28]. The Chief Information Officer also contains a leadership role responsible for managing the company's data assets [29]. There is no adequate separation of the individual areas of responsibility between these two management roles. In general, both roles can work on improving information management [30].

The Data Governance Office forms the central hub of data governance in a company. Exemplary areas of activity are scheduling data-related workshops or dealing with data stakeholders, and providing for their needs. Besides, the Data Governance Office should promote transparency [26, 27]. The Data Governance Coordinator is part of the Data Governance Office and the head of operations related to data governance. This role sets up all data governance practices [23] and is accountable for the implementation and operationalization of the data governance program [25] and preferably one of the management executives [31]. Furthermore, the Data Governance Coordinator manages the operational tasks for data stewards and reports on data governance performance [32]. The Data Governance Office can be differentiated from the Data Governance Working Group, comprised of business and IT data stakeholders [27].

The Data Team is composed of Data Stewards. They are responsible for all data management activities, including executing data management systems, defining protocols, and harmonizing all standards and procedures [26].

The Business Data Stewards operate in a first context to maintain conformity with data quality and corporate policies. They are often liable for documenting data problems to the client and are subject-matter specialists from different industries [23, 32]. Technical Data Stewards are IT professionals who serve as Business Data Stewards counterparts. They must grasp the program framework, system connections, data processing approaches, data protection, and code quality [23]. Operational Data Stewards are liable for routine entering and updating the operational data transactions [23]. English [33] also creates a hierarchy within the data stewards level and introduces the Strategic Information Steward or Lead Steward, responsible for the whole Data Team.

Besides the Data Stewards, there is a second widely accepted role, the Data Owners. They are often business executives and are responsible for their business division or unit [1]. In this context, the Data Producer generates the data or collates and preserves the generated data, a prerequisite for functioning as a Data Owner. The Data Owner is usually a senior client stakeholder liable for one or more data sets [34]. Besides, Fadler and Legner [35] introduce the Data Platform Owner with a platform-related task focus and the Data Product Owner, who takes care of product-related data issues.

A Data Stakeholder is interested in how data is collected, processed, manipulated, reported, or archived [36]. Kooper, Maes, and Lindgreen [37] describe this role as Data Consumers who are just data users in an organization.

Furthermore, upcoming data protection regulations require a Data Protection Officer who deals with all kinds of data security issues at a personal data level [38]. Besides, the Enterprise Data Architect should be tightly associated with data engineering as other specialists in technology development are hybrids bridging IT and company realms [39]. In this sense, Al-Ajmi [40] suggests the role of a Data Maintainer. This function is responsible for conducting daily system analysis, end-user service, upgrading a master database with new data, and maintaining specified change management procedures.

5.2   Allocation of Network Management Requirements (ANMR)

Fundamental network management requirements of the core roles of Knight and Harland [11] are allocated to appropriate intra-organizational data governance roles. The allocation of tasks establishes a basis for designing the role model (Fig. 2). The current intra-organizational roles and relationships are located in the left section of the model (white background). Based on the prior findings, these are extended across company boundaries (shaded background) by three selected roles (Chief Data Officer, Data Governance Coordinator, and the Data Governance Board).

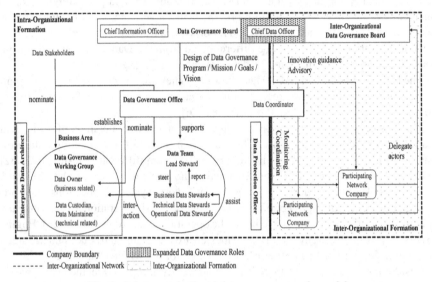

Fig. 2. Inter-organizational data governance role model

ANMR1: As the Innovation Facilitator covers promoting and facilitating product and process innovation [11], the linked tasks should be combined with the functions of the Chief Data Officer, as this role deals with innovation to enhance competitive value [30]. The Chief Data Officer is suggested participating with other executives in an Inter-Organizational Data Governance Board.

ANMR2: The Coordinator should be represented by the Data Governance Coordinator, as both roles have a coordinative task profile [11, 32]. Since the Data Governance Coordinator is part of the Data Governance Office [23], this organization entity will move closer to the company boundaries.

ANMR3: The Policy Maker should merge with the Data Governance Coordinator, and that role is responsible for developing the data governance standards. As the intra-organizational Data Governance Board provides strategic guidance, it should act as Advisor [11].

ANMR4: The network-related aim of the Advisor is the comprehensive consultation of individual actors within networks. For the appropriate allocation of the Advisor, the superior position of the Data Governance Board [24–26] lends itself.

ANMR5: The Information Broker appears as a center for transferring and distributing information within the inter-organizational network [11]. As this corresponds to the task profile of an executive, this role could be filled by the Data Governance Board [24–26] or through the role of a Chief Data Officer/Chief Information Officer [28, 30].

ANMR6: The Data Governance Coordinator represents the Network Structuring Agents. Both roles have monitoring and structuring responsibilities [11, 32]. The Data Governance Coordinator will act as boundary role and coordinates IODG projects with stakeholders from other organizations.

6 Discussion and Conclusion

For the next few years, IODG could present a crucial stream in IS research [9]. The entry of companies into networks is now occupying researchers with governance approaches for inter-organizational formations to assist corporate practice and government institutions in entering such ecosystems in a way that is data value-oriented and compliant with data protection. The initial contributions in recent years [41, 42] provide an excellent foundation for further developing this research stream. The present work aims to contribute to the young research field by suggesting inter-organizational role formations for future IODG endeavors. Therefore, this study examined the current knowledge of data governance roles and responsibilities by conducting a literature review. The identified roles were synthesized to provide an intra-organizational data governance role model with mutual relations between the included functions. That role model was extended by merging identified network management requirements and the initial results of the present literature review. Finally, these findings were introduced by designing a comprehensive IODG role model. This extension also answers the fielded research question on expanding existing data governance roles towards an inter-organizational environment.

Furthermore, this work expands previous research, primarily dealing with an intra-organizational focus on data governance roles and responsibilities. The findings also highlight the contribution of this paper first to take up and synthesize all existing data governance roles in the literature. It is also a systematic attempt to extend a data governance role model beyond organizational boundaries.

Literature has previously admitted many positive effects for organizations set up in networks. These findings underline the importance of research ventures in that field to develop a method to counteract the increasing data quantity and complexity on the one hand and structural heterogeneity of networks on the other hand.

Besides, Knight and Harland discussed network management roles [11] which form our requirements to form the presented IODG role model. Nevertheless, their research is based on empirical results within the National Health Service (United Kingdom) supplier network, which undoubtedly constitutes a particular form of a network. Therefore, the validity and applicability of both concepts in the context of networks in other industries have to be questioned, which would impact the designed model in the present study and therefore is a main limitation of the study. This limitation could be challenged by evaluating the present model within existing IODG projects. Typically, some publications also may remain undiscovered within the literature search due to a lack of the used keywords.

In summary, the findings of this short paper have demonstrated that the inter-organizational analysis of data governance roles offers plenty of room for further examination on conceptual and practice-oriented research.

References

1. Cheong, L., Chang, V.: The need for data governance: a case study. In: Proceedings of the 18th Australasian Conference on Information System. Toowoomba, Australia, pp. 999–1008 (2007)
2. Alter, C., Hage, J.: Organizations Working Together. Sage Publ, Newbury Park, Calif (1993)
3. Ghani, J.A.: Task uncertainty and the use of computer technology. Inf. Manag. 22(2), 69–76 (1992)
4. Weber, K., Otto, B., Oesterle, H.: One size does not fit all—a contingency approach to data governance. ACM J. Data Inf. Qual. 1(4), 1–27 (2009)
5. Khatri, V., Brown, C.V.: Designing data governance. Commun. ACM 53(1), 148–152 (2010)
6. Lis, D., Otto, B.: Towards a taxonomy of ecosystem data governance. In: Proceedings of the 54th Hawaii International Conference on System Sciences, p. 6067 (2021)
7. Lis, D., Otto, B.: Data governance in data ecosystems – insights from organizations. In: AMCIS 2020 Proceedings, p. 12 (2020)
8. Tiwana, A., Konsynski, B., Bush, A.: Research commentary—platform evolution: coevolution of platform architecture, governance, and environmental dynamics. Inf. Syst. Res. 21(4), 675–687 (2010)
9. Oliveira, M.I.S., Barros Lima, G.d.F., Farias Lóscio, B.: Investigations into data ecosystems: a systematic mapping study. Knowl. Inf. Syst. 61(2), 589–630 (2019)
10. Webster, J., Watson, R.T.: Analyzing the past to prepare for the future: writing a literature review. MIS Q. 26(2), xiii–xxiii (2002)
11. Knight, L., Harland, C.: Managing supply networks. Eur. Manag. J. 23(3), 281–292 (2005)
12. Weill, P., Ross, J.: IT governance on one page. CISR Working Paper (349), 1–15 (2004)
13. Brüning, A., Gluchowski, P., Kaiser, A.: Data Governance–Einordnung, Konzepte und aktuelle Herausforderungen (2017)
14. Panian, Z.: Some practical experiences in data governance. World Acad. Sci. Eng. Technol. 62, 468–475 (2010)
15. Sandkuhl, K., Filipe, J., Cordeiro, J., Cardoso, J.: Information logistics in networked organizations: selected concepts and application. In: International Conference on Enterprise Information Systems. Funchal, Madeira, pp. 43–54 (2009)
16. Powell, W.W.: Neither market nor hierarchy: network forms of organization. Res. Organ. Behav. 12, 295–336 (1990)
17. Huckvale, T., Ould, M.: Process modeling-who, what and how-role activity diagramming. In: Business Process Change: Concepts, Methods and Technologies. Idea Group Publishing, Harrisburg, PA, pp. 330–349 (1995)
18. Segars, A.H., Grover, V., Kettinger, W.J.: Business Process Change: Reengineering Concepts, Methods, and Technologies. (Grover, V., Kettinger, W.J., Review). Interfaces 26(1), 138–140 (1996)

19. Carleton, T., Leifer, L.: Stanford's ME310 course as an evolution of engineering design. In: Proceedings of the 19th CIRP Design Conference - Competitive Design, pp. 1–8 (2009)
20. Snow, C.C., Miles, R.E., Coleman, J.R.: Managing 21st century network organizations. Organ. Dyn. **20**(3), 4–20 (1992)
21. Mintzberg, H.: The manager's job: folklore and fact. Harv. Bus. Rev. **53**, 49–51 (1975)
22. Rowe, F.: What literature review is not: diversity, boundaries and recommendations. Eur. J. Inf. Syst. **23**(3), 241–255 (2014)
23. Yulfitri, A.: Modeling operational model of data governance in government: Case study: Government agency X in Jakarta. In: 2016 International Conference on Information Technology Systems and Innovation (ICITSI). Bandung, Indonesia, pp. 1–15. IEEE (2016)
24. Dyché, J., Levy, E.: Customer Data Integration. Reaching a Single Version of the Truth, 1st edn. Wiley, New York, NY (2006)
25. Loshin, D. (ed.): Master Data Management: The MK/OMG Press. Morgan Kaufmann, Boston (2009)
26. Thomas, G.: The DGI Data Governance DGI Data Governance Framework (2006). http://www.datagovernance.com/wp-content/uploads/2020/07/wp_how_to_use_the_dgi_data_g overnance_framework.pdf. Accessed 23 Mar 2021
27. Mosley, M., Brackett, M., Earley, S. (eds.): The DAMA Guide to the Data Management Body of Knowledge. (DAMA-DMBOK Guide). Technics Publications LLC, Bradley Beach, NJ (2010)
28. Lee, Y., Madnick, S.E., Wang, R.Y., Wang, F., Zhang, H.: A cubic framework for the chief data officer: succeeding in a world of big data. MIS Q. Exec. **13**(1), 1–13 (2014)
29. Thuraisingham, B., Kantarcioglu, M., Bertino, E., Bakdash, J.Z., Fernandez, M.: Towards a privacy-aware quantified self data management framework. In: Proceedings of the 23nd ACM on Symposium on Access Control Models and Technologies. SACMAT 2018. ACM, New York, NY, USA, pp. 173–184 (2018)
30. Kettinger, W., Zhang, C., Li, H.: Information Management capabilities in the digital era: the senior manager's perspective. In: Proceedings of the Fortieth International Conference on Information Systems. Munich, Germany, pp. 1–15 (2019)
31. Dreibelbis, A., Hechler, E., Milman, I., Oberhofer, M., van Run, P., Wolfson, D.: Enterprise Master Data Management: An SOA Approach to Managing Core Information. Pearson Education, India (2008)
32. Informatica: Holistic Data Governance: A Framework for Competitive Advantage (2012)
33. English, L.P.: Information Quality Applied. Best Practices for Improving Business Information, Processes and Systems, 1st edn. Wiley, New York, NY (2009)
34. Askham, N.: What's the difference between data owners and data custodians? https://www.nicolaaskham.com/blog/2019/4/12/whats-the-difference-between-data-owners-and-data-cus todians. Accessed 22 Mar 2021
35. Fadler, M., Legner, C.: Who owns data in the enterprise? Rethinking data ownership in times of big data and analytics. In: Proceedings of the Twenty-Eigth European Conference on Information Systems. Marrakesh, Morocco, pp. 1–16 (2020)
36. Young, A., McConkey, M.: Data governance and data quality: is it on your agenda? J. Instit. Res. **17**(1), 69–77 (2012)
37. Kooper, M.N., Maes, R., Lindgreen, E.E.O.R.: On the governance of information Introducing a new concept of governance to support the management of information. International Journal of Information Management 31(3), 195–200 (2011)
38. IT-Governance Privacy Team: EU General Data Protection Regulation (GDPR): An Implementation and Compliance Guide, 2nd edn. IT Governance Publishing, Cambridgeshire (2017)
39. Zornes, A.: Hybrids are hot. Inf. Manag. **17**(4), 45 (2007)

40. Al-Ajmi, H.Z.: Case: Big geosciences data validation challenges and achievements. In: 2017 IEEE International Conference on Big Data (Big Data), Boston, MA, pp. 3024–3030. IEEE (2017)
41. Lee, S.U., Zhu, L., Jeffery, R.: Data governance decisions for platform ecosystems. In: Bui, T. (ed.) Proceedings of the 52nd Hawaii International Conference on System Sciences. Grand Wailea, Maui, Hawaii, pp. 6377–6386 (2019)
42. De Prieëlle, F., De Reuver, M., Rezaei, J.: The role of ecosystem data governance in adoption of data platforms by internet-of-things data providers: case of dutch horticulture industry. IEEE Trans. Eng. Manag. 1–11 (2020). https://doi.org/10.1109/TEM.2020.2966024

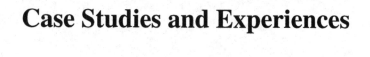

Case Studies and Experiences

Can SysML Be Used for Enterprise Modelling?

Kimberly Lai[✉] and Michael Gruninger

Department of Mechanical and Industrial Engineering, University of Toronto, Toronto, Canada
kimberly.lai@mail.utoronto.ca, gruninger@mie.utoronto.ca

Abstract. Although a variety of specialised formalisms have been proposed specifically for enterprise modelling, the use of existing modelling languages has not received as much attention. In this paper, we demonstrate that the systems modelling formalism SysML is in fact not sufficient to act as a standalone language for enterprise modelling. To demonstrate this claim, we show that there are four key enterprise modelling scenarios that cannot be addressed while adhering to SysML semantics: temporal representation, timing and scheduling, collaborations between two or more teams and decision trees .

Keywords: Enterprise modelling · SysML · Civil aircraft system case study

1 Introduction

Within academia and industry, there are many different modelling formalisms or languages that can be use in enterprise modelling, including UML [1], SysML [2], BPMN [3] and the IDEF modelling language family [4]. Depending on the purpose and context of a model, different languages are chosen as each has its own strengths and weaknesses. In practice, an enterprise model is often made up of a combination of models and hence comprises of a combination of languages. Certain modelling languages are used to model certain aspects of the enterprise while another language is used to model another aspect. This results in a lot of inconsistency as concepts may not be clearly defined and interpretations can differ. Thus, in an ideal scenario, having one modelling language that can cover all aspects of the enterprise would solve this problem.

On the other hand, it is postulated in academia that an enterprise can be considered as a system. Treating an enterprise as a system and using a systems engineering approach can result in a more efficient and effective running of the enterprise [5]. In terms of a modelling language for system models, SysML is the standard modelling language that has been tailored for systems engineering applications. It supports the specification, analysis, design, verification, and validation of a wide range of complex systems [6].

As a result, it would be reasonable to hypothesise that SysML can act as a standalone language for enterprise modelling. However, in this paper, we claim that although SysML can be used to model many aspects of an enterprise, it is in fact not sufficient to provide a full depiction. There are four key enterprise modelling scenarios that cannot

© IFIP International Federation for Information Processing 2021
Published by Springer Nature Switzerland AG 2021
E. Serral et al. (Eds.): PoEM 2021, LNBIP 432, pp. 257–266, 2021.
https://doi.org/10.1007/978-3-030-91279-6_18

be addressed while adhering to SysML semantics: temporal representation, timing and scheduling, collaborations between two or more teams and decision trees. This will be demonstrated using example diagrams in the context of an enterprise that designs and manufactures civil aircraft systems, with a specific focus on the system development and safety assessment processes.

2 Background and Related Work

2.1 Enterprise Modelling and Systems Modelling

Enterprise modelling is a field that has been gaining attention for the last few decades. As a result of digitalisation and globalisation, enterprises must become increasingly agile and continuously adapt to change in order to survive. One approach to remain competitive and achieve agility is to create an enterprise model to represent the organisation. As defined in [7], an enterprise model is a computational model that illustrates "the structure, activities, processes, information, resources, people, behaviour and goals of an enterprise". It provides all the information and knowledge necessary to achieve model-driven enterprise design, analysis, and operation.

Using a model-based approach to run an enterprise can bring about many benefits. This includes better integration and communication between various departments within an enterprise, as well as an improved understanding of the enterprise as a whole. It also results in better decision making as analysis can be performed before execution and the consequences of any sudden changes can be traced throughout the enterprise.

There are two key aspects that must be determined before any models are built. The first is the enterprise architecture/modelling framework which dictates how the enterprise will be broken down and represented. This is achieved by organising the model into various views or layers such as the business view, operations view, conceptual view, technical view and implementation view. Currently, there are a variety of existing frameworks that have been designed to support various modelling purposes and levels of granularity. Examples include: DoDAF, TOGAF, the Zachman Framework and CIMOSA [8]. The second key aspect is the modelling language that is used to draw the diagrams that make up the enterprise model. The modelling language dictates how certain concepts are graphically represented and the type of information that is presented in various types of diagrams. Examples of modelling languages include UML, which is used in software engineering, SysML which is used in systems engineering, and BPMN and IDEF3 which are used for process modelling.

It is often suggested in academia that an enterprise can be considered as a system. In the Handbook of Systems Engineering and Management [5] it discusses how treating an enterprise as a system and using a systems engineering approach can lead to a more efficient and effective running of the enterprise. Rouse [9] also suggests that understanding enterprises as systems is critical to addressing strategic challenges such as achieving growth and responding to change. Understanding interactions between different functions within an enterprise is also essential to fully leveraging an enterprise's assets. Following on from this logic, enterprise modelling can be considered as a variant of systems modelling and hence using SysML as an enterprise modelling language could be possible.

2.2 The Systems Modeling Language (SysML)

SysML is a visual modelling language that provides the semantics and notations for modelling a system. It was developed by the Object Modelling Group (OMG) specifically for systems engineering applications and is an extension of the Unified Modeling Language (UML), which was first developed as a generic modelling language in the software field. As it was developed specifically for systems engineering applications, there are certain concepts and diagram types that are introduced to support activities such as requirements specification and trade studies for design analysis. The diagrams defined by SysML semantics are also classified into four pillars: Behaviour, Structure, Parametric and Requirements.

SysML is well accepted by industry and academia as the de-facto standard for systems modelling. According to [10] it supports the "specification, analysis, design, verification and validations of systems that include hardware, software, data, personnel, procedures and facilities". Hence, it can describe a complex system from concept development and requirements writing all the way to design, implementation, verification, and validation activities.

SysML also has a profile extension mechanism that allows users to customise its profile so that it can be modified to suit the users' needs. This is a very useful capability, especially in the context of enterprise modelling, as every enterprise will have its preference for domain-specific vocabulary. With SysML, the names of pre-defined stereotypes can be modified, and specialisations of stereotypes can also be created to match the language typically used in the organisation. For example, for an enterprise that produces complex mechanical products, the requirement stereotype can be specialised into a functional requirement, performance requirement and constraint requirement to better capture all the requirements that need to be satisfied.

By examining the definitions of enterprise modelling and SysML, it can be seen that there is a large amount of overlap between the concepts covered by these formalisms. Hence, if systems modelling is indeed a variant of enterprise modelling, it is logical to consider SysML as a plausible language for enterprise modelling.

2.3 Related Work on Enterprise Modelling Languages

Ongoing and existing research in the field of enterprise modelling languages largely fit into two categories. The first category involves exploring how multiple languages representing different domains can be integrated together to cover all aspects of an enterprise model. For example, TOGAF provides a framework to integrate various domains within an enterprise including business, data, and technical architectures [11]. The second category is the introduction of a new modelling language that has been specifically created for the purpose of enterprise modelling. For example, the use of the Unified Enterprise Modelling Language (UEML) is proposed in [12] which acts as a simple universal language that functions as a standard user interface on top of existing languages and systems. Domain-specific models can then be translated into UEML models and interact with other domain models. On the other hand, The Open Group also introduce the use of the ArchiMate modelling technique [13] for describing enterprise architectures.

Works that contribute to assessing enterprise modelling techniques focus mostly on enterprise architecture/modelling frameworks. For example, [14] evaluates whether these frameworks provide a structure that will allow all aspects of an enterprise to be modelled. There has also been some work done on evaluating the adequacy of languages that have been specifically created for enterprise modelling purposes. For example, [15] evaluates how well ArchiMate responds to common enterprise modelling challenges.

However, beyond the work in [16], limited research has been performed on evaluating whether modelling languages that are already widely used in industry, such as BPMN or SysML, can be used for enterprise modelling purposes instead. If an existing language is already sufficient for enterprise modelling, this would greatly simplify the most common challenge of language inconsistency for enterprise models. Therefore, since it is often suggested that an enterprise can be considered as a kind of system, an evaluation on the adequacy of SysML as an enterprise modelling language is needed.

3 Case Study

3.1 Method

To investigate if SysML can be used as a standalone language for enterprise modelling, the following steps were performed. First, a list of common enterprise modelling scenarios was created by examining existing enterprise modelling frameworks such as GERAM and CIMOSA. These scenarios were then modelled using SysML on the Papyrus tool, which is an open-source graphical editing tool developed by Eclipse that has been designed to support SysML and adheres to all its semantics and rules. Finally, each of the scenarios were then analysed in order to determine whether SysML was able to adequately portray all the intended information.

Table 1 below provides a summary of common modelling scenarios that contribute to describing an enterprise as well as the corresponding type of SysML diagram that was used to represent them. Of these scenarios, there are three that cannot be represented accurately which are indicated in bold below: interaction between entities/teams, process interaction and decision tree. The conclusions drawn and challenges faced from modelling these scenarios will be discussed in Sect. 3.3.

Table 1. Summary of modelling scenarios.

Enterprise modelling scenario	Type of SysML diagram to use
Organisation hierarchy	Block definition diagram [bdd]
Process breakdown	Block definition diagram [bdd]; Internal block diagram [ibd]
Interaction between entities/teams	**Activity diagram [act]**
Process interaction	**Activity diagram [act]**

(continued)

Table 1. (*continued*)

Enterprise modelling scenario	Type of SysML diagram to use
Context andStakeholders	Use case diagram [uc]
Deliverable lifecycle	State machine diagram [stm]
Decision tree	**State machine diagram [stm]**
Requirements flow down	Requirement diagram [req]
Trade studies	Parametric diagram [par]
Task allocation	Allocation table [alloc]

3.2 Context: System Development and Safety Processes for Civil Aircraft

The example scenarios shown in this paper are performed from the perspective of an enterprise that is involved in the development of civil aircraft systems. In particular, some of the information related to the system development and safety assessment processes for a civil aircraft system are modelled. Standard documentation of these processes can also be found in ARP4754A [17] and ARP4761 [18].

3.3 Diagrams

The purpose of this paper is to identify and describe the inadequacies of SysML as an enterprise modelling language. Therefore, in this section, only the three scenarios mentioned above that could not be adequately portrayed using SysML will be presented. The challenges faced when using SysML semantics to represent the desired information will also be discussed below. For reference, the scenarios that were successfully represented using SysML can be found in the full paper **here**.

Interaction Between Entities. For an enterprise to operate smoothly and efficiently, multiple entities within an enterprise will often work together to achieve a common goal. As such, the representation of interactions between various entities is a crucial part of an enterprise model. An *Activity Diagram*, such as Fig. 1, can be used for this purpose, where swim lanes can be used to represent the different entities, and activities are used to represent the activities, tasks and processes that are performed. A swim lane can be used to represent either a specific individual, a team, or even an entire department, and hence it is suitable for detailing high level processes as well as low level ones.

However, one major drawback is that representing activities that are performed in collaboration between two or more entities or teams is impossible without violating SysML rules. In the context of aircraft system safety processes, the activities "System Level FHA" and "ASA" should be a collaborative effort by the Airframer and Aircraft System Supplier. Hence, as shown above, the activity is placed in between two swim lanes to reflect this. However, this could only be accomplished by disabling the simulation and model checking feature in Papyrus as placing an activity between two swim lanes is prohibited by the modelling tool. According to SysML semantics, placing an activity within a particular swim lane is equivalent to allocating that activity to the actor or

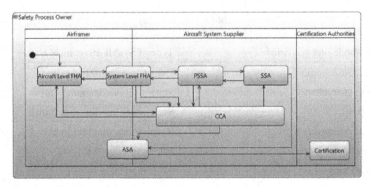

Fig. 1. Interaction between entities

element the swim lane represents and hence, only one allocation can be made. Therefore, despite successfully showing the intended information, Fig. 1 is semantically incorrect.

An alternative to an *Activity Diagram* is to use a *Sequence Diagram* to represent interactions between processes, with each lifeline representing a different entity. However, the same problem exists as each activity can only be drawn on top of one lifeline and cannot span across two or more.

Process Interaction. The representation of interactions between processes is another scenario that must be included within an enterprise model as it contributes to defining the operations of an enterprise. Of all the SysML diagram types, an *Activity Diagram* is best suited for this purpose. Processes can be represented by *Activities*, and *swim lanes* can represent the larger overarching super-process that a certain group of processes contribute to. For example, in Fig. 2 the diagram describes how the two major processes, the system development process and safety process, interact with one another and what type of information is transmitted. By using swim lanes, it can be shown that the Aircraft level FHA, System level FHA and PSSA are all sub-processes of the overall Safety Process.

However, one major problem in this representation is the lack of any temporal information. This diagram provides a great overview at all the important processes and how they interact, however, SysML semantics does not account for being able to represent the duration of each process. Knowing the expected duration of each sub-process and being able to predict the amount of time needed for completion can be extremely important, especially for time sensitive projects or tasks. Furthermore, without the support of temporal information, planning and scheduling is not possible, and hence this is another major drawback of SysML.

Moreover, it became apparent while drawing this diagram that the figure could very quickly become quite complex and visually confusing. SysML semantics dictate the use of *merge* and *split nodes* when one type of information needs to go from one element to two different ones or vice versa, thus adding to the complexity of the diagram. For scenarios of a higher complexity with much more information transfer than is shown in Fig. 2, the diagram would become very dense and disorganised which is impractical.

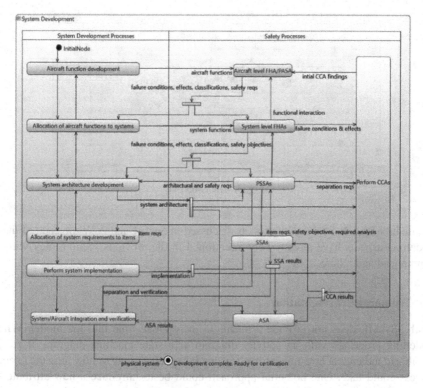

Fig. 2. Process interaction

Decision Trees. Decision trees are useful in providing a common guideline on how certain actions or decisions are made within an enterprise. For example, it is specified in ARP4761 [18] that once failure conditions are identified as part of the FHA process, there are three possible next steps. This is determined by a decision tree which has the FHA failure conditions as the top-level input as shown in Fig. 3. A *State Machine Diagram* can be used to represent this, yet this only works visually. In terms of SysML semantics, what is shown in this diagram is not correct; it violates SysML semantics and cannot be executed. State machines are meant to represent states, operations, and events, and hence drawing a diagram in this format where the decision nodes are used to represent questions in a decision tree is not valid. Therefore, the conclusion can be reached that SysML fails to support the modelling of decision trees.

4 Challenges of Using SysML for Enterprise Modelling

In summary, by drawing various enterprise model scenarios using SysML, we have identified four key enterprise modelling aspects that SysML is unable to represent. Although this may not be exhaustive, it is enough to demonstrate some counterexamples that prove that SysML cannot be used as a standalone language for enterprise modelling

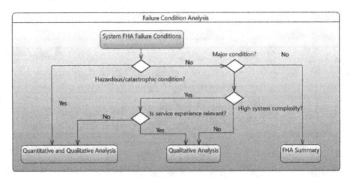

Fig. 3. Decision tree

despite it being a logical assumption as discussed in Sect. 1 and 2. While each of these modelling aspects have already been mentioned in the previous section, they will be summarised again here.

4.1 Temporal Representation

Firstly, SysML does not provide a means to incorporate time into the model. When modelling processes with an activity diagram or a state machine diagram, it is not possible to indicate of how much time is needed for each activity or how long the overall process could take. One potential approach could be to introduce a new attribute to represent time and use simulation to calculate how much time is needed for certain processes. However, from a graphical standpoint this does not solve the problem and is a very impractical method. There would still be no indication of time when looking at the diagram and the user would have to manually explore the properties of each model element to retrieve this information.

4.2 Timing and Scheduling

Similarly, representing timelines and creating schedules is also something that SysML cannot do. By definition, an enterprise model should supply the information and knowledge necessary to support the operations of the enterprise. Scheduling plays a crucial part in planning the operations of an enterprise and thus, without the capability to do so, this is quite a significant aspect of an enterprise model that cannot be represented.

4.3 Collaboration Between Teams

Representing activities as a collaboration between two or more teams is another scenario that SysML is unable to handle. In large organisations that have multiple teams, the scenario where multiple teams or individuals are responsible for one activity or deliverable is particularly common. Therefore, being able to indicate that something is under the joint responsibility of two or more stakeholders is necessary to avoid any confusion or misunderstandings. As discussed in Sect. 3.3, it is impossible to place an activity between two swim lanes without breaking SysML semantics that are implicitly enforced in the Papyrus tool. Figure 1 was only achieved by making the model non-executable, however this is obviously not an ideal solution as the diagram is no longer valid.

4.4 Decision Tree

Finally, is the challenge of representing a decision tree using SysML. Decision trees are useful in standardising how certain decisions are made in an enterprise and how to approach various scenarios. It can also be used to facilitate business decision making as they can be used to calculate probabilities and outcomes. A state machine diagram can be used to present the decision-making information graphically, however this causes the diagram to be semantically incorrect and invalid. As such, it can be concluded that SysML semantics do not support the generation of decision trees either.

5 Conclusion and Future Work

In conclusion, SysML is not sufficient to act as a standalone language for enterprise modelling. As demonstrated by this paper, there are several scenarios that should be described by an enterprise model which cannot be represented while still adhering to SysML semantics. In order to construct an enterprise model that will describe all the information necessary to support the operations of an enterprise, SysML will need to be supplemented with other languages or frameworks to help represent aspects that SysML cannot. For example, SysML could be combined with TimeML [19], a specification language developed for event and temporal expressions, or an ontology framework such as the Process Specification Language (PSL) [20] ontology which also supports temporal concepts [21].

Considering that the findings presented in this paper are a result of the authors' experience and expertise, this raises the challenge of being able to derive formal results about the expressiveness of modelling languages. In particular, how can one *prove* that temporal constraints and various other aspects cannot be represented by SysML?

Another question worth considering for further research efforts is whether an enterprise can indeed be regarded as a kind of system. As previously discussed, it is suggested by literature that an enterprise can in fact be treated as a system and using a systems engineering approach for an enterprise can result in a more efficient and effective running of the enterprise. Therefore, if an enterprise is considered a kind of system, then the results of this paper suggest that SysML is in fact not sufficient as a systems modelling language and needs to be extended such that all use cases are covered. Alternatively, an enterprise could instead be regarded as an extension of a system and hence it is only logical that SysML is not sufficient as an enterprise modelling language. Nevertheless, further exploration is needed on how an enterprise can be considered as a system and what sort of transformations need to be carried out for this to be true. Following from that, the shortcomings of SysML identified here will need to be evaluated once more to see if they are still valid.

References

1. Object Management Group: Unified Modeling Language v2.5.1, Dec 2017. https://www.omg.org/spec/UML/2.5.1/PDF. Accessed June 2021

2. Object Management Group: SysML v1.6, Nov 2019. https://www.omg.org/spec/SysML/1.6/PDF. Accessed June 2021

3. Object Management Group: Business Process Model and Notation (BPMN), version 2.0, Jan 2011. https://www.omg.org/spec/BPMN/2.0/PDF. Accessed June 2021

4. Menzel, C., Mayer, R.: The IDEF family of languages. In: Menzel, C., Mertins, K., Mayer, R. (eds.) Handbook on Architectures of Information Systems. Springer, Heidelberg, pp. 215–249 (2006).https://doi.org/10.1007/978-3-662-03526-9_1

5. Sage, A.P., Rouse, W.B.: Handbook of Systems Engineering and Management, 2nd edn. Wiley, New York (2009)

6. Object Management Group: SysML Open Source Project. https://sysml.org/. Accessed 10 Mar 2021

7. Gruninger, M., Fox, M.S.: The logic of enterprise modelling. In: Bernus, P., Nemes, L. (eds.) Modelling and Methodologies for Enterprise Integration. ITIFIP, pp. 140–157. Springer, Boston, MA (1996). https://doi.org/10.1007/978-0-387-34983-1_10

8. Urbaczewski, L., Mrdalj, S.: A comparison of enterprise architecture frameworks. Issues Inf. Syst. **VII**(2) (2006)

9. Rouse, W.B.: Enterprises as systems: essential challenges and approaches to transformation. Syst. Eng. **8**(2), 138–150 (2005)

10. Hause, M.: The SysML modelling language. In: Fifth European Systems Engineering Conference (2006)

11. The Open Group: The TOGAF Standard, Version 9.2. https://pubs.opengroup.org/architecture/togaf9-doc/arch/welcome.html. Accessed June 2021

12. Vernadat, F.B.: UEML: towards a unified enterprise modelling language. Int. J. Prod. Res. **40**(17), 4309–4321 (2020)

13. Visual Paradigm: What is ArchiMate? https://www.visual-paradigm.com/guide/archimate/what-is-archimate/. Accessed June 2021

14. Leist, S., Zellner, G.: Evaluation of current architecture frameworks. In: SAC 2006: Proceedings of the 2006 ACM Symposium on Applied Computing (2006)

15. Gils, B.v., Proper, H.A.: Enterprise modelling in the age of digital transformation. In: PoEM 2018 (2018)

16. Tsadimas, A.: Model-based enterprise information system architectural design with SysML. In: 2015 IEEE 9th International Conference on Research Challenges in Information Science (RCIS), Athens, Greece (2015)

17. SAE Aerospace, SAE4754A: Guidelines for development of civil aircraft and systems. (2010)

18. SAE Aerospace, ARP4761: Guidelines and methods for conducting the safety assessment process on civil airborne systems and equipment

19. Pustejovsky, J., et al.: TimeML: A Specification Language for Temporal and Event Expressions. Kluwer Academic Publishers, Netherlands (2003). Accessed Sept 2021

20. Schlenoff, C., Lubell, J., Gruninger, M., Tissot, F., Valois, J., Lee, J.: The process specification language (PSL) overview and version 1.0 specification, Gaithersburg, MD: NIST Interagency/Internal Report (NISTIR), National Institute of Standards and Technology (2000). Accessed Sept 2021

21. Sriram, R., Brady, M.: Ontology for big systems: the ontology summit 2012 communique. Appl Ontol. **8**(3) (2013)

A Collaborative Model for Connecting Product Design and Assembly Line Design: An Aeronautical Case

Alex Aquieta Nuñez[1], Anouck Chan[2], Alberto Donoso-Arciniega[1],
Thomas Polacsek[2(✉)], and Stéphane Roussel[2]

[1] ISAE, Toulouse, France
[2] ONERA, Toulouse, France
thomas.polacsek@onera.fr

Abstract. In business or in industry, some entities are in collaboration with each other when they work together with or without common objectives. In this paper, we are interested in this collaboration relationship in the context of aeronautics. More precisely, we focus on a use case in which two actors' objectives are respectively to design an aircraft and to design the assembly line for this aircraft. Following some previous work on coopetition, we analyse the dependency relationship between these actors and propose i^* models. In order to solve dependency cycle issues, we introduce a third actor that is in charge of realising trade-offs between the two designs. Finally, we show how existing methodology could be applied for supporting this trade-off activity.

Keywords: Goal modelling · Collaboration · Aeronautical case study · Enterprise modelling · Industry 4.0

1 Introduction

Collaboration means that different actors work jointly together, but not necessarily for the same objectives. The actors share resources, knowledge or can work together, to achieve their own goals which may or may not be common. In the context of business, the notion of cooperation has been extended with the concept of *coopetition* [4]. In coopetition, actors are in a competitive situation, but choose to work together in order to increase their profit. They are simultaneously in cooperation and in competition. Their objective is to maximise personal benefits and minimise personal cost through cooperation and competition. Coopetition relationship between actors is a common configuration in industrial environment. In fact, distinct organizations may need to combine their strengths to reach some of their objectives while there are rivals for others.

Recent works have focused on modelling goals and dependencies between actors in the context of coopetition [17,18]. Indeed, within this context, an actor

© IFIP International Federation for Information Processing 2021
Published by Springer Nature Switzerland AG 2021
E. Serral et al. (Eds.): PoEM 2021, LNBIP 432, pp. 267–280, 2021.
https://doi.org/10.1007/978-3-030-91279-6_19

collaborates with partners who contribute to provide her what she needs. Therefore, a dependency is established between the partners. This dependency relies on the partners' involvement level in the coopetition.

In this paper, we follow these approaches and focus on the notion of dependency among actors in a collaboration environment. The investment and sharing of resources within a cooperation framework may be more or less interesting, depending on the goals of each actor. Thus, it can be interesting to characterize the dependency in order to support the actors in making choices between satisfying the goals of the collaboration and their internal goals.

Even if we use quite simple modelling in this paper, we believe it helps to understand and solve a real practical problem without the need for extensive and complex systems modelling. In fact, modelling is here used as a thinking aid and not a technical simulation.

We specifically focus on an aeronautical case study, presented in Sect. 2. This case study consists of designing an aircraft and designing a factory (an assembly line) which produces this aircraft. It involves two actors, namely aircraft designers and assembly line designers. Even if the two actors belong to the same company, they have different goals and must therefore be handled as two separate entities. However, these actors are not rivals for any of their goals. Therefore, they really are in a collaborative context.

In Sect. 3, we follow previous methodological approaches developed for coopetition to elicit and propose several models of dependencies between the actors. The first model represents the current relationship of the actors, which is a subordinate relationship. The second model represents the desired relationship between them, which is a collaboration relationship. We show that there are some cycle issues with such a model. Therefore, we present a third model in which we introduce a new actor in order to realise trade-offs between the two actors and solve the cycle issues.

Then, in Sect. 4, we focus on a specific part of the aircraft and its assembly process and the trade-off that can be made between the two actors. We formalise the associated dependencies in order to be able to assess the impact of the actor's choices on another in the final approach. More specifically, we adapt an approach to support actors in making choices that affect collaboration in a way that maximises their goals.

Section 5 is dedicated to the conclusion and perspectives.

2   An Aeronautical Case Study

For some complex products, such as an aircraft, some cars or some satellites, the definition of the means of production starts after the definition of the product. In other words, the product specifications are used to define its manufacture. The main risk with this type of approach is that the means of production may face blocking constraints that, sometimes, could easily be solved by changing the design of the product. For instance, in the context of an aircraft, one might have a first design with the air conditioning going through the centre of the cockpit and a second design with the air conditioning split on the right and on the left of the cockpit. These two designs might be equivalent in terms of performance of the aircraft but very different in the way they are produced. In fact, the first design could be hard to produce as it would require several assembly tasks in a busy area of the aircraft whereas the second one allows tasks parallelisation.

This problem of *manufacturability* is a key element in Industry 4.0 [25]. One of the ways to manage the manufacturability problem is *Design for Assembly* (DFA) [2,15], which consists of the designing of products for ease of assembly. DFA takes into account the constraints inherent to the means of production, whether it is the prohibitive cost of certain elements or the physical impossibility of producing some designs due to the lack of specific tools. The philosophy of DFA is to solve manufacturing problems at the design stage and thus drastically reduce costs. DFA brings manufacturing and assembly restrictions into product development, it is strictly one-way from production to product design. But production is not only a source of problems, it can also provide new design possibilities. Indeed, new manufacturing methods such as robotics or additive manufacturing open up new possibilities in terms of design, while imposing constraints (size of what can be printed, materials used, *etc.*). Thanks to additive manufacturing special characteristics, designs using it are sometimes very different from conventional designs.

Therefore, it is increasingly crucial to integrate manufacturability early in the development cycle to understand the multiple interactions between design and manufacturing. This is exactly what concurrent engineering, or simultaneous engineering, aims to do. The idea of having the design office and production work together is not new [23]. This approach has been used for a long time in the context of spare parts in the automotive industry [12], but its implementation in the context of more complex systems, particularly in aeronautics [19,20], raises many problems. The aeronautical industry is precisely the focus of our case study. The aircraft development follows a cascading cycle, from high-level goals, which come from market studies, airlines and also from societal expectations (such as green or noise reduction), to requirements and then to specifications. The production system and its specification are mostly defined after the engineering activities. Manufacturing systems of an aerospace factory is a complex layout of different types of production equipment (forging/bending presses, welding stations, riveting machines, coordinate measuring machines, assembly jigs, *etc.*) that accommodates both flow and batch production process architectures [13]. So, aircraft manufacturers are faced with the challenges of flexibility, productivity, as well as the ever-growing pressure for cost reduction and better performance. As such, concurrent engineering approaches integrating product development and production system development are now a hot topic.

In this work, we focus on the high-level goals for the design of an aircraft and for the design of its production system. The goals we express are based on our experiences in the field. It covers both goals for the aircraft in terms of performance, noise, consumption, and goals for the production system in terms of cost and production capacity. Based on these goals, we apply a method that allows us to make choices both in the design of the aircraft and in the design of the production system. We consider the concept of regional transport aircraft, with an average range of 600 km, 150 seats and a cruising speed around Mach 0.8 [22]. This aircraft has the particularity to have a completely electric propulsion thanks to a set of electric motors integrated in the wing and powered by two turbines located at the back of the fuselage. The technical aspects related to the problems studied in this use case will be detailed in the following sections.

3   Product and Production Designers: Two Actors Trying to Work Together

In this section, we try to characterise, through goal-oriented modelling, the collaboration relationship among the different actors that build the DRAGON and its assembly line. To do this, we first highlight that there currently exists a dependency relationship between the actors. Then, we focus on the dependencies in the case of a collaboration relationship and we show that it raises some cycle issues. Finally, we propose a possible solution to allow actors to collaborate together.

3.1   Aircraft and Assembly Line Goals

Optimising the interaction between product and production system development requires first an analysis of the relations and inter-dependencies of both fields. To do this, it is necessary to elicit the requirements, or more precisely the goals, of each stakeholder. There are various frameworks for doing this, such as SysML [11], Kaos [8] or i^* [7].

Inspired by the work done by Pant and Yu [17,18] on coopetition we have chosen to use i^*. In the context of our study, we build a Strategic Dependency diagram which aims to elicit intentional relationships between actors. The diagram representing the current dependencies is given in Fig. 1. Legend of i^* elements that we use are recalled in Fig. 1.

In our case, we have two collaborating actors: *DRAGON designers* and the *Assembly line designers*. Both have their own actor's boundary, which is a graphical container for their intentional elements together as well as their interrelationships. They are not rivals for any resource, but, as within the coopetition relationship, the satisfaction of elements in one actor may depend on the satisfaction of elements in the other.

Regarding goals, for the DRAGON designers' side, we focus on four goals which are range, passenger capacity, cruising speed and the main objective of DRAGON, which is to have an electric propulsion. All these goals are fulfilled by task *do DRAGON design*. In addition, there is one *soft goal*[1]: DRAGON must use as little fuel as possible and perform better on this criterion than the present-day aircraft (*have lower consumption than current aircraft* in Fig. 1). Soft goal is a goal with no clear-cut criteria, *i.e.* a goal that cannot be clearly and formally qualified as satisfied [6]. The *lower consumption* objective is not quantified, so

---

[1] For the purposes of legibility, we have chosen to use the term *soft goal* instead of the term *quality* used in i^* 2.0.

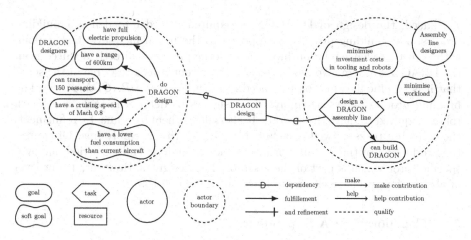

Fig. 1. Current relationship between DRAGON designers and assembly line designers

its satisfaction is necessarily subject to interpretation. In this diagram, the soft goal is linked to the task by a *qualify relationship*, it means that the task should take into account the soft goal when being performed [7].

From the assembly line designer's side, there are one goal and two soft goals. The task of the designers here is to design an assembly line, but not just any assembly line, an assembly line that must build the DRAGON aircraft. This is why the task *design a DRAGON assembly line* is qualified by the goal *can build DRAGON* attached to the task *design an assembly line*. Regarding the soft goals, the first one is to *minimise investments costs in tooling and robots*. The second is to minimise a specific operational cost: the workload (*i.e.* hourly labour).

Of course, many other important aspects should also be considered. For example, because of the noise pollution, DRAGON must make as little noise as possible, or even less noise than the current aircraft. Regarding building the assembly line, the non-recurring costs associated with the construction of the factory, of the workstations or land purchase could also be taken into account. For the sake of readability, we have chosen to keep a limited number of elements for both actors.

The dependency relation (represented by the D-arrow) connects two actors, here the two design teams, through elements. It expresses that an actor (the *depender*) depends upon another actor (the *dependee*) for something (the *dependum*). In other words, it describes the fact that one actor needs another one in order to satisfy or do an element. In the i^* model presented on Fig. 1, assembly line designers depend on DRAGON designers to have the *DRAGON design* in order to design the assembly line to build the DRAGON aircraft. Assembly line designers are the depender, DRAGON designers are the dependee and *DRAGON design* is the dependum.

Indeed, the design of DRAGON is required in order to define a building process. The building process corresponds to the list of high-level tasks, along with their precedence relationship. The building process is directly deduced from the DRAGON design. We have chosen to represent it as a resource in the sense that it is specific information produced from the task *do DRAGON design*. The building process allows assembly line designers to define the tools, machines, robots required to build the aircraft. It also allows them to define, by refinement, the assembly tasks as well as a first planning of the assembly line. Of course, the production of the building process is not automatic and is carried out by a specific actor which is part of the assembly line designers. However, at our level of abstraction, we have chosen to leave out these details.

3.2   Collaboration: A Dependency Cycle

In a concurrent engineering logic, the design of the factory and the product must be conceived together. Indeed, aircraft designers do not just want to make a aircraft, they want to have an aircraft design easy to produce. This is materialised by the addition of a new soft goal for the DRAGON designers (see Fig. 2). In the concurrent engineering context, the aircraft and assembly line designers must work together collaboratively to support each other. So, we have dependencies between actors. In our case study, we choose to model the collaboration with two dependency links. The first dependency is the one described previously, where the assembly line depends on the DRAGON design. For the second dependency link, it is the product design that depends on the factory. Indeed, in order to have an aircraft design easy to assemble, DRAGON designers must know the design of the factory (with its capacities, its know-how, *etc.*). The overall *i** model is presented on Fig. 2.

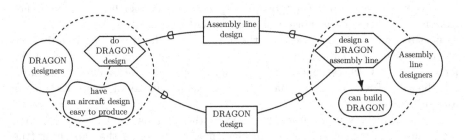

Fig. 2. Cyclical dependence between DRAGON design and assembly line design

Adding this new dependency results in a cycle of dependencies between DRAGON design and assembly line design. On the one side, assembly line designers need to know how the aircraft is designed before planning their own. On the other side, DRAGON designers need to understand what constraints their design will impose on the assembly line to conceive the aircraft. Thus, at the same time both design teams expect and need information and knowledge from the other team: this is a deadlock problem.

In practice, this problem can be circumvented by an iterative process. The aircraft design is created, then the factory design, which in turn feeds into the aircraft design and so on. Nevertheless, such a process still does not really correspond to a true collaboration relationship in which the factory and the product are designed together. It is more a DFA approach where the aircraft designer must take into account the constraints and objectives of the assembly line.

If we want a true collaboration in which the aircraft and its factory are jointly designed, we are in a deadlock: each actor, at the same time, needs an action to be done by the other in order to execute its own. This is cyclical form of dependence where each actor is waiting for the other to satisfy the element of its expectation. So, we must find a way to address this circular dependency problem, *i.e.* to break the cycle of dependency and propose a win-win solution for both actors.

3.3   Addition of a Third Actor

In Pant and Yu work, a similar circular dependency problem is stated as both actors face a blocking situation [17,18]. However, in their articles the dependency problem is not due to a simultaneous need for the dependum but to the presence of lose-lose or win-lose strategies. Despite this difference, a similar solution can be used, namely adding a third actor. In their problem, the authors chose to introduce a knowledge-sharing facilitator.

In the same spirit, we propose to introduce here a new actor to mitigate our circular dependency: *Global designers* (see Fig. 3). The global designers actor is able to perform the task *trade-off between DRAGON/assembly line designs*, which consists in a trade-off between both designs. This actor can be seen as a collaboration facilitator. In fact, the global designers actor is a team composed of people from the product design team and people from the production design team. Together, they collaborate to perform trade-offs between the aircraft and assembly line.

Before describing more precisely this third actor, we briefly describe why other approaches that do not involve this actor are not suited for our use-case.

A first simple solution that does not involve a third actor would be to get the two actors around a table to work out a draft of collaborative designs together. However, in our use-case, the two actors are not two individuals but entire departments. If a solution based on interaction between the department that designs the aircraft and the one that designs the factory was still possible a few decades ago, this solution is unfortunately unfeasible today. Indeed, due to the complexity of current systems, the number of stakeholders and the diversity of fields involved, it is necessary to find other ways to recreate a full collaboration between the product design and the assembly line design.

Another solution would be to use qualitative or quantitative satisfaction analysis techniques on the As-is diagram, to propagate the impacts of the alternatives on the goals of our actors, as presented in [14]. Then, the trade-offs between the goals could be made with trade-off analysis tools as described in [1,10]. Nevertheless, some issues make the previous proposals difficult or even impossible to realise. Firstly, for the sake of simplicity, we chose to not give importance to our goals but we could use the importance addition to i^* presented by Vik Pant in [16]. However, in our problem, the order of importance between soft goals is not fixed and may change depending on their satisfaction. For instance, *minimise workload* could be high-level priority soft goal at the beginning of the process, but once it is Weakly Satisfied, its priority would become lower than the one of the soft goal *minimise investment costs in tooling and robots*. Secondly, at this level of conception, we do not have enough information about contribution of alternatives to the goals to assess their impact with techniques of quantitative satisfaction analysis. We need expert intervention to define them. In addition, softer techniques such as qualitative ones are not precise enough for the designer to make a decision based on their recommendations. Finally, another choice of simplification in our model is to not represent all the alternatives allowing the satisfaction of the goal, *i.e. do DRAGON design* OR-refinement. In fact, there is a multitude of possible design alternatives, some of which may not yet exist at the beginning of the process. They are constructed by Global designers through the use of the Integrated Morphological Chart presented in Sect. 4.

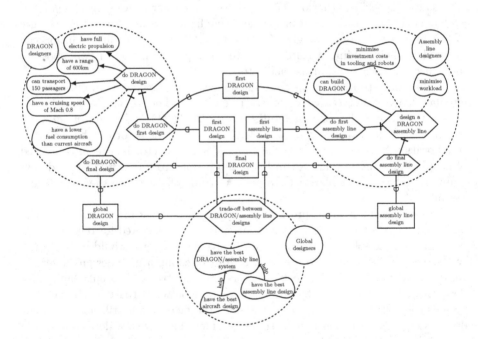

Fig. 3. Addition of the actor *Global designers* for solving the collaboration dependency cycle

As shown in Fig. 3, the only task performed by the global designer achieves one soft goal: *have the best DRAGON/assembly line system*. Indeed, unlike the other actors, global designers do not aim at optimising one design, but the quality of the combination/union of the two. To do this, the trade-off task performed by designers must fulfil all the goals of DRAGON designers and assembly line designers and also maximise all their soft goals. Rather than overloading the diagram with dependency or part-of links, we decided to simply indicate all these relationships by adding two sub-soft goals of the main goal: *have the best aircraft design* and *have the best assembly line*. These two new soft goals are a refinement of the main global designers' soft goal.

In this new model, the designs of the DRAGON aircraft and its assembly line follow three main steps. At first, as in the model given Fig. 1, we consider the one-way dependency from DRAGON to assembly line designers. So DRAGON designers propose a first DRAGON aircraft design and assembly line designers use it to propose a first assembly line design. Next, global designers optimise the global system from these first designs by realising trade-offs between them and propose better alternatives to each design team, denoted *global DRAGON design* and *global assembly line design* on Fig. 3. Finally, the two other teams can build their final design by optimising their own soft goals. In this last step, the one-way dependency between the two original actors is back again. In fact, each DRAGON design choice has an incidence on the assembly line design. Thus, at this last step the collaboration is broken. Nevertheless, we are still not in a competitive configuration since DRAGON designers have no interest in hurting the other actors. Our proposition in Fig. 3 allows designers to reach a more satisfying solution than the one presented on Fig. 1 as the worst scenarii is discarded. It would possible to reach an even better solution for the global system by iterating the *first design - trade-off - final design* again with global designers, until an optimal solution is achieved.

In this new proposal, the soft goal *have an aircraft design easy to produce* is removed of DRAGON designers boundary since global designers actor is now the one who works for this goal through the goal *have the best DRAGON/assembly line system*. It should be noted that this approach is motivated by the fact that technical teams are not familiar with goal modelling approaches, and even less with the *i** language. Therefore, we try to avoid complex modelling with several sorts of dependencies among DRAGON design and assembly line design and cover them by adding an intermediary human role to deal with them. As presented later in the paper, we also provide a realistic tool to assist in rationalising the type of decisions to be made for this intermediate role.

4   Building the Collaboration Between Design and Production

The introduction of the new actor *Global designers* and its associated goals and tasks raises new problems with regards to the evaluation of the system, *i.e.* the aircraft and its assembly line. One such new problem is that a trade-off must be made between the two designs. In this section, we focus on this trade-off capacity and apply an existing methodology that could be seen as a first step in defining framework and support tools for the global designers team.

4.1   The Integrated Morphological Chart Method

Stoffels and Vielhaber introduce the use of an *Integrated Morphological Chart* (IMC) as a method for multi-criteria evaluation of product alternatives with production system solutions [24]. In their work, the authors evaluate and refine existing product/production development methods. Their objective is to improve existing methods in the context of concurrent engineering. They propose IMC as a decision support tool for considering together product and production. Their cae study is the optimisation of the energy consumption of the product and production life cycles.

The first step for the creation of an IMC is the proposal of possible product solutions and production solutions. These solutions must, of course, satisfy all the goals but they do not necessarily satisfy all the soft goals in the same manner, *i.e.* with the same level of satisfaction. The second step is the definition of several evaluation criteria by the decision maker in order to assess all combinations of solutions. Then, domain experts give a value between 0 and 3 (3 being the optimal value) to each solution combination (*i.e.* for each product solution and for each production solution) and for each criterion. This score represents how optimal each combination is with regards to the criteria. So, for each criterion, a view of the best combinations of product/production solutions is obtained. Finally, as done classically for multi-criteria problems, it is possible to define an aggregation method to globally evaluate each combination of solutions. The objective is that the decision maker can make an informed and optimal decision by choosing for each criterion the solution that best satisfies the cross-domain goals.

4.2   Application to the DRAGON Case Study

We have adapted the IMC methodology to our case study. More precisely, we focus on two aircraft designs alternatives for the connection between the electric fans positioned at the rear of the wing and the inverters positioned at the front of the wing. Inverters are devices that change direct current into alternating current. They are wired to the fans by an electric harness. This harness can be installed either by drilling through the wing (first design alternative) or by following the shape of the wing (second design alternative). For the assembly line side, we consider two alternatives. The first one is to use manual tools and the second one to automate the assembly process with robots. It is important to understand that each of these design alternative is contained in the tasks *Design the DRAGON aircraft* and *Design an assembly line*. In fact, *drill through the wing* and *follow the shape of the wing* are subtasks that refine *Design the DRAGON aircraft*. The same holds for the assembly line tasks. The idea behind the adaptation of the IMC methodology is to allow the global designer actor to perform trade-offs among different design alternatives.

The relevant criteria for trade-offs come from the i^* goal model. Indeed, this model elicits the set of soft goals to be optimised. Note that the goals must be met and there is therefore no associated negotiation. Therefore, the criteria studied in our IMC are:

C1 minimise investment costs in tooling and robots, *i.e.* the cost of machines and production equipment; (assembly line designers soft goal).

C2 minimise workload, *i.e.* the cost of labour. In practice, it comes to minimise the number of hours worked to build the aircraft (assembly line designers soft goal);

C3 have a lower fuel consumption than current aircraft. Fuel consumption is directly related to the aircraft design and more specifically to its aerodynamics and weight (aircraft designers soft goal).

Based on the two alternatives for each product and production, we build an IMC matrix, given in Table 1. The values for each combination of alternatives are assigned by experts.

Table 1. Integrated Morphological Chart (IMC) matrix

Product solution 1	Product solution 2	Assessment according different product / production				
		AC1/AL1	AC2/AL1	AC1/AL2	AC2/AL2	
AC1 = Drilling through the wing	AC2 = Follow the shape of the wing	2	3	1	1	C1
		2	1	3	2	C2
		2	1	2	1	C3
		AL1 = Manual Production solution 1		AL2 = Robot support Production solution 2		

The use of robots is inherently costly and requires additional electricity resources. Therefore, the usefulness of using robots depends on the benefits it provides with respects to a specific task.

Concerning *tooling and robots cost* (C1), robots are expensive regardless of the aircraft design solution. Thus, in our study, in terms of investment costs, solutions without robots are always preferred. When considering the use of *manual tools* (AL1), *following the shape of the wing* (AC2) is the preferred option. This is because the equipment needed to drill the wing is much more expensive.

Regarding workload, the proposed solutions are to use *manual tools* or to automatise the process with *robots support*. In our case, using robots, is always beneficial for *workload reduction* (C2). For this criterion, *drilling through the wing* (AC1) appears to be a slightly better solution than *following the shape of the wing*. This is due to the speed of the process. We also find this same difference in the case of the use of *manual tools* (AL2).

After performance study, the experts came to the conclusion that *drilling through the wing* consumed less fuel (C3). Indeed, laying a cable on the leading edge of an aircraft's wing is not good for aerodynamic performance and therefore for fuel consumption. However, none of the solutions is optimal for the experts, as drilling weakens the structure of the wing. It is important to note that the structural criterion is not taken into account in our study (but it should be in the future). Unsurprisingly, the manufacturing alternatives have no impact on the fuel consumption criterion, judging only by the criterion *have a lower fuel consumption than current aircraft.* Thus it is equivalent to drill the wing with the help of robots, or with hand tools.

If we consider all the criteria, three configurations emerge: *drilling through the wing with manual tools, follow the shape of the wing with manual tools* and *drilling through the wing with robots support.* All of them are Pareto optimal, *i.e.* none of these solutions is better than the others on all criteria. For instance, the second solution (AC2/AL1) is the most efficient on the costs criterion (C1), while the third one is the best on the workload criterion (C2).

Since no solution is optimal on all criteria, many multi-criteria aggregation methods can be used to make a choice [3]. They all have their advantages and their drawbacks and choosing one is out of the scope of this article.

Note that, the IMC matrix could be further expanded when considering additional soft goals for product and production. Advantages of this methodology are its scalability, and its potential for cross-domain integration. New soft goals can be added each with its set of possible solutions, whose combinations have to be assessed in the context of each given criteria and integrated on a global assessment.

5   Conclusion and Perspectives

In this paper, we have shown how to model, in a goal-oriented approach, the collaboration relationship between the product design and manufacturing teams for an aeronautical case study. This collaboration can only really take place through the mediation of a new actor who has a more global vision of the system and who is therefore able to make the right trade-offs. In addition, to support this new actor, we have presented a possible trade-off method, related to our goal modelling.

Our work has so far been limited to a single case study. We now need to apply it to more complex cases, whether they are whole aircraft or other products such as satellites. This might allow us to generalise a method which starts from high level goals and systematically introduces a mitigating actor like the global design team.

Future work could also focus on the structure of this new actor, the global designers. Multidisciplinary teams of experts in fields such as architecture, manufacturing, procurement and sales have recently proposed work on similar issues in their respective industries [9]. Moreover, it is not easy to get people with different skills and areas of expertise to work together. The work on *tiers-lieu* could be an approach to the implementation of such a team [21].

Finally, with regards to manufacturing in particular, further work could seek to integrate elements of the value chain beyond the basic assembly objectives to consider the whole assembly system [5].

References

1. Amyot, D., Ghanavati, S., Horkoff, J., Mussbacher, G., Peyton, L., Yu, E.: Evaluating goal models within the goal-oriented requirement language. Int. J. Intell. Syst. **25**, 841–877 (2010). https://doi.org/10.1002/int.20433
2. Boothroyd, G.: Product design for manufacture and assembly. Comput. Aided Des. **26**(7), 505–520 (1994)
3. Bouyssou, D., Marchant, T., Pirlot, M., Tsoukiàs, A., Vincke, P.: Evaluation and Decision Models with Multiple Criteria: Stepping Stones for the Analyst, vol. 86. Springer, Boston (2006). https://doi.org/10.1007/0-387-31099-1
4. Brandenburger, A.M., Nalebuff, B.J.: The right game: Use game theory to shape strategy. Harv. Bus. Rev. **73**(4), 57–71 (1995)
5. Buergin, J., et al.: Local order scheduling for mixed-model assembly lines in the aircraft manufacturing industry. Prod. Eng. **12**(6), 759–767 (2018)
6. Chung, L., Nixon, B.A., Yu, E., Mylopoulos, J.: Non-Functional Requirements in Software Engineering. International Series in Software Engineering, vol. 5. Springer, Boston (2000). https://doi.org/10.1007/978-1-4615-5269-7
7. Dalpiaz, F., Franch, X., Horkoff, J.: iStar 2.0 language guide. CoRR abs/1605.07767 (2016)
8. Dardenne, A., van Lamsweerde, A., Fickas, S.: Goal-directed requirements acquisition. Sci. Comput. Program. **20**(1–2), 3–50 (1993)
9. Demoly, F., Yan, X., Eynard, B., Rivest, L., Gomes, S.: An assembly oriented design framework for product structure engineering and assembly sequence planning. Robot. Comput. Integr. Manuf. **27**(1), 33–46 (2011)
10. Elahi, G., Yu, E.: Requirements trade-offs analysis in the absence of quantitative measures: a heuristic method. In: Chu, W.C., Wong, W.E., Palakal, M.J., Hung, C. (eds.) Proceedings of the 2011 ACM Symposium on Applied Computing (SAC), pp. 651–658. ACM (2011)
11. Friedenthal, S., Moore, A., Steiner, R.: A Practical Guide to SysML: The Systems Modeling Language. Morgan Kaufmann, San Francisco (2014)
12. Göpfert, I., Schulz, M.: Logistics integrated product development in the German automotive industry: current state, trends and challenges. In: Kreowski, H.J., Scholz-Reiter, B., Thoben, K.D. (eds.) Dynamics in Logistics, LDIC 2012, pp. 509–519. Springer, Heidelberg (2013). https://doi.org/10.1007/978-3-642-35966-8_43
13. Grigoriev, S., Kutin, A., Turkin, M.: Modelling complex production processes in aerospace industry based on dimensional analysis. Procedia CIRP **7**, 473–478 (2013)
14. Horkoff, J., Yu, E.: Comparison and evaluation of goal-oriented satisfaction analysis techniques. Requir. Eng. **18**, 199–222 (2011)
15. Molloy, E., Yang, H., Browne, J., Davies, B.: Design for assembly within concurrent engineering. CIRP Ann. **40**(1), 107–110 (1991)
16. Pant, V.: Strategic coopetition - a conceptual modeling framework for analysis and design. Ph.D. thesis, University of Toronto, March 2021
17. Pant, V., Yu, E.: Modeling simultaneous cooperation and competition among enterprises. Bus. Inf. Syst. Eng. **60**(1), 39–54 (2018)
18. Pant, V., Yu, E.: A modeling approach for getting to win-win in industrial collaboration under strategic coopetition. Complex Syst. Inform. Model. Q. **19**, 19–41 (2019)

19. Polacsek, T., Roussel, S., Bouissiere, F., Cuiller, C., Dereux, P.-E., Kersuzan, S.: Towards thinking manufacturing and design together: an aeronautical case study. In: Mayr, H.C., Guizzardi, G., Ma, H., Pastor, O. (eds.) ER 2017. LNCS, vol. 10650, pp. 340–353. Springer, Cham (2017). https://doi.org/10.1007/978-3-319-69904-2_27

20. Polacsek, T., Roussel, S., Pralet, C., Cuiller, C.: Design for efficient production, a model-based approach. In: 13th IEEE International Conference on Research Challenges in Information Science, RCIS (2019)

21. Ralyté, J., Léonard, M.: Exploring the concept of "tiers-lieu" for information services: the value of conceptual modeling. In: Panach, J.I., Guizzardi, R.S.S., Claro, D.B. (eds.) Proceedings of the ER Forum and Poster & Demos Session. CEUR Workshop Proceedings, vol. 2469, pp. 98–107. CEUR-WS.org (2019)

22. Schmollgruber, P., et al.: Multidisciplinary exploration of dragon: an ONERA hybrid electric distributed propulsion concept. In: AIAA Scitech 2019 Forum, p. 1585 (2019)

23. Shenas, D.G., Derakhshan, S.: Organizational approaches to the implementation of simultaneous engineering. Int. J. Oper. Prod. Manag. **14**(10), 30–43 (1994)

24. Stoffels, P., Vielhaber, M.: Methodical support for concurrent engineering across product and production (system) development. In: DS 80–4 Proceedings of the 20th International Conference on Engineering Design (ICED 2015) Vol 4: Design for X, Design to X, Milan, Italy, 27–30 July 2015, pp. 155–162 (2015)

25. Wortmann, A., Barais, O., Combemale, B., Wimmer, M.: Modeling languages in industry 4.0: an extended systematic mapping study. Softw. Syst. Model. **19**(1), 67–94 (2020)

Assignment of Actors to Activities at Process-Oriented Applications: A Research Agenda

Thomas Bauer[1]([⊠]) and Ralf Laue[2]

[1] Hochschule Neu-Ulm, Wileystr. 1, 89231 Neu-Ulm, Germany
thomas.bauer@hnu.de
[2] Westsächsische Hochschule Zwickau, Kornmarkt 1, 08056 Zwickau, Germany
ralf.laue@fh-zwickau.de

Abstract. Current process management systems (PMS) use graphical modelling languages such as BPMN for modelling the control flow. Almost no program code has to be written by business process designers for defining the possible order of activities. For another important aspect of business processes – assigning actors to activities – no such simple and standardized way of modelling exists. This causes problems at business process implementation projects in practice. We explain such aspects and shortcomings of current commercial PMS that lead to these problems. For each aspect, it is analysed whether appropriate scientific solutions exist, or whether it is an unsolved research question.

Keywords: Organisational perspective · Actor assignment · Organizational model · Metamodel · Escalations · Substitutions · Research questions

1 Motivation

Modelling of business processes (BP) consists of the specification of several perspectives. This concerns business-oriented BP modelling (i.e. the business view, cf. ARIS) as well as BP implementation (the technical view) based on a process management system (PMS). The control-flow can be modelled graphically as a process graph and there exist standardized modelling languages for this perspective (e.g. BPMN). In the following we focus on the organizational perspective that describes which users are assigned to which activities and for which purpose. For each activity (that shall be performed by a person), an *actor assignment* defines the potential actors who are allowed to execute this activity. In addition, the behaviour in exceptional situations may be defined. For instance, an *escalation* shall be triggered in case of a delayed execution of the activity, or the long-term absence of its regular actors may be handled by a *substitution* mechanism. The organizational perspective is relevant at business-oriented BP design not only for the purpose of a complete BP documentation, but also for the training of the process participants and for process simulation; e.g. to calculate the expected workload of users.

E. Serral et al. (Eds.): PoEM 2021, LNBIP 432, pp. 281–291, 2021.
https://doi.org/10.1007/978-3-030-91279-6_20

At BP implementation, an even more detailed modelling of this perspective is necessary since the PMS must be able to calculate exactly the users who shall perform a specific activity, escalation, or substitution. For this purpose, the BP engine sends a query to the organizational database that stores the organizational model. This procedure requires that, at BP design time, rules are modelled that exactly define how to calculate the desired users.

In order to fulfil all requirements that occur in practice, it must be possible to model sophisticated rules for this purpose. Currently, however, there does not exist a standard for organizational modelling (cf. BPMN) and, as we will show, several commercial PMS do not support this appropriately. That means, it is not possible to define complex rules in an easy to use manner; e.g. graphically as possible with BPMN for the control-flow perspective. We present aspects where scientific concepts that would enable this are still missing. Thereby, the focus is on aspects that cause the problems we have identified in projects from practice and at current PMS. The reason for this decision was that defining the organizational perspective causes much effort in existing PMS. Sometimes it is not possible to define a required assignment rule at all, or the assignment must be realized by writing program code (despite BP designers normally do not possess programming skills). As we observed in real life implementation projects, in the worst case, this may result in the decision not to realize a process-aware application (PAIS) at all (but only a data and function-oriented application).

2 Basic Requirements for the Organizational Perspective

We explain relevant requirements and resulting problems that the first author has observed in real-life projects during ten years of practical experience with BP management at a large German vehicle manufacture. Then, we describe whether and how these requirements are fulfilled at some commercial PMS.

Project Experiences - Actor assignments: The purpose of (regular) actor assignments is to define the users who shall perform a specific activity. In practice, many types of actor assignments are required that do not only use roles but also groups, competences, departments, etc. It must be possible to define expressions combined with Boolean operators, e.g. "role = *Software Developer* ∧ group = *Development S-Class*". Furthermore, dependent actor assignments may refer to preceding activities or process instance data, e.g. "not same actor as at Activity X". Ideally, a PMS should offer all required actor assignments in an easy to use manner; e.g. using graphic modelling or by combining arbitrary textual templates provided by the modelling tool.

A problem at the observed projects was that the PMS did not support all required types of actor assignments. Especially, combined expressions and dependent actor assignments were not possible or could be only realized by writing program code (e.g. JavaScript). Furthermore, there does not exist a standard for the modelling of actor assignments. Therefore, even the transformation of the business view (for instance created with ARIS) to the technical implementation causes high effort, since the actor assignments were defined with a different modelling method, using different object types, and with insufficient details at the business view.

Metamodel of the Organizational Database: The potential actors that are allowed to perform a specific activity are calculated by a query to the organizational database. Such a database needs a comprehensive metamodel to support all required types of organizational objects (i.e. roles, groups, skills, teams, etc.). Ideally, the same organizational database should be used by all process-aware applications (even if they are based on different PMS) as well as by all traditional applications (the user directory).

Some metamodels of the organizational databases did not possess the required comprehensiveness (missing object types). Furthermore, no standard exists for such a metamodel. Hence, before starting with the main part of the BP implementation project, it was necessary to develop an appropriate metamodel in an external database or to extend the database of the PMS (e.g. with work-arounds). This causes delays as well as effort for the project, and represents an initial hurdle for the realization of a process-aware application. Because of the missing standardization and the absence of products providing a generally usable process-oriented organizational database, it was not possible to use the same data with different PMS. Having multiple organizational databases, however, results in high effort for their creation and maintenance.

Escalations: If an activity is not started or completed in time, an escalation is used, for instance, to inform other users or to change the set of its potential actors. For such an escalation, several parameters have to be defined; e.g. the time when it shall be triggered, the action that has to be performed, and the set of target persons. For the last aspect, complex rules may be required to define escalations as, for instance, "assign the activity to a colleague with the same role after two hours and to the supervisor after one day". At this informal description of a rule, "colleague" stands for a different person with the same role and from the same department; i.e. a complex formal rule has to be defined in order to specify such an escalation. Since different target persons may be responsible for escalations concerning different activities, multiple such rules have to be defined; i.e. they are activity-dependent.

At the observed projects, escalations were respected very seldom. A reason may be that escalations normally were not part of business-oriented BP models; i.e. the business view created during the requirement analysis phase. Therefore, it would be necessary to capture escalations by a separate analysis; e.g. later at the BP implementation phase. If a project avoids this effort, the resulting application will not contain any escalations. Furthermore, the limited escalation functionality of the respective PMS was an additional argument not to realize escalations at all. Since escalations should be implemented by a core component of the PMS, it would be much effort to realize sophisticated escalation mechanisms at the application level (i.e. as work-around).

Substitutions: Another exceptional situation is that actors are absent for a long time. Then, substitutions may be used to transfer the activity to other users. Additionally to the information required for escalations, the BP designer has to define, for instance, whether the substitution shall be activated when one, a given quota, or all potential actors are currently absent. Furthermore, since different departments may use different substitution strategies, different target person rules may be necessary for different original actors. Since this results in high effort, an efficient modelling technique is required that allows the flexible definition of the target persons of substitutions.

Similar to escalations, at most observed projects, the business view did not contain substitution rules. But a difference was that during BP implementation it was well-known that some kind of substitution is necessary to avoid that an activity is inserted solely into worklists of users who will be absent for a long time. Furthermore, it was obvious that the substitution mechanisms offered by the PMS are insufficient to realize all requirements of the project. To solve these problems, organizational work-arounds were analysed as the definition of several fixed substitutes for an actor for all activities or the definition of a manager as a potential actor who has solely the job to delegate the activity manually if the regular actors are absent. That means, additional effort became necessary to identify and realize an acceptable work-around.

Commercial PMS[1] - Actor Assignments: With K2, it is possible to define an actor assignment that consists of several parts. A condition (if) is assigned to each part of the rule to specify when it shall be used. However, no dependent actor assignments are supported. Programming of an actor assignment is not possible. Instead, the only way to realize an actor assignment is to fill out the form "Recipients Rule". With Signavio, actor assignments can be defined by filling a form as well. Additionally, two types of dependent actor assignments are offered: It is possible to define that an activity has to be assigned to the same actor as a preceding activity. Separation of duties can be modelled as well. The only possibility to define further actor assignments is to write JavaScript code. Bizagi enables the creation of complex rules (with Boolean operators) in a graphical editor and arbitrary actor assignment rules can be defined with XPath expressions. IBM Business Process Designer allows assigning an activity to a participant group, the actor of a preceding activity, or the starter of the process instance. Additionally, Routing Policies enable defining complex rules with conditions that use process variables and Boolean operators. But Routing Policies are no longer available in the succession product IBM Business Automation Workflow. Here, JavaScript code must be written to realize complex actor assignments: Team retrieval services can be realized to calculate the IDs of the appropriate users; e.g. by using functions of the product API or by calling an external service. Team filter services get the UserIDs of a participant group as input. Then, program code can be written that eliminates not intended users (e.g. wrong department, separation of duties).

Metamodel of the Organizational Database: The IBM metamodel comes with the fewest possibilities to structure organizational data since only so-called participant groups are offered. Signavio additionally enables the usage of roles. This is extended by K2 and Bizagi with competences and organizational units inclusive the possibility to define a hierarchy (e.g. team, department, center).

Escalations: Bizagi does not support any escalations. Signavio is able to send an email to a user in case of a missed deadline. In addition, K2 can transfer the activity to another user, but only a single user can be specified as target person (i.e. no group). IBM offers notifications via email and transferring an activity to other actors as well. Such escalations can be addressed to multiple persons.

---

[1] We inspected the PMS Bizagi Studio V.11.2.3, IBM Business Process Designer V.8.0.1 and V.8.6.0 as well as the succession product IBM Business Automation Workflow V.20.0.0.2, K2 Cloud V.4.0, and Signavio Workflow Accelerator V.13.6.0 (for details see [5]).

Substitutions: Bizagi and Signavio do not offer substitution mechanisms. K2 enables defining different substitutes for different activities. IBM allows to select for each activity whether it shall be transferred to a substitute or not. Only one list of substitutes can be defined for each original actor, i.e. the substitutes cannot depend on the concerned activity or process data.

3 Scientific State of the Art and Resulting Research Questions

In the following, scientific work is discussed that addresses these problems of the projects and the shortcomings of PMS. Thereby, the goal is to identify approaches, which have the potential to solve these topics, and not to present a complete overview on the literature concerning the organizational perspective of BP. Therefore, we will discuss literature that handles aspects causing these problems for practice. One the one hand, we want to identify which problems can be solved with existing scientific approaches. In such cases, the conclusion is that these approaches are solely not realized by current PMS technology. On the other hand, for the remaining problems, the conclusion must be that currently no appropriate scientific solution exists, and therefore, this is an unsolved research question.

Actor Assignments: A fundamental work on resources in BP are the workflow resource patterns [20]. This work describes various ways how activities are assigned to actors. It includes basic patterns such as role-based distribution of activities as well as more complex constraints such as separation of duties (4-eyes-principle) and assigning an activity to the user who has already performed a specific preceding activity.

[6] develops a language for the definition of additional constraints for actor assignments. They can be used, for instance, to realize separation of duties. [14] mentions some requirements for dependent actor assignments, e.g. that the potential actors may depend on process instance data (i.e. application data).

BPMN offers XPath as a method to define actor assignments. Thereby, the XPath expressions have to be defined by the BP designer. This is a similar difficulty as writing such a rule using a programming language. In addition, it is not possible to use the actor specification as a means to discuss the process among the stakeholders.

Some approaches enable additional types of actor assignments by extending standardized BP modelling languages as BPMN and UML: [12] extends the data model of BPMN in order to cover all types of actor assignments mentioned in the workflow resource patterns [20]. [23] develops a metamodel that allows to store the organizational perspective. Again, these classes extend the metamodel of BPMN. The paper, however, does not suggest concrete new object types as, for instance, roles, departments, or capabilities. [24] extends BPMN to enable the definition of additional constraints for actor assignments. The approach allows the definition of simple constraints for actor assignments (e.g. same actor as a preceding activity, separation of duties), as well as very complex rules (e.g. the same user is only allowed to perform max. 5 activities of the process instance). The constraints are defined by threshold values (i.e. numbers). For BP designers, this method is at least unusual. [22] extends UML activity diagrams with an organizational perspective. The authors suggest so-called "Business Activities" in order to enable the BP designer to define role-based access control (RBAC). [15] extends UML use case diagrams to realize actor assignments, delegations, and substitutions. This concept allows a transformation of the Platform Independent Model (PIM) into a Platform Specific Model (PSM). The latter is used by the PMS to control BP execution at runtime.

Some work addresses special types of actor assignments: [7] enhances the idea of separation of duties with advanced requirements, for instance, by respecting conflicts between roles and users. To give an example, a family member of a requestor may not be allowed to perform the corresponding approval activity. [1] extends the organizational model with a team concept. Thus, one activity can be performed by several persons (commonly), instead by a single actor. In addition to the (normal) actors, [9] assigns additional persons to an activity for control, information, and support of its execution (cf. RACI matrix). [10] extends the language RAL in order to define dependencies between actors of activities that belong to different process instances. In [21], an actor assignment may contain soft constraints. A soft constraint shall be respected if possible (i.e. it can be ignored); e.g. if it would result in a missed deadline.

Some approaches develop methods that shall enable the simple definition of actor assignments: [3] suggests to extend the metamodel of BPMN with actor assignments. They are defined as constraints expressed in Object Constraint Language (OCL). However, this means that such constraints would have to be written in a formal and less intuitive language by the BP designers. [8] develops the language RAL to assign resources to activities. It uses organizational objects with specific types (Role, Capability, etc.). The advantage of this language is that it is powerful and easy to read (i.e. simple), but again, formal expressions must be written. [11] enhances this approach with the graphical notation RALph. It covers all resource patterns mentioned in [20]. Furthermore, it allows combining parts of rules with Boolean operators in order to define even complex actor assignments. Therefore, important types of actor assignments can be realized. While we think that RALph should be easy to understand, experiments and studies evaluating its understandability are still missing.

Conclusion: Several authors develop techniques with the goal to simplify the modelling of actor assignments. However, we found no studies that evaluate which modelling technique is best suited; e.g. graphic modelling, textual specification (cf. RAL, OCL), or the combination of pre-defined textual templates (cf. the Routing Policies of IBM). Thereby, understandability for the BP designers is a crucial aspect. It may be necessary to distinguish modelling at the business-oriented level and at the technical level (workflow implementation) since the respective BP designers typically have very different IT skills. Furthermore, the resulting modelling technique has to cover dependent actor assignments and the combination of partial expression with Boolean operators. In order to ease the usage of business-oriented modelling tools and PMS from different manufacturers, a standard should be developed for this functionality.

Several papers suggest a set of actor assignment types, some by extending BPMN or UML, and some even respect special requirements as team tasks. But there exist no studies that analyze which types of actor assignments are required in practice, typically. Such studies, however, are required as foundation to develop the set of actor assignments that is offered to the BP designer with the selected modelling technique (see above).

Furthermore, no studies analyze whether the same types of actor assignments are required at different business domains; e.g. BP of hospitals, vehicle development, and marketing. Only if this applies, it makes sense for a PMS to offer a pre-implemented mechanism for the definition of actor assignments. Otherwise, using a programming language (e.g. JavaScript) cannot be avoided in most cases.

The missing studies concerning the appropriate modelling technique and the required set of actor assignments may be a reason that currently there does not exist a standard for the definition of actor assignments. Furthermore, we assume that the tool manufacturers boggle the implementation effort because of the risk that the resulting mechanisms are inadequate or not sufficient for many business domains. At the development of such a modelling method and standardization, the different requirements of the business and the technical level have to be respected. That means, the method for business modelling shall be simple to understand, but not too vague, in order to enable the direct transformation of the actor assignments into a BP implementation. For instance, even at the business level, it should be possible to define dependent actor assignments; i.e. the target must be to develop a comprehensive approach that may be used in all phases of a development project.

Metamodel of the Organizational Database: The W3C ORG Ontology deals with organizational units, membership, roles, posts, and reporting but does not include information that is fundamental for resource assignment such as competencies.

[20] presents several patterns for the organizational perspective incl. a metamodel for the organizational database: Users (human resources) have a position in an organizational unit and may belong to temporarily assigned groups. They may have assigned roles, capabilities, an organizational level, and subordinated persons. This means, the metamodel contains a variety of object types that can be used to define many types of actor assignments. [17] presents a metamodel that additionally contains competences, skills, and knowledge. In addition to users, other types of resources are respected.

The focus of [3] is the integration of actor assignments into the BPMN standard. The paper presents an organizational metamodel as well, but this contains organizational and functional roles inclusive a hierarchy only. Other object types (e.g. capabilities) are not considered. [23] extends BPMN with an organizational perspective too. For this purpose, it presents a graphical visualization for some types of organizational objects. The metamodel allows assigning arbitrary parameters to resources that can be queried at runtime to perform resource assignments. However, such an abstract approach leaves the responsibility to deal with the parameters and the rules how to use them for calculating actor assignments completely to the BP designer.

Approaches for enterprise modelling (e.g. ArchiMate, DEMO, MEMO, VDML) have the goal to enable the planning and improvement of the organization and its IT. For example, ArchiMate uses the concepts business actor and business role for defining the persons who are responsible for executing a task. However, assigning actors at runtime is out of scope; i.e. the approaches do not solve the need for an organizational database for the calculation of actor assignments used by a PMS at runtime.

Conclusion: The best situation for a BP implementation project would be that there already exists a complete and generally usable metamodel for the organizational model, since its organizational types are required to define actor assignments at the business and the technical level. Unfortunately, no such metamodel is proposed in literature. Even worse: there exist no studies that examine whether the same types of organizational objects are required at different business domains. In addition, no comprehensive metamodel is developed in literature. We assume that the types of organizational objects, proposed by the presented papers, are not sufficient (at least for some scenarios) since aspects as, for instance, worker protection cannot be modelled; i.e. cannot be respected in actor assignments.

The development of a comprehensive metamodel, however, would be a prerequisite for the standardization. Without such a standard, PMS use proprietary metamodels. This prevents the realization of a central organizational database for all process-aware applications (based on different PMS). Furthermore, we believe that a standard or concept for such a database should be based on or at least be integrable with regular user directories (e.g. LDAP, Microsoft Active Directory).

Escalations: They are mentioned in PMS literature (e.g. [12, 20]), but there does not exist any work that considers specifically the issue of how to define the target persons efficiently and flexibly. Some literature handles special aspects of escalations:

[2] suggests to react to delays not only if it is already too late. Instead, it considers expected durations for completion of activities and process instances in order to be able to react before a deadline is actually missed. Additionally, an escalation may concern several activities and process instances, e.g. if all activities of a user are delayed because of the same reason. The escalation mechanism can be selected automatically or manually and multiple escalation levels may be activated in sequence, with each level resulting in a different escalation mechanism. Several escalation mechanisms are presented. Hence, the paper describes a very powerful escalation approach that fits very well to the presented scenario of too high workload at a call center.

[18] improves the management of escalations with the goal to minimize their number. An algorithm adjusts deadlines of activities in order to compensate already occurred delays and, therefore, to avoid escalations at succeeding activities. Costs that are caused by not avoidable escalations are minimized by predicting whether an escalation will occur despite these adjustments. In this case, the escalation is triggered as early as possible (in the BP) since costs for early escalations are typically lower.

Conclusion: [2] and [18] present very advanced concepts that are not in our focus since they do not directly solve the mentioned problems of PMS in practice. The other papers mention the necessity of escalations but do not develop solution concepts. This is acceptable for many aspects of escalations that are quite simple as, for instance, the selection of the escalation mechanism (e.g. email vs. worklist entry) or the definition of the escalation deadline (e.g. measured from the availability or reservation time of the activity till its start or completion). The definition of the target persons of an escalation, however, requires a more sophisticated concept: They shall not only depend on the concerned activity and the process context, but also on the original actor of the activity (e.g. at an escalation to the supervisor). Furthermore, even different rules for different original actors may be required (e.g. escalation to the team leader for actors who belong to department X and to the department leader otherwise). It would result in too much effort for the BP designer, however, to define separate rules for each relevant combination of concerned activity and original actor. Therefore, a concept has to be developed that significantly differs from normal actor assignments.

Substitutions: [4] presents several requirements: It shall be possible to model rules that depend on the absent person and the concerned activity. It must be definable, whether the substitution shall be activated when one or all potential actors are currently absent, or when they have actively demanded to be substituted. Furthermore, multi-level substitutions may be desired (if substitutes are absent too) and activities may be revoked from a substitute when the original actor returns. Additionally, for all these cases, algorithms are presented that calculate the resulting substitutes. The work, however, does not contain a concept that enables "efficient" modelling of such substitution rules. That means, similar as at escalations, high effort may result for the BP designers to define many separate substitution rules.

Other papers do not offer solutions for this issue as well: The resource patterns [20], consider substitutions not as a separate topic, but as a delegation that is performed by the PMS. [16] describes a simple substitution mechanism: An (eventually restricted) access to the worklist of the substituted person is granted. The substitutes can solely be defined with roles. [13] only mentions that substitutions are necessary. However, no detailed requirements and no solutions are presented. [19] describes a metamodel for the organizational perspective that contains substitutions as well. The corresponding substitution rules, however, cannot depend on the concerned activity. Despite the necessity of context-related substitutions is mentioned, no concept for the modelling of such substitution rules is presented.

Conclusion: Compared to escalations, there exist more papers that handle substitutions. Additional requirements are presented, as for instance multi-level substitutions or revoking a substitution. As well, corresponding solution concepts were published. But again, there remains the unsolved topic, how to define the target persons efficiently: Different substitution rules are required for different activities and original actors. In addition, multi-level substitutions may require further or modified substitution rules. Therefore, there remains the unsolved research question, how to avoid the definition of many different rules in order to reduce the effort for the BP designer; i.e. how to re-use and adapt such rules (e.g. for different departments with slightly different substitution strategies).

Resulting Research Questions: The organizational perspective is essential to model a BP comprehensively and to enable a PMS to control the BP execution. Unfortunately, there occur several problems at the implementation of BP in practice. The following unsolved topics (i.e. research questions) still exist: (i) Researching which requirements for resource assignment exist in different business domains; i.e. which types of actor assignments and organizational objects are required. (ii) Based on these results: Developing a comprehensive modelling method and establishing a standard for actor assignment; i.e. a uniform organizational metamodel and easy to use actor assignments for all business domains. (iii) Creating formalisms and algorithms for the identified requirements, especially an efficient method for defining the set of target persons for escalations and substitutions that considers the non-trivial requirements as well. (iv) Evaluating and comparing the expressiveness, understandability, and usability of the formalisms resulting from (ii) and (iii).

References

1. van der Aalst, W.M., Kumar, A.: A reference model for team-enabled workflow management systems. Data Knowl. Eng. **38**(3), 335–363 (2001)
2. van der Aalst, W.M., Rosemann, M., Dumas, M.: Deadline-based escalation in process-aware information systems. Decis. Support Syst. **43**(2), 492–511 (2007)
3. Awad, A., Grosskopf, A., Meyer, A., et al.: Enabling Resource Assignment Constraints in BPMN. Hasso Plattner Institute, Potsdam (2009)
4. Bauer, T.: Substitution rules for task actors in process-oriented applications. Datenbank-Spektrum **9**, 40–51 (2009) (in German)
5. Bauer, T., Laue, R.: State of application-related research and technology for the organizational perspective of business processes. In: Proceedings of ZuGPM, pp. 605–619 (2020) (in German)
6. Bertino, E., Ferrari, E., Atluri, V.: The specification and enforcement of authorization constraints in WfMS. ACM Trans. Inf. Syst. Secur. **2**, 65–104 (1999)
7. Botha, R.A., Eloff, J.: Separation of duties for access control enforcement in workflow environments. IBM Syst. J. **40**(3), 666–682 (2001)
8. Cabanillas, C., Resinas, M., Ruiz-Cortés, A.: RAL: a high-level user-oriented resource assignment language for business processes. In: Daniel, F., Barkaoui, K., Dustdar, S. (eds.) BPM 2011. LNBIP, vol. 99, pp. 50–61. Springer, Heidelberg (2012). https://doi.org/10.1007/978-3-642-28108-2_5
9. Cabanillas, C., Resinas, M., Ruiz-Cortés, A.: Automated resource assignment in BPMN models using RACI matrices. In: Meersman, Robert, Panetto, Hervé, Dillon, Tharam, Rinderle-Ma, Stefanie, Dadam, Peter, Zhou, Xiaofang, Pearson, Siani, Ferscha, Alois, Bergamaschi, Sonia, Cruz, Isabel F. (eds.) OTM 2012. LNCS, vol. 7565, pp. 56–73. Springer, Heidelberg (2012). https://doi.org/10.1007/978-3-642-33606-5_5
10. Cabanillas, C., Resinas, M., Ruiz-Cortés, A.: Designing business processes with history-aware resource assignments. In: La Rosa, M., Soffer, P. (eds.) BPM 2012. LNBIP, vol. 132, pp. 101–112. Springer, Heidelberg (2013). https://doi.org/10.1007/978-3-642-36285-9_12
11. Cabanillas, C., Knuplesch, D., Resinas, M., Reichert, M., Mendling, J., Ruiz-Cortés, A.: RALph: a graphical notation for resource assignments in business processes. In: Zdravkovic, Jelena, Kirikova, Marite, Johannesson, Paul (eds.) CAiSE 2015. LNCS, vol. 9097, pp. 53–68. Springer, Cham (2015). https://doi.org/10.1007/978-3-319-19069-3_4
12. Großkopf, A.: An Extended Resource Information Layer for BPMN. Hasso-Plattner-Institute for IT Systems Engineering, Potsdam (2008)
13. Hochmüller, E., Dobrovnik, M.: Flexibility issues in workflow management systems. Proc. Bus. Process Model. Dev. Support **5** (2005)
14. Künzle, V., Reichert, M.: Integrating users in object-aware process management systems: issues and challenges. In: Rinderle-Ma, S., Sadiq, S., Leymann, F. (eds.) BPM 2009. LNBIP, vol. 43, pp. 29–41. Springer, Heidelberg (2010). https://doi.org/10.1007/978-3-642-12186-9_4
15. Link, S., Hoyer, P., Schuster, T., et al.: Model-driven development of human tasks for workflows. In: Proceedings of 3rd International Conference on Software Engineering Advances, pp. 329–335 (2008)

16. zur Mühlen, M.: Organizational management in workflow applications – issues and perspectives. Inf. Technol. Manag. J. **5,** 271–291 (2004)
17. Oberweis, A., Schuster, T.: A Meta-model based approach to the description of resources and skills. In: Proceedings of Americas Conference on Information Systems (2010)
18. Panagos E, Rabinovich M (1998) Reducing Escalation-Related Costs in WFMSs. In: Doğaç A., Kalinichenko L., Özsu M.T., Sheth A. (eds.) Workflow Management Systems and Interoperability. NATO ASI Series (Series F: Computer and Systems Sciences), vol. 164, pp. 107–128. Springer, Heidelberg (1998). https://doi.org/10.1007/978-3-642-58908-9_6
19. Rosemann, M, zur Mühlen, M.: Modelling of the organizational structure in workflow management systems. EMISA-Forum, pp. 78–86 (1998) (in German)
20. Russell, N., van der Aalst, W., ter Hofstede, A., Edmond, D.: Workflow resource patterns: identification, representation and tool support. In: Pastor, Oscar, Falcão e Cunha, João. (eds.) CAiSE 2005. LNCS, vol. 3520, pp. 216–232. Springer, Heidelberg (2005). https://doi.org/10.1007/11431855_16
21. Stefansen, C., Rajamani, S., Seshan, P.: SOFTALLOC: A work allocation language with soft constraints. In: Proceedings of IEEE International Conference on Web Services, pp. 441–448 (2008)
22. Strembeck, M., Mendling, J.: Modeling process-related RBAC models with extended UML activity models. Inf. Softw. Technol. **53,** 456–483 (2011)
23. Stroppi, L.J.R., Chiotti, O., Villarreal, P.D.: Defining the resource perspective in the development of PAIS. Inf. Softw. Technol. **59,** 86–108 (2015)
24. Wolter, C., Schaad, A.: Modeling of task-based authorization constraints in BPMN. In: Alonso, G., Dadam, P., Rosemann, M. (eds.) BPM 2007. LNCS, vol. 4714, pp. 64–79. Springer, Heidelberg (2007). https://doi.org/10.1007/978-3-540-75183-0_5

Author Index

Printed in the United States
by Baker & Taylor Publisher Services